The New Monteverdi Companion

The New
Monteverdi Companion

edited by
DENIS ARNOLD
and
NIGEL FORTUNE

faber and faber
LONDON·BOSTON

First published in 1985
by Faber and Faber Limited
3 Queen Square London WC1N 3AU

Phototypeset by Wyvern Typesetting Limited, Bristol
Printed in Great Britain by
Redwood Burn Limited, Trowbridge
All rights reserved

© 1985 Faber and Faber

British Library Cataloguing in Publication Data

The New Monteverdi companion.
1. Monteverdi Claudio
I. Arnold Denis   II. Fortune, Nigel
780'.92'4   ML41.M77

ISBN 0-571-13148-4
ISBN 0-571-13357-6 Pbk

Library of Congress Cataloging in Publication Data
Main entry under title:

The New Monteverdi companion.

Rev. ed. of The Monteverdi companion. 1968.
Bibliography: p.
1. Monteverdi, Claudio, 1567–1643.   I. Arnold, Denis.
II. Fortune, Nigel.   III. Monteverdi companion.
ML410.M77N5   1985   784'.092'4   85–6845
ISBN 0-571-13148-4
ISBN 0-571-13357-6 (pbk.)

Contents

Illustrations

Preface

The Monteverdi Companion was conceived as part of the celebrations in 1967 of the quatercentenary of the composer's birth. Although a number of life-and-works volumes had appeared by then, serious studies of various aspects of Monteverdi's music and its contexts were comparatively rare, especially those intended for students and general readers. The quatercentenary helped to change this situation: conferences, performances, books, and articles in journals abounded in the late 1960s; since then, other useful studies have appeared, and Monteverdi's music has been still more regularly performed than hitherto, and not just in an antiquarian spirit or context. When we were asked to prepare a new edition of the *Companion* it seemed important to reflect the new enthusiasm for Monteverdi displayed through scholarship and performance alike.

Our original translation of a selection of Monteverdi's letters has been superseded by Denis Stevens's definitive version of the complete surviving corpus (1980), based on scrutiny of the originals; the anthology in the present volume has been drawn from his complete edition by Denis Stevens himself. The material in Parts II and III has been substantially retained, in somewhat revised form; the chapter on the later madrigals, however, is new. So too is virtually everything in the book from this point on: the operas especially seemed to merit new consideration in the light of recent developments; and the interest in 'authentic' performance required an appropriate additional chapter. The bibliography obviously needed to be brought up to date, so we have reconsidered the principles underlying the previous one and in the case of periodical articles in particular have abandoned the ideal of completeness and omitted the more ephemeral items from earlier years to make room for items published since 1967. We hope that we have included all the more important editions of Monteverdi's music and literature concerning him.

Finally, we express our gratitude to Patrick Carnegy of Faber and Faber for his support, and to Rosemary Roberts for her meticulous editorial help in the later stages of the preparation of the manuscript.

Oxford/Birmingham　　　　　　　　　　　　　　DENIS ARNOLD
September 1983　　　　　　　　　　　　　　　NIGEL FORTUNE

Bibliographical Note

The standard complete edition of the works of Monteverdi is *Tutte le opere di Claudio Monteverdi*, ed. Gian Francesco Malipiero, i-xvi (Asolo, 1926–42); 2nd, rev. edn. (Vienna, 1954–68); supplementary vol., xvii (Venice, 1966); it is referred to throughout the book by the short title *Tutte le opere*.

Similarly, the following standard works of reference are cited respectively as *Il nuovo Vogel* and *The New Grove*: Emil Vogel, Alfred Einstein, François Lesure and Claudio Sartori, *Bibliografia della musica italiana vocale profana pubblicata dal 1500 al 1700* ([Geneva], [1978]); and Stanley Sadie, ed., *The New Grove Dictionary of Music and Musicians* (London, 1980).

I

Selected Letters of
Monteverdi

DENIS STEVENS

Selected Letters of Monteverdi
Translated and with Commentaries

Introduction

Although the following selection of letters differs somewhat from that in
The Monteverdi Companion, there is a certain amount of overlapping
because of the undisputed importance of some of them. The general
principle of selection remains the same as before. Any perceptible shift
of emphasis derives from my intention to reveal more of the man within
the context of his social and musical background. Minor changes and
improvements to the translations originally published in *The Letters of
Claudio Monteverdi* (London, 1980) have in some cases been incorporated into the present text, from which the often lengthy salutations and
perorations have been excised except in Letters I and XXXVIII.

The letters are here numbered from I to XL. The numbers in *The
Letters of Claudio Monteverdi* and the page numbers in the best available
Italian edition, *Claudio Monteverdi: lettere, dediche, e prefazioni*, edited by
Domenico De' Paoli (Rome, 1973), are given (except in the case of the
new letter, no. XXXVIII) in parentheses after the heading of each letter,
in the following way: *Stevens No. 2; De' Paoli, p. 21*.

For generous assistance in revision I am indebted to Dr Éva Lax of
the L. Eötvös University of Budapest, who hopes to make the
correspondence available in Hungarian.

NOTE ON MONEY VALUES

Exchange rates for the gold ducat and the debased gold scudo varied
considerably in Italy, depending on time and place. Mantua used ducats
in the sixteenth century but changed to scudi by the early seventeenth,
so that a salary designated in scudi would have to be discounted by about
10 per cent in order to measure up to Venetian ducats. The ducat was
worth about 7 Mantuan lire, and the scudo 6 lire. (There were 20 soldi
to the lira, and 12 denari to the soldo.)

I

The earliest of Monteverdi's letters in the Mantuan archives is an application, dated 28 November 1601, for the post of director of music to Vincenzo Gonzaga, fourth Duke of Mantua. This request was granted in 1602, and in the same year the composer acquired Mantuan citizenship. Early in 1603 he and his wife Claudia moved to a house in the parish of S. Pietro, in order to be nearer to the ducal palace, which was the main centre of his duties. In May 1604 their son Massimiliano was born, and a young singer from Rome—Caterina Martinelli—came to live with the family and study singing. The Duke believed in placing promising vocal talent in the hands of his very capable *maestro*, but the financial rewards hardly made up for all the extra work and responsibility. Not only were Monteverdi's wages being paid so late as to cause serious hardship, but the same was happening to his wife and her father, both of whom were also employed as court musicians. Monteverdi's letter to the Duke explains the root of the problem—a cunningly uncooperative treasury official, who proved to be mainly responsible for the consistently late payments. It was this lamentable state of affairs that finally brought the composer's patience to breaking point, yet throughout this exceptionally trying period he continued to write one masterpiece after another: madrigals, church music, ballets and operas. As with Mozart, external pressures seemed to have no adverse effect upon the quality of his inspiration or his need to create.

I

Mantua, 27 October 1604; to Duke Vincenzo Gonzaga, at Casale Monferrato. *(Stevens No. 2; De' Paoli, p. 21)*

Most Serene Lord, my Most Respected Master,[1]

As final recourse it is indeed proper that I appeal to Your Highness's infinite virtue, since it is that which in the end directs your will concerning the salary[2] granted to me by your kindness. I therefore kneel before you with the greatest possible humility, and beg you to be so good as to cast your gaze not upon my boldness (perhaps) in writing this letter, but rather upon my great distress, which is the reason for my writing; not upon the Lord President,[3] who on numerous occasions has given an affirmative order so very kindly and politely, but rather upon Belintento,[4] who never wanted to carry it out except when it pleased him, and now that it has come down to this, I have almost had to accustom myself to being beholden to him—and not to the infinite virtue of Your

Highness, who through his boundless good will grants favours even to servants of little merit such as I am compared with the widespread regard for Your Highness's great merit—although behaving in a most unmannerly **way** towards me when he did not want to give me such payments.

This humble petition of mine comes to you with no other aim but to beg Your Highness kindly to direct that I receive wages amounting to a total of five months, in which situation my wife Claudia and my father-in-law[5] also find themselves, and this sum grows even larger since we do not see any hope of being able to get hold of future payments save by the express command of Your Highness, without which support all that I have been building up will be ruined and undone, since misfortunes continue to overwhelm me day in and day out, and I have not the means to remedy them.

Nevertheless, to obtain these payments (at least of one month only, if not all) I have used nothing if not prayers, humility, and politeness morning and night, by virtue of which exertion I have lost and am still losing practically all the time for study that I ought to devote to the taste and requirements of Your Highness, finding myself as I do in a responsible position and favoured by you, and yet I can obtain nothing.

If I am worthy to receive it of Your Highness's infinite virtue, I beg you from the bottom of my heart to grant me this particular favour, which is not only that I be paid, but (and this I shall feel each time as an even greater favour) that I not be paid by the hand of this Belintento, for I am sure that Your Highness could find someone other than him who would give me some satisfaction, at least in words if not in deeds, at least in honour if not in results, at least once if not every time. Nor do I know why this man goes on behaving thus towards me.

If this favour of yours were to extend over the customs duties of Viadana,[6] we would be entirely satisfied; and I being thus assured by Your Highness's infinite virtue and by the many other outstanding graces and kindnesses granted to me, hope also to be favoured (by virtue of such graces and kindnesses) with that which I have requested of Your Highness. Being capable of no more, I shall pray that Our Lord grant a long life to Your Highness, to whom I bow and make a most humble reverence.

from Mantua, 27 October 1604

Your Most Serene Highness's

most humble and most grateful servant
Claudio Monteverdi

[1] The opening and closing salutations are given here in their complete form as an example of normal epistolary style in addressing superiors. They have been omitted from the remaining translations, except in the case of the newly discovered letter, no. XXXVIII.

[2] Salary, as opposed to payment in kind.

[3] Alessandro Striggio.

[4] Ottavio Benintendi.

[5] Giacomo Cattaneo.

[6] The town, not the composer.

II, III, IV

The next three letters were all written from Cremona, where the composer with his ailing wife Claudia and their children were lodging with his physician father, Baldassare Monteverdi. Although token contact was maintained with the Gonzaga court, Monteverdi felt no overpowering desire to return there and risk further spells of overwork and exhaustion. Each letter is written to a different councillor—Iberti, Chieppio and Striggio, for these were the men who at various times shared the task of controlling the artistic life of the court. Striggio, the youngest of the three, had already provided the libretto for Monteverdi's *Orfeo* in 1607 and was to become his special ally and protector throughout the troubled years at Mantua. The sonnets referred to in Letter II are in all probability *Zefiro torna e'l bel tempo rimena* and *Ohimè, il bel viso*, later published in his sixth book of madrigals.

The death of his wife on 10 September 1607 dealt Monteverdi's health and spirits a severe blow. His father wrote to the Duke and Duchess requesting an honourable dismissal for the grief-stricken composer. But this plea went unnoticed, for Chieppio, acting on orders from Vincenzo, instructed Monteverdi to return to his duties. Letter III shows the extent of his resentment and disappointment, contrasting as it does all the drawbacks of Mantuan service with the advantages enjoyed by other composers. The release for which he so passionately longed was not to be granted for another three years or more. Letter IV is of unusual interest since it portrays the composer in two relatively unfamiliar roles: as a person responsible for hiring wind-players for Prince Francesco's private band; and as a judge of musicianship and compositions, for the same Prince had expressed a wish to know as much as possible about Galeazzo Sirena, an organist who might just prove suitable for the vacant position at Casale Monferrato.

II

Cremona, 28 July 1607; to Annibale Iberti, at Genoa [Sampierdarena].
(Stevens No. 4; De' Paoli, p. 27)

As soon as His Highness[1] left Mantua, I too went away—to see my father in Cremona, where I still am—which is why I did not receive Your Lordship's letter earlier than the 20th of this month, and so on seeing His Highness's commission, I straightway began setting the sonnet to music, and was engaged in doing this for six days, then two more what with trying it out and rewriting it. I worked at it with the same devotion of mind that I have always had in regard to every other composition written by me in order the more to serve His Highness's most delicate taste.

But I did not work with comparable physical strength, because I was a little indisposed. Nevertheless I hope that this madrigal is not going to displease His Highness, but if by chance (to my misfortune) it were to obtain an unfavourable result, I beg Your Lordship to tender my apology based on the above-mentioned reason.

Here then is the music I have composed; but you will be doing me a kindness by handing it over, before His Highness hears it, to Signor Don Bassano[2] so that he can rehearse it and get a firm grasp of the melody together with the other gentlemen singers, because it is very difficult for a singer to perform a part which he has not first practised, and greatly damaging to the composition itself, as it is not completely understood on being sung for the first time.

I shall send Your Lordship the other sonnet, set to music, as soon as possible—since it is already clearly shaped in my mind—but if I should spin out the time even a little, in His Highness's opinion, please be good enough to let me know and I shall send it at once.

[1] Vincenzo Gonzaga, fourth Duke of Mantua.
[2] Bassano Casola, the assistant director of music.

III

Cremona, 2 December 1608; to Annibale Chieppio, [at Mantua].
(Stevens No. 6; De' Paoli, p. 33)

Today, which is the last day of November, I received from Your Lordship a letter from which I learned of His Highness's[1] command:

that I come as soon as possible to Mantua. Most Illustrious Signor Chieppio, if he orders me to come and wear myself out again, I assure you that unless I take a rest from toiling away at music for the theatre, my life will indeed be a short one, for as a result of my labours (so recent and of such magnitude) I have had a frightful pain in my head and so terrible and violent an itching around my waist, that neither by cauteries which I have had applied to myself, nor by purges taken orally, nor by blood-letting and other potent remedies has it thus far been possible to get better—only partly so. My father[2] attributes the cause of the headache to mental strain, and the itching to Mantua's air (which does not agree with me), and he fears that the air alone could be the death of me before long. Just think then, Your Lordship, what the addition of brainwork would do.

If His Highness orders me to come and receive graces and favours from his kindness and clemency, I tell Your Lordship that the fortune I have known in Mantua for nineteen consecutive years has given me occasion to call it inimical to me, and not friendly; because if it has done me the favour of receiving from His Highness the Duke the honour of being able to serve him in Hungary, it has also done me the disfavour of saddling me with an extra burden of expense from that journey, which our poor household feels almost to this very day.

If fortune called me to His Highness's service in Flanders, it also crossed me on that occasion by making my wife Claudia, living at Cremona, bring expense to our household with her maid and servant, she having at that time still only 47 lire a month from His Highness, beyond the money my father quietly gave me.

If fortune did me a good turn in that His Highness the Duke then increased my allowance from 12½ scudi in Mantuan currency to 25 a month, it also went against me by making the aforementioned Lord Duke decide subsequently to send me word, by Don Federico Follino, that out of this increase he intended that I should pay the expenses of Signor Campagnolo, then a boy, and because I did not want this trouble it was necessary for me to give up 5 scudi a month for those expenses. So I was left with the 20 scudi which I now have.

If fortune favoured me last year by making the Lord Duke invite me to assist with the musical events for the marriage, it also did me a bad turn on that occasion by making me perform an almost impossible task, and furthermore it caused me to suffer from cold, lack of clothing, servitude, and very nearly lack of food (through the stopping of my wife Claudia's allowance and the onset of a serious illness), without my being in the slightest degree favoured by His Highness with any public mark of esteem, though Your Lordship knows very well that the favours of great princes help servants both in regard to honour and what is useful to them, particularly on an occasion when there are visitors.

If fortune granted me a livery from His Highness, to wear at the time of the marriage, it also let me down badly by making me have it of cloth which was woven from silk and floss-silk, with no overcoat, no stockings and garters, and no silk lining for the cloak, wherefore I spent out of my own pocket 20 scudi in Mantuan currency.

If fortune has done me a favour by letting me have so very many opportunities of being commissioned by His Highness, it has also caused me this loss, that the Lord Duke has always spoken to me about hard work, and never about bringing me a little pleasure or profit.

If lastly (to go on no longer) fortune has looked kindly upon me by making me think I had a pension from His Highness of 100 scudi in Mantuan currency from the captaincy of the piazza, it showed its black side even then because when the marriage ceremonies were over there were not 100 scudi but only 70 (along with the loss of my commission and loss of money from the previous months), as if perhaps it were amazed by the 100 scudi being too much; and those added to the 20 I am getting made about 22 ducatoni a month. Even if I had received them, what then would I have set aside for the use of my poor sons?

Orazio della Viola would have had to work very hard to get an income of 500 scudi a year, without the usual perquisites, if he had nothing but the aforementioned every month. Similarly Luca Marenzio would have had to work quite hard to become as rich, and likewise Philippe de Monte and Palestrina, who left his sons an income worth more than 1000 scudi. Luzzaschi and Fiorino[3] would have had to work quite hard to get an income of 300 scudi each, which was then left to their sons; and lastly (to say no more) Franceschino Rovigo would have had to toil away to save 7000 scudi, as he did, if he had nothing but the aforementioned wages, which hardly suffice to pay the expenses of a master and servant and clothe him; for I don't know about his having two sons as well, which is the case with me. So, Your Lordship, if I have to draw the conclusion from the premises I shall say that I am never going to receive graces and favours at Mantua, but rather expect the final blow from ill fortune to be on its way.

I know full well that His Highness the Duke has the very best of intentions towards me, and I know that he is a very generous prince; but I am extremely unlucky at Mantua, and this Your Lordship will discover from the following account, for I do know that His Highness—after the death of my wife Claudia—made a resolution to leave me her allowance. However, on my arrival in Mantua he suddenly changed his mind and thus gave no such order (unluckily for me), wherefore up till now I happen to have lost more than 200 scudi, and every day I go on losing. He also decided—as I said before—to give me 25 scudi a month, but lo and behold he suddenly changed his mind, and unluckily for me five of them fell by the wayside; so that my ill fortune, Your Lordship, is openly acknowledged to be at Mantua.

What clearer proof do you want, Your Lordship? To give 200 scudi to Messer Marco da Gagliano, who can hardly be said to have done anything, and to give me nothing, who did what I did. Therefore I beg you for the love of God, Most Illustrious Signor Chieppio, knowing as you do that I am unwell and unfortunate in Mantua, please let me have an honourable dismissal from His Highness, for I know that from this I shall derive true happiness. Don Federico Follino promised in one of his letters, inviting me from Cremona last year to Mantua for the wedding preparations—I tell you he promised me what Your Lordship can see in this letter of his that I am sending you; and then at the end of it all nothing happened, or if indeed I had something, it was 1500 lines to set to music.

Dear Sir, help me to obtain an honourable dismissal, for it seems to me that this is the best possible thing, because I shall have a change of air, work and fortune; and who knows, if the worst comes to the worst what else can I do but remain poor as I am? As regards my coming to Mantua to secure my dismissal with His Highness's kind approval, unless he wish it otherwise this much will I do, assuring Your Lordship that I shall always proclaim His Highness as my lord and master, wherever I am, and I shall always acknowledge him with my humble prayers to Almighty God; more than this I cannot do. Then when it comes to considering the graces and favours received time and time again from the Most Illustrious Signor Chieppio, you may be sure that I never think about this matter without blushing, remembering how troublesome I have been to you; but where my feeble powers cannot reach, at least my heart and voice will succeed in proclaiming your infinite kindnesses and my everlasting indebtedness to Your Lordship.

[1] Vincenzo Gonzaga, fourth Duke of Mantua.
[2] Baldassare Monteverdi.
[3] Luzzasco Luzzaschi; Ippolito Fiorini.

IV

Cremona, 10 September 1609; [to Alessandro Striggio, at Mantua].
(Stevens No. 8; De' Paoli, p. 43)

On the 9th of this month I had a letter from Your Lordship enjoining me
not to engage those wind-players without further advice, but rather to
keep them buoyed up with a little hope. This much I did, and this much I
would have done without being advised; in any event I shall so continue
with greater confidence now that I have it as an order. I said to these
people three days ago: 'If the commander or governor of the castle knew
that you wanted to leave, would he give you permission?' They replied
that not only would he not give permission, but he would hinder them in
every way so that they could not leave. 'And if the need should arise, how
would you leave?' They answered: 'We would go without saying
anything.' I did not discuss the matter further; but Your Lordship has
now heard about the difficulties of their departure.

On the 4th of this month I also had a letter from His Highness the
Prince,[1] written to me from Maderno.[2] This mentions that I am to
enquire whether a certain Galeazzo Sirena, composer and organist,
would come and serve His Highness, and what salary he would like; and
that I am to let the said prince know about his capability and intelligence.
And because I am very well acquainted with the said Galeazzo—indeed
he comes daily to see me at home, so that through this I know him
intimately—I performed this task as soon as the commission was
received.

The man at once replied that he had no mind to go and serve princes,
but was keen to go and live in Milan as director of music at the church
of La Scala[3] (especially since certain Milanese singers promised to
make that post available to him), because with a chance like that he
says he could earn his living by teaching, making music for the city,
composing for the nuns, and having guitars and harpsichords made
for sale; and so by this means he would hope to become rich in a
short time.

To this I replied that I wanted him to think a little about what I had
said to him, and then if he did not wish to enter the service of that prince,
he might at least tell me what excuse I should offer. So, after seeing him
several times and nothing having come of it, I thought it proper to write
to Your Lordship as to who this man is, so that you may inform His
Highness; for if I insist on waiting until Galeazzo answers me and then

write to His Highness, I am afraid he may think that by being tardy I am negligent in doing what he commands.

I therefore tell Your Lordship that this Galeazzo is a man thirty-seven years old, poor, with a wife and children, a father who works as a labourer in the carriage and sedan-chair trade, and a mother very much poorer who has to spin at the mill all day. This man has an all-round talent, and when he concentrates he does not do badly. He set himself to make a psaltery and made it very well; he set himself to make a theorbo and again he made it very well, and likewise a harpsichord and many other handmade things. In music he is certainly intelligent, but self-opinionated; and he insists that whatever comes out of his head is the most beautiful of its kind, and if others are not quick to say so, he himself is the first.

Of his work I have only heard—from two eight-part masses—the *Kyrie* and *Gloria* of one, and all of the other except the *Sanctus* and *Agnus* (for more than this he has not composed), and a *Credo* from another four-part mass, a twelve-part *Dixit*, and some four-part canzonas to be played on string or wind instruments, these being very practical, technically well worked out, and of a certain novel invention. As for the masses and *Dixit*, however, they are written in a style that is certainly opulent but difficult to sing, because he persists in hunting down certain voice-parts and rests, which greatly tires and worries the singers.

I genuinely believe that he would still accommodate himself to what His Highness is looking for, but since I have not heard any of it—any of his work in this vein—I prefer not to give my opinion, because I rather think that before he could gain familiarity with the theatre it would cost him no little effort, having spent his time on music of the ecclesiastical type; and even in this he still finds it hard to be successful with his own works, since he tends to be stubborn.

So, knowing him to be very well endowed both as regards the poverty and the conviction of his thought, and not being sure that he would give complete satisfaction to His Highness, I said to him: 'Since I know that you would want to be well paid, and so that His Highness may know upon whom he has to lay out such moneys, it will give you little trouble to do what His Highness commands. Consequently, if you would like to go and live in Mantua on a trial basis for three months and there display your worth, I will see to it that you are given a room, service, food, and something of a gratuity as well; and in this way you can arrange the contract yourself.' But to this he replied that he did not want to, so I added: 'You do not have anything in print about which an opinion can be given concerning your worth, nor do you even want to come on trial, nor have you ever composed theatrical music; so how can one possibly form any idea of this without first-hand knowledge?'

As Your Lordship has realized, he is of this nature: he has ample conviction, but no idea of making himself liked by the singers, for those in Cremona are not happy singing under him, although they respect him; and he readily speaks ill of a third party. Next, about his organ playing: he performs in accordance with his knowledge of counterpoint, but certainly not with elegance of hand, since he has not the touch to bring off runs, trills, appoggiaturas or other ornaments, and he himself admits to not making a profession of it, although he plays the organ in S. Agostino here in Cremona; but he does this because he is poor.

After two or three days he asked me to tell him (if he were to go and serve His Highness) whether the Prince wanted him as his director of music, or for some other post, to which I replied that I did not know his intention. So, Signor Striggio, I thought I would write to Your Lordship a few words about the things that make me uneasy, because I mean the Prince is entitled to do just what seems right and pleasing to His Highness, but by taking either him or others as director of music (if indeed he wants to give him such a title, and that I don't know), on the death of the Duke, and should Almighty God allow me to survive—the Prince having a director of music—what would you wish me to do: go away from Mantua then?

I want to find out, if you please, Your Lordship (in that discreet manner which I know will be better seen to by you than explained by me), whether His Highness has this intention, so that I may know what to do. Forgive me if I have been too long, but blame my ignorance which has prevented me from learning to speak concisely.

[1] Francesco Gonzaga.
[2] Now known as Toscolano-Maderno; it is on the west shore of Lake Garda.
[3] S. Maria della Scala.

V, VI, VII

Although the majority of Monteverdi's letters are addressed to Striggio, a handful came directly to the attention of Duke Vincenzo and his sons. The three following letters, sent from Mantua to the Duke, and to the Princes Ferdinando and Francesco, indicate the nature of this personal contact between the composer and his patrons and the reasons for its existence. Letter V provides a detailed and highly informative report on a 'contralto' (actually a male singer with a high tenor range) who wished to join the growing number of the Duke's musicians. As Vincenzo was on holiday at Maderno on the gentle shores of Lake Garda, the letter was sent to him there, bypassing the usual and formal administrative channels. Monteverdi emerges as a resourceful and much respected director of music in Letter VI (dated January, not June as shown in *The Letters of Claudio Monteverdi*), which tells with loving care and justifiable pride about his performances of secular music at court. In Letter VII we learn what was expected of a wind instrumentalist wishing to serve a prince: once again Monteverdi's role is that of a well-informed judge.

V

Mantua, 9 June 1610; [to Duke Vincenzo Gonzaga, at Maderno].
  (Stevens No. 9; De' Paoli, p. 48)

I was entrusted by Messer Pandolfo[1] (on behalf of Your Highness) with hearing a certain contralto, come from Modena, desirous of serving Your Highness, so I took him straightway into S. Pietro[2] and had him sing a motet in the organ gallery. I heard a fine voice, powerful and far-reaching; and when he sings on the stage he will make himself heard in every corner very easily and without strain, a thing that Brandino[3] could not do as well.

He has a very good *trillo* and decent ornamentation, and he sings his part very surely in motets, so I hope he will not displease Your Highness. He has a few small defects, that is to say, he sometimes swallows his vowel a little, almost in the manner of Messer Pandolfo, and sometimes sends it through his nose, and then again he lets it slip through his teeth, which makes the word in question unintelligible; and he does not really strike the ornamentation as would be needful, nor does he soften it at certain other places.

But I am of the sure opinion that he could rid himself of all these things as soon as they are pointed out. I have not been able to hear him in madrigals, because he was all ready to set out and place himself at Your Highness's disposal, so that I am reporting to Your Highness what I have heard him in, and since you have ordered me to do nothing else, I end my letter here.

[1] Pandolfo Grandi of Modena.
[2] The cathedral of Mantua.
[3] Antonio Brandi, a male alto.

VI

Mantua, 22 January 1611; [to Cardinal Ferdinando Gonzaga, at Rome].
(Stevens No. 12; De' Paoli, p. 57)

I have just now received Your Eminence's very kind letter together with
the two most beautiful madrigals set to music; and I read and re-read the
letter, I at once sang the music to myself over and over, and kissed the
one and the other again and again with extreme rejoicing, seeing in that
letter how great Your Eminence's affection is towards one of his lowliest
servants, as I am, who deserve nothing.

Every Friday evening music is performed in the Hall of Mirrors.
Signora Adriana[1] comes to sing in concert, and lends the music such
power and so special a grace, bringing such delight to the senses that the
place becomes almost like a new theatre. And I think that the carnival of
concerts will not end without His Highness the Duke[2] having to post
guards at the entrance, for I swear to Your Eminence that in the
audience this last Friday there were not only Their Highnesses the
Duke and Duchess, the Lady Isabella of San Martino,[3] the Marquis and
Marchioness of Solferino,[4] ladies and knights from the entire court, but
also more than a hundred other gentlemen from the city too.

On a similar splendid occasion I shall have the theorbos played by the
musicians from Casale,[5] to the accompaniment of the wooden organ
(which is extremely suave), and in this way Signora Adriana and Don
Giovanni Battista[6] will sing the extremely beautiful madrigal *Ahi, che
morire mi sento*, and the other madrigal to the organ alone. Tomorrow I
shall take the aforesaid compositions and present them to Signora
Adriana, and I know how precious they will be to her, yet I do not want to
tell her the composer's name until she has sung them. I shall then send a
report to Your Eminence of the entire outcome.

I shall not fail to see to it that Franceschino[7] my son, and Your
Eminence's most humble servant, may learn three virtues: first, to serve
God with all diligence and fear; second, the art of letters; and third, a
little music, for until now it seems to me that he manages both *trillo* and
ornaments quite well, so that by means of Your Eminence's support he
may obtain from God and His Holiness[8] the favour which I beg for him
every day in my feeble prayers.

I do not know, Most Illustrious Lord, whether it would be too bold of
me to ask you—the bishopric of Novara being vacant, which has an
income of 8000 scudi—whether you would be kind enough to put in a

word here about the allowance for this son of mine, since it would pay for
his board and lodging, amounting to at least 100 golden scudi. If in fact I
have been too forward in troubling you, forgive me for the love of God,
but if I could indeed receive the favour, what content I would feel in my
heart! It would seem as if I had acquired all the gold in the world.

[1] Adriana Basile.
[2] Vincenzo Gonzaga, fourth Duke of Mantua.
[3] Isabella di Novellara, widow of Don Ferrante Gonzaga di Bozzolo.
[4] Cristierno Gonzaga di Solferino and his wife Marcella.
[5] Probably the brothers Orazio and Giovanni Rubini of Casale Monferrato.
[6] Giovanni Battista Sacchi.
[7] Francesco Monteverdi.
[8] Pope Paul V.

VII

Mantua, 26 March 1611; [to Prince Francesco Gonzaga, at Casale
Monferrato]. *(Stevens No. 11; De' Paoli, p. 54)*

Your Highness left instruction with Messer Giulio Cesare[1] the
Cremonese (who plays the cornett) that if someone could be found who
would play the recorder, cornett, trombone, flute and bassoon—for
want of a fifth part in Your Highness's wind band—you would be
pleased to take him on. I therefore approach with this letter of mine to let
Your Highness know that there is a young man here of about twenty-six
or twenty-eight (I do not know whether he is passing through or has
come on purpose) who can play on the aforementioned instruments very
readily at least, and with assurance, because I have heard him play both
recorder and cornett; moreover he says that he can also play the gamba
and the viola.

At first glance I find him full of great probity and good manners. I
sounded him out on my own initiative about his requirements in case it
should happen that Their Highnesses[2] might be pleased to engage him.
Never, as far as I have been able to ascertain, has he wanted to come
down to any other particular than this: that if he were worthy of such a
favour, he would consider all that might be given to him as great good
fortune, since he has no other or greater desire than to learn, and to
serve, and to become fit to be allowed to serve.

I sounded him out on my own account and told him: 'If His Highness
the Prince were pleased to take you on, this gentleman very much likes
not only to hear a variety of wind instruments, he also likes to have the

said musicians play in private, in church, in procession and atop city walls; now madrigals, now French songs, now airs and now dance-songs.' And he told me in reply that he would do everything, as he will always consider it great good fortune, this becoming fit to be allowed to serve the likes of Their Highnesses in some way. He says that he will stay in Mantua for Easter; consequently Your Highness can give such instruction as may please you in this matter.

At this point in my letter I am also praying that Our Lord grant you a happy Easter, and I beseech you to be so kind as to accept the *Dixit* for eight voices which Your Highness ordered me to send, together with which I am also sending you a little motet for two voices to be sung at the Elevation, and another for five voices for the Blessed Virgin. Once Holy Week is over I shall send a couple of madrigals, and anything else that I understand may be to Your Highness's taste.

You will do me a special kindness by letting my brother[3] see these compositions a little before Your Highness may condescend to hear them, so that my brother, the singers and the players can—as a group—get acquainted with the melody of the said songs, for Your Highness will then be less offended by this feeble music of mine.

[1] Giulio Cesare Bianchi.
[2] Francesco Gonzaga and Margherita of Savoy.
[3] Giulio Cesare Monteverdi.

VIII, IX, X, XI

Just as Monteverdi's sojourn in Mantua witnessed much in the way of sorrow and disappointment, despite his artistic triumphs, so did his leave-taking feature an unhappy incident when he and his sons and their maidservant were robbed on the road to Venice, near the village of Sanguinetto, some four miles east of Nogara. Letter VIII, besides its value as a social document, provides an excellent example of Monteverdi's feeling for dramatic narration. Fortunately for music, all the passengers escaped with their lives, though they lost money and personal possessions. Once they were established in an apartment in the canonry of St. Mark's, a new kind of life began. Monteverdi took his duties as director of music seriously, yet he continued to correspond with Mantua about entertainment, especially stage works. Letter IX discusses the production, performance and instrumentation of the ballet *Tirsi e Clori*, later published in the seventh book of madrigals. Letters X and XI, addressed to Striggio, deal with further dramatic projects: a maritime fable which brings out the shrewd critic within the composer, and a ballet whose music seems not to have survived.

VIII

Venice, 12 October 1613; [to Annibale Iberti, at Mantua]. *(Stevens No. 13; De' Paoli, p. 62)*

I am writing to let Your Lordship know how, being in the company of the Mantuan courier and leaving with him for Venice, we were robbed at Sanguinetto (not in the actual place, but rather two miles away from it) by three ruffians—bandits—in this manner. Suddenly from a field adjoining the main road there came two men of a brownish complexion, not much beard, and of medium height, with a long musket apiece (the flint-wheel type) and its firing-pin down. Then, one of these approaching on my side to frighten me with the musket, and the other holding on to the bridle of the horses—which went along quietly—they drew us aside into that field without saying a word.

And making me kneel down as soon as I had dismounted, one of the two who had the muskets demanded my purse, and the other demanded the cases from the courier. They were pulled down from the carriage by the courier, who opened them for him one by one, that assassin taking what he liked, and having everything given to him promptly by the courier. I was still on my knees all the while, guarded by the other one who had a gun, and in this manner they took whatever they wanted, as the third of the three assassins, who had a spike in his hand and had acted as lookout, was continuing to do this, making sure that nobody should enter from the road.

When they had well and truly turned over all the goods, the one who was looking into the things obtained from the courier came up to me and told me to undress myself because he wanted to see whether I had any other money. Having made sure that I did not, he went over to my maidservant for the same purpose, but she—helping her cause with all manner of prayers, entreaties and lamentations—made him leave her alone. Then, turning to the things and the cases, he made a bundle of the best and finest, and while looking for something to cover himself with he found my cloak—a long one of serge, brand new—which I had just had made for me in Cremona.

He said to the courier, 'Put this cloak on me'; but when the assassin saw that it was too long for him, he said: 'Give me another one.' So he took my son's, but finding it too short, the courier then said, 'Look, master, it belongs to that poor seminarian—give it to him'; and he complied. The courier also found the said boy's suit and did the same, and then when he asked with many entreaties for the maidservant's things as a gift, the ruffian handed them over to him. They made a huge bundle of the remainder, took it on their shoulders, and carried it away. Then we picked up the things that were left and went off to the inn.

On the following morning we filed a charge at Sanguinetto, then we left (I being much upset) and reached Este. We took a boat for Padua, which held us up all Thursday night and nearly the whole of Friday in silt, nobody worrying about the fact that we finally got away at 1 p.m.,[1] in heavy wind and rain, on an uncovered barge, and with none other rowing in the stern but our courier, who made a really hard job of it. We arrived at Padua, but it was as much as we could do to get in by 6 p.m.

After rising early on Saturday morning to leave for Venice, we waited more than two hours after sunrise to get under way, and during the time we were in Padua, the courier put his arm in a sling saying that this happened because of that business about the cloaks, when he was robbed. I, knowing that nothing of the coachman's was touched or even looked at, was beside myself to say the least. This act of the courier aroused suspicion among all who were with us, because they had previously seen him without any injury at all.

And there was someone in the Padua boat who said to the courier, 'What kind of tale is this, brother?', and being about to add further words (I would say, perhaps, as a jest) the courier dropped out of the conversation. So we reached Venice in the boat at 5 p.m. on Saturday, while he was joking and laughing, then he stayed for barely two hours and left again for Mantua. This was the affair in detail; and because the other Mantuan courier was here at my house reproaching me by saying that he understood I suspected the last courier, I told him in reply that I suspected nothing and that I take him to be a good man. But it is true that he did do that act you know about—putting his arm in a sling on Saturday morning because of the incident that happened on the previous Wednesday evening, and yet nobody touched him and he was rowing all day Friday.

I am writing to let Your Lordship know that I suspected nothing about this man, because if such a thought were to have entered my mind I would at once have given notice of it to Your Lordship. I am really saying that in regard to this act of the courier's—putting his arm in a sling—he gave us something to think about, and if there is something to be thought about, I leave it to the very prudent opinion of Your Lordship, for as for myself I think of nothing and look for nothing unless from the hand of

God. I assure you, Most Illustrious Lord, that they robbed me of more than a hundred Venetian ducats in goods and money.

When I was in Mantua, I enjoyed the favour from the Lord President of having six months' salary, and I am also due for another, due three months ago. I told him of my great misfortune. If you were to try and put in a good word for me with the Lord President[2] (although I know that the Lord President's kindness is great), I would regard it as the greatest favour because, Sir, I have infinite need of it.

---

[1] This and later references to times of the day have been adjusted to the *ore italiane*, which have been overlooked in previous translations (including my own).

[2] Lord President [of the Magistracy], at that time Alessandro Striggio.

IX

Venice, 21 November 1615; [to Annibale Iberti, at Mantua]. *(Stevens No. 18; De' Paoli, p. 79)*

His Highness[1] of Mantua's Most Illustrious Resident[2] dwelling in Venice, very much my master, commissioned me recently through Your Lordship's letter (at the command of His Highness of Mantua, my particular Lord) to set a ballet to music; but the commission did not go into any other detail, unlike those of the Most Serene Lord Duke Vincenzo—may he be in glory!—who used to demand of me such productions either in six, eight or nine movements, besides which he used to give me some account of the plot, and I used to try and fit to it the most apt and suitable music, and the metrical schemes that I knew.

However, believing that a ballet of six movements should turn out to be to His Highness's liking, I straightway tried to finish the enclosed, of which two movements were lacking; and this in fact I began in recent months in order to present it to His Highness, thinking that I would be in Mantua this past summer for certain business affairs of mine.

While I am sending it off by the hand of the Resident to Your Lordship, to present to His Highness, I also thought it a good idea to accompany it with a letter of mine addressed to Your Lordship, to tell you at the same time that if His Highness should want either a change of tune in this ballet, or additions to the enclosed movements of a slow or grave nature, or fuller and without imitative passages (His Highness taking no notice of the present words which can easily be changed, though at least these words help by the nature of their metre and by imitating the melody), or if he should want everything altered I beg you to act on my behalf so that His Highness may be so kind as to reword the commission, since as a most devoted servant, and most desirous of acquiring His Highness's favour, I shall not fail to carry it out in such a way that His Highness will be satisfied with me.

But if by good fortune the enclosed should be to his liking, I would think it proper to perform it in a half-moon, at whose corners should be placed an archlute and a harpsichord, one each side, one playing the bass for Chloris and the other for Thyrsis, each of them holding a lute, and playing and singing themselves to their own instruments and to the aforementioned. If there could be a harp instead of a lute for Chloris that would be even better.

Then having reached the ballet movement after they have sung a dialogue, there could be added to the ballet six more voices in order to make eight voices in all, eight *viole da braccio*, a contrabass, a *spineta arpata*,[3] and if there were also two lutes, that would be fine. And directed with a beat suitable to the character of the melodies, avoiding overexcitement among the singers and players, and with the understanding of the ballet-master, I hope that—sung in this way—it will not displease His Highness.

Also, if you could let the singers and players see it for an hour before His Highness hears it, it would be a very good thing indeed. It has been unusually precious to me, this present opportunity, not so much for showing myself very prompt in obeying His Highness's commands, which I so much desire and long for, as to commend myself to Your Lordship as a loyal servant, praying that you may wish to maintain me, and condescend to command me.

[1] Ferdinando Gonzaga, sixth Duke of Mantua.
[2] Camillo Sordi.
[3] A harp-shaped spinet.

X

Venice, 9 December 1616; [to Alessandro Striggio, at Mantua] *(Stevens No. 21; De' Paoli, p. 86)*

I received Your Lordship's letter from Signor Carlo de Torri[1] with most hearty rejoicing, also the little book containing the maritime fable *Le nozze di Tetide*. Your Lordship writes that you are sending it to me so that

I may look at it carefully and then give you my opinion, as it has to be set to music for use at the forthcoming wedding of His Highness.[2] I, who long for nothing so much as to be of some worth in His Highness's service, shall say no more in my initial reply than this, Your Lordship—that I offer myself readily for whatever His Highness may at any time deign to command me, and always without question honour and revere all that His Highness commands.

So, if His Highness approves of this fable it ought therefore to be very beautiful and much to my taste. But if you add that I may speak my mind, I am bound to obey Your Lordship's instructions with all respect and promptness, realizing that whatever I may say is a mere trifle, being a person worth little in all things, and a person who always honours every virtuoso, in particular the present Signor Poet[3] (whose name I know not), and so much the more because this profession of poetry is not mine.

I shall say, then, with all due respect—and in order to obey you since you so command—I shall say first of all in general that music wishes to be mistress of the air, not only of the water; I mean (in my terminology) that the ensembles described in that fable are all low-pitched and near to the earth, an enormous drawback to beautiful harmony since the continuo instruments will be placed among the bigger creatures at the back of the set—difficult for everyone to hear, and difficult to perform within the set.

And so I leave the decision about this matter to your most refined and most intelligent taste, for because of that defect you will need three archlutes instead of one, and you would want three harps instead of one, and so on and so forth; and instead of a delicate singing voice you would have a forced one. Besides this, in my opinion, the proper imitation of the words should be dependent upon wind instruments rather than upon strings and delicate instruments, for I think that the music of the Tritons and the other sea gods should be assigned to trombones and cornetts, not to citterns or harpsichords and harps, since the action (being maritime) properly takes place outside the city; and Plato teaches us that 'the cithara should be in the city, and the tibia in the country'[4] —so either the delicate will be unsuitable, or the suitable not delicate.

In addition, I have noticed that the interlocutors are winds, cupids, little zephyrs and sirens: consequently many sopranos will be needed, and it can also be stated that the winds have to sing—that is, the zephyrs and the boreals. How, dear Sir, can I imitate the speech of the winds, if they do not speak? And how can I, by such means, move the passions?

Ariadne moved us because she was a woman, and similarly Orpheus because he was a man, not a wind. Music can suggest, without any words, the noise of winds and the bleating of sheep, the neighing of horses and so on and so forth; but it cannot imitate the speech of winds because no such thing exists.

Next, the dances which are scattered throughout the fable do not have dance measures. And as to the story as a whole—as far as my no little ignorance is concerned, I do not feel that it moves me at all (moreover I find it hard to understand), nor do I feel that it carries me in a natural manner to an end that moves me. *Arianna* led me to a just lament, and *Orfeo* to a righteous prayer, but this fable leads me I don't know to what end. So what does Your Lordship want the music to be able to do? Nevertheless I shall always accept everything with due reverence and honour if by chance His Highness should so command and desire it, since he is my master without question.

And so, if His Highness should order it to be set to music, I would say that—since deities have more dialogue than anyone else in this fable, and I like to hear these deities singing gracefully—as regards the sirens, the three sisters (that is, Signora Adriana and the others)[5] would be able to sing them and also compose the music, and similarly Signor Rasi[6] with his part, and Signor Don Francesco[7] as well, and so on with the other gentlemen; in this way copying Cardinal Mont'Alto,[8] who put on a play in which every character who appeared made up his own part. Because if this were something that led to a single climax, like *Arianna* and *Orfeo*, you would certainly require a single hand—that is, if it led to singing speech, and not (as this does) to spoken song.

I also consider it, in this respect, much too long as regards each of the speaking parts, from the sirens onwards (and some other little discourse). Forgive me, dear Sir, if I have said too much; it was not to disparage anything, but through a desire to obey your orders, because if it has to be set to music (and were I so commanded), Your Lordship might take my thoughts into consideration.

[1] Probably a Mantuan gentleman visiting Venice.
[2] Ferdinando Gonzaga, sixth Duke of Mantua.
[3] Scipione Agnelli, later Bishop of Casale Monferrato.
[4] 'cithara debet esse in civitate, et thibia in agris' (*Republic*, I).
[5] Adriana Basile and her sisters Margherita and Tolla.
[6] Francesco Rasi, the eminent tenor.
[7] Francesco Dognazzi, who became director of music at Mantua in 1619.
[8] Alessandro Peretti Damascene, a patron of music and of Monteverdi. The play referred to is Jacopo Cicognini's *Amor pudico*.

XI

Venice, 9 February 1619; [to Alessandro Striggio, at Mantua]. *(Stevens No. 31; De' Paoli, p. 110)*

I have received Your Lordship's previous letter and the present one, but with this delay, however, because I went with my elder son Francesco to Bologna (as the first feast-days of Christmas were over) and had the chance to remove him from Padua—to remove him from the splendid time which the Most Illustrious Lord Abbot Morosini[1] was kindly giving him so as to enjoy a little of the boy's singing. And in the long run he would have turned out to be a good singer with all the other additions (as one would say—though it is better to keep quiet about that), rather than an average doctor; and yet my way of thinking would prefer him to be good in the second profession and mediocre in the first, as if it were an ornament.

So, for the sake of helping the boy (as indeed I have done) and for my own satisfaction, I went—as I said—to settle him in Bologna as a boarder with the Servite fathers, in which priory they read and debate every day. And I was there for this purpose for about fifteen days, so that what with going and coming back and stopping there, I can say that I had hardly reached Venice when Your Lordship's aforementioned first letter was handed over to me.

And even if I had not received this second one from the post a moment ago—as the debtor I was as regards replying to Your Lordship's most kind letter—I had determined to let Your Lordship know (by the courier who is returning) just what I have told you above in this letter. I hope that, as a very kind person, you will accept this my true excuse as legitimate; and I do assure you that if I had received the first letter in time, and had not been hindered by an urgent duty, I would already have carried into effect what you were kind enough to command me.

But since Your Lordship is pleased to have the ballet for this Easter, you may be sure of receiving it, for I would not tolerate so great a deficiency in myself (in not doing all I can to serve you) if I wanted to maintain myself, through results, as much your servant as I profess to be, both in speech and in writing.

[1] Monsignor Giovanni Francesco Morosini, Abbot of Leno and canon of Padua.

XII, XIII, XIV

Monteverdi's principal correspondents at the Gonzaga court, Striggio and Marigliani, were both active as librettists in addition to their work as bureaucrats, yet much of their output has vanished along with the music that was written to accompany it. The next three letters are mainly concerned with the progress of *Apollo*, an eclogue by Striggio, and Marigliani's play *Andromeda* (the text of which has recently been discovered: see below, 285–6). Working on them simultaneously, though in fits and starts because of the piecemeal delivery of the verse, Monteverdi appears to have regarded them as a mixed blessing: they assured him of work that brought a tangible reward even though it was not in itself rewarding, but at the same time they increased his worries and his artistic responsibilities. Nevertheless, the lament from *Apollo* found plentiful admirers at some of the soirées given by Giovanni Matteo Bembo, who was one of the leading musical patrons in Venice. Its loss is all the more regrettable in view of the other laments, madrigalian and operatic, which helped the composer to a pinnacle of fame.

XII

Venice, 9 January 1620; [to Alessandro Striggio, at Mantua]. *(Stevens No. 38; De' Paoli, p. 124)*

I am sending Your Lordship the lament of Apollo. By the next post I shall send you the beginning, up to this point, since it is already almost finished; a little revision in passing still remains to be done. At the place where Amore begins to sing, I would think it a good idea if Your Lordship were to add three more short verses of like metre and similar sentiment, so that the same tune could be repeated (hoping that this touch of gladness will not produce a bad effect when it follows—by way of contrast—Apollo's previous doleful mood), and then go on as it stands, changing the manner of expression in the music, just as the text does.

I would have sent Your Lordship this song by the last post, but Signor Marigliani[1] (in a letter addressed to me) has passed on a formidable request from Signor Don Vincenzo:[2] that I finish the *Andromeda*—already begun—a fable by the aforementioned Signor Marigliani, so that it can be performed for His Highness this carnival time, on his return from Casale. But just as I am having to do a bad job through being obliged to finish it in a hurry, so too I am thinking that it will be badly performed and badly played because of the acute shortage of time. I am also greatly surprised that Signor Marigliani wishes to involve himself in such a dubious enterprise, since even if it had been begun before Christmas, there would hardly be time to rehearse it, let alone learn it.

Now consider, Your Lordship: what do you think can be done when more than 400 lines, which have to be set to music, are still lacking? I can envisage no other result than bad singing of the poetry, bad playing of the instruments, and bad musical ensemble. These are not things to be done hastily, as it were; and you know from *Arianna* that after it was finished and learned by heart, five months of strenuous rehearsal took place.

Therefore if I could be certain that, through Your Lordship's influence, the Prince's[3] choice might fall upon Your Lordship's ballet (assuming however that this meets with your approval) I would expect this to be sufficient and would really succeed because I would have just enough time for such a short work. Then, at my convenience, I could finish off the *Andromeda*, and you could have it learned in ample time (afterwards letting it be heard to good effect) so that I could attend with more care and thought to that ballet of yours I am talking about.

Otherwise, being obliged to serve Signor Don Vincenzo and Your Lordship in so little time, I continue to think that the music I send will certainly be unsuitable rather than suitable; and I know you will admit that I am right, because you will take into account the fact that my ecclesiastical service has somewhat alienated me from the musical style of the theatre, and so before the style has become familiar again (what with the shortage of time and the need to write much) I shall have to send mere notes rather than something appropriate.

I am however most heartily eager to serve the Prince, Your Lordship and Signor Marigliani, and because of this I am going to beseech Your Lordship to arrange the matter so that it comes out to everybody's satisfaction, otherwise I shall do whatever I can with all my heart. You will honour me by letting me know whether this music is to your liking; and if not, send me word so that I may try and do what I can to serve you.

[1] Ercole Marigliani, court secretary and librettist.
[2] Don Vincenzo Gonzaga, younger brother of Duke Ferdinando.
[3] Referring to Don Vincenzo.

XIII

Venice, 1 February 1620; [to Alessandro Striggio, at Mantua]. *(Stevens No. 41; De' Paoli, p. 129)*

I have received Your Lordship's very kind letter and understood the reason for the delay, and what you wish from me. I reply to Your Lordship that, believing you did not want to do anything else, I gave up work for the time being. Now that you tell me you are about to have it performed, I assure you that if you do not receive from me, by the next post, everything that is outstanding, little will remain in my hands to finish.

You have only to let me know—once the verses are finished—what more I have to do, because if you wanted the ballet to be sung as well, let Your Lordship send me the words, for which I shall try (in setting them) to invent something in the metre that you give me; but should there be one metre in all the verses, I shall certainly change the tempo from time to time.

The lament of Apollo has been heard by certain gentlemen here, and since it pleased them in the manner of its invention, poetry and music, they think—after an hour of concerted music which usually takes place these days at the house of a certain gentleman of the Bembo family, where the most important ladies and gentlemen come to listen—they think (as I said) of having afterwards this fine idea of Your Lordship's put on a small stage. If I have to compose the ballet for this, would Your Lordship send me the verses as soon as possible? But if not, I shall add something of my own invention so that such a fine work of Your Lordship's can be enjoyed.

I was thinking of travelling to Mantua to present my books[1]—which I have now had printed—dedicated to Her Highness[2] (to take an advantageous road that may lead me to the goal I so much desired and worked for) so as to be able, once and for all, to get possession of that small donation which His Highness Duke Vincenzo,[3] of beloved memory, was kind enough to grant me.

But remembering that Signor Marigliani's play would have fallen entirely on my shoulders—and knowing that with the passage of time a feeble branch can bear a huge fruit, so that in no time at all the ability to hold up without breaking would be out of the question—in order not to break myself (in my feeble state of health) I did not want to come at such short notice to sustain this impossible weight, because something other than haste is needed to do justice to such a plot, and it is no small matter to make a success of it even with plenty of time.

Wherefore I have resolved to stay, and I am sorry about it because of my own interests, but in order to avoid dying I would give up whatever worldly interests you like. Your Lordship's work was a delight to me because I had already thought carefully about it beforehand. Besides this, it was very short, so that I would on that account have considered it a favour to be able to serve you, just as it always will be whenever you are so kind as to command me.

[1] The part-books of the seventh book of madrigals.
[2] Caterina Medici Gonzaga.
[3] Vincenzo Gonzaga, fourth Duke of Mantua.

XIV

Venice, 8 February 1620; [to Alessandro Striggio, at Mantua]. *(Stevens No. 42; De' Paoli, p. 132)*

I have received Your Lordship's very kind letter, and have remarked how constantly you continue to make me worthy of your grace, since you always show by your courteous expression of thanks that my service is not displeasing to you. Wherefore I am so bold as to send off to you the other remaining pieces of music for Your Lordship's very fine and beautiful eclogue.[1] The part of the River[2] is still to be done, and this—now that I know Signor Amigoni[3] will be singing it—I shall dispatch by the next post; and perhaps to my greater satisfaction too, since I shall compose it more to the mark now that I know who is going to sing it.

I further understood that you will be glad, up to this point, to give me an opportunity to serve you further at present since he has finished learning the aria already written. If however you are unable at present to honour me with further commands, I shall still not refrain from begging you a favour, which is that you may be so kind as to present, in my name, to Her Most Serene Ladyship[4] those madrigals dedicated to her, which I thought of presenting in person had I been able to come to Mantua; but the obvious impediments prevent me from doing so.

I shall arrange for these books (if you will so kindly do me the honour of assisting me) to be handed over personally to Your Lordship by my father-in-law.[5] More than this I was not hoping to do even if I came myself, other than to commend myself to Her Highness's favour and protection, so that one of these days I might be rewarded by His Highness the Duke[6] so as to be able to have my capital, from which I could draw my annual pension; for apart from the fact of rewarding a servant who toiled hard for so many years, and is of some renown in the world, it would also relieve the ducal chamber of such a duty.

If Your Lordship in his kindness may be willing to lend a little help in such a matter, you know my story as well as I do; and what the Prince[7] can do in such a matter, if he will be so kind, will help my two sons who are studying—sons indeed of the city of Mantua and subjects of Their Highnesses. And I am hoping that one day they will let themselves be seen by their rightful lords as not unworthy of their grace, since one is aiming at a doctorate in law, and the other in medicine.

Without the favour of Their Highnesses I cannot obtain the past half-yearly payments at the right time, and in consequence I cannot help them with these sums of money as I would do if I had them. If I am asking too much of Your Lordship's grace, blame your own kindness which has given me such a guarantee, and blame my very great need of your grace, which will ever be revered and honoured, by me no less than by my sons, and to which I—a servant—devote myself as is my wont.

[1] *Apollo.*
[2] Peneus.
[3] Giovanni Amigoni was a bass at Mantua.
[4] Caterina Medici Gonzaga.
[5] Giacomo Cattaneo.
[6] Ferdinando Gonzaga, sixth Duke of Mantua.
[7] Don Vincenzo Gonzaga, younger brother of Duke Ferdinando.

XV, XVI

In the late autumn of 1619, and well into the early months of 1620, the Gonzagas tried by various means to tempt Monteverdi in two ways: one was designed to persuade him to write a new work for the celebrations attendant upon the Duchess of Mantua's birthday, while the other—aiming at long-term results—sought to cajole him back into his old post as court musician. Both attempts failed, as one might expect, for Monteverdi was too firmly established in Venice ever to want to leave. But if he evaded the problems and pressures of writing a new work, he acquiesced in refurbishing an old one: the original score of *Arianna* was taken down from its shelf and recopied under his close personal supervision. Letter XV, besides mentioning *Apollo* and the seventh book of madrigals once more, hints at a much more serious topic than music. The Gonzagas have again made Monteverdi an offer, and true to type he writes to Striggio requesting further time for reflection and stringent security measures. He is anxious that no rumour of this offer should be put about in the profession, and admits that his reluctance even to visit Mantua for a short time stems from a cursory but caustic remark made by his dean. Letter XVI, remarkable for its length and frankness, shows that a week of careful thought had brought the composer not only to a better appreciation of his current advantages at St. Mark's, but to a pitch of rhetoric that gave rise to a strong indictment of the Gonzagas and their mean and devious ways. That such words should have been addressed to his friend Striggio undoubtedly caused Monteverdi some embarrassment, yet he knew that the statement had to be made, and made quickly.

XV

Venice, 8 March 1620; [to Alessandro Striggio, at Mantua]. *(Stevens No. 48; De' Paoli, p. 145)*

I shall become so indebted to you in my lifetime, Your Lordship, that even if I were to give up my life-blood (as it were) I know for sure that I would not pay off the debt. I shall always pray God that wherever my feeble forces are powerless, His Divine Majesty may come to my aid.

Your Lordship's very kind letter came late into my hands, so you will be doing me a favour by giving me time until the next post to think about that second paragraph, though I am quite certain that (passing through Your Lordship's hands) it could not possibly have any other result than my betterment and my peace of mind. Nevertheless, the fact that you may be content to wait until the next post for my reply will be the greatest favour of all.

I implore you however that this proposal, made to me by His Highness's[1] infinite goodness, may in no wise (whether the outcome is successful or not) be guessed at by any singer, player, or other of His Highness's musicians whatever, for you can be sure that no sooner would they hear about it than they would straightway noise it abroad in Venice, and everything would turn out to my ruin.

And this was one of the main reasons why I did not try in any way to discuss the said business with Signor Don Francesco Dognazzi,[2] when he was here in Venice this past November to do me this outstanding favour on behalf of His Highness, which was likewise the matter of offering me employment. But he, through being in the profession, was in consequence capable of getting excited about it, and did not keep it to himself, so that not long after his departure I heard it rumoured that I was returning to Mantua. And what is more, a month ago, when I let it be known that as soon as Their Highnesses returned from Casale I wanted to bring and present to them those books[3] of mine, the Most Illustrious Primicerius,[4] son of the Most Excellent Lord Procurator, My Lord of the House of Cornaro,[5] said to me: 'This business of your going to Mantua—they say you are going there for good!'

And this, perhaps, was one of the main reasons that kept me from bringing those books in person, because (dear Sir) the substance is bound to be dearer to me than the shadow. Now that the matter is in the hands of Your Lordship, who has all the qualities one looks for in negotiating everything to my advantage and without any harm to me, I shall accordingly tell you what I think by the next post, trying to base my thoughts upon such justice that even if I were not to succeed, I hope it will do me no harm—neither to my present position nor to my relationship with His Highness, which I honour and revere as much as the greatest blessings I can possibly have in this world.

I have heard about the success that my feeble music has won—helped, protected and raised up as it was by the great and infinite merit of Your Lordship's most beautiful words; no less admired and honoured by those illustrious gentlemen than I predicted (and I say this with a true and sincere heart), and no less raised up to the favour of His Highness as much as by the infinite kindness of Your Lordship, so that with good reason indeed I am still bound to be ever grateful in the manner I have already mentioned to Your Lordship.

[1] Ferdinando Gonzaga, sixth Duke of Mantua.
[2] Director of music since 1619.
[3] The part-books of the seventh book of madrigals.
[4] Marc'Antonio Cornaro, the principal dignitary of St. Mark's.
[5] Giovanni Cornaro (elected 1609).

XVI

Venice, 13 March 1620; [to Alessandro Striggio, at Mantua]. *(Stevens No. 49; De' Paoli, p. 148)*

I am writing to answer the second paragraph of Your Lordship's letter, about which I took time to reply until the present post. In the first place, Your Lordship, I must say that the singular honour which His Highness has accorded to my person, in doing me this particular favour of offering me employment once again, has been so heart-warming and of such kindness that I confess myself lacking in words to give expression to so remarkable a favour—inasmuch as the years of my youth spent in that Most Serene service have in such wise planted in my heart a memory of gratitude and goodwill and reverence towards that Most Serene House—so that as long as there is life in me I shall pray to God, and desire for it the greatest happiness that a servant bowed down and indebted to it can wish and long for.

And certainly if I had no other concern but for myself alone, Your Lordship may be sure that I would be compelled to fly if I could, not just run, to His Highness's commands without any other thought or expectation. But what with this Most Serene Republic, and the fact that my sons[1] oblige me to entertain second thoughts, perhaps you will allow me to run on a little about these two points, as I still believe myself to be aided by Your Lordship's kindness in this matter likewise, and know of what great worth it is in regard to prudence and brotherly love.

I shall therefore submit for Your Lordship's consideration the fact that this Most Serene Republic has never before given to any of my predecessors—whether it were Adriano or Cipriano,[2] or Zarlino,[3] or anyone else—but 200 ducats in salary whereas to me they give 400; a favour that ought not to be so lightly set aside by me without some consideration, since (Most Illustrious Lord) this Most Serene Signory does not make an innovation without very careful thought.

Wherefore—I repeat—this particular favour ought to command my utmost respect. Nor, having done this for me, have they ever regretted it: on the contrary they have honoured me, and honour me continually in such manner, that no singer is accepted into the choir until they ask the opinion of the director of music; nor do they want any report about the affairs of singers other than that of the director of music; nor do they take on organists or an assistant director unless they have the opinion and the report of that same director of music; nor is there any gentleman who does not esteem and honour me, and when I am about to perform either chamber or church music, I swear to Your Lordship that the entire city comes running.

Next, the duties are very light since the whole choir is liable to discipline except the director of music—in fact, it is in his hands, having a singer censured or excused and giving leave or not; and if he does not go into chapel nobody says anything. Moreover his allowance is assured until his death: neither the death of a procurator nor that of a doge interferes with it, and by always serving faithfully and with reverence he has greater expectations, not the opposite; and as regards his salary money, if he does not go at the appointed time to pick it up, it is brought round to his house.

And this is the first particular, as regards basic income: then there is occasional income, which consists of whatever extra I can easily earn outside St. Mark's, of about 200 ducats a year (invited as I am again and again by the wardens of the guilds) because whoever can engage the director to look after their music—not to mention the payment of 30 ducats, and even 40, and up to 50 for two Vespers and a mass—does not fail to take him on, and they also thank him afterwards with well-chosen words.

Now let Your Lordship weigh in the balance of your very refined judgment that amount which you have offered me in His Highness's name,[4] and see whether—on good and solid grounds—I could make the change or not; and please consider in the first place, Your Lordship, what harm it would do to my reputation with these Most Illustrious Gentlemen and the Doge[5] himself if I were to agree that these present moneys that I have for life should change into those of the Mantuan treasury, which dry up on the death of a duke or at his slightest ill-humour—besides abandoning 450 [scudi] of Mantua (which I am getting from the treasury here in Venice) to come and pick up 300, as Signor Sante[6] had—what would these gentlemen not say about me, and with reason?

It is true that you are adding on as well, on behalf of His Highness, 150 scudi from lands that will be my freehold. But to this I reply that the Duke does not have to give me what is mine: there will not be 150 but rather 50, since His Highness already owes me the 100; wherefore what I have already acquired during an earlier period of my life, with sweat and endless toil, should not be taken into account. So, there would be in all but 350, and here I find myself with 450, and 200 more from extra work.

And so, Your Lordship may therefore see that the world would—without fail—have a great deal to say against me; and without mentioning others, what would Adriana[7] not say, or a brother of hers,[8] or Campagnolo,[9] or Don Bassano,[10] who up till now have been very much more recognized and rewarded! And what embarrassment would I not suffer because of them, seeing them to have been rewarded more than me! Moreover, the city of Venice—I leave it to Your Lordship's consideration! What was offered me by His Highness, through Signor Campagnolo, was of greater benefit—when on the death of Signor Sante I was in Mantua, staying at the house of the said Signor

Campagnolo—which was 300 scudi income from lands, 200 of which would have been understood as mine until my death, and 100 as payment from my property rent or donation.

But because I said that I did not wish to have anything to do with the treasury he offered me a further 200 as a pension, which amounts in all to about 600 Mantuan ducats, and now His Highness would like me to settle for less by far, along with the business of going to Signor Treasurer's office every day to beg him to give me what is mine.

God forbid! I have never in my life suffered greater affliction of mind than when I had to go and ask for my pay, almost for the love of God, from Signor Treasurer. I would sooner be content to go begging than return to such indignity. (I beg Your Lordship to forgive me if I speak freely; and on account of my friendship—as I am a true-hearted servant—to be pleased this once to listen to me with the ear of your infinite kindness, and not with that of your singular merits.) When the Most Excellent Lord Procurator Landi[11]—together with the other Most Excellent Lords—once again increased my salary by 100 ducats, this gentleman said these precise words: 'Most Excellent Lords and Colleagues: whosoever wishes a servant to be honoured must also deal with him honourably.'

So, if the Duke has a mind that I should live honourably it is right and proper that he treat me in such a manner, but if not I beg him not to trouble me, since I live honourably as Your Lordship can ascertain. I say nothing about the point concerning my sons because I am speaking to Your Lordship, who is also the father of a family;[12] you know very well what consideration a father needs, who desires (and who ought by the laws of nature to desire) honour for himself and for the family he leaves behind him.

My conclusion, Most Illustrious Sir, is this: that in regard to Claudio, he already submits himself completely to the will and command of His Highness; in regard however to his having considered the afore-mentioned points, he cannot—with the honour he has—change employment unless he changes for the better, so that he could take leave of these Most Excellent Lords to his genuine satisfaction (having been so honoured and favoured by these Lords) through not being laughed at even by those who have earned much through little merit, and not being censured either by society or by his sons.

Indeed, His Highness—now that the Lord Bishop of Mantua[13] has passed to a better life—would easily be able to give satisfaction with stipends and with a little more land, without delivering up Monteverdi to the vexations of the treasury, and to its uncertainty. In short, 400 Mantuan scudi as salary and 300 from lands would mean little to His Highness, but to Claudio it would mean true and undisputed quiet. But is this perhaps asking the impossible? In a word, he asks for even less than Adriana used to get, and perhaps Settimia;[14] but he asks only for what he gets now.

I see no other disagreement but that bit of property, since it is really my duty to leave a little something to my sons, and if I leave something given by the Most Serene House of Gonzaga it will also be to the everlasting honour of that house, for having helped a servant of so many years standing; nor indeed was he disdained by rulers. But if this were to seem too much to His Highness, let him do me the honour of assigning to me my little bit of land, as I shall be content with the capital since the 400 ducats I have here are like a pension. And His Highness will have paid his servant well and truly, for if he will be pleased to command me he will see that in order to serve him, that servant will get out of bed in the middle of the night to render greater obedience.

Forgive me, Your Lordship, if I have gone on for too long. There remains nothing for me to do at present other than to thank Your Lordship from the bottom of my heart for the singular favour done to me in having presented my madrigals to Her Highness, and I am sure that through the most honourable medium of Your Lordship they will have been much more acceptable and welcome.

[1] Francesco was at this time eighteen-and-a-half, Massimiliano nearly sixteen.
[2] Adrian Willaert; Cipriano de Rore.
[3] Giuseppe Zarlino.
[4] Ferdinando Gonzaga, sixth Duke of Mantua.
[5] Antonio Priuli.
[6] Sante Orlandi, late director of music to the Mantuan court.
[7] Adriana Basile.
[8] Probably referring to Adriana's brother Giovanni Battista, a poet.
[9] Francesco Campagnolo, a tenor.
[10] Don Bassano Casola, singer and assistant director of music.
[11] Antonio Landi, one of the four procurators who had appointed Monteverdi in 1613.
[12] Striggio had eleven children.
[13] Mgr. Francesco Gonzaga (died 11 March 1620).
[14] Settimia Caccini, singer, married to Alessandro Ghivizzani.

XVII, XVIII, XIX, XX

The following group of four letters allows us a glimpse of Monteverdi's continuing involvement with a régime that he knew to be basically treacherous and unreliable, yet his correspondents in Mantua were chosen with sufficient care to ensure a ready audience in times of need or stress. Even though the composer occasionally wrote a personal letter to the Duchess, he relied for the most part on the frequent intercession of Striggio, whose loyalty and patience were never in doubt. From this triangular interchange there emerges a distinct feeling of goodwill, contrasting radiantly with the darker side of the Monteverdi–Gonzaga relationship. In Letter XVII Monteverdi thanks the Duchess for giving him a valuable necklace—a reward for the dedication to her of his seventh book of madrigals. He is also grateful to Striggio, in Letter XVIII, for presenting the part-books, but continues to express his indignation over the delay in payment of his pension. Once mentioned, however, this peculiarly toxic topic causes an immediate reaction, a feeling of guilt that prompts Monteverdi to excuse himself for being tiresome while at the same time reminding Striggio of all that he has done—and can do in the future. Letter XIX continues in similar vein, though a silver lining of contentment lightens the gloom as Monteverdi expresses his pride and pleasure on hearing from the Duchess, and his sense of relief about the cancellation of *Arianna*. He seems genuinely pleased to know that Jacopo Peri's music will be heard, and it is possible that he held it in high esteem, indeed far higher than what he knew of Gagliano's. Letter XX reveals his belief that the Duchess has power to assist him in finding a place for his son Massimiliano at Cardinal Montalto's college in Bologna.

XVII

Venice, 4 April 1620; [to Caterina Medici Gonzaga, Duchess of Mantua, at Mantua]. *(Stevens No. 54; De' Paoli, p. 161)*

It was my bounden duty this carnival time, Most Serene Madam, to appear promptly before you and to lay at Your Highness's feet these poor songs of mine; but some illness having stricken me in the meantime, I was therefore compelled to ask—as indeed I did most earnestly—the Most Illustrious Lord, Count Alessandro Striggio,[1] my special protector as regards the favour of Your Most Serene Highnesses, to be so kind as to present them to Your Highness in my stead, begging you to be so good as to accept them favourably as a sign that Your Highness did not disdain my admittedly poor but genuinely devoted and reverent service, since it had also been deemed worthy by the entire Most Serene House of Gonzaga.

But Your Highness, who cannot favour the very least of her servants (as I am indeed) in any other way than in lofty proportion to your great mind—for this reason Your Highness has not only been so kind as to consider me excused for my failings, and indeed to receive this feeble token of my devoted service with a happy countenance, but (more than all this) has wished to honour me with a gift of a fine necklace.

Wherefore, being so overcome with grace, I have not been able to refrain from coming to Your Highness's feet with this letter of mine, to offer you the best thanks of which a humble, devoted, and grateful servant of Your Highness is capable.

[1] Striggio had recently been made Count of Corticelli.

XVIII

Venice, 18 April 1620; [to Alessandro Striggio, at Mantua]. *(Stevens No. 55; De' Paoli, p. 165)*

I am writing to beg Your Lordship not to exert yourself, please, if you have to go to some trouble in getting the money from that voucher, for I know how tiresome a business it is, coping with extraction of money from the treasury. But I so much value that Prince's[1] goodwill and your own peace of mind that the money would almost be unimportant to me, or rather definitely so, if any trouble or vexation might ensue.

But, Your Lordship, it seems to me very strange that in my donation these precise words are to be found: 'We command the President of Our Magistracy that he execute this our donation and obligation without any other mandate or commission, this being our well-considered wish.'

And yet I have always been obliged—and am now to a greater extent even more obliged—either to come and ask His Highness to grant me the favour of an order that they be given to me (always with travelling expenses of 25 ducats), or that I beg the likes of you to be so kind as to put themselves out for me in asking, on my behalf, for something that should not have to be requested. For truly, Your Lordship, I sometimes cannot decide what causes the greater suffering in my heart: the dislike of wholly giving up such sums of money to them, or (because of a claim) seeing troubles of this kind for the likes of you, and expenses and inconvenience for me if I try to come and take possession of it.

And as for me, Your Lordship, if in future the affair goes on in this way, I wish to renounce the said donation for my sons; for if they do receive it, well and good; but if not, it may also be to their detriment. It will be better for the mind to calm down once and for all, than try to hold on continually to a hope which may only come to an end, with all the expenses and the fatigue and the inconvenience and the obligations, after my death.

I begged His Highness when I was at Mantua last year that he might be so good as to arrange for these moneys to reach me as quickly as possible, for the maintenance of my children[2] in their studies. I certainly had a reply, full of kindness and benevolence, but nevertheless I am worse off than before. That is the way my luck goes in Mantua. And because I know it to be thus, I once again beg Your Lordship simply to give the task to someone else, since your infinite humanity and kindness so ordains, for if it were not thus I could never have been so bold.

If it is possible, well and good; if not, however, let us leave it to whatsoever time may be pleasing to God. With regard to my promptness in obeying the orders of His Highness and, at the same time, of Your Lordship—whenever you may be so good as to give me the slightest hint about my helping with *Arianna* or anything else, you will see and know from the results my genuine willingness, and the great desire I have, to show myself no less a very humble servant of His Highness than I desire to be an affectionate and grateful servant to Your Lordship.

As for the future, Your Lordship, do not bother yourself further about setting to rights the troubles of the likes of me, for they are numerous because of the constant necessity that besets me, and if one of them is taken care of today, another comes up tomorrow—just as it happens to a poor man who has old clothes: as soon as one hole is repaired he discovers another that has to be mended. Allow yourself to reckon it up, and you will discover the truth. First there was the inconvenience to Your Lordship over the books; now the voucher has suddenly turned up; after this comes the request for money, with all that inconvenience—and so I never cease troubling you with it all.

Do it then as I say, I beg you, by not taking on troubles like these, and be content that I am your servant because of past favours.

[1] Ferdinando Gonzaga, sixth Duke of Mantua.
[2] Francesco and Massimiliano.

XIX

Venice, 10 May 1620; [to Alessandro Striggio, at Mantua]. *(Stevens No. 56; De' Paoli, p. 168)*

At every moment I keep receiving infinite favours from Your Lordship's generous hand; and so, every day, I keep considering myself so much the more indebted to Your Lordship's noble ways. Would that I could make the outcome equal to my devotion, so that I might perhaps be more worthy than I am of Your Lordship's commands! But fortune goes on tormenting me in this delightful manner, while it makes me worthy of favours and not of merit.

I received a most gracious reply to my letter, through Her Ladyship's[1] infinite kindness, and this singular favour alone was (without any other recognition) sufficient to make me perforce her lifelong servant. But I am not so modest a connoisseur of the truth as not to realize that the greater part of my credit as regards Her Highness's favour springs from Your Lordship's special protection, so that I must therefore remain no less obliged to Your Lordship in recognition of your assistance than I must to Her Highness in recognition of her patronage.

I shall try to entertain much greater hopes for the future (aided by the favour of Her Highness and that of Your Lordship) than I had for the past, in the belief that I shall be made worthy of that little bit of capital which I claim for myself, by favour (not by merit) of the generous hand of the Most Serene Lord Duke of Mantua,[2] as much a kind master as he is a just one. And I shall hope to be able, before I die, to enjoy once and for all that favour which the kindness of the Most Serene Lord Duke Vincenzo[3] (may he be in glory!) granted to me.

It was a good decision that the Most Serene Lord Duke made, in not letting *Arianna* (and also that other composition by Signor Zazzerino)[4] be put on the stage at such short notice, because really and truly haste is far too harmful to such projects, inasmuch as the sense of hearing is too general and too delicate—all the more so in company where the presence of great princes such as himself has to be taken into account. And Her Ladyship has shown great prudence by deciding on the ballet, for the presence of great subject matter is enough to provide what is needful for festivals like this, but in others it does not work out in this way.

For then Signor Zazzerino may be given a chance to show that he too is a servant worthy of Her Highness's favour. Not only does he possess all the qualities about which you write to me, but the gentle and healthy rivalry will give the others a better chance to do something else in order to gain favour for themselves; for without knowledge of the way one cannot arrive at the place decided upon. I assure you, however, that Your Lordship's affection, which you continue to show me in every way, goes on binding me immeasurably closer in the knot of service.

If I am also presumptuous in accepting that favour (so much more necessary now for looking after my sons than for myself) which through your spontaneous goodwill you offer me in this very kind letter of yours—which is that my father-in-law[5] may put in an appearance at Your Lordship's, who will see to it that the voucher of mine which he now has in his hands will be paid—blame my very great need and your kind nature (since the former has made me bold and the latter has led me on) and not my temerity, for indeed I knew only too well that it had inconvenienced you.

You will therefore be seeing my father-in-law at your house; and do forgive him the intrusion.

[1] Caterina Medici Gonzaga.
[2] Ferdinando Gonzaga, sixth Duke of Mantua.
[3] Vincenzo Gonzaga, fourth Duke of Mantua.
[4] Jacopo Peri, whose long reddish-blond hair earned him this nickname. The other composition referred to is his *Adone*.
[5] Giacomo Cattaneo.

XX

Venice, 7 August 1621; [to Caterina Medici Gonzaga, Duchess of Mantua, at Mantua]. *(Stevens No. 67; De' Paoli, p. 190)*

Most Serene Lady, I have a son aged sixteen-and-a-half years[1]—a subject and most humble servant of Your Highness—who has now left the seminary at Bologna, having completed there the course in humanistic studies and rhetoric. I would like him to go on to the other sciences in order to obtain a doctorate in medicine. He has always been under the discipline of tutors who have kept him in the fear of God and on the right lines of study.

Considering his liveliness and the licentious freedom of students (because of which fact they fall oftentimes into bad company, which diverts them from the rightful path, causing great sorrow to their fathers and tremendous loss to themselves), and in order to ward off the great harm that could come about, I thought that a place in the college of the Most Illustrious Lord Cardinal Mont'Alto[2]—which he has in Bologna—would be a real boon to me, and the salvation of my son; but without a royal hand to aid me in so great a need it would not be possible for me to obtain such an outstanding favour.

Knowing therefore that Your Highness is by nature a princess full of infinite kindness towards everyone, in particular towards her respectful subjects, as is this poor boy, and to servants (though lowly) like myself, I have on this account been so bold as to beg Your Highness with most heartfelt sincerity (as I am doing) and with the most humble respect of which I am capable, that you may be so kind as to write in recommendation of such a place for the aforementioned son in the aforesaid college in Bologna to the said Cardinal Mont'Alto, so that he may receive so lofty a favour.

But if at present all the places are filled, the first vacancy would still be in time.

[1] Massimiliano, who later practised medicine in Mantua.
[2] Grand-nephew of Pope Sixtus V, and a patron of music.

XXI, XXII, XXIII

The last ten weeks of 1622 saw Monteverdi heavily involved in a delicate and complex manoeuvre that was somewhat removed from his normal sphere of activity: helping his friend Lorenzo Giustiniani to persuade a group of actors in Mantua to put on a series of plays in Venice. Unfortunately for the composer, who was ill enough to be confined to his apartment, this basically simple plot soon degenerated into a vexatious and time-consuming farce. Giustiniani had elicited at least a show of interest from the leading actor G. B. Andreini, only to find that the problems and politics of the theatrical world stood in the way. Andreini was ready to move, but his wife Virginia (who had created the role of Ariadne in 1608) had other ideas. She wanted him to give up the role of actor–director and play the buffoon. Furthermore one of his leading men, Tristano Martinelli, disliked the idea of appearing in a city where a rival actor—Pier Maria Cecchini—enjoyed great popularity. Monteverdi's part in this affair was to contact Striggio and ask him to use his influence in resolving the difficulties. In the meantime Giustiniani continued to contact individual actors and found that Martinelli would accept only if Francesco Scattolone agreed to join him. Letter XXII indicates that Cecchini was trying to prevent the rival company from appearing in Venice, and that Giustiniani went to Padua to persuade (and even threaten) Scattolone. Although Striggio's first reply raised the hopes of Monteverdi and Giustiniani, the actors suddenly left for

Paris, and Letter XXIII hints at the assembly of a substitute company. At the same time, a Mantuan organist was trying to obtain a vacant position at St. Mark's, and Monteverdi hastens to assure Striggio that he does not wish to become embroiled since it would be unfair to his former employers.

XXI

Venice, 21 October 1622; [to Alessandro Striggio, at Mantua]. *(Stevens No. 72; De' Paoli, p. 198)*

Three days ago the Most Illustrious Signor Giustiniani,[1] a gentleman of great authority in this Most Serene Republic and a very good patron of mine, paid a special visit to my house in company with many other very distinguished gentlemen, to tell me how only a few days previously he arranged for an invitation to be written to Signor Lelio Andreini[2] the actor, so that he might make himself available—together with Signora Florinda and all his company—to come to Venice and produce plays for the general public; provided however the Duke did not wish to make use of him, for in such a case he would in no wise wish to negotiate.

He received a reply to the effect that Andreini was as ready as could be; all the more so because the Lord Duke[3] had already let it be known that he would not wish to make use of him. The only thing lacking was for Arlecchino[4] to say yes, for without this—to avoid loss of reputation through having to act in the place where Fritellino[5] was also acting (even though in another hall)—he could not agree to come. So, this most illustrious gentleman had a letter sent to the said Arlecchino, and received a reply saying that if His Highness were not making use of him, and would grant him official leave also, he would come on the understanding that a certain Doctor Gratiano,[6] who is now in Savoy, were to come.

But while this gentleman is trying by negotiations to set everything straight, lo and behold Signor Lelio writes him a letter, saying that as far as he is concerned personally he stands in complete readiness to be of service, and that he offers himself as a most humble servant, but nevertheless makes it known to His Lordship that Signora Florinda does not wish to act, and that he has got it into his head to perform as a buffoon on his own (even in other companies) for two years, and no longer as head of a company, in view of the fact that so many unpleasant things happen and there are so many problems in trying to run a company.

This gentleman, having gathered from the letter that the negotiation had almost collapsed, and knowing how very humble a servant I am of His Highness and of Your Lordship, begged me (as also did those other gentlemen who were with him) that I try with a letter of mine—still assuming His Highness is not about to make use of him—to ask Your Lordship most urgently to persuade this Signor Lelio to oblige the gentleman, and if Signor Lelio should insist on making excuses because of the shortage of actors in his company, this gentleman offers him Gratiano and Zanni[7] and Doctor,[8] and any other part that might be lacking.

I am therefore writing to beg Your Lordship, or rather (to put it better) I am writing to entreat Your Lordship's infinite kindness to honour me by asking Your Lordship to try and be so kind as to perform this service of requesting the said Signor Lelio to place himself at the disposal of this most illustrious gentleman, for he will show himself full of kindness towards Signor Lelio's person, both with gifts and with payment of travel costs and so on; and also to bring Signora Florinda, and others of whom he approves.

But if he does not want to, would you ask Signor Lelio to consider that as a result of the expectations already raised by his letters, Signor Giustiniani will not only be hindered in his search for another company, but his theatre will be prevented (because of Lelio) from giving performances—a disappointment which he can well imagine.

Your Lordship's authority will, I know, be such as can take care of everything perfectly, and I shall always be most grateful to Your Lordship for a favour I have so long desired, and which I know will make it clear to these most distinguished gentlemen how much you hold my servitude dear to your grace. Do not look, I beg you, upon my modest worth, but marvel rather at your own kindness in deigning to have a request made to Signor Lelio, persuading him with the gentleness of your favour.

[1] Lorenzo Giustiniani.
[2] Giovanni Battista Andreini, actor, author, and director of I Fedeli.
[3] Ferdinando Gonzaga, sixth Duke of Mantua.
[4] The role created by Tristano Martinelli.
[5] Pier Maria Cecchini, actor, and director of a rival company.
[6] Francesco Scattolone.
[7] Gianni (or Arlecchino).
[8] In fact the same character as Gratiano.

XXII

Venice, 3 December 1622; [to Alessandro Striggio, at Mantua]. *(Stevens No. 74; De' Paoli, p. 202)*

This morning (which is the 3rd of the present month) the Most Illustrious Signor Giustiniani,[1] my lord, came expressly to call on me in my own room and tell me about a certain ticklish situation, which has come about through fear that Fritellino[2] has been busy with some of his intrigues in order to remain supreme in Venice (although little appreciated), so that the arrival of the Mantuan actors—very much looked forward to by the entire city—can be thwarted, inasmuch as they are late; and all the more so through having heard that Dr Gratiano[3] was so much to His Highness's liking as to be rewarded with a present of 100 scudi, living expenses, and other steady maintenance, but Signor Giustiniani (this approval being what it is) would not want the skill of the said Fritellino to have been able to prevail.

As regards the other matter: having already seen Your Lordship's letter (which you were so kind as to send me in reply) confirming the arrival of the aforementioned actors with the Duke's full approval, but not so far having seen letters brought by the courier from any of those actors—which however gives us hope that they may come—it is nevertheless assumed that the desired favour will be received. This most illustrious gentleman certainly deserves to have his mind set at rest about the matter by His Highness, for (believe me, Your Lordship) he has not failed to apply himself to it with all diligence and affection, so that His Highness also might be pleased by having actors sent to fill the company's need.

Not only did he go to the trouble of arranging for these leading actors to come, and still more, of making Franceschina[4] decide; but as regards the Doctor—who would not answer 'yes' to mild but insistent entreaties—he decided on the opposite approach, changing entreaties into threats, whereby the said Doctor would have to get into a gondola with him and be taken to Lizza Fusina,[5] with the idea of forcing him to come. But the Doctor having sworn to His Lordship that he would come, he was content just to have someone accompany him.

On account of His Lordship's having exerted himself with such enthusiasm—both because of the promise which Your Lordship made to him in your letter by way of reply to mine, and because of not having seen letters to the contrary in the present delivery—he lives in greatest hopes; but since he so much desires this favour he has again instructed me to write and ask Your Lordship, so that in case of need you may be so kind as to assist him. But even if (as he believes) they would have come without any further inconvenience to Your Lordship, he still asks you to try and set his mind at rest with the latest news of their certain arrival, which would still be in time if it were (as he hopes) within ten or fifteen days.

That most illustrious lord also added that if he could have written to Your Lordship—since he knows very well that gentlemen such as he cannot write to ministers of princes without leave—he would already have demonstrated the obligation that he owes to Your Lordship.

[1] Lorenzo Giustiniani, a Venetian gentleman.
[2] Pier Maria Cecchini, an actor.
[3] A stock character in the *commedia dell'arte*, the role to be played by Francesco Scattolone.
[4] The name usually given to the wife of Zanni.
[5] The embarkation point on the mainland for the journey to Padua.

XXIII

Venice, 31 December 1622; [to Alessandro Striggio, at Mantua]. *(Stevens No. 76; De' Paoli, p. 206)*

At the time when I received Your Lordship's two letters by the most recent post, a man was waiting here for what you were so kind as to write—the messenger of the Most Illustrious Signor Giustiniani.[1] After I had read them and given them to the messenger so that he could take them for his master to see, he returned to my room with the letters and requested that I write to Your Lordship in the name of the Most Illustrious Signor Giustiniani, to the effect that he acknowledges himself to be as much obliged to you as if he himself in fact had received the favour.

And he begs you to command him if you consider him in any way suitable for serving Your Lordship, both with his person and with his possessions, inasmuch as he is again enquiring of Your Lordship's kindness (having heard that there is a company of Spanish actors in Mantua) and whether, with such a favourable situation and with that diplomatic manner Your Lordship can adopt, our aim might be achieved—His Highness[2] being perhaps more pleased with the said Spaniards than with the Italians—for the favour would always be welcome. Nevertheless he wants everything to be done with Your Lordship's approval.

Aside from this, I am even more grateful to Your Lordship since you have been so kind as to show in writing that you are not ashamed of your fondness for me, weak as I am in this world of ours; therefore I shall always feel bound to pray God that He bless and preserve Your Lordship, and that He make me worthy to deserve Your Lordship's commands, so that I may prove myself a worthy servant of yours by the results.

Most Illustrious Lord, already a month and a half ago an organist of St. Mark's[3] passed to a better life, and a little while after his death Signor Ottavio Bargnani[4] wrote to me complaining that I did not let him know about this vacancy, so that he could apply for the post. I replied to him: 'Dear Signor Bargnani—I am very fond of you, but since you are a servant of that Prince who is as much my master and lord, I would never have considered (let alone risked) writing such a thing to you, for it would have amounted to a desire that you leave that service which I so much revere and honour. You will therefore do me a kindness by discussing with me any matter other than that one.'

So the affair quietened down, and when I thought it had been dropped, lo and behold only the other day I was summoned to the Procuratia by the chief representatives of the procurators; and when I arrived, they immediately had a letter read out from Signor Bargnani (I do not know where they got it) who is trying to obtain the aforementioned post, which is still not filled. The letter having been read, they asked me whether this person would be acceptable, and I answered 'yes'. They then asked me to write him a letter on behalf of Their Excellencies to the effect that he should come for an audition at his convenience, for they assure him that if he is the kind of man he says he is, they would not seek to harm his reputation, although there are still five others who are interested in the post, so that a competition will be necessary.

Thinking to myself that such a letter (without first letting Your Lordship know about it, so that you may in turn tell His Highness) would greatly injure me in His Highness's grace—which I esteem and shall esteem as long as I live, in boundless respects—I have for this reason told Your Lordship about the matter, begging you to let me know by the next post as to what I can do, with His Highness's approval, in the event that Signor Bargnani hints in his letter that he would be able (also with His Highness's approval) to come and serve at St. Mark's. I wanted to place the matter in Your Lordship's hands, because I know that everything will be done discreetly, and without embarrassment to me.

[1] Lorenzo Giustiniani, a Venetian gentleman.
[2] Ferdinando Gonzaga, sixth Duke of Mantua.
[3] Giovanni Battista Grillo (died *c.* 15 November 1622)
[4] An organist from Brescia who served at S. Barbara, Mantua.

XXIV, XXV, XXVI

Ranging over the years 1624–7, these three letters are addressed to three different Mantuan personages, all of whom at various times asked for Monteverdi's musical advice, while he in turn looked to them for moral or political support of one kind or another. Letter XXIV responds to a request from Duke Ferdinando, who not only wanted a good castrato singer for his chapel and chamber music, but preferably one trained by Monteverdi himself. There is indeed a likely candidate, but he must be eased away from Salzburg on the pretext of improving his talent in Venice. Then perhaps he would be ready for a transfer to Mantua. Another singer is mentioned in passing—a member of an academy in Ferrara—but Monteverdi makes it clear that he does not quite trust his source of information. On the other hand, his former student Campagnolo can be relied upon to give a report on the situation, as he belongs to the élite among the well-travelled virtuosos. Letter XXV appeals to Ercole Marigliani, a court secretary who (like his senior colleague Striggio) turned out librettos for ballets, plays and *intermedi* such as *Andromeda* and *Le tre costanti*, dabbling in alchemy on the side, as is apparent from an exchange of letters earlier in 1625. This appeal concerns a lawsuit over a house given by a widow to Monteverdi's father-in-law, Giacomo Cattaneo, the problem being that on Cattaneo's death the house would revert to the granddaughter of the original owner. It is not clear why Monteverdi thought that he had rights to the property, or whether some member of his family persuaded him to put forward a claim. But Marigliani was unable to help him, and the claim failed. Letter XXVI informs Striggio in plain terms of the composer's intense dislike of having to work hastily on a musical commission, in this case a play whose title is not divulged. Instead he offers *Armida*, already composed, or a new work based on Strozzi's *La finta pazza Licori*.

XXIV

Venice, 2 March 1624; [to Duke Ferdinando Gonzaga, at Mantua].
(Stevens No. 81; De' Paoli, p. 217)

I am writing to offer Your Highness the greatest thanks I most reverently and possibly can, with all my heart and mind, for the special honour which you have deigned to do me, namely by honouring me with your commands, which I shall always look upon as sent by the hand of God, and the greatest honour and good fortune I could receive.

At present, Most Serene Lord, there is no suitable individual here in Venice; however I heard of the following possibility through a monk attached to San Stefano, in Venice (a singer at St. Mark's), who told me ten days ago that he has a brother—a young castrato with a very good voice, ready ornamentation, and a *trillo*—in the service of the Most Illustrious Lord Bishop of Salzburg.[1] But because nobody in that establishment is capable of improving his talent, this monk would be glad for him to come and stay in Venice if there were an opportunity to do something useful.

I replied that he should have him come here, for I would not fail to help him as regards employers and with a little advice too. This very morning (as it so happened) before I received Your Highness's command, he told me in chapel that he had written and asked him to come. Now that I know what I have to attend to, in regard to Your Highness's pleasure, I shall not be neglectful in keeping myself most carefully informed about it, and should it be appropriate I shall not fail to press the matter so that I can show by the results—over and beyond my most ready intent—how I long to be a servant of Your Highness.

Nor shall I limit myself merely to this—indeed I shall not forget to look elsewhere for further possibilities about which I shall at once inform Your Highness if they come to my notice. I believe that Signor Campagnolo,[2] as one who has been in those parts, would perhaps be able to give Your Highness a report.

During the past few days I heard that in Ferrara, in the service of the community of Santo Spirito,[3] there is a man with a very fine voice and good vocal graces who has been giving by no means ordinary satisfaction. Since the Most Serene Lord Prince of Modena[4] is beginning to enjoy music the way he does, and since he is not slow in hiring the best, yet finds them only with difficulty, for this very reason I do not entirely believe those who have told me about this man from Ferrara.

Nevertheless I did not wish to refrain from mentioning it to Your Highness, so that (if it please God) you would be served as I desire.

[1] Count Paris Lodron (installed 3 March 1621; died 15 December 1653).
[2] Francesco Campagnolo, a tenor who had studied with Monteverdi.
[3] The Accademia di Santo Spirito, where Monteverdi's assistant Alessandro Grandi had been in charge of the music from 1610 until 1616.
[4] Alfonso III d'Este, Prince of Modena (1591–1644).

XXV

Venice, 22 November 1625; [to Ercole Marigliani, at Mantua]. *(Stevens No. 85; De' Paoli, p. 228)*

Having received from the Most Excellent Signor Bagozzi,[1] my solicitor, the present letter in which—as Your Lordship can see—he notifies me as to how Signor Belli[2] uses all manner of means to take action against me in every way he wishes and finds possible (which is something I did not believe, in view of the words you were good enough to write to me in your previous letters; namely, my goods being sold, he would have gone about it in such a way that everything would have been settled), I turn to you once again and beg you to make him calm down and wait for the result of what you are trying to accomplish through the one party or the other.

I know it will be better for you to act than for me to speak, therefore I entrust myself in every respect to your love and great prudence, putting it to you that what I have been trying to get hold of is an endowment of Signora Claudia's,[3] given to me by the Lord Duke,[4] of which I have had little or nothing; and that if I have been trying to get hold of that house, and it could not rightly be mine, the other party has lost nothing of his own because of this, since he possessed it anyway.

If now from my nothing I were to have to pay 200 or more scudi beyond the expenses—another 200—and, it seems to me, Signor Belli having given me nothing of his own except tyranny and ill-will, past injuries would be quite enough without adding more. If only I had been in Mantua, the affair that went off in one way would certainly have gone off in another. You can help me, and I know you will use your influence to free me from such unimaginable and unthinkable vexation.

Dear Signor Marigliani, my lord, may you honour my request and make that man of little conscience keep quiet so that (by God) you will add merit to your soul. And I earnestly request your reply about this matter, so that I may know in what state of mind I should be.

[1] Dr Giulio Bagozzi, a Mantuan lawyer.
[2] Ippolito de Belli, Monteverdi's adversary in the lawsuit.
[3] Monteverdi's wife, who had died in 1607.
[4] Vincenzo Gonzaga, fourth Duke of Mantua.

XXVI

Venice, 1 May 1627; [to Alessandro Striggio, at Mantua]. *(Stevens No.
92; De' Paoli, p. 240)*

Your Lordship will forgive me for not being in time to respond by the
previous post to your very kind and precious letter, inasmuch as time was
not available—partly through late receipt of the letter, and partly
because of the many tasks I still had at that juncture—for it was the Vigil
of St. Mark, a day which kept me extremely busy looking after the music.

Be so kind, therefore, Your Lordship, as to accept this letter of mine
in lieu of the previous post, and by way of an addition to the present one;
and please rest assured that I shall never receive a greater boon from my
good fortune than being made worthy of His Highness's commands.[1]
Indeed I shall pray to God that He grant me to an even greater extent the
power of being able (with better results than I alone could achieve) to
show myself that much more worthy of such conspicuous favours, ever
rendering infinite thanks and obligations to Your Lordship for such
honour received.

I would wish, however, to pray and beseech Your Lordship that His
Highness, graciously allowing me to set to music the play which you
mention, might deign to take two points into consideration: one, that I
should have ample time to compose it; the other, that it should be
written in an excellent style. For I would no less have to put up with
considerable worry and little peace of mind (indeed, very great distress)
by setting tawdry verses to music, than I would if I had to compose in a
hurry—this lack of time being the reason why I almost killed myself
when writing *Arianna*.

I know that it would be possible to do it quickly, but speed and quality
do not go together. So, if there were time, and again if I were to have the
work of production from your most noble intellect, you may be very sure
that my joy would be boundless, because I know what facility and
propriety Your Lordship would bring to it. If the project related to
intermedi for a full-length play, its birth would be neither so tiring nor so
long-drawn-out, but a sung play which says as much as an epic poem, to
be set in a short time—believe me, Your Lordship, it cannot be done
without falling into one of two dangers: either doing it badly or making
oneself ill.

However, I happen to have set many stanzas of Tasso—where
Armida begins 'O tu, che porte parte teco di me, parte ne lassi',[2]

continuing with all her lament and anger, with Rinaldo's[3] reply; and these perhaps would not be displeasing. I also happen to have set to music the fight between Tancredi and Clorinda. Again, I have carefully considered a little play by Signor Giulio Strozzi, very beautiful and unusual, which runs to some 400 lines, called *Licori finta pazza innamorata d'Aminta*, and this—after a thousand comical situations— ends up with a wedding, by a nice touch of stratagem.

Both these and similar things can serve as short episodes between other pieces of music. They do not come off too badly, and I know they would not displease Your Lordship. Then, if church music were needed, either for Vespers or for Mass, I rather think I might have something of this kind that would be to His Highness's liking.

[1] Vincenzo Gonzaga, seventh Duke of Mantua.
[2] *Gerusalemme liberata*, XVI, 40.
[3] The original letter has 'Ruggiero' in error.

XXVII, XXVIII, XXIX, XXX

Monteverdi's friendship with the poet and librettist Giulio Strozzi may have begun in the early 1620s, but their first serious collaboration dates from 1627, when from May until September they were in constant contact with each other about a comic opera, *La finta pazza Licori*. In 1628 they worked together on *I cinque fratelli*, and in 1630 came *Proserpina rapita*, a wedding piece for Leonardo Giustiniani and Giustiniana Mocenigo, daughter of one of Monteverdi's most important patrons. The opera was never completed, and the other two scores disappeared, with the exception of one song (*Come dolce oggi l'auretta spira*) from *Proserpina rapita*, which was printed in the ninth book of madrigals. Striggio's rejection of the comic opera is especially regrettable, for the relevant letters leave no doubt as to the composer's great enthusiasm for the project and his constant attention to every detail of interpretation. Letter XXVII outlines the character of Licoris, the girl who feigns madness and who must be ready to appear first as a man, then as a woman; in short, the part requires a superb actress as well as a highly competent singer. Margherita Basile is Monteverdi's first choice for this difficult role, though at first he may have entertained some doubts as to its final success, for he also offers a play by Rinuccini as an alternative. Letters XXVIII, XXIX and XXX give an unusually careful assessment of the vocal talents of a young singer from Bologna, Giovanni Battista Bisucci, who eventually went on to Mantua until the political situation drove him back to Venice, where he frequently appeared in the newly opened opera theatres. Not only is Bisucci's character discussed, but also the range of his voice, his potential for chamber music and for the stage, and his command of ornamentation. Yet the letters continue to mention the progress of the libretto, and Strozzi's willingness to modify and augment the story when Monteverdi sensed a need for changes.

XXVII

Venice, 7 May 1627; [to Alessandro Striggio, at Mantua]. *(Stevens No. 93; De' Paoli, p. 243)*

I am sending off to Your Lordship *La finta pazza Licori* by Signor Strozzi (as you stipulated in your very kind letter), so far neither set to music, nor printed, nor ever acted on the stage; for as soon as the author had completed it he himself straightway gave me, with his own hands, a copy of it, which was in fact this one.

If the aforementioned Signor Giulio gets to know that it might be to His Highness's[1] taste, I am quite sure that with extreme promptness of thought and deed he will put it in order—divided into three acts, or however His Highness wishes—desiring beyond all measure to see it set to music by me, and rejoicing to see his most honoured literary works clothed with my modest music. For truly both in the beauty of its verse, and in its ideas, I have found it indeed a most worthy subject, absolutely ready for setting, so that if such a story were to Your Lordship's taste, you need pay no attention to its present form, because I know for sure that the author will arrange it to your complete satisfaction in a very short space of time.

In my opinion, the story is not bad, nor indeed is the way it unfolds; nevertheless the part of Licoris, because of its variety of moods, must not fall into the hands of a woman who cannot play first a man and then a woman, with lively gestures and different emotions. Therefore the imitation of this feigned madness must take into consideration only the present, not the past or the future, and consequently must emphasize the word, not the sense of the phrase. So when she speaks of war she will have to imitate war; when of peace, peace; when of death, death, and so forth.

And since the transformations take place in the shortest possible time, and the imitations as well—then whoever has to play this leading role, which moves us to laughter and to compassion, must be a woman capable of leaving aside all other imitations except the immediate one, which the word she utters will suggest to her. All the same, I believe that Signora Margherita[2] will be best of all.

But to give further proof of my heartfelt affection (even though I know

1. Monteverdi in his later years by Bernardo Strozzi (1581–1644).

2. The first page of Monteverdi's letter of 13 March 1620 to Alessandro Striggio.

3. Mantua with its lakes, from a seventeenth-century engraving.

Veduta del Piaza di St. Marco di Venezia vista verso il porto

4. St. Mark's, Venice, from a seventeenth-century engraving.

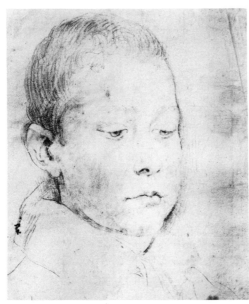

5.
Prince (later Duke)
Ferdinando Gonzaga,
chalk drawing (*c.* 1601)
by Rubens (1577–1640).

6. A *carro* forming part of the wedding celebrations in Mantua in 1608
depicted in Federico Follino, *Compendio delle sontuose feste fatte l'ann*
M.DC.VIII nella Città di Mantova (Mantua, 1608).

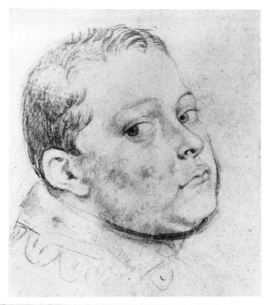

7.
Prince (late Duke)
Francesco Gonzaga,
chalk drawing (*c.* 1601)
by Rubens (1577–1640).

ɹale & fuochi Trionfali fatti nelle Reali & feliciſſime nozZe del Ser.ᵐᵒ Prençipe di Mantᵃ
ɹ l'architettura di Gabriele Bertazzolo Ingeonero, delle Alt Ser.ᵐᵉ di Mantᵃ l'anno i 6 o ɹ

8. Part of the ritornello for double harp in 'Possente spirto'
in Act III of *Orfeo* (1609 edition).

9. Kent Opera's 1976 staging of *Orfeo*, with Peter Knapp in the title role. Producer, Norman Platt; designer, Martyn Bainbridge; conductor, Roger Norrington.

10. Philippe Hüttenlocher in the title in *Orfeo* as staged by the Zurich Opera. Production and design, Jean-Pierre Ponnelle and Per Halmen; conductor, Nikolaus Harnoncourt.

11. *Il ritorno d'Ulisse* at Glyndebourne, 1974, with Janet Baker as Penelope.
Producer, Peter Hall; designer, John Bury; conductor, Raymond Leppard.

12. *L'incoronazione di Poppea*, with Anne Pashley (left) as the soprano Nero
and Sarah Walker (right) as Poppea, Kent Opera, 1974. Producer,
Norman Platt; designer, Nadine Baylis; conductor, Roger Norrington.

for sure that the task would be more difficult for me) I am sending you the enclosed *Narciso*, a play by Signor Ottavio Rinuccini,[3] which has never been set to music, or actually produced. This gentleman, when he was alive (how fervently I pray that he is now in heaven!), did me the favour not only of giving me a copy but also of asking me to take it on, for he liked the work very much, and hoped that I might have to set it to music.

I have had a go at it several times, and turned it over to some extent in my mind, but to tell Your Lordship the truth it would not, in my opinion, succeed so powerfully as I would wish for, because of the numerous sopranos we would have to employ for so many nymphs, and the numerous tenors for so many shepherds, and nothing else by way of variety. And then a sad and tragic ending! However, I did not want to neglect sending it so that Your Lordship could look it over and give it the benefit of your fine judgment.

I have no copy of either work other than the present ones I am sending off to Your Lordship. When you have read everything please do me the favour of sending back the aforementioned originals so that I can make use of them should some occasion arouse my interest, for as you may know they are very precious to me.

[P.S.] As regards reminding Your Lordship of some bass singer who might be suitable and to His Highness's taste; and of the need for excellent singers—about which His Highness is particular—for the sopranos assigned to those female roles, I must say I would not know whom to mention. I have heard, however, by chance (as it were) that there is somebody-or-other good in Milan, in the cathedral. Here, for chamber music, we have nobody better than Rapallino[4] the Mantuan, whose name is Don Giacomo; he is a priest, but a baritone and not a bass. Nevertheless he lets his words be heard clearly, he has something of a *trillo*, some graces, and he sings boldly. I shall however be on the lookout for a better one, and here make another bow to Your Lordship.

[1] Vincenzo Gonzaga, seventh Duke of Mantua.
[2] Margherita Basile, the younger sister of Adriana.
[3] Florentine poet and librettist.
[4] Don Giacomo Rapallino, chaplain to Girolamo Mocenigo and baritone.

XXVIII

Venice, 13 June 1627; [to Alessandro Striggio, at Mantua]. *(Stevens No. 97; De' Paoli, p. 256)*

Six days have already elapsed since I gave *La finta pazza* to Signor Giulio Strozzi, who promised to adapt it at once to your liking; but today, Saturday, when I paid a special visit to his house to see the adaptation and let Your Lordship know about it in detail, and at the same time to get hold of it myself in order to start sending the music to Your Lordship, I found that he had gone to Padua for two or three days for the feast of the saint which is being celebrated tomorrow,[1] and for this reason I cannot inform you properly before the next post. I know for certain, however, that he is in the process of touching it up and adding to it with great enthusiasm, because he very much wants the other lady singers to take part, as indeed I told Your Lordship in my other letter.

Just now a certain young man has arrived here in Venice from Bologna.[2] He is about twenty-four years old, wears long breeches, composes a little, and professes to sing light bass parts in chamber music. I have heard him sing a motet of his in church, with a few short runs here and there, and little ornaments, with a decent *trillo*: the voice is very pleasing but not too deep. He articulates the words very clearly, his voice goes up into the tenor range very smoothly indeed, and as a singer he is very reliable.

A certain Tarroni,[3] who entices musicians to Poland, is after him with offers of employment, but he would like to stay on at St. Mark's in order to continue living in Venice. He is not aware that I am telling Your Lordship about him, and this I swear to you by God. As a most reverent and (as I profess to that Most Serene Highness) most grateful servant, I thought it a good idea to point him out to Your Lordship, so that if anything were asked of me, I would know what to do about it.

And even if Your Lordship does not instruct me, it will matter very little because—as I said to Your Lordship—he has no idea of this report of mine.

[1] St. Anthony of Padua (13 June). This letter may have been begun on 12 June.
[2] Giovanni Battista Bisucci.
[3] Antonio Tarroni, priest and musician.

XXIX

Venice, 20 June 1627; [to Alessandro Striggio, at Mantua]. *(Stevens No. 98; De' Paoli, p. 259)*

I shall let Your Lordship know, by the next post, the results of what you have deigned to command me regarding the negotiations for basses, since I have been unable in so short a time to find the opportunity to speak tactfully to the person you asked about, a service I must perform myself and not through someone else. But I can tell Your Lordship (as I also mentioned in another of my letters, submitting it for your consideration) that Rapallino[1] gets, I believe, 80 ducats from the chapel, 60 or 70 from Masses, and 40 for being chaplain to a Most Excellent Lord Procurator,[2] without counting the unknown sums for singing around the city in performances that take place there.

The young man who has come to Venice[3]—the Bolognese—does not have anything certain as yet; but he does manage, by asking frequently, to come into chapel. He is not a priest: he is a young man of good stature, but dresses in long breeches; he sings with more charm of voice than Rapallino, and more reliably, since he composes a little. Not only does he pronounce his words extremely well, he sings ornaments very nicely, and has something of a *trillo*.

He does not go down too far, nevertheless for chamber and theatrical music he would not, I hope, displease His Highness.[4] This young man came to Venice with letters of recommendation so that he could be helped in his various plans; among them there was even one addressed to the Most Illustrious Resident Rossi,[5] from His Majesty—that is, the Emperor.[6] If you were to entrust such a negotiation as this to the said Signor Rossi, it would seem to me very good, for then these singers could not say that I was turning other singers away, and I tend to think that Your Lordship will approve of this.

Signor Giulio Strozzi has returned from Padua, and even though he was absent, he has not on that account forgotten to improve his *Finta pazza Licori*, which he has rearranged in five acts. Within four days he will either give it to me completely finished, or give me about two or three completed acts by way of a beginning, so that by Saturday week at the latest I hope to send some of it to Your Lordship with the music added. And I hope you will see something to please you greatly, because Signor Giulio is a worthy subject, courteously and willingly following my ideas, a convenience which makes it very much easier for me to set it to music.

[1] Don Giacomo Rapallino, chaplain to Girolamo Mocenigo and baritone.
[2] Giovanni Battista Foscarini.
[3] Giovanni Battista Bisucci.
[4] Vincenzo Gonzaga, seventh Duke of Mantua.
[5] Nicolò Rossi, Venetian Resident of the Imperial Court.
[6] Emperor Ferdinand II.

XXX

Venice, 24 July 1627; [to Alessandro Striggio, at Mantua]. *(Stevens No. 101; De' Paoli, p. 266)*

I beg you to forgive me for missing the previous post, not having replied to Your Lordship's most kind and courteous letter; because the many tasks I had last Saturday (the post day) were the reason for my failure. There were two tasks: one was having to provide chamber music from 1 p.m. until 4 p.m. for the Most Serene Prince of Neuburg,[1] who is staying incognito in the house of the English Ambassador;[2] and this music being over, I then had to go—pressed by the entreaties of many friends—to the Carmelite church, as it was the day of First Vespers of the Most Holy Madonna of that Order, and stay there fully occupied until almost 9 p.m.

I am writing this now to let Your Lordship know what great delight I had on reading, in your very kind letter, of the pleasure you received from the first act of the brave *Licoris* of Signor Giulio Strozzi. I now have it all in my hands, given me by the same Signor Giulio, and full of many beautiful variations. At present I am having it written out at home, so that no copies, either partial or complete, can be taken.

I have already completed practically all the first act, and would be even further ahead if I had not had that little trouble with my eyes that I told Your Lordship about, and if I had not had some church music to write. From now on I shall work harder at it, and if you would like to see it, that is to read the whole of it, I shall send it off to Your Lordship when I have copied it, so that you can give it a glance, and you will see that Signora Margherita[3] will have a great deal to do on her own.

I took note of what Your Lordship proposed for the young bass,[4] and it seems to me that he has firmly decided to enter His Highness's[5] service, but I really think that the allowance is more generous than he deserves, because although it is true that he performs with assurance, he sings nevertheless in a somewhat melancholy manner; and regarding the ornaments, he does not separate them too well because he fails most of the time to join the chest voice to the middle voice, for if the middle fails the chest voice, the ornamentation becomes harsh and hard and offensive; if the chest voice fails that of the middle, the ornamentation becomes unctuous, as it were, and almost continuous in the voice, but when both function, the ornamentation comes off both sweetly and separated, and is most natural.

Although he is not in the chapel, this going around earning fees here and there (since both major and minor feasts are celebrated a great deal in this city, especially at this time) pleases him, seeing a few small coins coming into his purse, as they do come in this delightful kind of liberty. Otherwise I can give no explanation. The young man's nature is very calm, modest, and humble.

[1] Wolfgang Wilhelm, Count Palatine of the Rhine.
[2] Sir Isaac Wake.
[3] Margherita Basile, the younger sister of Adriana.
[4] Giovanni Battista Bisucci.
[5] Vincenzo Gonzaga, seventh Duke of Mantua. Bisucci was, however, appointed a bass in the choir of St. Mark's on 23 January 1628 at an annual salary of sixty ducats.

XXXI, XXXII, XXXIII, XXXIV

It is ironic that the sack of Mantua in 1630 by the merciless imperial troops caused the destruction of precious musical scores known to have been sent to the Gonzaga court (*Arianna, Armida, Le tre costanti, La finta pazza Licori*), but at the same time overlooked the archives in which all the correspondence—including Monteverdi's—was carefully housed. Nevertheless, he undoubtedly wrote many more letters than now survive, for nothing remains of his correspondence with members of his family: his parents, his father-in-law, his sons, his brother. A hint of the prolific nature of his letter-writing can be gathered from the three examples sent on the same day (10 September 1627) to three different people—a marquis, a count and a councillor. Each one of them, for different reasons, is given information about a new and considerable undertaking that was to occupy the composer for the next sixteen months: a commission from Parma to write the music for a prologue and five *intermedi* for Tasso's *Aminta*, and, as if that were not enough, a tourney, *Mercurio e Marte*, all to be part of the celebrations at the wedding of Odoardo Farnese and Margherita de' Medici, which eventually took place towards the end of 1628. Letter XXXI, to the Marquis Enzo Bentivoglio (son of Cornelio Bentivoglio and the singer Isabella Bendidio), is of importance in that it proves how Monteverdi sometimes liked to request the 'sensitive aid' of a patron in matters practical and artistic. Letters XXXII and XXXIII, to Striggio and Marigliani respectively, show that the composer was not slow to inform his Mantuan correspondents about lucrative and prestigious commissions received from rival courts. Letter XXXIV contains the first faint suggestion of a misfortune in Mantua—almost certainly his son Massimiliano's troubles with the Inquisition, which seem to lead naturally to his preoccupation with the character of Discord in the *intermedio* about Dido and Aeneas.

XXXI

Venice, 10 September 1627; [to the Marquis Enzo Bentivoglio, at Ferrara]. *(Stevens No. 105; De' Paoli, p. 277)*

Yesterday, which was the 9th of this month, I received from the courier Your Excellency's package in which there was an *intermedio*[1] and a letter from Your Excellency, doing me infinite kindness and honour, together with a copy of a paragraph from a letter of the Duchess of Parma,[2] written to Your Excellency, in which she deigns to honour me by commanding me (through Your Excellency) to set to music what will be ordered by Your Excellency. I have hardly been able to read the said *intermedio* twice before having to write—this being the day when the courier leaves—yet I have seen so much beauty in it that, truth to tell, I was deeply moved and captivated by so fine a work.

Although time has been short, I have not been entirely useless in this respect, for I have already begun work, the modest results of which Your Excellency will see by next Wednesday. I have already taken into account the four kinds of music that will be used to adorn the said *intermedio*: the first, which starts at the beginning and goes so far as the onset of the quarrel between Venus and Diana, and between their arguments; the second, from the beginning of the quarrel until the arguments are over; the third, when Pluto comes in to establish order and calm, lasting until Diana starts to fall in love with Endymion; and the fourth and last, from the beginning of the said falling in love until the end.

But believe me, Your Excellency, there are passages which—without your sensitive aid—could, as you will see, cause me no little trouble, and I shall give Your Excellency more detailed information about this on Wednesday. For the moment I intend to do nothing more than to give thanks to God first of all, for having made me worthy of being able to receive such distinguished commissions from such eminent gentlemen and patrons, praying Him at the same time to make me worthy as much by the results as by my devotion, which will surely seek to serve patrons with the greatest power of which it is capable.

¹ *Diana e Venere*, the third of five *intermedi* by Ascanio Pio di Savoia.
² The Dowager Duchess Margherita, widow of Ranuccio Farnese.

XXXII

Venice, 10 September 1627; [to Alessandro Striggio, at Mantua].
(Stevens No. 106; De' Paoli, p. 273)

I am sending off to Your Lordship the remainder of *La finta pazza Licori*. I did not send it by the previous post, as the copyist was unable to let me have it in time for the departure of the courier. I have also paid heed to what Your Lordship was kind enough to tell me, yet even if you had not ordered me to be silent—since it was a matter such that talking about it could even have caused harm to my present occupation, for strange things go on amongst our crowd of singers—this ability to control myself would have been desirable for that very reason; but all the more so now that you ask it of me through your innate kindness.

The Marquis Bentivoglio, very much my master for many years past, wrote to me as long as a month ago asking if I would set to music some words of his, made by His Excellency for use in a certain very important play that would be written for performance at a princely wedding. These would be *intermedi*, not a play sung throughout. As he was very much my special master I replied that I would do everything possible to carry out His Excellency's orders. He answered with particular appreciation and told me it was going to be used at the wedding of the Duke of Parma.¹ I replied that I would do whatever he would be so kind as to ask of me.

He at once informed Their Highnesses² of this, and I received a reply telling me to start work on the assignment, so he at once sent me the first *intermedio*.³ I have already half finished it, and shall compose it easily because they are almost all soliloquies. Their Highnesses do me great honour with such a commission, for I have heard that about six or seven applied for the appointment, but of their own accord these gentlemen were so kind as to elect myself, and that was how it happened.

I now reply to the paragraph that mentions the kind and special affection of the Most Serene Lord Duke Vincenzo,⁴ my special master, for so he surely will be in every time and condition, and in no matter what circumstances, because of the particular reverence in which I shall always hold that Most Serene House, and which I hold now; and because of the special obligation I have to that Most Serene Highness, as I have received particular favours from his infinite kindness. And I shall affirm that His Highness will always be my master and patron without any expectation on my part other than His Highness's good grace, since I know for sure that he would not consent to my ruin or unhappiness.

Considering what I have, I have most securely whilst I live, whether or not I am able to work, because this security operates in such a way, that (as with the Director of Music, so with the singers themselves) they would never try to make anyone do what he cannot, never! I shall also affirm that I am very unlucky (and believe me truly, Your Lordship) in that my ill fortune—to play a joke on me—should interfere with the allowance which His Highness[5] deigned to grant me: nine times out of ten there would be no money for me in the treasury. And so, thanks to this major misfortune I could in a short time be ripe for some internal illness, not to mention the misfortunes attendant upon death, which would in fact leave me without any allowance whatever.

Nothing could give my soul peace with satisfaction except to have a canonry at Cremona, in addition to my lands, without anything of benefit from the treasury; and I could have that canonry at once by means of an order from Her Majesty the Empress[6] to the Governor of Milan,[7] or to the Cardinal of Cremona[8] himself. The canonry would provide me with about 300 scudi in that currency. Thus feeling secure on this firm basis, and with the addition of my estate, I could be sure—after serving as long as I were able—of then having somewhere to retire, honourably and in godly manner, for the last days of my life.

Otherwise, as I told Your Lordship, I would always be in fear of some colossal trick that my ill fortune might play on me, and I could certainly expect it because I am no longer young. With this end in mind—of the said canonry—before its patronage was allowed by His Majesty,[9] I was on the point of passing through Mantua to ask for letters of recommendation from His Highness to Her Majesty the Empress (since I was about to present her with some of my compositions, expressly in order to be favoured with that canonry), since the Prince of Poland[10] became very involved in the matter; but ill luck called on me, because I did not wish to present his letters for a certain reason.

I am certainly not rich, but neither am I poor; moreover I lead a life with a certain security of income until my death, and moreover I am absolutely sure of always having it on the appointed pay-days, which come every two months without fail. Indeed, if it is the least bit late, they send it to my house. Then as regards chapel I do as I wish, since there is the sub-director, called Assistant Director of Music;[11] and there is no obligation to teach. Also, the city is most beautiful, and if I want to put myself to minimal trouble I come up with a further 200 good ducats.

Such is my condition: nevertheless the Lord Duke will always be my master, and I shall be his most faithful and most humble servant in every place and condition.

[1] Odoardo Farnese.
[2] Duke Odoardo and the Dowager Duchess Margherita.
[3] Actually the third of five, but the first to be sent.
[4] Vincenzo II Gonzaga, seventh Duke of Mantua.
[5] Vincenzo I Gonzaga, fourth Duke of Mantua.
[6] Eleonora Gonzaga, wife of Ferdinand II, Holy Roman Emperor.
[7] Don Gomez Suarez di Figueroa e Cordova, fourth Duke of Feria.
[8] Pietro Campori, elected Bishop of Cremona in 1621.
[9] Emperor Ferdinand II.
[10] Sigismund III, King of Poland.
[11] Giovanni Rovetta, appointed in 1627.

XXXIII

Venice, 10 September 1627; [to Ercole Marigliani, at Mantua]. *(Stevens No. 107; De' Paoli, p. 279)*

I have received Your Lordship's most esteemed and courteous letter, enclosing one from Signor Alessandro,[1] husband of Signora Settimia,[2] in which he speaks of little else but his certainty about the shortness of time for what those Most Serene Princes[3] intend to do, for as yet nothing in the way of poetry or any kind of beginning is to be seen.

Once again he kindly assures me that he will not allow his wife to obey anyone else but myself in singing, and that I should not be surprised about his having replied to Signor Sigismondo,[4] since he could not suffer the friend he loves to be hurt by anyone, either rightly or wrongly, beseeching me that if I knew anything I might try and pass the word on to him; and at the end of that letter he tells me that he is not one of His Highness's musicians, and would I please no longer give him the title of Musician to His Highness. Little wonder that I had erred, not knowing about this; but when writing to him again (as I shall do by the next post) I shall try not to fall into my former error. But what made me err was seeing those precise words in his letter: 'If anybody—other than you yourself—has a right to look after that music, I should do so more than anyone else, because I am not inferior to the aforesaid (whom you mention) in any aspect of the art, so much the more because of the particular merits of my wife and my many years of service to that Most Serene House.'

And, I repeat, since looking after music suits the musician and not the doctor, I have asked him this for these basic reasons; but when writing to him I shall be able to correct my error, and may he forgive me for it, since his letter was full of the greatest love and kindness.

I am invited to go to Mantua by the Most Illustrious Lord Count Alessandro Striggio, very much my master, because of his desire to speak with me. The Feast of the Rosary[5] being over, and His Highness back from Maderno,[6] it will be easy for me to get to Mantua, and it will be most welcome to me, as much to enjoy that country which I so love, as to cheer myself up with Signor Marigliani, very much my master, ever rejoicing (as I shall ever go on doing) in his every complete happiness, which Our Lord grant him always.

[1] Alessandro Ghivizzani, composer.
[2] Settimia Caccini, singer.
[3] Duke Odoardo Farnese and the Dowager Duchess Margherita.
[4] Sigismondo d'India, composer.
[5] 7 October.
[6] Now known as Toscolano-Maderno; it is on the west shore of Lake Garda.

XXXIV

Venice, 18 September 1627; [to the Marquis Enzo Bentivoglio, at Ferrara]. *(Stevens No. 109; De' Paoli, p. 282)*

I am hoping, without more ado, to send Your Excellency by the next post, Saturday, the *intermedio* of Dido[1] in its entirety. I thought that I might even send it by the present post, but a misfortune came upon me and has prevented me from composing for two days. I do hope this *intermedio* will not displease Your Excellency, for not much has to be done to complete the first one. I further acknowledge receipt from Your Excellency, by courier, of the verses sent to me for the use of the tournament.[2] These I have not read thoroughly as yet because of insufficient time, and because of my concentration on writing the said *intermedio* of Dido.

I have, however, taken a quick glance at the Months and how they speak, and I have also looked at Discord. I have also thought a little about the representation of the aforementioned Discord, and it seems to me that it will be a little difficult. The reason is this: since the Months have to sing together in mellow harmony—and I shall seek out the kind that will provide the most plausible representation of each—I am going to assign the opposite kind of music to Discord (I mean opposite to that which is suitable for the Months). I cannot for the moment think of anything else but to have her declaim in speech and not in music.

This however is a first thought, which I wanted to let Your Excellency know about, so that with your most refined judgment you can assist my ability the better to serve Your Excellency's pleasure, which I desire with all my heart. Yet I would not deny that those speeches of the aforementioned Discord might be intensified by music; that is, she would have to speak just as if she were actually singing, but this singing of hers would not however be based on any instrumental harmony, and this (it seems to me) would be the way to represent Discord.

I would look upon it as the greatest favour to hear from Your Excellency regarding the time I can have for writing these songs, in order to fulfil your wishes in time, for here in Venice there is talk that the wedding of those Most Serene Princes[3] will take place next carnival time, in 1628.

[1] The second of five *intermedi* by Ascanio Pio di Savoia.
[2] *Mercurio e Marte*, by Claudio Achillini, a Bolognese lawyer and poet.
[3] Duke Odoardo Farnese and Margherita de' Medici.

XXXV, XXXVI, XXXVII

Monteverdi's younger son, Massimiliano, had followed the profession of his paternal grandfather and had begun a medical practice in Mantua in 1626. In little more than a year he had fallen foul of a jealous colleague or acquaintance who had denounced him to the Inquisition for supposedly reading a prohibited scientific book, and he was at once imprisoned. His Mantuan friends, shocked by the suddenness of the tragedy and stunned by their own inability to assist, had the news conveyed to Monteverdi, who was so overcome with grief that he was unable to compose for two days. To make matters worse, he knew that it would be virtually impossible for him even to visit his son and offer some comfort. So he turned once again to his friends at court, Striggio and Marigliani, beginning with the latter in the hope that a ranking councillor could deal not only with the Father Inquisitor—who required 100 ducats as a security payment—but with the Mantuan treasury, which was supposed to supply the money from the composer's yearly allowance. He should have known that such a hope was foredoomed. Now, in Letter XXXV, he appeals to the more powerful Striggio, and offers to have the money sent from Venice. Even during this time of anxiety, however, he finds time to discuss the recopying of *Armida* and to think about suitable singers for his Mantuan patron. In Letter XXXVI he reverts to the sorry tale, assuring Striggio that the funds will be forthcoming and begging him to speak to the Father Inquisitor so that Massimiliano can be released. Striggio in fact advanced the money, and the release was duly obtained. Letter XXXVII reveals the extent of Monteverdi's joy at the news of Striggio's elevation to the marquisate. *Armida* is mentioned for the last time, and Parma becomes once more the main topic for discussion.

XXXV

Venice, 18 December 1627; [to Alessandro Striggio, at Mantua]. *(Stevens No. 115; De' Paoli, p. 295)*

I received at Parma two of Your Lordship's letters: in the one you instructed me to let you have *Armida*, which was so much to the liking of the Most Serene Lord Duke[1] my master, and likewise that I should come to Mantua; and in the other Your Lordship instructed me to busy myself getting hold of a male soprano of the best quality. I answered neither the one nor the other because I was doing my best, day after day, to return to Venice and serve you from there.

On my return to Venice three days ago, I at once handed over *Armida* for recopying: I shall be sending this to Your Lordship by the next post, and informing you about the castrato, for in Parma the best is said to be Signor Gregorio,[2] who is in the service of His Eminence Cardinal Borghese, but could (with considerable effort) get away, I should think. There is also Signor Antonio Grimano,[3] but you could hardly hope to engage him. There are two others who have also come from Rome: some castrato who sings in St. Peter's,[4] but he seems not very good to me because he has a voice that suffers from catarrh—not too clear, stiff ornaments, and very little *trillo*; then there is a boy of about eleven,[5] but he seems not to have a pleasing voice either—he can do little ornaments and something of a *trillo*, but everything is pronounced with a somewhat muffled voice.

Regarding these two, I shall put out a feeler if Your Lordship wishes, but concerning the others I think I would not do anything. Nevertheless I have let them know about it, and since I am returning (if it please God) on the 2nd or 3rd of next month, I shall be better able to inform Your Lordship, as I have been late in receiving Your Lordship's very kind letters.

About my coming to Mantua, I shall also have to be excused at present, for because of my reputation I am not allowed to go there since my son Massimiliano is in the prisons of the Holy Office. He has been there for three months, the reason being that he read a book which he did not know was prohibited. He was accused by the owner of the book, who got himself imprisoned, and was deceived by the owner who said that the book dealt only with medicine and astrology. As soon as Massimiliano was in prison, the Father Inquisitor wrote to me saying that if I gave him a pledge of 100 ducats for being legally represented until the case was dispatched, he would release him at once.

In one of his letters, Signor Ercole Marigliani, the councillor, offered of his own accord to protect my son, and because of this known partiality of his, I begged him to pass on the task of arranging for my security payment to the Father Inquisitor to come out of the annual income paid to me by that Most Serene Prince my master, but since two months have gone by without my receiving an answer either from the Father Inquisitor or from Signor Marigliani, I am turning (with the greatest possible reverence) to Your Lordship's protection in delegating this particular matter to Signor Marigliani, in Massimiliano's favour and in accordance with his interests.

If he does not wish to undertake this security settlement, I shall always be ready to deposit 100 ducats so that my son can be released. I would indeed have done this already had I received a reply from Signor Marigliani. While Your Lordship will be helping my son (and of this I am most certain), I shall pray Our Lord for your well-being on this most holy feast of Christmas, and for a happy new year.

[1] Vincenzo Gonzaga, seventh Duke of Mantua.
[2] Gregorio Lazzarini (died Rome, 1686).
[3] A castrato in the service of Cardinal Ciampoli.
[4] Pietro, a young singer accompanied by his teacher.
[5] Marc'Antonio Malagigi.

XXXVI

Venice, 1 January 1628; [to Alessandro Striggio, at Mantua]. *(Stevens No. 116; De' Paoli, p. 298)*

You will be doing me a favour, Your Lordship, to forgive me for not sending by the previous post an immediate reply to Your Lordship's most kind and courteous letter, the reason for this being that the postman did not give me mine until the outgoing post had left.

I am however writing now—not having been able to do so before—to give your Lordship boundless thanks for such a favour as you have shown yourself so willing to do me by helping that poor unfortunate son of mine, Massimiliano, so that he may come out of prison: a favour so great that I do not know how I shall ever be able to repay even the smallest part, for it will hold me so indebted that I shall always be bound at least to pray God for the continual preservation and exaltation of yourself and of all your most illustrious house.

The favour that I now beg of Your Lordship's great authority, with all due affection, is this: only that you may be so kind as to influence the Father Inquisitor so that he lets Massimiliano go back home, by virtue of the pledge that he himself requested of me. I desire nothing else of Your Lordship's grace, since I have handed over a necklace worth 100 ducats to Signor Barbieri (a rich dealer in precious stones who is here in Venice, both a countryman of mine, and a close friend for many years) so that he may write by this post asking Signor Zavarella,[1] who looks after the customs duties of His Most Serene Highness of Mantua[2] and is a very close friend of the aforesaid Signor Barbieri, to come to Your Lordship and offer to look after the said pledge personally.

I do not intend to inconvenience you, or beg for anything, otherwise than to induce the Father Inquisitor to let Massimiliano go back home. If I am too bold with Your Lordship's grace, blame the great need that I have of your favour, and blame that great kindness and gentleness of yours which gave me a mind to be so bold.

To change the subject, I heard with extreme sorrow of the death of the Most Serene Don Vincenzo[3] (may God receive him in heaven!) not only because of the special affection I bore to all those noble masters, in particular to this Most Serene Lord—because of that spontaneous goodwill with which he was moved to remember my feeble self, by showing that he took pleasure both in seeing me and in my poor compositions—but also because I hoped that through his kindness I might get the capital sum for that pension or remittance of mine, of 100 scudi.

So, to obtain that favour with greater ease, I endeavoured to put on one side a few small sums of money, and it was for this reason—to add a little more—that I went as I did to toil away for those Princes of Parma.[4] But my fate, which has always been rather more unfavourable than otherwise, insisted on giving me this great mortification when least expected. Thank God I have not lost both my master and that little security which, through grievous toil, has been granted me by God,

whom I pray and beseech with all my heart that the present Most Serene
Lord may live in blessed tranquillity.

For as I am very sure that he is very just, being of that Most Serene
house, I do not believe nor ever will believe that he would take away what
is mine, so reliant am I upon the favours of Your Lordship, who (I
confidently hope) will be most gracious in helping me if the need arise.
Dear Sir, comfort me with a word about this matter, because it will give
me life.

[P.S.] I said above that Signor Zavarella will come to Your Lordship to
take care of the pledge, but I now have to say that it will not be him, but
rather Signor Giovanni Ambrosio Spiga,[5] His Highness's jeweller. It
will be this man who will come to take care of the pledge. For the love of
God, forgive me for such inconvenience: again I turn to make you a most
humble reverence.

[1] Giulio Cesare Zavarella.
[2] Carlo Gonzaga of Nevers, eighth Duke of Mantua.
[3] The seventh Duke had died on 25 December 1627.
[4] Duke Odoardo Farnese and the Dowager Duchess Margherita.
[5] A Milanese goldsmith who settled in Mantua.

XXXVII

Parma, 4 February 1628; [to the Marquis Alessandro Striggio, at
Mantua]. *(Stevens No. 118; De' Paoli, p. 303)*

The news given me by the Most Illustrious Marquis Enzo,[1] who has just
passed through Mantua and arrived at Parma, about Your Lordship's
having been made a marquis by the new duke, cheers and comforts my
heart. The infinite obligation that I owe, and shall owe as long as I live,
and the long and unbroken friendship of which you have always deigned
to make me worthy, by offering me continual proofs of particular and
extraordinary favours; and the long service which I have ever professed
to maintain by always desiring to be worthy of being known, through
your grace, as your true and genuine servant; let them plead and speak
for me, and assure Your Lordship of my consolation.

I beg you most urgently to be so kind as to keep me in that same state
of grace, in the future also, assuring Your Lordship that if I cannot serve
you in any other way (being a most feeble subject) I shall never fail in my

feeble prayers to pray the Lord that He maintain and prosper you in this and greater happiness by His holy grace.

How distressing it was, then, for me to receive Your Lordship's renewed instructions that I send *Armida*, because of my being (as I am) in Parma, and having *Armida* in Venice—may God be my witness! I refrained from sending it to Your Lordship this Christmas, because of the death of the Most Serene Lord Duke Vincenzo (may he be in glory!) as I would never have thought that you might wish to enjoy it at carnival time. This failure on my part, if Your Lordship could see into my heart, upsets me very much, believe me truly. *Armida* is however in the hands of the Most Illustrious Signor Mocenigo,[2] my very affectionate and special master.

Now by this post, which leaves today for Venice, I am writing very urgently to the said gentleman, that he honour me with a copy of it, and that he give it to Signor Giacomo Rapallino[3] the Mantuan, very much Your Lordship's servant, a singer at St. Mark's and my very dear friend, to whom I am now writing persuasively to see if he can get it from the aforesaid Signor Mocenigo (very much his master and much befriended by him), and without loss of time—if possible—send it off in my name to Your Lordship. And knowing this nobleman to be most polite, and Signor Rapallino to be very keen on having himself known as Your Lordship's servant, I have not the slightest doubt, Your Lordship, that as soon as ever possible it will be sent to you.

Here in Parma the music is being rehearsed, having been written by me in haste—Their Most Serene Highnesses[4] believing that the noble wedding might have to take place some time before the appointed date—and these rehearsals are being held because in Parma there are Roman and Modenese singers, instrumentalists from Piacenza, and others. Since Their Highnesses have seen how these musicians fulfil their needs, and the success they are having, and their confident outlook upon the event that they are preparing in a very few days, it is considered that we—all of us—could go home, until firm news of the outcome, which they say could be this May, though others favour this September.

There will be two most beautiful entertainments—one a complete spoken play, with the *intermedi* set to music (there is no *intermedio* that is not at least 300 lines in length, and each has a different character, the words having been written by the Most Illustrious Don Ascanio Pio, son-in-law of the Marquis Enzo, and a most worthy and gifted nobleman); the other will be a tourney, in which four squadrons of knights will take part, and the master of ceremonies will be the Duke himself. Signor Achillini[5] has written the words for the tourney, and there are more than a thousand lines, which is very nice for the tourney but very long-drawn-out as regards the music. They have given me a great deal to do.

Just now they are rehearsing the music for this tourney.[6] Whenever I could not find enough emotional variety, I tried to change the instrumentation, and I hope this will give pleasure. I entrusted Signor Barbieri, a rich merchant of Venice, to do his best to relieve Your Lordship of the pledge made for Massimiliano, and to this end he is keeping on hand for you a necklace worth 100 ducats. I am waiting for a reply about this: may Your Lordship forgive me for the delay.

[1] Enzo Bentivoglio of Ferrara.
[2] Girolamo Mocenigo, a Venetian patron of the arts.
[3] Baritone, and chaplain to Mocenigo.
[4] Duke Odoardo Farnese and the Dowager Duchess Margherita.
[5] Claudio Achillini, a Bolognese lawyer and poet.
[6] *Mercurio e Marte.*

XXXVIII

The rediscovery of this letter came too late for it to be included in the 1980 volume. It is presented in the format there adopted in case readers who wish to make the collection more complete care to copy it and insert it after page 401.

121a

Forlì, Biblioteca Comunale Aurelio Saffi, Fondo Piancastelli, Autografi sec. XII-XVIII, *ad vocem* Monteverdi. Folio, 1 p. [to the Marquis Enzo Bentivoglio, at Ferrara]. *Enclosure:* a canzonetta. *(9 March 1630).* Vitali, 411.

The rediscovery of this letter, apparently yet another that may have formed part of Giuseppe Antonelli's collection deriving from the archives at Ferrara, was first announced by Carlo Vitali in 'Una lettera vivaldiana perduta e ritrovata; un inedito monteverdiano del 1630 e altri carteggi di musicisti celebri, ovvero Splendori e nefandezze del collezionismo di autografi', *Nuova rivista musicale italiana,* xiv (1980), 404–12. The opinion there expressed with regard to the most likely recipient of the letter—Enzo Bentivoglio—is borne out not only by the references to Parma and to

Goretti, who had given so much in the way of moral and practical assistance to Monteverdi while the Farnese music was being composed, copied and rehearsed, but also by the initial, medial and final salutation formulae. Indeed they correspond exactly with those employed in Letters 105 [XXXI], 109 [XXXIV], 111 and 113; and by the same token they reconfirm the supposition that Letter 121 was written to a person of slightly less exalted rank than the marquis. A comparison of the final phrases of 121 and 121a suffices to show that Monteverdi found it expedient, in the latter case, to adopt a more elaborate and flowery cadential formula.

Despite the coincidence that Letters 121 and 121a both mention delays in the composition of a canzonetta, it is clear that Monteverdi is working on two different canzonettas for two different patrons; and in case they might happen to know one another (as they would if the recipient of Letter 121 were Ascanio Pio, Bentivoglio's son-in-law), he gives two separate excuses: music for the nuns of S. Lorenzo, and a bad leg. This is the first time we hear of a leg hurt at Parma, but it comes as no great surprise because the letters written by Francesco Guitti, Francesco Mazzi and Antonio Goretti make it clear that Monteverdi often went on tours of inspection to ensure that the two amphitheatres at Parma could really and truly accommodate his musicians.[1] It would not have been difficult for a 61-year-old man to fall while attempting to reach some of the more inaccessible and dangerously placed balconies, and apparently the accident was serious enough to cause pain more than a year after it had happened.

[1] Lavin, 126, 131, 134, 146.

121a [XXXVIII]

Venice, 9 March 1630: [to the Marquis Enzo Bentivoglio, at Ferrara].

My Most Illustrious and Most Excellent Lord and Most Respected Master,

You will forgive me if I have been a little tardy in sending Your Excellency the canzonetta[a] which you kindly requested of me, for (much to my displeasure) it was advisable for me—because of my leg—to stay in bed for a few days; and again it is the leg which I slightly damaged at Parma, as indeed Signor Goretti[b] can confirm to Your Excellency.

Please God that I may have found favour with your most refined taste, but if not, may there be some recompense in that I did not know what it was really intended for; otherwise I would have written it more suitably. And my mind—with which I long to serve you with the greatest integrity in everything—will be what would intervene to assist me; with which also I pray fervently for Your Excellency's greater happiness and

pleasure, while with all my heart I make a most humble reverence and
kiss your hand.

from Venice, 9 March 1630
Your Most Illustrious Excellency's
Most humble and most grateful servant
Claudio Monteverdi

[a] A different canzonetta from the one mentioned in Letter 121, but possibly printed later in Book IX.

[b] Antonio Goretti, composer and collector of instruments at Ferrara.

XXXIX, XL

In the early 1630s the eminent Florentine scholar Giovanni Battista
Doni—at that time Secretary of the College of Cardinals in Rome—
launched a large-scale correspondence with experts on ancient music, both
in Italy and beyond its borders, in the hope of drawing together information
that could be used in his *Trattato della musica scenica*, which steadily occupied
him from about 1632 until 1638. In the interim he published the *Compendio
del trattato de' generi e de' modi della musica* (Rome, 1635). Wishing to contact
Monteverdi, Doni wrote a letter to him and sent it to an old acquaintance,
Marc'Antonio Cornaro, Bishop of Padua, who as a former dean of St.
Mark's had known Monteverdi well. Letter XXXIX, almost certainly to
Doni, gives ample evidence of the composer's enthusiasm for a new project,
a book about word-setting, harmony and rhythm with the provisional title of
Melodia, ovvero Seconda pratica musicale. He never completed the book, but
was glad enough to exchange ideas with Doni, who knew much of
Monteverdi's published and unpublished work. Letter XL, also presumably
to Doni, continues the theoretical discussion and expresses a sincere hope
that the two could meet in Rome; but whether this meeting ever took place is
a matter for conjecture. In later life Monteverdi's distaste for travel
intensified, and though Doni returned to Florence in 1640 it is unlikely that
the composer visited him there. Nevertheless the letters demonstrate a
kinship of spirit and idea that looks forward to later musical developments.

XXXIX

Venice, 22 October 1633; [to Giovanni Battista Doni, at Rome]. *(Stevens
No. 123; De' Paoli, p. 320)*

Enclosed with a most kind letter from the Most Illustrious Lord Bishop
Cornaro,[1] my particular lord and most revered master, sent to me from
Padua, there was one from Your Worship addressed to me, so

abundantly fruitful in honour and praise of my feeble self that I was
almost lost in wonder at it; but considering that from a most virtuous and
kindly tree such as Your Worship's person there could grow no other
fruit but that of like nature, I kept quiet, accepting the harvest not so
much because I was worthy of it, but rather to preserve it for the singular
merits of Your Worship, knowing myself to be something of a green
shrub, and of such kind that I produce nothing other than leaves and
flowers without scent.

Please be so good, therefore, as to accept from me by way of reply the
praises that your most noble letter deserves, for I deem it a great favour
that you do me the honour of accepting me as your most humble servant.
Monsignor the Vicar of St. Mark's,[2] who was so kind as to tell me about
Your Worship's noble qualities and particular virtues, mentioned that
you were writing a book on music;[3] at which point I added that I too was
writing one, though with fear that through my weakness I would fail to
reach the desired conclusion. This gentleman being very devoted to the
Most Illustrious Lord Bishop of Padua, I imagine that this is how His
Grace may have heard of my writings, for I know of no other way, and I
make no effort to let people know. But since His Grace has been kind
enough to honour me so in Your Worship's favour, I beg you to consider
the rest of what I have to say.

You should know, therefore, that I am indeed at work—but under
compulsion, however, inasmuch as the event which years ago spurred
me to begin was of such a kind that it caused me unawares to promise the
world something that (once I had become aware of it) my feeble forces
could not manage. I promised, as I said before, in a printed work of mine
to let a certain theoretician[4] of the First Practice know that there was
another way (unknown to him) of considering music, and this I called
the Second Practice. The reason for this was that he had been pleased to
criticize (in print!) one of my madrigals,[5] as regards certain of its
harmonic progressions, on the basis of tenets of the First Practice (that
is to say, the ordinary rules, as if they were exercises written by a youth
beginning to learn the first species of counterpoint) and not according to
a knowledge of melody.

But on hearing of a certain exegesis published in my defence by my
brother,[6] he calmed down in such a way that from thenceforward not
only did he stop overruling me, but—turning his pen to my praise—he
began to like and admire me. Since the promise was public, I could not
neglect it, and for this reason I am compelled to pay the debt. I beg you
therefore to consider me excused for my boldness.

The title of the book will be as follows: *Melodia, ovvero Seconda pratica musicale.* I mean the second as regards numerical order, in modern style; first in order, in the old style. I am dividing the book into three parts corresponding to the three aspects of Melody. In the first I discuss word-setting, in the second, harmony, and in the third, the rhythmic part. I keep telling myself that it will not be unacceptable to the world, for I found out in practice that when I was about to compose the lament of Ariadne—finding no book that could show me the natural way of imitation, not even one that would explain how I ought to become an imitator (other than Plato, in one of his shafts of wisdom, but so hidden that I could hardly discern from afar with my feeble sight what little he showed me)—I found out (let me tell you) what hard work I had to do in order to achieve the little I did do in the way of imitation, and I therefore hope it is not going to be displeasing, but—let it come out as it will in the end—I shall be happier to be moderately praised in the new style than greatly praised in the ordinary; and for this further presumption I ask fresh pardon.

Well, what pleasure I felt on learning that in our own times a new instrument had been invented![7] May God be my witness—whom I pray with all my heart to maintain and bless the most virtuous person of the inventor, who was none other than Your Worship—I have indeed often thought about the reason for its discovery, on which (I mean to say, where) the ancients based their ideas in order to find so many differences in it (as they did), because not only are there many that we use, but many that have been lost. Nor has there been even one theorist of our times (yet they have professed to know all about the art) who has shown even one to the world. I hope, however, in my book, to say something about this point that perhaps will not be displeasing.

From the pleasure I have told you about, Your Worship can decide for sure whether it will be precious to me—the favour promised me in due course through your kindness—that is, in being favoured with a copy of such a worthy treatise, containing new and recondite things.

[1] Marc'Antonio Cornaro, Bishop of Padua from 1632 until his death in 1636.
[2] Benedetto Erizzo, Abbot of S. Crisogono of Zara.
[3] *Compendio del trattato* (Rome, 1635).
[4] Canon Giovanni Maria Artusi, of Bologna.
[5] *Cruda Amarilli* (Book V).
[6] Giulio Cesare Monteverdi, in the *Dichiaratione* printed at the end of the *Scherzi musicali* of 1607.

⁷ The *lyra barberina*, whose three sets of strings could be tuned to the Dorian, Phrygian and Lydian modes.

XL

Venice, 2 February 1634; [to Giovanni Battista Doni, at Rome]. *(Stevens No. 124; De' Paoli, p. 325)*

I have received two letters from Your Worship: one before Christmas—at a time when I was entirely taken up with writing the mass for Christmas eve (a new mass being expected of the director of music according to a custom of this city)—and the other one two weeks ago from the courier, who found me not properly recovered from a catarrhal descent which started to appear over my left eye just after Christmas, and this kept me far not only from writing but also from reading, for many a long day. Nor am I yet free from it, in fact, for it still keeps troubling me to some extent, and because of these two real impediments I am writing to beg Your Worship to forgive this fault of mine in replying so tardily.

Only two weeks ago I read Your Worship's first letter, most courteous and most helpful, from which I gathered the most kindly advice, all of it worthy of my careful consideration; and for this I am sending you my infinite thanks. I have however seen the Galilei[1]—not just now, but rather twenty years ago—the part where he mentions that scant practice of ancient times. I valued seeing it then, perceiving in that same part how the ancients used their practical signs in a different way from ours, but I did not try to go any further in understanding them, being sure that they would have come out as very obscure ciphers, or worse, since that ancient practical manner is completely lost.

Whereupon I turned my studies in another direction, basing them on the principles of the best philosophers to have investigated nature. And because, in accordance with my reading, I notice that the results agree with those reasonings (and with the requirements of nature) when I write down practical things with the aid of those observations, and really feel that our present rules have nothing to do with those requirements, I have for this basic reason given my book the title *Seconda pratica*; and I hope to make this so clear that it will not be censured by the world, but rather taken seriously.

I keep well away, in my writings, from that method upheld by the Greeks with their words and signs, employing instead the voices and characters that we use in our practice, because my intention is to show by means of our practice what I have been able to extract from the mind of those philosophers for the benefit of good art, and not for the principles of the First Practice, which was only harmonic.

Would to God that I might find myself near to Your Worship's singular affection and singular prudence and advice, for I would tell you all, by word of mouth—begging you to hear me out, I mean in everything—as much about the plan, as about the principles and the divisions of the parts of my book; but my being far away prevents it. Because of a special favour received of the Most Holy Virgin's consummate goodness in the year of the plague at Venice, I am bound by a vow to visit the Most Holy House of Loreto. I hope soon, with the Lord's help, to fulfil it; on which occasion I would come on to Rome (if it please the Lord to grant me the favour) in order to be able to present my service personally to Your Worship, and enjoy both the sight and the most beautiful sound of your most noble instrument, and be honoured by your most brilliant conversation.

I have seen a drawing of the instrument on the piece of paper you sent me, which—far from diminishing my eagerness—has on the contrary made it grow. But since in the aforesaid second letter you ask me to engage the services of Scapino[2] in order that I may send Your Worship drawings of the many extraordinary instruments that he plays, because of my great desire to find an opportunity of serving you, and being unable to do this as he is performing in Modena, not in Venice, I therefore feel very disappointed.

Nevertheless I have used a little diligence with certain friends so that they can at least describe to me the ones they are able to remember, and so they gave me the enclosed sheet of paper which here and now I am sending off to Your Worship. Nor did I neglect to write to a friend[3] about trying to obtain drawings of those most different from the ones in use. I have never seen them myself, but from the little information I am sending, it seems to me that they are new as regards shape but not in sound, since all fit in with the sounds of the instruments that we use.

What I did see in Mantua thirty years ago, played and put together by a certain Arab who had just come from Turkey (and this man was lodged at the court of the Duke of Mantua,[4] my master) was a cittern, the size of ours, strung with the same strings and similarly played, but it had this difference—its belly was half of wood around the part near the neck, and half of sheepskin around the underneath part, well stretched and glued about the rim of the cittern, the strings of which were attached rather to

its lower rim, and rested upon a bridge which was placed in the centre of
that sheepskin; and the small finger of the quill hand making the said
sheepskin dance while he stopped the chord, those chords came out
with a tremolo motion which gave a very pleasing effect. I have heard
nothing more novel that was to my liking.

I shall remain alert, and if I am notified of anything that might bring
you pleasure I shall not fail to send you a little drawing at once.

[1] Vincenzo Galilei, Florentine composer and theorist.
[2] Stage name of the actor–musician Francesco Gabrielli.
[3] Probably Bellerofonte Castaldi of Modena, artist and musician.
[4] Vincenzo Gonzaga, fourth Duke of Mantua.

II

The Musical Environment

DENIS ARNOLD

Monteverdi and his Teachers

Some, perhaps many, composers seem to know little of other men's music; and that little is often a curious selection of our heritage, chosen to help the individual solve his problems of technique and style, without much thought of its intrinsic worth. It is rare for a Mozart to find inspiration in the work of Johann Sebastian Bach, or a Haydn to receive a renewed impetus from Mozart. The chosen guide is just as probably a Sarti or Wagenseil, who serves the somewhat narrow purpose of the composer just as well.

Monteverdi, by contrast, was extremely well informed. Scattered throughout his letters, prefaces, and the documents relating to his life, there are references to no fewer than three dozen composers. Some are men he may have known personally. Of the list of composers mentioned in the preface of the *Scherzi musicali* of 1607 as involved in the development of the new manner which Monteverdi called the *seconda prattica*, all had been at courts neighbouring that of the Gonzagas: Luzzaschi and Gesualdo at Ferrara, where Cipriano de Rore had also worked; Bardi, Alfonso, Fontanella, Cavalieri and the other members of the Camerata academy at Florence. Marc'Antonio Ingegneri had been his teacher at Cremona, Giaches de Wert was for some time his immediate superior at Mantua. Such is the common acquaintance of musicians. But the list of *prima prattica* composers is a different matter. Ockeghem, Josquin, Pierre de La Rue, Mouton, Crecquillon, Clemens non Papa, Gombert and Willaert were part of the distant past. They had little to offer any musician of the early seventeenth century and least of all to the 'modern' composer of up-to-date madrigals and dramatic entertainments.

The impeccable taste of Monteverdi's choice from musical history arouses our suspicions. His taste in contemporaries was mixed enough. Mingling with the admittedly great masters are minor, even insignificant composers whose names were soon to perish and whose music today has little interest. The old Netherlanders were without exception great composers, quoted as authorities by all the writers of treatises to display their learning. Could Monteverdi have copied their names from some

august theoretician without really knowing their work by anything
except reputation? To this the reply must surely be to affirm
Monteverdi's honesty. The motets and masses of Gombert and most of
the others were in the library of the Duke's chapel at Mantua for
Monteverdi's study. His parody mass *In illo tempore* shows that he had a
thorough grasp of the old manner, and the fact that the Roman publisher
Masotti invited him to edit Arcadelt's ever-popular madrigals for four
voices in 1627 suggests that he was known to have an interest in the
music of the early sixteenth century. Remembering that Monteverdi
possessed a copy of Zarlino's *Istitutioni harmoniche*[1] and was acquainted
with Bottrigari's theoretical writings, we can build up the picture of a
man thoroughly versed in his art, interested in its many branches, and
one of the first historically minded composers.

   Great composers rarely owe much to their teachers, but Monteverdi's
breadth and astonishing technical competence from a very early age
surely indicate that his Cremonese master, Ingegneri, was a man of
extraordinary ability. Not that he was an outstanding worldly success.
The cathedral *maestro di cappella* was never as fashionable or as well paid
as the court composer or virtuoso; and Cremona was no great centre of
music-making or high society. Ingegneri was not particularly successful
in his published works either. He was clearly a reasonably fluent
composer of secular music, who could produce eight books of madrigals
during the twenty years of his maturity. Yet scarcely a dozen of his pieces
were included in the popular anthologies in his lifetime, a sign that he
was not in the main stream of north Italian music. Only one of his
madrigal books (significantly an early collection) achieved the distinction of being reprinted more than once, and this at a time when a single
collection by Marenzio usually went through half-a-dozen Italian
editions before being taken up by the foreign presses, and even an
anthology of pieces by a group of Mantuan mediocrities achieved a
reprinting, so fashionable was the genre.[2]

   Ingegneri was as competent as any of the composers of the 1570s and
80s—a great deal more so than many—but there is a simple explanation
for his neglect. Tastes changed rapidly in his lifetime. Andrea Gabrieli's
light touch transformed the semi-serious madrigal form from a 'learned'
style, based essentially on extended melodic lines, to one based on easily

---

[1] See Gustave Reese, *Music in the Renaissance* (London, 1954), plate IV.
[2] *L'amorosa caccia de diversi eccellentissimi musici mantovani nativi a cinque voci*
   (Venice, 1588).

memorable tags and short phrases. For those demanding more earnest essays in the modern manner, Marenzio managed to bring the resources of clear-cut harmony and dramatic chromaticism to the form, without completely disrupting it. Ingegneri remained of a previous generation, not unlike Lassus, who came to his peak of stylistic development in the period just before 1575, and thereafter became something of an anachronism. And like Lassus he is best thought of as belonging to the post-Rore generation, for he undoubtedly took up the basic philosophy of that master without making radical changes. Ingegneri was proud of his indebtedness, for in dedicating his *Primo libro de madrigali a sei voci* to the Duke of Parma in 1586, he thanks him because 'the favours and patronage which you as liberally gave in former times to M. Cipriano de Rore of happy memory were favour and patronage to all practitioners of his art; since under your protection and with the opportunity which he received from you, he made such advances that he became an everlasting example and master to all in the craft of perfect composition. But those who more especially and heavily than the others must remain obliged to Your Highness are those who could at that time, when he flourished at your most happy court, be on friendly terms with M. Cipriano, and talked with him, and personally received his tuition.'[3]

There were two basic lessons that were to be learned from Rore, and both were well mastered by Ingegneri. The prime importance attached by Rore to the expression of the words infected all the succeeding composers. Some interpreted this as a licence to try extreme experiments; but, like the master himself, Ingegneri found it possible to maintain the musical interest while matching the detail of the verse. A melisma to make the lips part in a smile to express the word 'rise', as in *Quasi vermiglia rosa*:[4]

Ex. 1

Quan-d'il ciel ri - - - - - - - - - - se

---

[3] For the original Italian, see *Il nuovo Vogel*, 852.
[4] *Il quinto libro de madrigali a cinque voci* (Venice, 1587).

or a broken line to express the trembling of the apprehensive lover:

Ex. 2

do not essentially interrupt the musical thought of a craftsman-composer. Nor is there any departure from musicality in the second instructive feature of Rore's music, the use of chromaticism, in the way it is applied in the madrigals of Ingegneri. Tonality is not disintegrating but merely widening in the occasional use of D flat and A flat chords in *Hore sacre*,[5] or in the imitations of the chromatic tetrachord of *Ah tu Signor*:[6]

Ex. 3

And more than anything else Ingegneri is like Rore in that musical form is one of his prime interests. Far from breaking the genre into segments for the better expression of the contrasts of the verse, as Marenzio and later composers were to do, his madrigals show a basic unity of mood. This is achieved by an equally basic unity of texture, and by the working-out of contrapuntal material at sufficient length to make the enigmatic, dramatic changes of the final phase of the madrigal quite unthinkable. Even in his most mature works, written at a time when the 'modern' style was well established, this feeling for the general rather than the particular was kept well to the fore. In *La verginella*,[7] for

[5] *Il primo libro de madrigali a quattro voci* (Venice, 2/1578).
[6] *Il quarto libro de madrigali a cinque voci* (Venice, 1584).
[7] *Il quinto libro de madrigali a cinque voci* (Venice, 1587); in *Adriano Willaert e i suoi discendenti*, ed. Gian Francesco Malipiero (Venice, 1963), 23.

example, published in the year in which Monteverdi's first madrigals also appeared, the main preoccupation is with pattern. In the very first phrase, the lower parts may enter with different words to prevent too great a length, but four out of the five voices enter with the same musical theme. The second section uses up its words quickly too, in a number of close imitations between the voices; but then the whole section is virtually repeated to give the correct musical proportions. The final paragraph is given a similar treatment so that the musical material is spread over some thirty bars—nearly half the madrigal. Repetition of concluding sections is, of course, quite common in early madrigals (the most famous of all of these, Arcadelt's *Il dolce e bianco cigno*, shows how it was usually done), and Ingegneri uses it no fewer than two dozen times throughout his madrigal books. What is unusual about *La verginella* is that the thematic material of this conclusion is a deliberate development of that of the beginning of the madrigal. The canzona motif ♩ ♩ ♩ becomes first 𝄾 ♩ ♩ ♩, then 𝄾 ♩. ♪♩|♩ and finally ♩ ♫. There is no reason for this in the verse. The musician's desire to shape predominates; and if the *da capo* idea was well known to musicians of Ingegneri's generation through the popularity of the French chanson, there is no doubt that here it is applied with subtlety and skill.

   Ingegneri, then, was a worthy master for such a pupil as the young Monteverdi. Yet he was so old-fashioned that, at first sight, he would appear to be the kind of model young men tend to ignore. Certainly so sagacious a critic as Alfred Einstein thought that the older man had little deep effect on his pupil, and a preliminary glance at Monteverdi's *Il primo libro de madrigali* apparently confirms the disparity between the two. A closer examination reveals more similarities, for Monteverdi has many of the solid musical interests of his master. If the contrasts of texture, the pathetic dissonance of the fashionable pastoral madrigal have proved too attractive to ignore, his attention to shape and the adequate development of musical sections is still of paramount importance. Last sections are often repeated *in extenso*. Earlier passages are equally not devoid of thematic links between sections to make for smooth musical development. In *Amor, per tua mercè*, there is even the same use of the chanson motif as in Ingegneri's *La verginella* with the ♩ ♩ ♩ changing first to ♩ ♫ and 𝄾 ♩ ♩ ♩—although Monteverdi is less sure of himself, and the madrigal scarcely explores the possibilities of either the verse or the contrapuntal tags at all thoroughly. And if there is any doubt about the relationship of master and pupil, a comparison of their settings of the fashionable poem *Ardo sì, ma non*

t'amo and its reply, *Ardi e gela*,[8] will remove it. Again at first sight
Monteverdi appears much more modern. He prefers the lighter colours
provided by the use of the upper voices (the lowest part is written in the
tenor clef), and this feeling for contrasts of colours, revealed in the
concertante play of various groupings of them, is something Ingegneri is
too old to appreciate. Then the similarities appear. The opening motifs
are virtually identical:

Ex. 4

(*a*) Ingegneri

Monteverdi covers the ground of the verse more speedily than does his
master, but even so, until the closing section of the madrigal, when he
invents a 'modern' short motif to work out, his vocal lines are smooth
and well developed. He also accepts the final hint of the older man.
Ingegneri binds his two madrigals together by using the same thematic
material. The suggestion has come from the repetition of the word
'sdegno', and since the concluding section of the first madrigal has been
repeated at great length, some return of its tag seems natural if the two
pieces are to become an artistic entity. The composer is not unsubtle
about this. The material used may be the same; its treatment is not.
Having displayed it at great length in its exposition, the restatement is
necessarily more concise. Monteverdi is a shade more obvious. He not
only repeats his concluding section in his first part, he repeats the
concluding section of the second part also; and as the two are virtually
identical, even the least educated of the noble dilettanti can hardly have
failed to notice the device. Nevertheless, Monteverdi has his own touch
of sophistication. The first madrigal ends with a definitive cadence. The
lover is quite sure that he has said the final word: 'I burn with anger and
not with love'. The reply 'Burn and freeze just as you will . . .' startles

[8] Malipiero, ed., op. cit., 31.

him. After this, there is no certainty, and the second madrigal ends with an inconclusive cadence, which, however common in the early part of the sixteenth century, by the 1580s was distinctly unusual in the up-to-date madrigal. Equally, when Monteverdi adds yet a third madrigal to the group, a *contrarisposta*, he adds to the air of dissension with a similarly unsure ending. Again we notice his interest in pattern, for having used the *risposta* as a middle section, he opens his third piece with an inversion of the opening theme of *Ardo sì*:

Ex. 5

A composer of 23, with four published volumes behind him, does not admit to his pupillage without good reason, and the fact that Monteverdi put 'discepolo del Sig. Marc'Antonio Ingegneri' on the title-page of his *Secondo libro de madrigali* in 1590 proves that he held his master in high regard. Probably the main lesson he had learned from him was that the craft of music was just as important as inspiration or philosophy. In an age when the amateur composer (albeit often the professional performer) was rife, it was a necessary lesson. It went deeply into Monteverdi's mind. To his final years he remained a craftsman when craftsmanship was comparatively little esteemed, at least among the general public. That he later took to the duet rather than the solo song is a symptom of his attitude. The duet requires more craft, less hedonistic melody.[9] And it is no coincidence that in as late a work as *L'incoronazione di Poppea*, the famous ensemble of Seneca's friends, 'Non morir, Seneca', is a madrigal very similar in both its attitude and technique to the chromatic works of Rore and Ingegneri.

If he had gone directly to Florence from Cremona, it is just possible that the path on which Monteverdi had started would have been diverted into the byways of monody and operatic experiment. As it was, by finding his first job in Mantua he ensured for himself a second thoroughly professional master, Giaches de Wert. No documents tell us that Wert was active in the development of the young man's style, but, as Bernard Berenson has said, 'in this [finding out what spirit influenced an artist], the really vital matter, historians with their documents seldom give us any help. It is a matter which we must establish for ourselves by the study of the artist's own works, and by determining their relation to

[9] See below, 190–1.

those of his predecessors.'[10] And there can be absolutely no doubt that
the 'eccellente Giaches', to quote Monteverdi's earliest known letter,
was one of the most influential of his associates. By the time Monteverdi
met him, he was probably well into his fifties, a man of great experience
and much respected by the musical world. A Netherlander, he had come
to Italy in his early twenties and had visited and worked at several courts
before becoming *maestro di cappella* to Guglielmo Gonzaga in 1565. He
remained in Mantua for the rest of his life, building up the distinguished
musical establishment which was to reach its highest point in the last
decade of the century. Wert died in 1596 and was buried in the ducal
chapel of S. Barbara.

It is easy to understand why Monteverdi was deeply affected by him,
for Wert was one of the great original madrigal composers of the
century. He arrived in Italy at a time when the vogue for Rore's style was
at its height, so it is remarkable to find him taking a somewhat different
attitude to the problems of secular composition. In a few early works he
shows his northern upbringing. Such a madrigal as *Chi salirà per me
madonn'in cielo*,[11] from his *Primo libro de' madrigali a quattro voci* of 1561,
is in the old polyphonic tradition, its motifs worked out as skilfully as
anyone could wish. Only the thoroughly professional composer would
have thought of the opening of *Quand'io mi volgo*[12] in his second book for
five voices (published in the same year), with the inversion of the
soprano theme given out simultaneously by the second voice:

Ex. 6

[10] Bernard Berenson, *Rudiments of Connoisseurship* (New York, 1962), 25;
originally published as *The Study and Criticism of Italian Art*, 2nd ser. (London, 1902).
[11] *Giaches de Wert, Collected Works*, xv, ed. Carol MacClintock (American Institute of Musicology, 1972), 62.
[12] *Collected Works*, ii, ed. MacClintock (1962), 53.

But even at this time, Wert was fully aware of Rore's innovations and was in fact prepared to take them a stage further. His inventiveness in creating musical imagery to catch the detail of the words was from the beginning quite remarkable. There are the usual symbols to express such words as 'alto' ('high') or 'lungo' ('long' or 'slow'); conventional figures such as the sighing rest to precede 'sospiro' or the smiling melisma for 'riso' are the commonplaces of his style. He will invent a natural fanfare motif suggested by 'Accend'i cor a l'arme' ('The heart is stirred to take up arms') and expand it into a section remarkably reminiscent of a Monteverdian *madrigale guerriero*:

Ex. 7

Still more impressive is his economy of means in this expression of the verbal image. The opening of *Cantai, or piango*[13] (also from the second book of five-voice madrigals) at first looks conventionally polyphonic, with its suggestion of inversion between soprano and tenor. Within half-a-dozen bars it has established the fluctuating emotions of the manic lover. His joy ('cantai': 'I sang') reveals itself in the *note nere*, the fast movement still comparatively new and up-to-date around 1560. His gloom ('piango': 'I weep') brings about a violent contrast, requiring dissonance and slow motion, in the original made the more startling to the singer who sees the page by the use of open 'white' notes in the ligatures (see Ex. 8). So vivid an equation of words and music continues throughout the madrigal. 'Dolcezza' and 'dolce' call forth consonance; 'canto' has a melisma; 'altezza' displays a rising motif; 'amaro' ('bitter') finds expression in an unusual intensity of dissonance. Such mastery of the idiom is remarkable in a man in his mid-twenties.

[13] Ibid., 32.

Ex. 8

The mastery was Wert's; the idiom (as far as these characteristics are concerned) was essentially Rore's. Nevertheless, even in *Cantai, or piango* there are signs of another attitude to the problems of setting words. For after the opening section has set the mood (or rather moods), there follows an extended passage in which the audibility of the poem seems the prime concern. Declamation is careful and exact; and the texture is for the most part homophonic. What variety exists comes from the different groupings of voices, not from the interplay of the several voices. Most remarkable of all is the fact that the repetition of the individual phrases of the poem occurs comparatively rarely in this section. An examination of the uppermost part shows extraordinarily little 'laceration of the poetry' (to quote the Camerata's telling phrase). If each phrase of the poem that Wert repeats is italicized, the result is revealing:

> Cantai, or piango, e non men di dolcezza
> Del pianger prendo che del canto presi,
> *Ch'a la cagion* non a l'effetto intesi
> Son i miei sensi vaghi pur d'altezza.
> *Indi e mansuetudine e durezza*
> Et atti feri *et umili e cortesi*

Port'egualmente, nè mi gravan pesi,
Nè l'arme mie punta di sdegni spezza.

Even more revealing is a comparison with a more or less contemporary madrigal, a typical example of the epoch by Vincenzo Ruffo, published in 1558:

L'alto splendor *ch'in voi sovente infonde*
La fida aurora nell'aprir del giorno
E quel che i monti scalda *e i piani e l'onde*
Mentre gira felice il ciel adorno
Agguagliar non potrà mai lo splendore
Ch'ognor nel viso di Virginia splende.[14]

The difference lies less in the quantity of repetition than its relevance to the expression of the basic emotions of the verse. Ruffo repeats the phrases casually, with little thought for their importance, thinking mainly of the musical balance that is needed to work out the various contrapuntal tags. Wert, on the contrary, does this only to keep the traditional expansion of the last lines. His main repetition in the middle section is to show how intensely the lover feels, stressing the emotional words 'mansuetudine e durezza' ('gentleness and harshness'), which are given out in pure homophony. Again the mastery is astonishing, less this time for the composer's youth than for the fact that he was working in a foreign language and with some of its greatest poetry.

And again these features of his idiom are by no means unique to Wert. Another style common in the 1550s has clearly affected his thinking. This is the homophonic declamation of Willaert's *Musica nova*, published in the very year that these madrigals of Wert appeared—though declamation is perhaps too strong a term for any music by either composer. Rather is it that Wert shares with Willaert the understanding of the importance of clarity and emotional balance in setting words to music. Both were musicians first and last; neither seems to have attempted consciously to work out an academic theory, though such speculation was as popular in their time as in Monteverdi's. In neither is there a hint of amateurism; Monteverdi's lineage is based on the great professional traditions of the composers from the Netherlands.

Unlike Ingegneri, Wert was one of the great successes of his time. By virtue of his post as *maestro di cappella* at Mantua, he was at the top of his profession. He was prolific. He produced a dozen books of madrigals,

[14] Malipiero, ed., op cit., 14.

some canzonettas and a considerable body of church music. For years, the principal anthologies contained his music. Yet there is one aspect of his success that needs explanation. His early madrigal-books were reprinted many times. His first book of five-voice madrigals appeared five times, his second book four times. His later music was apparently not so well received. His eighth book achieved two editions, the ninth and tenth not even that. And whereas Marenzio's madrigals continued in favour well into the seventeenth century, by 1600 Wert's music was already in the process of being forgotten.

One reason for this seeming decline in popularity is suggested by the dedication of his *Ottavo libro de madrigali a cinque voci* to the Duke of Ferrara: 'I would have committed a most grave mistake if I had dedicated these compositions of mine to anyone else, since they were for the most part written in Ferrara ... And where in the world could they be better sung than at the court of Your Highness? ... To whom today is not known these marvels of both art and nature, the voices, the grace, the temperament, the memory and the other rare qualities of the three noble young ladies of Her Highness the Duchess of Ferrara?'[15] Not only could they not be sung better than in Ferrara; few courts had the requisite women singers who could cope with their difficulties. Quite a number of the madrigals in this book are thus occasional music for the renowned ensemble of the Este court. Without the art of Lucrezia Bendidio, Tarquinia Molza and Laura Peperara, with their gift for improvisatory decoration, their dexterity of voice and intelligence, these madrigals can hardly have made much effect. The opening of *Usciva homai*, in spite of the bright colours of the upper voices, seems to cry out for virtuoso decoration, not to mention the evenness of tonal quality to make such altitudes bearable:

Ex. 9

[15] Original in Emil Vogel, *Bibliothek der gedruckten weltlichen Vocalmusik Italiens* (repr. Hildesheim, 1962), ii, 343; incomplete in *Il nuovo Vogel*.

Mantua could perhaps rival the Ferrarese group; few other courts or cities could do so.

But there were other reasons for Wert's receding fashionableness. His development of both the Willaertian clarity of the words and the Roreian vividness of the musical image eventually became a little eccentric. His declamatory madrigals late in life became very austere. Whereas a piece such as *Aspro cor'e selvaggio* from the first book for five voices had been relatively short and achieved intensity because the variety of vocal grouping could maintain the interest throughout, the madrigal sequence *O primavera* of Book XI is so extended that it really requires all the resources of the madrigalist to underscore the emotions of Guarini's poem. This is precisely what is lacking in Wert's setting. In spite of some daring chromaticism and the occasional delicious touch of word-painting, it appears shapeless. The recitative-like progress, which setting a huge piece of verse in such a limited space entails, allows little contrast of rhythm. Even in lesser works, this is a serious drawback. So often it is the detail that stands out, rather than the overall effect, as in *Quel rossignol*, where an exquisite melodic idea at the beginning peters out before achieving the emotional potential inherent in the verse:

Ex. 10

If the declamatory madrigals seem a little dull because of a lack of musical incident, the unsatisfactory nature of some of the pictorial madrigals is the result of too much. Even in his earliest books there are roughnesses of style which are unusual for the second half of the sixteenth century. A little of this roughness comes from the harmony. Wert obviously had a liking for false relations, which lead him to use even an occasional 'English' cadence—although unlike the English he uses it for direct expression of the verse. But Wert's main asperities concern melody. At the beginning of his career there are some unconventional intervals in the vocal lines of some otherwise unremarkable madrigals. The augmented second is quite common, and no addition of *musica ficta* that is at all satisfactory will eliminate them. Leaps of sixths (not difficult for the professional singer but tricky for the

amateur) and of sevenths (not encouraged by the theorists at all) are not
unknown.

In Wert's early madrigals such awkwardnesses seem casual (though
with his splendidly sure technique he could have avoided them if he had
felt so inclined). In his later music, there can be no doubt of his
deliberate intent. Having invented a phrase using an unusual interval, he
lingers on it throughout the parts until it yields its full intensity. The use
of the diminished fourth in *Valle che de' lamenti miei*, to take an example
from the ninth book of madrigals, would be of little consequence if it
happened just once in the cantus; add the alto with the same interval,
and immediately a false relation occurs, to give still more atmosphere:

Ex. 11

Then Wert adds each voice in turn, all of them using the same melodic
trick, until the paragraph has expanded to some thirty bars of slowly
moving harmony. There is little actual dissonance, yet the melody has
done its work—to create a sombre, smouldering atmosphere. This kind
of melody reaches its farthest point in Wert's setting of Petrarch's
sonnet *Solo e pensoso*.[16] Again it is impossible to find a single interval
which by itself would cause any real trouble to the singer or listener. But
follow a downward perfect fifth by another perfect fifth (instead of the
conventional fourth) and the strangeness of mood immediately imparts
itself. Or use a succession of sixths, give them out in parallel motion in
three voices, and the effect is very odd:

Ex. 12

[16] *Collected Works*, vii, ed. MacClintock (1967), 32.

Finally, to make the bass voice sing the extreme notes of a two-octave range within the space of three bars, in the manner of Purcell's John Gostling, and it becomes clear why Wert's late madrigal-books never sold well.

Why did Wert do this? The romantic biographer would no doubt find the reason in his tragic love-affair with the singer Tarquinia Molza, a match not allowed to a mere musician and 'povero fiammingo'. A more realistic musicologist must search elsewhere—and probably in the lost archives (if indeed they ever existed) of the Accademia degli Intrepidi of Ferrara. For it was in the musical academies of Ferrara that the 'modern' style was forged. It was there that the *archicembalo* was created to try out the chromatic experiments of Vicentino, and was played by Luzzaschi and Gesualdo. It was at Ferrara that the new orchestral sonorities were tried out by Bottrigari and his associates. And it was in Ferrara that the singers existed to try out the various theories concerning the expression of the words, which derived from the Platonic ideas of universal interest to musicians in the later sixteenth century. That such ideas were to lead to monody and opera in the hands of the Florentines need cause no surprise, since the main revolution came from the amateurs, who were especially strong in Count Bardi's Camerata. The Ferrarese academies had started earlier and were more firmly orientated musically.

Wert's compromise style seems logically the result of some such compromise in thinking. So does Monteverdi's. The closeness of their relationship is seen most clearly in the latter's second, third and fourth books of madrigals. At first, as in *Ecco mormorar l'onde*, which resembles Wert's *Vezzosi augelli*[17] so closely, it was the realistic, Tassoesque elements that attracted him. It was the declamation and the violence of Wert's music that turned him to the style of the *Vattene* madrigal-cycle in which the older man's manner is not fully assimilated, and then to the agonies of the Guarini settings in the fourth book. Here Wert's experiments are finally fulfilled in a volume intended as a homage to Duke Alfonso d'Este, as was Wert's best music. And when, later, Monteverdi went appreciably beyond Wert's acerbities, his style still remained solidly based on the older man's principles. The difference between the Sestina, *Incenerite spoglie*, of Monteverdi's sixth book, published in 1614, and some of the madrigals of Wert's eleventh book, which appeared twenty years earlier, is one of degree, not of kind. The

[17] *Collected Works*, viii, ed. MacClintock (1968), 11.

very opening of Monteverdi's cycle indeed could have been written by Wert, as could the pastoral climax of the last section (based on an old-fashioned madrigalian tag); and if this is not true of the dissonance of the fourth section, *Ma te raccoglie*, it is hardly surprising, considering what had happened to the art of music in those intervening years.

From Ingegneri, Monteverdi had learned craftsmanship. From Wert he learned the art of expressing passion, and this was to be just as rare a quality in the early years of the seventeenth century. For although it is usually assumed that the term 'baroque' implies extravagance of feeling, this is certainly not true of most of the composers who flourished in what music historians have liked to call 'the early Baroque period'. The Camerata composers, for all their technical novelty, were emotionally restrained in comparison with some of the madrigalists who were working around the turn of the century. The Venetian church musicians who set the style of seventeenth-century church music were monumental rather than passionate in their stately motets. Only those who had learned their art in the later decades of the previous century—Gesualdo and Marco da Gagliano in vocal music, Frescobaldi in instrumental music—retained the grand excesses typical of those inbred north Italian courts. They are, in fact, mannerist rather than Baroque composers, and Monteverdi is the greatest of them.

DENIS ARNOLD

Monteverdi: Some Colleagues and Pupils

Few things could be worse than indifferent mannerism. Extravagance of the kind in which Wert and Monteverdi indulged demands genius; anything less seems merely eccentric. So perhaps it is not surprising that only one other of the Mantuan composers seriously attempted to follow this path (though nearby Ferrara had produced a greater crop of strange compositions over the years). Benedetto Pallavicino was a composer whom Monteverdi thought no more than competent,[1] but this is something not unknown with colleagues in any situation—the more especially in the claustrophobic atmosphere of a small court. Added to which, Pallavicino had been promoted to be *maestro di cappella* at Mantua when Monteverdi probably considered himself to be in the running for the job, although admittedly he was still only in his late twenties and should not have expected to gain it over the head of a man of much greater experience. But Pallavicino, having also come from Cremona, was no distinguished foreigner, and young men are apt to consider themselves as special cases, worthy of rapid promotion.

In the event, it is not difficult to understand the Duke's point of view, for long before Monteverdi had appeared on the Mantuan scene Pallavicino had proved himself a perfectly competent composer. By 1593 he had written seven books of madrigals, and from a casual sampling of these it is evident that he was thoroughly up-to-date, without being a revolutionary. The contents of the fourth book for five voices, for example, are not unlike those of Monteverdi's second book. Diatonic and short-breathed phrases make singing them a not too arduous pleasure. The tendency to repeat sections either exactly or with variations mainly of texture gives an air of easy memorability. The words are expressed by conventional symbols, and if there is no grand passion there is a quiet efficiency which is attractive. The concluding section of *Mentre che qui d'intorno* is typically modern and resembles that of Marenzio's *Dissi a l'amata*, a popular madrigal from a popular book

---

[1] See *The Letters of Claudio Monteverdi*, trans. and ed. Denis Stevens (London, 1980), 37. Further on Pallavicino, see Kathryn Bosi Monteath, *The Five-part Madrigals of Benedetto Pallavicino* (diss., U. of Otago, 1981).

published only a year or two earlier.[2] No wonder Pallavicino was esteemed at Mantua:

Ex. 1

In these earlier works there are few hints of the revolution to come and unexpectedly few signs of any influence of Wert. But, like Marenzio and Monteverdi, Pallavicino was to change greatly in the last decade of the century. His sixth book of madrigals for five voices, published in 1600, is as mannerist as any of Monteverdi's volumes and, in a different way, not unlike the extremist volumes of Gesualdo which were beginning to appear at this time. Not surprisingly in the work of an older man than Monteverdi, the Wertian characteristics are less strong than in the latter's third book, and perhaps better integrated. Even so, it was Wert who again provided the basis for the advanced style, and most of the traits of his eleventh book of madrigals for five voices reappear in Pallavicino's work. Again there are the signs of an attempt at choral recitative. The whole of the first section of his setting of Guarini's *Era l'anima mia* is written in pure homophony, with the usual elisions to give an exact declamation, and if here the atmosphere is somewhat lost because of this academicism (as a comparison with Monteverdi's superb but distinctly 'un-academic' setting makes clear), in *Deh, dolce anima mia* the downward sixth leap in the melody is as effective as it is in any of Monteverdi's madrigals:

[2] See Denis Arnold, *Marenzio* (London, 1965), 11.

Ex. 2

This downward sixth is one of the least disturbing of the melodic awkwardnesses that Pallavicino inherited from Wert. Others are more difficult to sing, sometimes because a false relation takes the harmony in an unexpected direction,[3] sometimes because the composer wants the interval itself to be a conscious asperity:

Ex. 3

Such melodic expression is the commonplace of Pallavicino's music just as much as it is of Wert's, although it does not draw attention to itself quite as much as do the similar progressions in Monteverdi's third book. But what is certainly not derived from Wert is the harmonic astringency which permeates the contents of Pallavicino's sixth book. In this it is hard to find an exact equivalent in any contemporary madrigalist. Even Monteverdi himself is scarcely as concerned to wring out the last drops of emotion from dissonance. Not only do we find the occasional unprepared discord of the type about which Artusi felt so keenly, but when quite conventional suspensions are used they are often strung out to form an almost continuous phrase of dissonant harmony. The following passage from *Lunge da voi* has after its opening scarcely a quarter of its time filled with actual consonances, and its opening, with the tenor's leap of a seventh, is hardly lacking in event:

Ex. 4

[3] See, for example, bars 43–4 of *Cruda Amarilli* in *Vier Madrigale von Mantuaner Komponisten*, ed. Arnold, Das Chorwerk, lxxx (Wolfenbüttel, 1961), 19.

The opening of *Cruda Amarilli*[4] is not much less pungent, and even the more ordinary madrigals of the book contain short sections of similar harmonic strain. In *Ohimè*, a cadential formula of a most conventional kind becomes far from harmless when it is repeated half-a-dozen times within ten bars, coupled with occasional suspensions and a bass line that thrives on what can only be considered pedal notes.

There is nothing amateurish in Pallavicino's use of dissonance, and the madrigals that rely extensively on this as a means of expression are worthy of consideration along with those of Monteverdi's magnificent fourth book. Where mannerism becomes dangerous is in the chromatic works, or rather works with chromatic progressions, for, whereas the dissonance is always logically developed, the chromaticism is often haphazard. Pallavicino has a liking for the contrast of major and minor chords closely juxtaposed. Where this does not interfere with the basic tonality, this is an effective device, and in the following example from *Ch'io non t'ami* the use of the minor to deny the major chord at the beginning of the bar adds to the meaning of the verse:

Ex. 5

Elsewhere the chromatic progressions are more eccentric, for they change the basic tonality without giving enough time for the new 'key' (as it must be called) to settle, as in these concluding bars of *Ohimè*:

Ex. 6

Nevertheless, in spite of a number of strange passages which scarcely seem to fit into the overall scheme, there is no doubt that Pallavicino was a worthy colleague for Monteverdi. The nervous discontinuity of his mannerist madrigals reminds us that Gesualdo's improvisatory pieces came out in 1596, and Pallavicino's music (with the later work of Wert and Marenzio and the third book of madrigals of Monteverdi) seems to belong in that interesting byway of musical history.

[4] Arnold, ed., loc. cit.

It is tempting to see Mantuan music solely in these terms; for the great palace set in the small town lends itself to the romantic fantasy and conjures up gothick gloom. The history of the Gonzagas as a dynasty is no less inspiring of a darkly glowering *Götterdämmerung* atmosphere. But, as far as music is concerned, such a view distorts the truth considerably, for among the composers of the court were excellent purveyors of light, cheerful music. Though Monteverdi seemingly found it hard to compose such music in his earlier Mantuan years, even Pallavicino produced the occasional madrigal meant for delight rather than emotional intensity. In his sixth book, *Hoggi nacqui ben mio* offers undemanding charm; and *Ch'io non t'ami*, for all its close attention to the detail of the words, is a frothy piece written with the bright sonorities of the Three Ladies of Ferrara much in mind. Considering that most of his colleagues had at one time or another written canzonettas or ballettos, this is hardly surprising, and in fact during the years surrounding Monteverdi's arrival various publications seem to indicate a sudden new interest in light music. Wert, until then a very serious-minded composer, published at the age of around 54 his first book of *Canzonette villanelle*, dedicating them to his patroness the Duchess Leonora Medici Gonzaga to congratulate her on the birth of the future Dukes Francesco and Ferdinando. In the same year of 1589 the principal instrumentalist at the court, Salamone Rossi, produced his first book of canzonettas, dedicated to the Duke himself; early the next year the organist at Mantua Cathedral, Lodovico Viadana, produced yet another set of canzonettas, and, although not a member of the court, Orazio Vecchi, the leading composer of light music at that time, dedicated a book of not too serious madrigals to the Duke of Mantua. Was it the accession of the new Prince Vincenzo that stimulated a new gaiety in Mantua? Or, perhaps more likely, was it Vincenzo's new interest in Agnes de Argotta of Cordoba, who (we may assume) became his mistress in this year?

In any case, Vincenzo was the dedicatee of the most popular volume of light music to be produced in the sixteenth century—Gastoldi's ballettos for five voices, which first came out in 1581, to be followed by no fewer than twenty reprints and new editions, published in Venice, Antwerp, Amsterdam, Paris and Nuremberg, not to mention the 'parodies' (to use a polite term for what was really 'pirating' in one or two cases) with which Thomas Morley commandeered the English market for the product in 1595. After a year, Gastoldi produced a set of canzonettas for three voices; in 1594 some more ballettos, this time for three voices; and in the following year a second set of canzonettas. All

these volumes went through a number of editions, and if they were not
quite as popular as his first light-music volume, there can be no doubt
that the director of music in the ducal chapel of S. Barbara was, however
inappropriately, known throughout the world as a composer of truly
popular songs.

'Songs', perhaps, is the wrong word; 'dances' would almost certainly
be better. For while it is difficult to think of some of Morley's imitations
of Gastoldi as anything but madrigals with fa-la refrains (an attempt at
dancing to *Fire, fire* would be amusing, to say the least), the originals are
so artless and naïve that they can hardly stand as 'pure' music. While
such a predecessor of the genre as Baldassare Donato's *Chi la gagliarda*[5]
places the dance rhythms in an interesting polyphonic context to make it
rewarding for everyone to sing, Gastoldi is too regular, too homophonic
and a shade too diatonic to be really interesting to performer or listener.
But for dancing his pieces are perfect, and we realize the truth of the
title-page of the volume: 'Dances for five voices with their verses, for
singing, playing and dancing'. The 'verses' are clearly an afterthought.
Dancing is the main *raison d'être.*

It seems perverse to connect these trifles with Monteverdi until we
realize that he too composed such music, much of which must have been
lost. The first volume of canzonettas for three voices of Gastoldi
contains a final number called a 'balletto'; and this piece, *Par che'l ciel
brami*, is subtitled '*Intermedio de Pescatori*'—in other words it was part of
an *intermedio* with fishermen. This *intermedio* was surely an interlude in a
play; and Monteverdi, as we know from his letters, composed many
dances for such entertainments. Nor is it a far cry from these to the first
two acts of *Orfeo*, not to mention such obviously ballet-like episodes as
the final *moresca* to accompany the ascent of Apollo and Orpheus to the
heavens. The song of the shepherds 'Lasciate i monti' in Act I, with its
interplay between the two upper voices and the role of filling in the
harmony taken by the lower parts, is very Gastoldian; so are the regular
rhythms and the very diatonic melody. Admittedly the working-out of
short imitative tags in the three lower voices is a typically Monteverdian
complication, but the delicious orchestration using both wind and
strings may tell us what the Gastoldi dance-songs really sounded like.
Monteverdi's pastoral chorus is surely one of the finest examples of a
balletto 'for singing, playing and dancing' and taken out of its context
might well have appeared in a volume of Gastoldi or Vecchi.

[5] Luigi Torchi, ed., *L'arte musicale in Italia*, i (Milan, 1897), 183.

Certainly on the occasions when he did contribute to two volumes of this kind, in 1594, when Antonio Morsolino (in his *Primo libro delle canzonette a tre voci*) printed four pieces, and in 1607, when Monteverdi's colleague Amante Franzoni put one of his canzonettas in his *Nuovi fioretti musicali a tre voci*, Monteverdi followed Gastoldi's style quite closely. In the earlier pieces[6] especially he found delight in the texture favoured by Gastoldi in his canzonettas for three voices. Two sopranos are widely separated from a bass to give an airy sound, and for the most part a homophonic texture stresses the strong dance rhythms. The tunefulness is emphasized by the sweetly moving thirds of the sopranos and the short, memorable phrases. The same things are to be found in Monteverdi's own volume of *Scherzi musicali* of 1607. Academic discussion of this volume has been bedevilled by Giulio Cesare Monteverdi's preface, which mysteriously refers to his brother's use of a French manner of singing or composition (*canto alla francese*). If there is any detectable French influence (and admittedly some of the *Scherzi* begin with the chanson ——— motif—but then so did many Italian pieces of the time) it is swamped by the Gastoldian atmosphere. The rhythms of, say, *I bei legami*, the opening number of the volume, are so like those of Gastoldi's canzonettas,[7] the texture and method of phrasing are so similar, that these *Scherzi* seem Mantuan rather than Gallic. And if the extensive use of the hemiola patterns has no exact precedent in Gastoldi, it must have been known to Monteverdi from the work of Vecchi, whose own *Canzonette a quattro voci* of 1593 contains balletti or 'scherzi' which use this essential feature of the galliard—and Vecchi was an Emilian from Modena, and no Frenchman. That this was fully acclimatized in Mantua can be seen from a canzonetta of Franzoni, the gentle modulatory harmony of which might have been written by either Gastoldi or Monteverdi:

Ex. 7

Lu-ci va-gh'e   se - re - ne, ca-gion d'o-gni   mio be - ne

Lu-ci va-gh'e   se - re - ne, ca-gion d'o-gni mio be - - ne

Lu-ci va-gh'e   se - re - ne, ca-gion d'o-gni   mio   be - ne

[6] *Tutte le opere*, xvii, 1. They are also printed in *Monteverdi: 12 composizioni vocali profane e sacre (inedite)*, ed. Wolfgang Osthoff (Milan, 1958).
[7] A good example is *Il invaghito* in *Collana di composizioni polifoniche vocali sacre e profane*, ed. Achille Schinelli, ii (Milan, 1960), 109. Also see 230ff., below.

Monteverdi was perhaps not as attractive a composer in this style as
Gastoldi, or Salamone Rossi, who adapted the balletto manner to
instrumental music to become one of the first composers of the trio
sonata. In *Prima vedrò* from Franzoni's collection of 1607, Monteverdi
seems to be showing his impatience with the restrictions of the
canzonetta when he interpolates passages of chanting in the manner of
Sfogava con le stelle, which, however appropriate to the madrigal, ruin the
dance rhythms of light music. In this, he may well have influenced
Franzoni, who tries out this *falsobordone* usage in two numbers of his
second book of *Fioretti musicali* (Venice, 1607)—*Ecco l'alba* and *Si
rid'amor.*

If Franzoni was influenced in this way, he was one of the earliest
composers really to be affected by Monteverdi's music, for there is little
evidence that Monteverdi had left much of a mark on the world at large.
He was still at this time mainly a local celebrity rather than an
international figure. He had been swimming with the tide rather than
striking out on his own. Most of his colleagues had been older men, and
even a nearer contemporary such as Salamone Rossi probably was not
much aware of the greatness of the Mantuan *maestro di cappella.*
Certainly Rossi's continuo madrigals, printed before Monteverdi
published his fifth book but perhaps (in view of the known delay in the
production of this volume) composed contemporaneously, show a quite
different approach to the problems of a new manner of composition.

The change came in 1608 with the opera festival at Mantua. Already a
year earlier his Venetian publisher had thought it worth while to bring
out new editions of Monteverdi's older madrigal-books, as a result of
the publicity acquired by the dispute with Artusi. With the production of
two operas and a major ballet, Monteverdi became really famous; and it
was *Arianna*, more than any other work, that made it impossible for any
progressive composer to ignore his style. The lament in this opera
became the model for countless compositions. Those which appeared in
the secular song-books indeed demand some mention in different
surroundings, and this will be found in a later chapter.[8] Here it need only
be said that the vogue lasted, especially in opera, until the very end of the
century. Even such a composition as the lament in Purcell's *Dido and
Aeneas* can trace its ancestry directly to Monteverdi's piece; and perhaps
Handel was not untouched by the same fashion in the following century.
Nor was religious music unaffected. Especially after the publication of a

[8] See below, 192–4.

religious contrafactum in which Ariadne has been transformed into the Blessed Virgin, sacred music took to the genre like a duck to water, and such pieces as Frescobaldi's *A piè della gran Croce* from his *Primo libro d'arie musicali* (Florence, 1630) and Domenico Mazzocchi's *Lamento della B. Vergine* in his *Musiche sacre e morali* of 1640 derive directly from Monteverdi's first great popular scena; not to mention the great set pieces in Carissimi's oratorios and dialogues, of which the 'Pianto della figlia' in *Jefte* and the central aria in the *Historia di Ezechia* must be mentioned in this context as two of the best examples of the genre.

What clearly cannot be derived directly from Ariadne's lament is the great variety of styles in which these pieces are written, for even by the 1640s Monteverdi's work was a masterpiece of an older musical manner; but a number of monodists were affected by its technique of melodic expression, and without its superb transmutation of the continuo madrigal into expressive arioso, the serious solo song might well have remained mannerist and purely virtuoso, incapable of further progress into the cantata. Something of the variety in Monteverdi's imitators can be seen by examining the music of two of his closest followers. Of these, Claudio Saracini was a noble Sienese, a dilettante typically attracted towards monody, and, because of the simplicity of the solo song, rather more successful than he would have been in the previous century, when he would have had to master the contrapuntal techniques of the madrigal. In his serious books of songs, there are several pieces that are virtually laments, one of which, in *Le seconde musiche* of 1620,[9] is 'dedicated to the most illustrious Claudio Monteverdi, Maestro di Cappella of the Most Serene Signory of Venice'. It is a setting of *Udite, lagrimosi spirti* from Guarini's *Il pastor fido* (reminding us from where Monteverdi obtained the idea of the lament); and in many details it shows the sincerest form of flattery. The repetition of the word 'perchè', the irregular movement between melody and bass, the resolution of a seventh by a leap on to a consonant note of the next chord in Ex. 8 require no comment. A later passage in the same piece equally has a marked similarity to a section of *Nigra sum*, Monteverdi's first published monody, but the taut organization of the original is beyond Saracini's grasp. Monteverdi's professionalism is a deciding factor in the quality of his monodic as well as his polyphonic compositions.

Saracini was not incapable of improvement, and a later lament,

[9] Facsimile reprint (Siena, 1933).

Io parto (*Le quinte musiche* (Venice, 1624)), is much more concentrated in its handling of what again is Monteverdian material, this time showing an understanding of the art of repeating phrases which was Monteverdi's main contribution to the arioso style. But for an equally vital handling of the genre we have to turn to another professional

Ex. 8

composer, Sigismondo d'India, whose noble origins and good voice do not seem to have diverted him from a mastery of his craft. The lament was for him a favourite medium, and his last two song-books contain no fewer than five of them, all surely deriving their inspiration from *Arianna*. The similarities of their technical detail have already been discussed elsewhere.[10] Here it may be said that d'India's basic attitude to monodic composition was reasonably like Monteverdi's. Both were concerned with the problems of finding a technique by which the recitative style of the Camerata was made capable of the highest emotional power, without relapsing into pretty tunes or being stolidly academic. Both succeeded to an astonishing degree. D'India's version of Dido's lament at first sight looks like the severest type of operatic recitative. In performance, it proves a worthy successor to the lament of Ariadne. Like Monteverdi, d'India understood not only how to organize his material so that it never becomes amorphous but also how excitement in a deliberately unmelodious style is achieved mainly by variations of speed and tessitura. While dissonance and awkward intervals have their part to play in keeping up the intensity, the overall control of emotional power is revealed in the contrast of pace and vocal registers in the following passage, which is too like the fourth part of Monteverdi's piece for the resemblance to be pure coincidence:

[10] Nigel Fortune, 'Sigismondo d'India, an Introduction to his Life and Works', *Proceedings of the Royal Musical Association*, lxxxi (1954–5), 29.

Ex. 9

When Monteverdi wrote *Arianna*, he was by no means half way through his career. Nevertheless, it is the music he composed in the years around this time that had most effect on the musical world. The madrigals of his mannerist style (which include those of Book VI, which represent its culmination) were reprinted time and again. His later music was less well diffused. In part the reason for this must be that tastes were changing more rapidly than was Monteverdi; and in part that he had changed from being primarily a composer of secular music to being one of church music. It was much more difficult to be a composer of mannerist church music, and it was perhaps because of this that the music of the Vespers volume of 1610 never really became popular. Not that it was so revolutionary as has been sometimes thought. The actual ingredients of the music were common enough in Mantuan church music. After all, Viadana was *maestro di cappella* at Mantua Cathedral when he published the first volume of concertato church music ever printed, so that this was no novelty. The use of *falsobordone* chanting, which is so much a feature of the psalm-settings, was seemingly the usual practice in Mantua, if we may judge from Viadana's *Vespertina omnium solemnitatum Psalmodia* (1588) and Gastoldi's *Salmi intieri che nelle solennità dell'anno al Vespro si canta* of 1607. The polychoral manner from which Monteverdi's work was to spring was not unknown there either, for not only was Viadana again one of its exponents but Pallavicino's *Sacrae Dei laudes*, published posthumously in 1605, are worthy examples of the style. The *Sonata sopra Sancta Maria* was no unique piece in the region, for Archangelo Crotti, a monk from Ferrara, published a similar item in his *Concerti ecclesiastici* of 1608[11] (it was also imitated by Franzoni in 1619). Even the elaborate ornamentation of the 'solo' motets has its counterpart in the Lamentations by Giovanni Francesco Capello, a Veronese who published these works in the same year of 1610. Nevertheless, the mixture of elements is unique to Monteverdi, and apparently not all that successful in worldly terms, for it was the 'pure' work of the collection, the mass *In illo tempore*, that achieved wider circulation,[12] not the Vespers music that has fascinated the twentieth century.

And when Monteverdi took up his appointment in Venice, he again seems to have swum with the tide. The concertato pieces that were published in the collections of Bianchi in 1620 closely resemble those of the composers left over from the Gabrielian period in St. Mark's. Giovanni Battista Grillo's *Sacri concentus ac symphoniae* of 1617 reveals a pupil of the younger Gabrieli, even to the extent of providing another *Sonata pian e forte*. Nevertheless, the concertato pieces resemble Monteverdi's early Venetian church music quite strongly, the more especially since Grillo has brought the traditional style a little more up to date by making the solo sections (inherited from such works as Gabrieli's *In ecclesiis*) into ornamented duets in the manner of Monteverdi's continuo madrigals from Book V.

The atmosphere in Venice began to change radically only a few years later when Monteverdi began to surround himself with his own discoveries—Alessandro Grandi and Francesco Cavalli, who were appointed in St. Mark's as singers in the period around 1617, Giovanni Rovetta, who started in the orchestra about the same time, and later Giovanni Pietro Berti, who became an organist of the basilica in 1624. These and some others who worked elsewhere in the city made its religious music thoroughly modern, and led the world in adapting methods developed in secular works to the needs of the Church. How much of this change of style can be attributed to the arrival of Monteverdi is problematical, for although his 1610 volume had been a pioneering venture, it was not unique in this way. But it is significant that

[11] See Arnold, 'Notes on two Movements of the Monteverdi "Vespers"', *Monthly Musical Record*, lxxxiv (1954), 59.

[12] Whereas the whole mass achieved a reprint in 1612 in a collection published by Phalèse, only two items of the Vespers music were reprinted (in *Reliquiae sacrorum concentuum Giovan Gabrielis, Iohan–Leonis Hasleri...*, ed. Georg Gruber (Nuremberg, 1615)).

Venetian music had been tending towards the conservative and was becoming out of touch with the 'modern' schools of Florence, Ferrara and Mantua before 1612. Its acquisition of the greatest of the progressive composers had its effect.

A great deal of this change of heart can only vaguely be ascribed to the influence of Monteverdi. Only in certain composers are the signs clear. Of these, Grandi was one who without doubt learned a great deal from the master and made good use of his knowledge. He was nearly twenty years younger than Monteverdi[13] and had never composed in the older pre-continuo style; indeed his first volume of motets, published in 1610, was already an accomplished collection in the post-Viadana manner. He produced a considerable amount of church music before he left Ferrara for Venice, but none of it shows anything much more than competence and a certain lyrical gift. Then, in Venice, this gift became something more, and since it flowered most particularly in his solo motets, Grandi's development can be ascribed either to the incentive given by the virtuoso singers of St. Mark's or to Monteverdi—or perhaps to both. For the virtuoso nature of these motets is not of the arid kind that stresses florid *gorgie*, but rather, like Monteverdi's, one that needs legato singing and understanding of the words. In *Vulnerasti cor meum*, published four years after Grandi came into Monteverdi's circle, the sensuous climax, with its repeated phrase, chromatics, and subtle dissonance, has the authentic mastery of arioso that stems from *Arianna* and another motet setting a passage from the Song of Songs—Monteverdi's *Nigra sum*:

Ex. 10

And Grandi's setting of the plainsong hymn *Veni Sancte Spiritus* could hardly have been written without his knowing the solo verses of that

---

[13] See James H. Moore, *Vespers at St. Mark's: Music of Alessandro Grandi, Giovanni Rovetta and Francesco Cavalli* (Ann Arbor, 1981), i, 6.

other part of the Vespers volume, the hymn *Ave maris stella*. Both use triple time and the rhythmic variety of the hemiolas to make a genuine tune which could well belong to the popular song-books of the time:

Ex. 11

This tunefulness indeed may have had its effect on Monteverdi himself, for the young men who were his colleagues were masters of it; and if we compare the 'alleluia' sections of two motets published in Leonardo Simonetti's *Ghirlanda sacra* in 1625 the explanation of Monteverdi's newly found gaiety may be found:

Ex. 12

(*a*) Grandi, *Cantabo Domino*

(*b*) Caralli, *currite populi*

But an invention that is Monteverdi's alone and that did intrigue the Venetian musical world was the *stile concitato*. He had developed it in the dramatic cantata (which is perhaps the nearest short description of it that seems apt) *Il combattimento di Tancredi e Clorinda*, where it had a particular significance, and in his eighth book of madrigals the style seems to be part of an academic manifesto, a demonstration of principles learned long ago which had dominated his thinking. To other composers, it was more of a trick, not to be taken seriously or employed with any consistency. Tarquinio Merula, in his *Curtio precipitato* published in 1638, starts his extended cantata *Curtio, ove vai* with a 'sinfonia ad immitatione d'un Cavallo' ('a symphony to imitate the sound of a horse') and proceeds to express the word 'armato' with the same sort of triple-time vocal arpeggios to which Monteverdi was so attached:

Ex. 13

Da   ca - po a
pie - di   ar - ma - to,   ar - ma - to

Earlier Grandi had found it a happy way to provide a realistic setting for the word 'conquassabit' in the psalm *Dixit Dominus*,[14] a usage justified by Monteverdi in his own settings of the *Magnificat*, where it is equally appropriate to 'put down the mighty from their seat'.[15] Schütz's use in his duet motet *Der Herr ist mein Licht und mein Heil* in his second book of *Symphoniae sacrae* (1647) is very similar and equally effective, for it is provided first by the phrase 'Wenn sich schon ein Heer wider mich leget' ('Though an host of men were laid against me') and then by 'Wenn sich wider mich erhebet' ('though there rose up war against me'), a reasonably logical use of pictorialism. Less satisfying was his contrafactum of Monteverdi's *Armato il cor* and *Zefiro torna* in the same volume. Schütz, in his second sabbatical year in Venice, was clearly fascinated by the novelty of it all. He may well have met Monteverdi, but it was the younger men whose style he really assimilated. His sacred symphonies are offshoots of the motets of Grandi, Rovetta and the rest, and *Es steh Gott auf,* for all its external trappings, shows a liking for the trick rather than the substance of the *stile concitato*. *Armato il cor* takes the phrases based on common chords about as far as they will go. Schütz needs two violins to add a new dimension of colour, for he makes the composition much longer than its original; and it is doubtful whether the material really can stand this. Its second part, an adaptation of Monteverdi's virtuoso chaconne, is more modestly treated, with good reason, for the original stretches its basic idea as far as it can go, and Schütz's shorter version matches his shorter text. Yet one must wonder

[14] *Salmi a otto brevi con il primo coro concertato* (Venice, 1629).
[15] *Tutte le opere*, xv, 659.

why he chose this composition to parody. *Zefiro torna* is essentially an illustrative piece, tolerable only when the aptness of each musical image for the image of the verse is appreciated. In fact, it is the very kind of piece to avoid when adapting something to another text.

Schütz's relationship to Monteverdi is significant of the position of the old man (for such was a sexagenarian at this time) in 1628. In secular music his juniors were writing pretty melodies and forgetting the mannerism of the early years of the century. In their operas they were no longer to attempt to envelop 'Renaissance man' in an art that wanted to create a whole new world. They were content to entertain a lesser mortal, and if to this end they were willing to borrow the external features of the Monteverdian art, it is doubtful whether they appreciated the philosophy behind it. A glance at a large choral lament from Loreto Vittori's *La Galatea*,[16] a Roman opera produced in 1639, is sufficient to recognize the opening of the madrigal version of Ariadne's lament; another glance is sufficient to realize, not necessarily that it is feebler, but that it is different. It has lost the sustained emotionalism so characteristic of the period of the younger Monteverdi:

Ex. 14

[16] See Hugo Goldschmidt, *Studien zur Geschichte der italienischen Oper im 17. Jahrhundert*, i (Leipzig, 1901/R1967), 288.

Nor is it hard to find the echoes of the *stile concitato* in dramatic music in the last decade of Monteverdi's life. A chorus of soldiers in Michelangelo Rossi's *Erminia sul Giordano* (1633) has the same sort of fanfare motifs, the same consonant harmony—but little sign of understanding of the strict rhythmic patterns which Monteverdi had derived from Platonic ideas. Even when the basic knowledge of Monteverdi's style is clearly there, some change of atmosphere is always to be found. Cavalli was surely as close a pupil as anyone could have been, employed by Monteverdi in St. Mark's from an early age. In both his church music and his stage works he shows evidence of learning from the master. His concertato motets and the *Magnificat* that was published in the posthumous collection of Monteverdi's church music are in some ways very similar to the older man's work. The lament from his opera *L'Egisto* (1643) is so like Monteverdi that at its dissonant climax the illusion of its being from *Poppea* or some other work of that period is almost complete:

Ex. 15

But only almost complete. A recollection of the *Lamento della ninfa* (Book VIII, 1638), with its background of men interjecting 'Ah, miserella', establishes the difference at once. Monteverdi is more complicated, more extravagant and more powerful. Cavalli's magnificence is colder, more Venetian. It is not surprising that he was one of the first composers to take opera to France.

The quintessential Monteverdi is to be seen in *L'incoronazione di Poppea*. Its composer is not blind to any element in his environment. He has learned from the young men, he has remembered his older colleagues and even his teachers. He is fully aware of what was successful in his earlier works. No doubt if we possessed the scores of those lost operas and *intermedi* from Mantua and Parma we could trace much of this masterpiece to some particular circumstance of his musical life. Certainly the smouldering, illogical, immoral and very human atmosphere could not have been produced except by a man who had been through the agonies of the Gonzaga court (we may suspect that there is more than a trace of Vincenzo in the cruelty of Nero). In that power to transcribe human experience into music lies the greatness of Monteverdi. For this, much was clearly forgiven him in his lifetime; and we must be grateful to many now forgotten composers who stimulated his overwhelming imagination and provided the means for its musical expression.

III

Thinker and Musician

CLAUDE V. PALISCA

The Artusi–Monteverdi Controversy

The debt music history owes to Giovanni Maria Artusi is only grudgingly recognized. Yet it is a great one, for he focused attention on one of the deepest crises in musical composition and stimulated the composer who most squarely confronted it to clarify his position. Without Claudio Monteverdi's letter in the fifth book of madrigals and his brother's glosses upon it in the *Scherzi musicali* (1607), Monteverdi's youthful creative thrust would have left a blunter mark in history. His stylistic profile without Artusi's criticism would be set less boldly in relief.

If the controversy between Artusi and Monteverdi gives us a valuable commentary upon music history in the making, it also affected the course of musical evolution. Claudio and his brother Giulio Cesare, by publishing their manifestos for the new or second practice, held up a banner for others to rally around. Their slogans echoed for half a century in the prefaces and pamphlets of the avant-garde. Nor is this the only significance of the controversy: it also gives us a glimpse into the way composers thought about certain points of technique, how they justified them, what precedents they recognized, how they viewed the act of composition itself.

What are the real issues of this debate? In one sense it was the usual battle of the generations. Monteverdi rebelled against the strictures of his masters; Artusi, a generation older, stood by the standards of composition taught by Gioseffo Zarlino, among whose followers he was one of the most eminent. He expected dissonances to be introduced according to the rules of counterpoint, and he insisted upon unity of modality within a piece. These conventions had been challenged already in the middle of the sixteenth century, and Artusi's offensive—or rather counter-offensive—was only one of a chain of attacks and counter-attacks that can be traced back to the debate between Nicola Vicentino and Vincenzo Lusitano in 1551. Artusi was not an arch-conservative through and through. His own books on counterpoint relaxed unnecessarily strict rules that were often honoured in the breach. He recognized, as Zarlino did not, that dissonances were of primary importance in composition and devoted a whole volume to them. He was

one of the first to take a strong position in favour of equal temperament
as a standard tuning for instrumental music. Yet it grieved him to see
counterpoint, which had reached a point of ultimate refinement and
control, become a prey to caprice and expediency. He honestly believed
that the patiently erected structure was under siege.

In another sense it was a battle between two contemporary points of
view. On one side were those like Monteverdi who accepted the
advances of concerted instrumental music, improvised counterpoint,
ornamented singing, the rhythms of dance music, and the enlarged
vocabulary of chromaticism blended with the diatonic. On the other side
were those like Artusi who felt that these innovations, mainly products
of relatively unschooled musicians, corrupted a pure, noble and learned
art. In one camp were those who held to a single standard of
counterpoint; in the other those who followed a double standard, one for
everyday sacred compositions and another for compositions on texts
expressing violent passions. From a long view, neither side won an
absolute victory. The strict standards backed by Artusi returned by the
mid-seventeenth century in a modified form, and the modifications
represented concessions to the other side.

Artusi printed and analysed in his dialogue of 1600 nine examples
from two madrigals of Monteverdi that he knew from manuscript
copies. He withheld both the composer's name and the texts. The
dialogue is divided into two *ragionamenti* or discourses, of which the
first, dealing with tuning, was probably Artusi's main pretext
for publishing the book. The second dealt with the anonymous
composer's madrigals.[1] Artusi saw no reason to print the words,
because he did not recognize a double standard of contrapuntal
correctness. To omit them also helped conceal the authorship of the
madrigals. Although Artusi knew the name of the composer, he
refrained from revealing it, because in view of his criticism to do so
would have been indelicate. To soften the blow further the author
expressed his opinion through one of the interlocutors, a fictitious

---

[1] *L'Artusi, overo Delle imperfettioni della moderna musica* (Venice, 1600). The first
ragionamento takes issue with Ercole Bottrigari's conclusions about tuning and
concerted instrumental groupings published in *Il Desiderio* (Venice, 1594). A
part of the second *ragionamento* is translated in Oliver Strunk, *Source Readings
in Music History* (New York, 1950), 393–404. Artusi had started the ball rolling
with his 'Opinione intorno alli conserti musicali' in *Seconda parte dell'Arte del
contraponto nella quale si tratta dell'utile & uso delle dissonanze* (Venice, 1589), Bk
2, chap. 17.

musician named Vario, who converses with a cultivated amateur named Luca.

Three years after this dialogue appeared Artusi, having received letters from a defender of the anonymous composer who signs himself 'L'Ottuso Academico', published a second book. In the first part of this he answers his correspondent's letters. In the *Considerationi* that follow he defends Francesco Patrizi's statements about Greek music against Ercole Bottrigari's criticisms.[2] Although now the discussion of the anonymous madrigals deals largely with the question of text expression, Artusi again omits texts when he prints examples by the anonymous composer and by L'Ottuso. The composer's identity was not made known in print until Monteverdi answered Artusi in the famous letter that opens the fifth book of madrigals of 1605. Of the madrigals criticized in the 1600 dialogue, *Anima mia, perdona* was not published until 1603 in the fourth book of madrigals and *Cruda Amarilli* and *O Mirtillo* not until 1605 in the fifth book. In addition to these, also under discussion in the 1603 book are *Era l'anima mia* and the second part of *Ecco Silvio*, both from the fifth book.

Throughout the controversy the treatment of dissonances was the most bitterly contested territory. The dissonant effects Artusi objected to in Monteverdi's madrigals are of three kinds: 1) those caused by the application of ornaments to a consonant framework; 2) those which, though accepted by usage in improvised counterpoint and instrumental music, were outside the norms of the severe style; 3) those outside these two categories that could be justified only in terms of the expressive demands of the text. The text, of course, was the principal motivating force behind all three kinds of dissonances. But it was possible to talk about the first two without the text, and this is what Artusi does in his first critique, even though some of his examples could not be explained adequately without the text.

Each of the examples cited by Artusi in the 1600 book violates one or more rules of the strict style as taught by Zarlino and Artusi in their counterpoint books.[3] Luca, who plays the advocate for Monteverdi,

---

[2] *Seconda parte dell'Artusi, overo Delle imperfettioni della moderna musica* (Venice, 1603); Francesco Patrizi, *Della poetica, La deca istoriale* (Ferrara, 1586); Bottrigari, *Il Patricio, overo De' tetracordi armonici di Aristosseno* (Bologna, 1593). By 1603 Artusi and Bottrigari had exchanged a number of acrimonious pamphlets and letters, both printed and manuscript. The urge to respond to Bottrigari may have provided a stronger motive for the 1603 book than continuing the criticism of Monteverdi.

[3] Gioseffo Zarlino, *Le istitutioni harmoniche* (Venice, 1558), Bk 3; Artusi, *L'arte*

pleads that modern composers excuse these lapses by various pretexts. The defences Luca timidly brings up are very revealing of the thinking of the time.

The composer in Ex. 1 is charged by Vario with failing to accord the upper parts with the bass:

Ex. 1. Monteverdi, *Cruda Amarilli*, bars 12–14

Luca argues that the example should be regarded as 'accented' singing: that is, it is a written example of an improvisational practice. Vario protests that no author has yet spoken of accented music or defined what accents are. Actually Lodovico Zacconi had spoken of these at length and defined them as follows:

> The graces (*vaghezze*) and accents (*accenti*) are made by splitting and breaking the note values when in a bar or half-bar is added a number of notes that have the property of being rapidly proffered. These give so much pleasure and delight that it appears to us that we are hearing so many well trained birds which capture our hearts and render us very happy with their singing.[4]

> For example, when a part has two semibreves or minims, particularly separated by a skip, the singer may fill the time or pitch interval with shorter notes.

> However, he should know that these notes are accompanied by certain accents caused by certain retardations and sustainings of the voice, which

[4] Lodovico Zacconi, *Prattica di musica* (Venice, 1596), Bk 1, chap. 66, f. 58. All the translations in this chapter are mine.

---

del contraponto ridotta in tavole (Venice, 1586); *Seconda parte dell'Arte del contraponto* (Venice, 1589); *L'arte del contraponto . . . novamente ristampata, & di molte nuove aggiunte, dall'-auttore arrichite* (Venice, 1598).

are accomplished by taking away a particle from one value and assigning it to another.[5]

Zacconi gives the following illustration:

Ex. 2

Girolamo dalla Casa, another exponent of florid singing, inserts the semiquaver runs shown in the following example:

Ex. 3. Cipriano de Rore, *Tanto mi piacque*, with diminutions from dalla Casa, *Il vero modo di diminuir* (Venice, 1584), ii, 48

If Monteverdi's passage in Ex. 1 is reduced to a hypothetical simpler framework (Ex. 4) and Zacconi's suggested *accenti* and runs similar to dalla Casa's are applied, we arrive at a version close to Monteverdi's and just as faulty from Artusi's point of view (Ex. 5):

Ex. 4

Ex. 5

[5] Ibid., Bk 1, chap. 63, f. 55. The ensuing example is at Bk 1, chap. 66, f. 62.

Luca finds the effect of the *accenti* attractive. Compositions embellished by such ornaments 'when played by various instruments or sung by singers skilled in this kind of accented music full of substitutions (*suppositi*) yield a not displeasing harmony at which I marvel'.[6]

Vario's answer is doctrinaire, as expected. Composers and singers who use these portamentos, delays and turns, while they may avoid offensive sounds by instinct or deceive the ear by the quickness of their embellishments, corrupt the good old rules with their mannerisms.

Another ornamental figure lies at the basis of the dissonances in Ex. 6 which are quoted by Artusi. A hypothetical simple version is shown in Ex. 7. Christoph Bernhard in a manuscript treatise of around 1660 shows how a similar passage can be embellished by means of the figure he calls *quaesitio notae* (searching note; Ex. 8).[7]

Ex. 6. Monteverdi, *Cruda Amarilli*, bars 35–8

Ex. 7

[6] *L'Artusi*, f. 41v.

[7] Christoph Bernhard, *Tractatus compositionis augmentatus*, chap. 33, printed in Joseph Müller-Blattau, *Die Kompositionslehre Heinrich Schützens* (Kassel, 2/1963), 81–2; trans. in Walter Hilse, 'The Treatises of Christoph Bernhard', *Music Forum*, iii (1973), 1–196.

Ex. 8

Only some of Monteverdi's licences can be passed as *accenti*. Luca
suggests another defence for others:

> these musicians observe their rule that the part making the dissonance
> with the lowest part should have a harmonic correspondence with the
> tenor, and that it [the first] accord with every other part, while the
> lowest part also should accord with every other part.[8]

A situation governed by this rule would arise in *contrapunto a mente* if a
bass and a higher voice were improvising against a *cantus firmus* in the
tenor. The two improvisers would be obliged to accord with the tenor
but not necessarily with each other. Tinctoris states as a rule that in
singing *super librum*, that is over a plainchant book, the part-singer needs
to observe the laws of consonance with respect to the tenor part alone,
while in *res facta*, that is written counterpoint, all parts must have regard
to one another. It is laudable, he says, when all the parts accord with one
another even in improvised counterpoint.[9] But this will happen only by
accident or through rehearsal. In the sixteenth century it was customary
to have the bass sing the *cantus firmus*. To judge by the profusion of
manuals or portions of them dedicated to the art of improvised
counterpoint towards the end of that century and the beginning of the
next, it was a widespread practice, particularly in the principal chapel
and cathedral choirs.[10]

Adriano Banchieri recalls with pleasure the wonderful effect,
peculiar charm and very tasteful sensation of the *contrapunti a mente*,
with their unexpected consecutive fifths and octaves, the dissonant
encounters and extravagant turns:

In Rome in the Chapel of our Holy Father, in the holy mansion of San

[8] *L'Artusi*, f. 43.
[9] Johannes Tinctoris, *Liber de arte contrapuncti*, Bk 2, chap. 20, printed in
Edmond de Coussemaker, *Scriptorum de musica medii aevi*, iv (Paris,
1876/R1963), 129; in *Johannis Tinctoris, Opera theoretica*, ed. Albert Seay,
Corpus scriptorum de musica, xxii/2 (American Institute of Musicology,
1975), 110.
[10] See Ernest T. Ferand, 'Improvised Vocal Counterpoint in the Late
Renaissance and Early Baroque', *Annales musicologiques*, iv (1956), 129–74.

Loreto and in countless other chapels when they sing *contrapunto alla mente* on a bass, no one knows what his companion is going to sing, but together through certain observances agreed among themselves they give a most tasteful sensation to the hearing. It can be stated as a general maxim that even if a hundred various voices (so to speak) were singing consonantly over a bass, all would agree, and those dissonances, fifths, octaves, extravagances and clashes are all graces that make up the true effect of *contrapunto alla mente*.[11]

So impressed was Banchieri with the possibilities of this effect that he made up a set of ten instructions for counterfeiting such counterpoints in writing. The trick, he shows, is to write each of the parts against the bass independently of the others.

Monteverdi accepts into written composition some of the fortuitous clashes that occur when parts are moving independently around some common focus. One of the passages Vario points to as following the relaxed rules of harmonic correspondence between parts is bars 41–2 of *Cruda Amarilli*. Ex. 9 divides the texture into two groups, each of which corresponds harmonically with the tenor, but parts of opposing groups may clash with each other:

Ex. 9

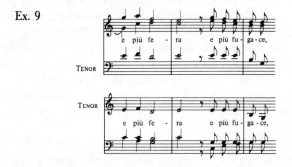

The composer takes advantage of the tolerance for free mixtures of intervals acquired through improvised music to introduce a variety of rhetorical effects. This device is particularly fitting to illustrate the word 'fugace' ('elusive'), as it affords at once smooth and independent voice movement. The diminished fifth and seventh on the word 'fera' ('fierce') serve both the musical function of providing a climactic cadence and to heighten the feeling of the word.

[11] Adriano Banchieri, *Cartella musicale nel canto figurato, fermo & contrapunto* . . . *novamente in questa terza impressione ridotta dall'antica alla moderna pratica* (Venice, 1614), 230.

Luca makes another significant remark about how musicians became receptive to the chance combinations that arise from rapidly and independently moving parts. In answering Vario's objection that in bars 42–3 some of the quavers do not correspond either to the bass or tenor, Luca says this licence is derived 'from perceiving that in instruments these [quavers] do not much offend the ear because of the quickness of movement'.[12]

Vincenzo Galilei in his manuscript treatise on counterpoint (1589–91) made precisely this observation about rapidly moving parts, which he found 'more appropriate for instruments than for voices'.[13]

Whenever two or more parts move over one another gracefully according to the decorum of the art of counterpoint, whatever dissonance occurs among them not only will be tolerated by the sense, but it will take delight in it.[14]

Although it was customary, he said, to alternate consonance and dissonance in writing such runs, he declined to make a hard-and-fast rule, showing rather that as many as three dissonances may occur in succession with impunity. By coincidence his example uses the very same progression as Monteverdi does in bars 42–3 of *Cruda Amarilli* between the two uppermost parts and the bass:[15]

 Ex. 10

Up to now I have been reviewing some of the arguments on behalf of Monteverdi adduced by Luca in the second discourse of Artusi's dialogue of 1600. In 1603, as we saw, Artusi published a defence of his criticism of Monteverdi in reply to letters from L'Ottuso Accademico. This book begins with the text of a letter Artusi purportedly wrote to L'Ottuso in response to one from him of 1599. In his letter Artusi

---

[12] *L'Artusi*, loc. cit.
[13] Vincenzo Galilei, *Il primo libro della prattica del contrapunto intorno all'uso delle consonanze*, Florence, Biblioteca Nazionale, MS Anteriore Galileo I, f. 78; Italian text ed. in Frieder Rempp, *Die Kontrapunkttraktate Vincenzo Galileis* (Cologne, 1980), 40. See Claude V. Palisca, 'Vincenzo Galilei's Counterpoint Treatise: a Code for the "seconda pratica" ', *Journal of the American Musicological Society*, ix (1956), 88.
[14] Palisca, 89, quoted from *Discorso intorno all'uso delle dissonanze*, MS Anteriore Galileo I, f. 143; ed. in Rempp, 152.
[15] *Discorso intorno all'uso delle dissonanze*, f. 126.

quotes selectively from L'Ottuso's reply, which, though not dated, is obviously subsequent to Artusi's dialogue of 1600, as it counters some points made there.

The mystery of L'Ottuso's identity has not been satisfactorily solved. Emil Vogel and others before him[16] simply assumed that he was Monteverdi, and later writers have generally followed suit. Several circumstances, however, militate against this assumption. Monteverdi begins his foreword to *Il quinto libro de' madrigali* (1605) with the remark: 'be not surprised that I am giving these madrigals to the press without first replying to the objections that Artusi made against some very minute portions of them.' He could not have made such a plea if his reply had already appeared in print under the name L'Ottuso. There is no resemblance between L'Ottuso's letter and Monteverdi's style of writing. Further, Artusi prints (ff. 50v–51) fourteen breve-bars taken from five-part madrigals of L'Ottuso—'passaggi fatti dall'Ottuso ne suoi Madrigali'—and these cannot be reconciled with any known works of Monteverdi. Besides, when Monteverdi is referred to in the correspondence it is always as 'Signor Etc.', not as L'Ottuso.

If L'Ottuso is not Monteverdi, who is he? Several possibilities need to be examined.

(1) L'Ottuso is a straw man contrived by Artusi to be knocked down as he refutes objections made to his earlier critique of Monteverdi.

(2) L'Ottuso is Ercole Bottrigari, to whom the book is dedicated and against whose *Patricio* half of it is directed.

(3) L'Ottuso is a composer and academician probably from Ferrara or Mantua.

Is L'Ottuso Artusi's creation? Just as Artusi invented the interlocutors Vario and Luca to argue the merits of the questions discussed in the

---

[16] See Emil Vogel, 'Claudio Monteverdi', *Vierteljahrsschrift für Musikwissenschaft*, iii (1887), 315. On p. 332 Vogel cites the authority of Zaccaria Tevo, *Il musico testore* (Venice, 1706), 175, to support the attribution of the letters to Monteverdi. Gaetano Gaspari (died 1881) in his manuscript notes appended to his own copy of the *Seconda parte dell'Artusi* now in Bologna, Civico Museo Bibliografico Musicale, also expressed the opinion that L'Ottuso was Monteverdi. This copy, which was the one used in this study, bears the signature of the official censor at the end of the *Considerationi* on p. 54 and the note that the author should be required to place his name and surname and native city on the title page. All of the more personally offensive passages, including the entire sarcastic letter of dedication addressed to Bottrigari and the letter to the reader, are struck out in this copy with a single stroke of the pen.

1600 dialogue, it is reasonable that he would invent an opponent against whom he could debate in the first person about Monteverdi's modernisms. L'Ottuso writes garrulously and redundantly like Artusi himself. He cites many classical and modern authors and has a command of the calculations of proportions every theorist, but not necessarily every composer, had to know. He makes a moderately good case for Monteverdi, something Artusi was perfectly capable of doing, because he understood the modernists even if he disagreed with them. It is even conceivable that Artusi might have gone to such lengths as fabricating excerpts from non-existent madrigals, which he claimed were sent to him from L'Ottuso's academy. If L'Ottuso's letter of 1599 was not faked later, why did Artusi not produce it in the dialogue of 1600, when it would have made a good pretext for attacking the modernist point of view in the first place? The dedication in Venice on 20 November 1600 shows that he had ample time to do so. The possibility that L'Ottuso was an invention of Artusi is, therefore, not to be excluded.[17]

May L'Ottuso be Bottrigari, to whom the 1603 book is dedicated? The whole second part of the book is a defence of statements about music, particularly on the Greek tunings, made by Francesco Patrizi in his *Della poetica, La deca istoriale* (1586) against the objections of Bottrigari in his *Il Patricio, overo De' tetracordi armonici di Aristosseno* (1593).[18] At the same time Artusi answers a pamphlet by Bottrigari entitled *Ant-Artusi*.[19] The possibility that L'Ottuso is Bottrigari is made unlikely by the fact that Bottrigari treats him as a real person. In his *Aletelogia*,[20] an answer to Artusi's book of 1603, Bottrigari says he will not refute what Artusi writes against L'Ottuso in his ninth 'Inconsideratione', because the academician is wise and capable and will defend himself with sagacity and valour. Bottrigari may have known his identity, having lived a long time in Ferrara and now in Artusi's own city of Bologna.

---

[17] John Harper, in 'Frescobaldi's Early *Inganni* and their Background', *Proceedings of the Royal Musical Association*, cv (1978–9), 11, has raised the possibility that Artusi concealed his own name in the similar sounding 'Ottuso' as an *inganno*.

[18] See n. 2 on p. 129.

[19] This pamphlet was mentioned by Artusi in his letter dedicating the *Seconda parte dell'Artusi* to Bottrigari.

[20] Bottrigari, *Aletelogia di Leonardo Gallucio ai benigni, e sinceri lettori, lettera apologetica D.M.I.S.C.H.B.* (1604), Bologna, Civico Museo Bibliografico Musicale, MS B–43, p. 72.

The most likely possibility is that L'Ottuso was a composer active in Ferrara or Mantua. Artusi introduces the first quotation from L'Ottuso's letter with the words:

finding myself in Ferrara in the year 1599, I was given a letter without proper name but with the signature 'L'Ottuso Academico'. Later from a good source I had the information that this was a man of much authority and that he was very much a musician.[21]

The pseudonym, meaning 'the obtuse one', fits the current style of academic names, which were often teasingly self-derogatory, like 'L'Ebbro' (the drunken one), 'L'Incruscato' (the crusty one, Giovanni Bardi's name in the Alterati), 'L'Affannato' (the breathless one, Marco da Gagliano's name in the Elevati and Scipione Gonzaga's in the Invaghiti), 'Lo Smemorato' (the forgetful one), and so on. As to which academy he may have belonged to there is no clue. The Accademia degli Intrepidi of Ferrara, to which Monteverdi dedicated his fourth book of madrigals, was founded in 1600,[22] too late for L'Ottuso to have acquired his academic name in it by 1599. Another Ferrarese academy, the Accademia dei Parteni, had as one of its councillors the composer Count Alfonso Fontanella and as its musical censors Count Alfonso Fogliani and Luigi Putti.[23] Fontanella, a man of culture and an accomplished composer, had the necessary qualifications to be L'Ottuso, but Anthony Newcomb finds the letters published by Artusi 'too hysterical, too learned . . . and too witless to be connected with the urbane, mildly cynical style of Fontanelli', and he could not locate any of the excerpts from L'Ottuso's madrigals quoted in the second letter among Fontanella's surviving works. However, he has not excluded altogether the possibility that Fontanella was the writer of the letters.[24] Another good candidate is the Ferrarese composer Antonio Goretti, at whose salon Artusi's dialogists Vario and Luca are represented as hearing Monteverdi's not yet published madrigals.[25]

---

[21] *Seconda parte dell'Artusi*, 5.
[22] Stuart Reiner, 'Preparations in Parma', *Music Review*, xxv (1964), 289, n. 78.
[23] Anthony Newcomb, 'Carlo Gesualdo and a Musical Correspondence of 1594', *Musical Quarterly*, liv (1968), 412.
[24] Idem, 'Alfonso Fontanelli and the Ancestry of the *seconda pratica* Madrigal', *Studies in Renaissance and Baroque Music in Honor of Arthur Mendel*, ed. Robert L. Marshall (Kassel, 1974), 67–8.
[25] There is a possibility, though not a strong one, that the correspondent was a member of an academy called 'degli Ottusi'. If he had been a member of such an academy, 'Accademico Ottuso' would have been more normal usage than

Stuart Reiner in a review of the first edition of this book[26] proposed that L'Ottuso may have been Giulio Cesare Monteverdi. This is an interesting suggestion and would merit further exploration if their styles of writing and thinking were not so diverse. Giulio Cesare speaks in generalities and with a certain touch of sophistry; L'Ottuso is very direct, concrete, cites his sources precisely, is innovative in his theoretical ideas, and extremely well read, citing not only numerous composers but poets such as Guarini and Tasso (to whom he refers as 'nostro', suggesting a Ferrarese connection), Ficino's *Compendium in Timaeum*, and the Pseudo-Aristotle *Problems*, and he refers to 'Monsignore Zarlino' rather than, as Giulio Cesare does, to 'Reverendo Zerlino'.

There was an academician L'Ottuso active as a court poet later in the century, but he is not likely as Monteverdi's supporter. A sacred play, *L'Ave Maria addolorata*, by him has a dedication to the Holy Roman Emperor Ferdinand III (reigned 1636–57) and signed 'L'Incognito Ottuso'.[27]

Although Artusi's credibility on this subject is naturally suspect, it should be recalled that he claims in his last discourse, written under the pseudonym Antonio Braccino da Todi, that the whole quarrel began because a number of friendly and civil letters Artusi wrote to Monteverdi remained unanswered, and instead Monteverdi replied through a third person (obviously meaning L'Ottuso).[28] It is clear, in any case, that Artusi never pretended that L'Ottuso was Monteverdi or that he was calling the composer a blockhead.

Whoever he was, L'Ottuso finally brought the debate around to the

---

[26] *Journal of the American Musicological Society*, xxiii (1970), 344–6.
[27] Vienna, Österreichische Nationalbibliothek, MS Pal. Vind. 13278. According to Maylender, op. cit., iii, 202–4, there had been two academies called 'Incogniti' in Italy in the sixteenth century, one in Naples between 1546 and 1548 and another in Turin, instituted in 1585 but short-lived. The Ottuso discovered by Reiner in the Roman Accademia degli Umoristi, the dramatist Girolamo Rocco, may be the same person as the Vienna poet.
[28] *Discorso secondo musicale di Antonio Braccino da Todi* (Venice, 1608), 6; facsimile reprint (Milan, 1924).

'L'Ottuso Accademico'. There were two academies so named. One was the Accademia degli Ottusi in Bologna, of which, unfortunately, nothing is known; see Michele Maylender, *Storia delle accademie d'Italia* (Bologna, 1926–30), iii, 173. The Accademia degli Ottusi of Spoleto seems to go no further back than 1610 (ibid., iv, 176).

main point—why the new harmonic effects were necessary. He is quoted as saying in his letter of 1599:

The purpose of this new movement of the parts (*modulatione*) is to discover through its novelty a new consensus (*concenti*) and new affections, and this without departing in any way from good reason, even if it leaves behind somehow the ancient traditions of some excellent composers.[29]

New affections call for new harmonic combinations to express them. This is the crux of the matter.

Artusi's retort deals in semantics. He first defines 'concento': 'it is a mixture of low and high notes intermediated in such a way that when sounded they produce an infinite sweetness to the ear'.[30] There are only four ways of mediating the interval between a low and high sound, through the arithmetic, geometric, harmonic and counterharmonic divisions. None of these will divide a seventh, one of the new combinations defended by L'Ottuso, consonantly. Therefore the new combinations are not *concenti*. Indeed no new *concenti* are possible, because the number of consonances is limited. So no new affections can be expressed by them.

L'Ottuso's second letter, written a month after Artusi's reply, is printed in full by Artusi.[31] L'Ottuso, not intimidated by Artusi's sophistry, insists that if Artusi can find something in Signor Etc.'s madrigals to complain about, it must come from the progression of the parts (*modulatione*), the consensus (*concenti*) resulting from it, or from the lines (*arie*) assigned to the various voices. If he finds these unusual and new, they are so because they must express new affections. The central argument is in this passage of L'Ottuso's letter:

It is therefore true that the new progression of the parts (*modulatione*) makes a new consensus (*concento*) and a new affection, and not (as you say) new confusion and discord. But Your Lordship himself admits in his [letter] that there is a new air (*aria*), a new stimulation to the ear, which, struck by the quickness and tardiness of movement, is affected now harshly, now sweetly according to the air that [Signor] Etc. has given to the parts. What is this, then, if not new part-movement (*modulatione*) full of new affection, imitating the nature of the verse and justly representing the true meaning of the poet? And if it appears that this somehow contradicts the authority of the very learned Monsignor Zarlino of reverent memory in the Second Part of the *Institutioni harmoniche*, nevertheless he himself confesses at the end of the

[29] *Seconda parte dell'Artusi*, loc. cit.
[30] Ibid., 6.
[31] Ibid., 13–21.

[twelfth] chapter that from this movement of the parts (*modulatione*) is born melody (*melodia*).[32]

The major barrier to communication between the two writers now becomes apparent. Artusi follows the terminology of Zarlino, while L'Ottuso uses such terms as 'modulatione', 'concento' and 'aria' loosely in the manner of the current musical jargon. By *modulatione* Zarlino meant the movement from pitch to pitch through various intervals by one or more parts with or without measured rhythm. *Modulatione*, properly speaking, that is *modulatione propria*, is the movement of two or more parts meeting in consonances through measured rhythm. This kind of *modulatione* produces *harmonia*.[33] *Harmonia*, according to Zarlino, can be of several kinds: *propria*, a mixture of two or more moving lines of low and high sounds that strikes the ear smoothly; *non propria*, a mixture of low and high sounds without any change of pitch; *perfetta*, in which the outer voices are mediated by one or more inner parts; *imperfetta*, when the outer two parts are not so mediated. When the parts meet in consonances, this is called *concento*. *Harmonia propria* has more power to move the passions than *harmonia non propria*, but it does not acquire its full power except through rhythm and text. 'Therefore from these three things joined together, that is *harmonia propria*, rhythm (*rithmo*) and text (*oratione*), arise (as Plato would have it) *melodia*.'[34] *Melodia*, then, is not melody but the synthesis of the musical, textual and expressive content of a composition. This usage of *melodia* not only clarifies what L'Ottuso wants to say in the excerpt quoted above but is also, as we shall see, a key to Monteverdi's preface.

So the difficulty was that L'Ottuso, though he had read Zarlino, had garbled his terms. Properly translated into Zarlinian, what he was saying is this. Monteverdi was striving for a *harmonia*, which when combined with the other two elements of Plato's triad, rhythm and text, would produce a *melodia* expressive of a particular text. When this text expressed new and violent passions, the *modulatione* that made up the *harmonia* had to be new to produce a new *melodia*.

The contradiction that bothered Artusi now becomes evident. Only mixtures of several lines that strike the ear smoothly can be considered *harmonia propria*. Monteverdi's mixtures sometimes did not. Moreover,

[32] Ibid., 14.
[33] See Zarlino, op. cit., Bk 2, chap. 14, p. 81.
[34] Ibid., Bk 2, chap. 12, p. 80. Artusi summarizes these definitions, paraphrasing Zarlino (*Seconda parte dell'Artusi*, 24ff.). Melody in the sense of a line that an individual part makes as it is 'modulated' is called 'aria'.

the *modulatione* was sometimes faulty by Zarlino's criteria; it used intervals not accepted into vocal music. So Artusi could say that Monteverdi's new *melodia* was no *melodia* at all, because it violated the standards of good *modulatione* and *harmonia propria*.

The usages to which Artusi took exception may be considered in two categories, then: irregularities of 'modulation' or melody-writing, and irregularities of 'harmony' or vertical combination.

Artusi objected to the following interval because it passes from a diatonic note to a chromatic one and is therefore unnatural to the voice, which, unlike instruments, is limited to a small number of consonant and dissonant intervals, through which it passes from one consonance to another:[35]

Ex. 11

This interval is made up of one tone (A–B) and two semitones (B–C and A–G♯). A 9/8 tone added to two 16/15 semitones results in an interval in the ratio 32/25. Artusi is assuming the syntonic diatonic tuning of Ptolemy advocated by Zarlino as the only possible tuning for voices singing unaccompanied. The interval C–G♯ is therefore a most dissonant interval. It is neither a major nor a minor third, and Artusi defies his correspondent to tell him what it is.

Whereas L'Ottuso should have challenged Artusi's assumption of the syntonic diatonic tuning, by then proved unserviceable by several authors,[36] he replies feebly: 'It is a new voice progression (*modulatione*) for the sake of finding through its novelty a new consensus (*concento*) and a new affection'.[37]

The interval occurs twice in the madrigal under discussion in these pages, *Era l'anima mia* (Book V)—at bars 28–9 in the quintus part at the words 'Deh perchè ti consumi?' ('Say, why do you waste yourself?') and at bars 58–9 in the tenor at the words 'Non mori tu, mor'io' ('Don't die yourself, I shall die'):

---

[35] This example appears in Artusi (p. 9) as follows: I have assumed a soprano clef.

[36] Cf. Vincenzo Galilei in *Dialogo della musica antica et della moderna* (Florence, 1581) and Giovanni Battista Benedetti in *Diversarum speculationum mathematicorum & phisicorum liber* (Turin, 1585). See Palisca, 'Scientific Empiricism in Musical Thought', *Seventeenth Century Science and the Arts*, ed. Hedley Howell Rhys (Princeton, 1961), 133ff.

[37] *Seconda parte dell'Artusi*, 15.

Ex. 12

Although L'Ottuso calls it new, he goes on to defend it by precedents (an inconsistency Artusi was quick to point out). Cipriano de Rore uses it in *Poi chè m'invita amore* at the words 'dolce mia vita'[38] and Giaches de Wert in *Misera, non credea* at the word 'essangue' (bars 79–84):[39]

Ex. 13

Another usage that Artusi criticizes and L'Ottuso defends is that of following a sharpened note by a descending interval and a flattened note by a rising one. Artusi does not cite any examples in Monteverdi; but many can be found.[40] All the *moderni* are doing it, says L'Ottuso, 'most of all those who have embraced this new second practice' (*questa nuova seconda pratica*).[41] This is the first time the expression 'seconda pratica' appears in the controversy, and it is introduced without fanfare, as if the term were already current in oral if not written discussions. The

---

[38] *Vive fiamme* (Venice, 1565). L'Ottuso quotes (p. 15) a fragment of the soprano. See *Cipriano de Rore, Opera omnia*, ed. Bernhard Meier, v (American Institute of Musicology, 1971), 79, bar 38.

[39] *Ottavo libro de' madrigali a cinque voci* (Venice, 1586); L'Ottuso quotes (p. 15) fragments of the soprano, tenor and alto. See *Vier Madrigale von Mantuaner Komponisten*, ed. Denis Arnold, Das Chorwerk, lxxx (Wolfenbüttel, 1961), 10; also see *Giaches de Wert, Collected Works*, viii, ed. Carol MacClintock (American Institute of Musicology, 1968), 32, bars 21–2.

[40] For example, in the fourth book: *Anima mia, perdona*, bars 38ff., second part, bar 17; *Luci serene e chiare*, bars 31, 34–5; *Voi pur da me partite*; *Ohimè, se tanto amate*, bar 6, flat rising, etc.

[41] *Seconda parte dell'Artusi*, 16.

particular examples cited by L'Ottuso[42] are: the beginning of Marenzio's
Dura legge[43] and *S'io parto*;[44] and Wert's *Misera, non credea* at the words
'parte tornò'.[45] In *S'io parto*[46] the step Bb–C is used constantly, as is to be
expected in any G minor piece. In the following example from Wert's
madrigal the progression to the dominant of D minor is entirely fitting to
the modern minor mode (bars 86–7):

Ex. 14

But it does not belong in the First or Second Mode, and Artusi expected
a composition to remain within the steps of a mode and its plagal form.
In this he was a loyal follower of Zarlino, who denounced inflections and
chromaticism in vocal music.

The issue of modal purity and unity had already come up in the
dialogue of 1600, when Artusi singled out *O Mirtillo* for attack because it
seemed to begin in one mode and end in another.[47] Then in his letter to
L'Ottuso, Artusi criticized *Cruda Amarilli* for having more cadences in
the Twelfth Mode (C plagal) than in the mode of its closing or opening,
namely the Seventh (G authentic). L'Ottuso's answer is weak.
Everybody knows, he says, 'that a mode is determined from the first and
last notes and not from the median cadences'.[48] Giulio Cesare
Monteverdi's gloss on his brother's letter is similarly naïve in replying to
the first attack. He justifies the disunity of mode in *O Mirtillo* on the
precedents of the mixed modes of plainchant and the mixtures of modes

[42] Ibid., 18; Artusi prints only fragments of the offending parts.
[43] Marenzio, *Il nono libro de madrigali a 5* (Venice, 1599).
[44] Marenzio, *Il sesto libro de madrigali a 5* (Venice, 1594); in *Luca Marenzio,
Sämtliche Werke*, ed. Alfred Einstein, ii, Publikationen älterer Musik, vi
(Leipzig, 1931), 103.
[45] *Wert, Collected Works*, viii, 32, bar 24.
[46] Printed in *Masterpieces of Music before 1750*, ed. Carl Parrish and John F. Ohl
(London, 1952), 102.
[47] *L'Artusi*, f. 48v.
[48] *Seconda parte dell'Artusi*, 21.

in compositions of Josquin, Willaert, Rore and Alessandro Striggio the elder.[49] The latter's *Nasce la pena mia*[50] is cited as being built upon four modes.

Artusi had reason to be shocked at this mixed bag of examples, which left him wondering if the commentator understood what mixed modes were. He replied for the traditionalists forcefully through 'Braccino da Todi' in 1608:

Now for the mixture of tones or modes, which the commentator seems to reproach Artusi for not knowing. What it is, how many kinds there are, what is rational and what is irrational, I shall tell you. If Monteverdi wished to write a composition in a single mode (*Tono*) such as the First, he could not, because perforce there would be a mixture of modes. For when a composer constructs a piece in the First Mode, he must keep to the following order. The tenor should proceed or 'modulate' by way of the notes of the First natural Mode or whichever mode he intends to construct it in . . . and the bass by way of its collateral [the plagal mode]. The cantus corresponds and 'modulates' an octave higher and by the same steps [and mode] as the tenor. The contralto regularly corresponds to the bass, but an octave higher. So all vocal compositions are mixtures of the authentic and plagal. But the mixtures of Monteverdi are not regular like these, but irregular. If he sets out to give one form to his composition, he ends up giving it another, because he exceeds the bounds of mixture. Therefore one may say that he throws the pumpkins in with the lanterns.[51]

Modal unity was of some moment to Artusi, because he, like Zarlino and Glareanus before him, believed that each mode had its special character. In his dialogue of 1600 Artusi had assigned an ethos to each of the modes and urged the composer to choose one suited to the subject of a composition and stick to it.[52]

Giulio Cesare's reply did not come to terms with the issue, because he lacked either the courage or conviction to proclaim the end of the tyranny of the modes. Galilei had already prepared their demise when he exposed the false humanism of the modal theorists in 1581[53] and again ten years later. In his counterpoint treatise he asserted that

---

[49] 'Dichiaratione della lettera stampata nel quinto libro de suoi madrigali', in G. Francesco Malipiero, *Claudio Monteverdi* (Milan, 1929), 83–4; trans. in Strunk, op. cit., 411–12. Also see *Claudio Monteverdi: lettere, dediche, e prefazioni*, ed. Domenico De' Paoli (Rome, 1973), 393–407.

[50] Striggio, *Il primo libro de madrigali a 6* (Venice, 1560).

[51] *Discorso secondo musicale*, 11–12.

[52] *L'Artusi*, f. 68v.

[53] One of the main points of the *Dialogo* was that the ecclesiastical modes had none of the virtues claimed for them by Glareanus and Zarlino.

modality had become more a matter for the eye than the ear, for no one now paid any attention to the internal cadences:

the best and most famous contrapuntists have used cadences on any step at all [of the mode] in their vocal compositions. Moreover . . . the sure identification of the mode is derived from the last note in the bass. That this is true is obvious every time this last note is hidden from the sight of the person studying the piece. . . . With the eyes, therefore, and not with the ears, do modern practitioners know the modes of their pieces. . . . Moreover, take any modern vocal piece in whatever mode and remove or add one or two notes at the end to make it terminate in other notes than the previous ones (without going to extremes, though), and practitioners today will say that there has been a mutation of mode. . . . And when Zarlino too would wish to persuade me again of the simplicities he writes, saying that among our modes one has a quiet nature, another deprecatory, others querulous, excited, lascivious, cheerful, somnolent, tranquil or infuriated and others yet different natures and characters, and finally that the modes as practitioners use them today have the same capacities as those he mentioned the ancient modes possessed, I would answer, convinced by experience, which teaches us the contrary, that these are all tales intended to confuse dunderheads. If our practice retains the smallest part of these aptitudes it does not derive them from the mode or the final note or the harmonic and arithmetic divisions but from the way contrapuntists make the parts progress in any of the modes according to what suits them best.[54]

It is usual to compose a sonnet, he continues, so that

each quatrain and tercet, indeed each particular verse, is of a different mode from the rest. Whoever does differently is taken for a satrap and is accused of indolence and of lacking inventiveness. The ancients sang a history, an action of a hero and an entire book in one same tone (*Tono*), but the goal of the ancients was to make men moderate and virtuous, and that of the moderns is to amuse them, if not to make them effeminate.[55]

Galilei's objective in criticizing the loose modality practised by composers in his time was the opposite of Artusi's. Galilei wanted to see modality abandoned in favour of tonal unity based on pitch level, on the model of the ancient Greeks. Monteverdi was heading pragmatically in the same direction, though unencumbered by Galilei's theoretical bias. To judge by Giulio Cesare's reply, which must have had his approval, Claudio could not yet foresee the theoretical implications of his creative impulses.

The controversy had begun around the use of dissonance. Luca's

[54] *Il primo libro della prattica del contrapunto*, ff. 100–100v; ed. in Rempp, 70–71.
[55] Ibid., f. 101; ed. in Rempp, 72.

rationalizations for its free employment fit only those combinations that seem to come about casually as a by-product of independent part-movement. But more characteristic of Monteverdi's style are dissonances deliberately planted in exposed situations. Some of the exposed dissonances illustrated in Artusi's eighth and ninth examples, both from *Anima mia, perdona*,[56] are the result of suspension. But the suspended note, instead of being held, is sounded again. Artusi fails to make this clear, because he omits bar 59 of the second part of this madrigal in the second of his examples; the repetition of the suspended C in the alto in bar 60 can be seen in the following example (bars 59–62):

Ex. 15

This repetition violated the regular suspension usage as analysed in Artusi's own counterpoint text, where one of the notes of a suspension is regarded as the 'patient' (*paziente*) and the other as the 'agent' (*agente*). The 'patient' remains stationary as it suffers the 'agent' causing the dissonance to move and strike against it.[57]

The reasons traditionally given for tolerating the suspension depend on this absorption of the shock of the dissonance by the sustained voice. Franchino Gaffurio speaks of the hidden and dulled nature of this dissonance.[58] Zarlino finds such a dissonance tolerable

because in singing the syncopated semibreve the voice holds firm, and a certain suspension is heard (*si ode quasi una sospensione*), a taciturnity that is noticed amidst the percussions that produce the tones and make them distinguishable from one another in time. So the ear barely notices this dissonance, not being sufficiently stimulated by it to comprehend it fully.[59]

Monteverdi's seventh in bar 60 of Ex. 15 does not crouch behind the consonances but steps out to be noticed. As Galilei put it, when a

[56] See Strunk, op. cit., 395.

[57] Artusi, *Seconda parte dell'Arte del contraponto*, Bk 2, chap. 1, pp. 27ff.

[58] *Practica musicae* (Milan, 1496), Bk 3, chap. 4: 'est item et latens discordia in contrapuncto praeter sincopatam scilicet inter plures cantilenae partes concordes continetur et obtunditur'.

[59] Zarlino, op. cit., Bk 3, chap. 42, p. 197; Eng. trans. from *Zarlino, The Art of Counterpoint*, trans. Guy A. Marco and Claude V. Palisca (New Haven, 1968/R1983), 97.

composer uses dissonances in this manner he does not expect them to

blend in harmony with wonderful effect; but rather that the sense become satisfied with them, not because they harmonize . . . but because of the gentle mixture of the sweet and the strong, which . . . affect our ears not unlike the way in which taste receives satisfaction from both sugar and vinegar.[60]

Even more prominent, of course, is the seventh in the top part in bar 61, which is not sounded in the previous bar. L'Ottuso admits that he can offer no theoretical demonstration to justify these usages. Yet he is convinced they are admissible, not only on grounds of precedent but also by virtue of the context or as a poetic licence. He is not driven, as Artusi implied, to call a dissonance a consonance—he realizes that a dissonance would always be a dissonance:

but by circumstance (*per accidente*) it can well be otherwise, for there is no dissonant interval which is in itself one that by circumstance cannot be made good with reference to the accompaniments among which it is placed. . . . As an accent, as a deception, or indeed as a dissonance, though sweetened by the accompaniment of the other parts, it [a seventh] will undoubtedly not only have a good effect but, being something new, will give greater delight to the ear than would the supposed octave. And since you desire a proof, you will draw it very easily from this: you allow an excellent poet the metaphor purposefully used; similarly the seventh is taken in place of the octave. [61]

The octave is understood or 'supposed' (*supposta*), but the seventh is heard in its stead. As the poet metaphorically takes one word for another, the composer takes one note for another. For example, Marenzio, 'who was not in the habit of staying within the narrow prescriptions of music theory', used the seventh above the bass in two of the madrigals of his ninth book of five-part madrigals:[62] in *E so come in un punto* at the words 'per le guancie' and 'ascoso langue', and in *Così nel*

---

[60] Quoted in Palisca, 'Vincenzo Galilei's Counterpoint Treatise', 87; ed. in Rempp, 39.

[61] *Seconda parte dell'Artusi*, 16. Angelo Berardi paraphrased this passage in his *Miscellanea musicale* (Bologna, 1689), Part II, chap. 12, p. 39: 'the moderns use the bare seventh (*settima nuda*) as a deception (*inganno*) and accent (*accento*), or as a dissonance, yes, but sweetened by the accompaniment of the other parts, as something new that produces a new affection in the ear.' He then cites the madrigals of Marenzio named by L'Ottuso.

[62] *Il nono libro de madrigali a 5* (Venice, 1599).

mio parlar[63] at the words 'maggior durezze' and in the second part at 'da i colpi mortali'. Here is the last of these:

Ex. 16

The word 'colpi' ('blows') is accompanied by a second and seventh above the bass instead of a third and octave. Like the figure of speech in which a word with stronger and richer associations replaces the normal one, the composer, L'Ottuso would have us believe, substitutes a sharp dissonance for the normal consonance. This notion has great potential, as Bernhard shows when he classifies many irregular uses of dissonance as rhetorical figures. But L'Ottuso fails to develop the thought. Nevertheless he is one of the very few Italian writers who associates musical licences with rhetorical figures.

The two principal sources for Monteverdi's free treatment of dissonance that emerge from Artusi's dialogue and the letters of L'Ottuso are the impromptu practices of singers and the pioneering efforts of Rore and his followers, and they are corroborated by Zacconi in the second part of his *Prattica di musica*, published in 1622. If someone were to ask him, he writes, whence came the practice of placing dissonances on the downbeat in the manner found throughout Monteverdi's works,

I would say that he took it from the second part of the motet of Cipriano Bora [i.e. Rore] *O altitudo divitiarum*, which uses this arrangement of notes. The first minim [see bar 94 of Ex. 17] is made dissonant as an affectation (*per affetto*), thereby making the second minim awaited by the melody so much the better. Or shall we say that, although he [Monteverdi] may have taken this practice from the aforenamed composer, he was not moved entirely by this but by that everyday habit singers have today of performing

[63] Printed in Einstein, 'Dante im Madrigal', *Archiv für Musikwissenschaft*, iii (1921), 414–20. From the four places in these two madrigals cited, Artusi (p. 17) prints the two voice parts that form the seventh.

things with the most grateful affectations (*affetti*) possibly to make themselves as pleasing as they can to listeners.[64]

Ex. 17. Rore, *O altitudo divitiarum*, from *Il terzo libro di motetti a 5* (Venice, 1549), bars 93–4

Throughout his replies, Artusi insists upon the rules, because, he says, they are based on nature, demonstration and the models of excellent composers. Although L'Ottuso too has recourse to the example of excellent composers, he challenges the principle of imitation. Every good painter, sculptor, poet or orator seeks to imitate the ancients and particularly the excellent ones, but there are also those who esteem invention more than imitation. Indeed, in music invention is much more esteemed than imitation, because only through invention can musical art advance. Signor Etc. (Monteverdi) is one of those dedicated to invention. *Era l'anima mia*, for example, in whose opening, staying for four bars on the chord of D minor, Artusi found nothing new, but rather a reminiscence of the *giustiniana*,[65] L'Ottuso defends as full of new harmonic progressions, elegant passages from plagal to authentic, ascents after accidental flats and descents after sharps, substitutions of unexpected notes for the expected, and other artful devices. 'If Your Lordship considered the madrigals of Signor Etc.', he pleaded, 'you will find them full of such flowers, embellished with such terse modulation, far from the common, indeed full of judicious deceptions.'[66]

So much of the effect of these licences depends on subtle nuances and emphases that, in L'Ottuso's opinion, compositions indulging in them had, in order to be judged fairly, to be sung by specially gifted musicians.

[64] *Prattica di musica seconda parte* (Venice, 1622), Bk 2, chap. 10, p. 63. Zacconi quotes of the alto and quintus parts the second half of bar 93 and the first half of 94. The motet is published in *Rore, Opera omnia*, ed. Meier, i (1959), 122.

[65] A type of villanella, common in Venice. On the opening of *Era l'anima mia* see also below, 206. Similarly, Artusi asks if the first eight bars, which he quotes, of *Ma se con la pietà*, the second part of *Ecco Silvio* in the fifth book, is the beginning of a *giustiniana* or a *spifarata mantovana*: *Seconda parte dell'Artusi*, 5.

[66] Ibid., 19.

You must remember that the singer is the soul of music, and it is he who, in sum, represents the true meaning of the composer to us. In this representation, according to the variety of the subject, the voice is sometimes reinforced, at other times sweetened. For this reason you have to hear this manner of clever composition sung by singers who are out of the ordinary. Your Lordship's grounds [for criticism] would then cease to exist, in that the harshness of these madrigals would be covered in such a way that the dissonances would not be heard.[67]

For Artusi L'Ottuso relied too much on deluding the ear and the judgment with deceptions, suppositions and artifices that have no basis in reality.

All those things that the modern confounders call suppositions, flowers (*fioretti*), deceptions, accents and artifices, which are against the good rules, the student knows for false, false suppositions against the nature of the thing, false deceptions, false flowers, false artifices, false accents, and never true things and true suppositions.[68]

Modern composers take too much refuge in the deficiencies of the senses. In their ambition to sway the emotions they resort to means that are unnatural and therefore cannot stimulate a natural process like moving the affections, for like responds to like. The only new effects that come across are those the singers make when they

turn the head slowly, arch their eyebrows, roll their eyes, twist their shoulders, let themselves go as if they want to die, and their many other metamorphoses, the likes of which Ovid never imagined. Indeed they make these grimaces just when they arrive at those dissonances that offend the sense to show what others ought to be doing. But instead of being moved [the listeners] are ruffled by the bitterness and discontent they feel, and, turning their heads, depart dissatisfied.[69]

The following concise and eloquent statement, printed in the fifth book of madrigals (1605), is the only public reply Claudio Monteverdi made to Artusi's criticisms.

Studious Readers:

Be not surprised that I am giving these madrigals to the press without first replying to the objections that Artusi made against some very minute portions of them. Being in the service of this Serene Highness of Mantua, I am not master of the time I would require. Nevertheless I wrote a reply to let it be known that I do not do things by chance, and as soon as it is rewritten it will see the light with the title in front, *Seconda pratica overo Perfettione della*

---

[67] Ibid., 19–20.   [68] Ibid., 47.   [69] Ibid., 40–41.

moderna musica. Some will wonder at this, not believing that there is any other practice than that taught by Zerlino [*sic*]. But let them be assured concerning consonances and dissonances that there is a different way of considering them from that already determined which defends the modern manner of composition with the assent of the reason and the senses. I wanted to say this both so that the expression *Seconda pratica* would not be appropriated by others and so that men of intellect might meanwhile consider other second thoughts concerning harmony. And have faith that the modern composer builds on foundations of truth.

Live happily.[70]

This is a statement full of promise. Monteverdi, though confident of his musical instinct, recognized the need for a theoretical rationalization of his new way of dealing with dissonances if it was to be generally accepted.[71] Like his predecessors Zarlino and Francisco de Salinas, he aimed to appeal to both the reason and the senses. The letter does not imply, as has sometimes been suggested, that Monteverdi considered the rules of the First Practice a theory, while the Second was a mere practice. He obviously knew the difference between *musica theorica* and *musica practica.* Zarlino's *Istitutioni* is a union of both, but its Book 3, which deals with the use of consonances and dissonances in counterpoint, is essentially a *musica practica.* Monteverdi promised to replace it with a second and different *musica practica.*[72]

Giulio Cesare Monteverdi's commentary on his brother's letter, published in the *Scherzi musicali* (1607), is one of the most important manifestos in the history of music. As with most manifestos it is richer in slogans than in original aesthetic ideas. But it does illuminate some of Claudio's remarks, even if we cannot assume that he would have stood behind every word of it.

From the first paragraph we learn that Monteverdi's letter of 1605 was answered by a discourse printed under the name of Antonio Braccino da Todi. No copy of this is extant, but its existence is further

[70] Italian text in Malipiero, op. cit., 71–2, and De' Paoli, op. cit., 391–2'.
[71] Monteverdi was apparently unaware of Galilei's counterpoint treatise, which for polyphonic music at least presents a new set of rules and considerations about consonance and dissonance on the basis of the works of some of the composers Giulio Cesare Monteverdi names as founders of the *seconda prattica.* See Palisca, 'Vincenzo Galilei's Counterpoint Treatise'.
[72] This numbering of the 'practices' is obviously short in hindsight, as Artusi points out in the *Discorso secondo musicale,* 15; but the latter's suggestion of calling it the third or fourth practice, depending on whether that of the Greeks and Romans is considered the first or the first and second, is not much better.

corroborated by the title of the discourse published under the same name in 1608, *Discorso secondo musicale di Antonio Braccino da Todi per la dichiaratione della lettera posta ne Scherzi musicali del Sig. Claudio Monteverde*. The author of these discourses has always been assumed to be Artusi, and there is no reason to contest this attribution. The explanation for Artusi's hiding behind a pseudonym is probably that here for the first time he names the composer whose madrigals he attacked and out of delicacy wished to remain anonymous, as before he kept the composer anonymous.

The principal contribution of Giulio Cesare's commentary is that he informs us of the *seconda prattica*'s pedigree, both in practice and philosophy. He names Rore the founder and lists the composers who developed it before his brother,[73] and he aligns it with the famous dictum of Plato, which put the text ahead of the other two components of music, 'harmony' and rhythm. Giulio Cesare and, we may assume, Claudio, conceived the second practice as a revival of Plato's ideal music. It renewed or revived this lost art through 'our notation', that is the mensural notation used in polyphonic music. Both Zarlino and Artusi had quoted the relevant passage from the *Republic*, but neither had emphasized the order Plato gave to the three elements. One writer who did call attention to the priority of the text was Giulio Caccini,[74] who significantly figured among those Giulio Cesare named as developers of the Second Practice.

Caccini was not the first to note this side of Plato's definition. Johannes Ott pointed to it briefly in a foreword to his masses of 1539,[75] and Bishop Jacopo Sadoleto commented upon it at length in a sweeping condemnation of the polyphonic music of his time in his *De liberis recte instituendis* ('Concerning the Proper Education of Boys') in 1533. A humanist churchman who as cardinal was a member of the pontifical commission for the reform of the church and the Council of Trent, he appealed to musicians to restore the verbal message to its sovereignty among the components of music. Elaborating on the famous Platonian

---

[73] These are Marc'Antonio Ingegneri, Marenzio, Wert, Luzzasco Luzzaschi, Jacopo Peri, Giulio Caccini and the 'Heroic School' of gentlemen-composers, which includes Carlo Gesualdo, Prince of Venosa, Emilio de' Cavalieri, Fontanella, 'the Count of the Camerata' (i.e. Bardi), Cavaliere Turchi and Tommaso Pecci.

[74] In his foreword to *Le nuove musiche* (Florence, 1602); trans. H. Wiley Hitchcock in Recent Researches in the Music of the Baroque Era, ix (Madison, 1970), 43.

[75] Cf. Strunk, op. cit., 256, note k.

passage in his dialogue, Sadoleto has the father, Jacopus, tell his son
Paullus:

If we inquire into what style is to be maintained in music, I believe that we
should bear all the following in mind. A chorus consists of three elements,
the sense of the words, the rhythm (which we call number) and tone. The
words are the first and most important of the three as being the very basis
and foundation of the others. By themselves the words have no mean
influence upon the mind, whether to persuade or restrain. Accommodated
to rhythm (*numerus*) and metre (*modus*) they penetrate much more deeply. If
in addition they are given a melodic setting, they take possession of the inner
feelings and of the whole man.[76]

Sadoleto missed this persuasiveness and feeling in the vocal music of his
day, which he characterized as consisting of nothing but variation and
patterns of notes. The music with text that he heard served only the
sense of hearing, and this made the mind a slave of the body.

   Giulio Cesare proclaims that the Second Practice has restored the
supremacy of the text, subordinating 'harmony' and leading to the
perfection of 'melody'. Without perhaps intending to, he gave a new
twist to Plato's words. He assigned to the word 'harmony' a modern
meaning, while attempting to cling to the ancient concept of 'melody'.
Zarlino had already planted the seed for this confusion, when he said (as
we saw above) 'from proper harmony (*harmonia propria*), rhythm
(*rithmo*) and text (*oratione*) arise (as Plato would have it) melody
(*melodia*)'.[77]

   The confusion resulted from the scant comprehension of Greek
music on the part of the early translators of Plato. The translation most
current in Italy was the Latin of Marsilio Ficino. Plato's phrase is
rendered: 'melodia ex tribus constare, oratione, harmonia, rhythmus'.[78]
And later: 'atqui harmonia et rhythmus orationem sequi debent'.[79]

---

[76] *Iac. Sadoleti De liberis recte instituendis liber* (Venice, 1533), f. 42v: 'Quod si
quaeratur qui modus sit in musicis tenendus, haec ego omnia attendenda esse
puto: cum constet chorus ex tribus, sententia, rhythmo (hic enim numerus
nobis est) & uoce, primum quidem omnium & potissimum sententiam esse,
utpote quae si sedes & fundamentum reliquorum, & per se ipsa ualeat non
minimum ad suadendum animo uel dissuadendum: numeris autem modisque
contorta penetret multo acrius: si uero etiam cantu & uoce fuerit modulata,
iam omnis intus sensus & hominem totum possideat'.
[77] Op. cit., Bk 2, chap. 12, p. 80; see above, 141.
[78] *Republic* 398c: *Plato, Opera*, trans. Marsilio Ficino (Venice, 1491), f. 201.
[79] *Republic* 398d.

In the original Greek, however, we read that *melos* ('song') consists of three things, *logos* ('the word', or 'that by which the inward thought is expressed'), *harmonia* ('agreement' or 'relation of sounds') and *rhythmos* ('time' or 'rhythm'). Plato was saying simply that a song consists of a text, an agreeable arrangement of intervals, and measured time; and of these the text is the leader.

But Giulio Cesare, and L'Ottuso with him, are saying that a modern polyphonic composition, like the ancient song or *melos*, should subordinate to the text (its meaning and rhythm) the arrangement of tones both successive and simultaneous (broadening of the concept of *harmonia*) and rhythm (now broadened to include tempo, metre and rhythm). This results in the perfection of 'melody', that is, expressive composition. He is not saying, as has sometimes been inferred, that melody in the sense of tune or monody should now take precedence over counterpoint or harmony. Melody in this sense is not even in question.[80]

The recognition that Monteverdi gave to the existence of two practices and their definition by Giulio Cesare were of resonant importance. Hardly a theoretical book was published after 1608 that did not help to confirm this dichotomy. It should be recalled, however, that the Monteverdi brothers underscored a dualism that already existed in both the music and the literature about it from the middle of the sixteenth century. The *musica nova* and *musica reservata* of the 1540s and 1550s broke the ground for the tradition that Giulio Cesare dates back to the madrigals of Rore.[81] Galilei in his counterpoint treatise contrasted the composers who followed the rules—the *osservatori*—and those who,

---

[80] Artusi quite rightly, if unduly harshly, scolded Giulio Cesare for distorting Plato's meaning: 'Plato does not treat nor ever did, nor had he any thought of treating of modern melodies or music, but I believe, rather, that he discussed those melodies that flourished in his time. It was possible to say then that the text had greater force than the harmony or rhythm, because that history, tale or whatever it may have been was recited to the sound of a single instrument. . . . But the melodies of Monteverdi of which the commentator writes are not similar to those used in the time of Plato; they are deformed. In those [of the ancients] the text was stirring, in these, if anything, the harmony; in those the text was intelligible, in these the harmony; then they worked many effects, now none. . . . There is no conformity or resemblance between the melody used in the time of Plato and that of our day. It is too diverse, too different. The quoted passage is out of the seminary, out of context, a chimera, malapropos' (*Discorso secondo musicale*, 9).
[81] See Palisca, 'A Clarification of "Musica Reservata" in Jean Taisnier's "Astrologiae", 1559', *Acta musicologica*, xxxi (1959), 133.

like the painters Michelangelo and Raphael, were guided only by their own judgment based on both reason and sense.[82]

Girolamo Diruta in 1609[83] and Adriano Banchieri in 1614 distinguished between the *contrapunto osservato* and the modern freer *contrapunto commune*. The *osservato*, Banchieri notes, was explained both as to theory and practice by Zarlino, Artusi and other writers, but of the *contrapunto misto* or *commune* writers had not produced a single rule or precept for accommodating the affections. Nor does he consider the subject one that could be written about.[84]

The writer who most faithfully communicates both the language and spirit of the Monteverdi brothers is Marco Scacchi. He synthesizes the ideas of the 1605, 1607 and 1638 prefaces in a single system of style classification. While the *musica antica*, Scacchi asserts, maintained the same style for all serious subjects, whether meant for sacred or secular functions, modern music employs two practices and three styles. In the First Practice the composer is guided by the principle *ut harmonia sit*

[82] *Discorso intorno all'uso delle dissonanze*, f. 142v; ed. in Rempp, 151: 'The greatness and majesty that is contained in that Canzone which begins *Hor ch'il cielo, et la Terra, e'l vento tace* [*Li madrigali cromatici a 5*, Book I (Venice, repr. 1562)], the loveliness and grace of *Anchor che col partire* [*Il primo libro de madrigali a 4* (Ferrara, 1550)], the varied sweetness and unusual sonority of *Cantai mentre ch'io arsi del mio foco* [*Li madrigali cromatici*], the sombreness of *Come havran fin le dolorose tempre* [*Primo libro a 5*, 1550] expressed with so much artfulness without any affectation: Cipriano did not learn the art of turning out such works as these in the books written about the rules of counterpoints, but it rested entirely on his own judgment.'

[83] *Seconda parte del Transilvano dialogo* (Venice, 1609), Bk 2, p. 3.

[84] Adriano Banchieri, *Cartella musicale*, 161ff. Already in an earlier publication, *Conclusioni nel suono dell'organo* (Bologna, 1609), 58–9, Banchieri had complained that the authors on counterpoint never gave 'any rule or precept that would show how in practice to imitate the affections when setting any kind of words [to music], whether Latin or vernacular, and in particular words signifying pains, passions, sighing, tears, laughter, question, error and similar circumstances. . . . There is no doubt that music, so far as harmony (*harmonia*) is concerned, must be subject to the words, since the words are those that express the conceit.' Galilei in 1591 made a similar complaint: 'In the variety of books which are in print today written on the subject of the art of modern counterpoint, which I have read diligently many times, I have never been able to know two very principal things. One of these pertains to the soul of harmony, which is the meaning of the words; and the other pertains to the body, which is the diversity of successive sounds and notes by which the parts proceed. Regarding the soul, no one so far as I know, as I have said, has yet taught the way to accompany the words, or rather the ideas behind them, with notes' (*Discorso intorno all'uso delle dissonanze*, f.105v; ed. in Rempp, 77).

domina orationis ('that harmony be the mistress of the text'). In the Second Practice he obeys the rule *ut oratio sit domina harmoniae* ('that the text be the mistress of the harmony').[85] Scacchi's three styles of music are indebted to the letter that precedes the *Madrigali guerrieri, et amorosi* (Venice, 1638). Here Monteverdi states: 'the music of grand princes is used in their royal chambers in three manners to please their delicate tastes, namely [music for] the theatre, for the chamber and for the dance'.[86]

Scacchi built upon this base a broader scheme of classification. The three styles of the modern or second practice are the church style (*ecclesiasticus*), the chamber style (*cubicularis*) and the theatrical style (*scenicus seu theatralis*). These categories break down into further divisions, as shown in the following chart:[87]

Ecclesiasticus	*Cubicularis*	*Scenicus seu theatralis*
1. 4 to 8 voices, no organ	1. madrigals *da tavolino* (*a cappella*)	1. *stile semplice recitativo* (without gestures)
2. polychoral with organ	2. madrigals with basso continuo	2. *stile recitativo* (with gestures)
3. *in concerto* (with instruments)	3. compositions for voices and instruments	
4. motets in modern style in *stile misto* (recitative with florid passages and arias)		

---

[85] Marco Scacchi, *Breve discorso sopra la musica moderna* (Warsaw, 1649), ff. C3v–C4v; ed. Palisca in 'Marco Scacchi's Defense of Modern Music (1649)', *Words and Music: the Scholar's View ... in Honor of A. Tillman Merritt*, ed. Laurence Berman (Cambridge, Mass., 1972), 204–5. This pamphlet is essentially a commentary on Giulio Cesare's 'Dichiaratione' in response to an opponent of the modern style, namely Romano Micheli. Scacchi comments on the Artusi–Monteverdi feud also in his *Cribrum musicum* (Venice, 1643).

[86] Malipiero, op. cit., 91.

[87] In this chart I have incorporated into the classification presented in the *Breve discorso* the more detailed division of church music Scacchi makes in a letter to Christoph Werner, published in Erich Katz, *Die musikalischen Stilbegriffe des 17. Jahrhunderts* (Freiburg, 1926), 83–7. This classification of church music is adopted by Berardi, a pupil of Scacchi, in his *Ragionamenti musicali* (Bologna, 1681), 134.

Scacchi's style system underwent further development at the hands of Christoph Bernhard,[88] who partly reconciled it with the terminology of Diruta and Banchieri:

Contrapunctus gravis	*Contrapunctus luxurians*
or *stylus antiquus*	or *stylus modernus*
or *a capella* or *ecclesiasticus*	1. *communis*
(*Harmonia Orationis*	(*Oratio* as well as *Harmonia Domina*)
Domina)	2. *comicus* or *theatralis*
	or *recitativus* or *oratorius*
	(*Oratio Harmoniae Domina*
	absolutissima)

Thus the slogans of Giulio Cesare Monteverdi still ring in the treatises and pamphlets of the mid-seventeenth century. The ripple started by Artusi's first stone reaches ever wider circles as the controversy over the two styles is stirred up in Rome, Danzig, Warsaw and Hamburg, among other places. In Rome Romano Micheli takes up Artusi's role as defender of the First Practice, while Marco Scacchi challenges him from Warsaw.[89] Their quarrel grows out of a local difference between the composers Paul Seyfert and Kaspar Förster the Elder in Danzig. Then, as Scacchi gathers testimonials for his point of view throughout Germany and Poland, many of the other musical centres of northern Europe are drawn into the fray. In the heat of these debates were tempered and forged the rules of the neo-severe style of the late seventeenth century.

[88] *Tractatus compositionis augmentatus*, chaps. 3 and 35, pp. 42–3 and 82–3; trans. Hilse, 34–5, 110–11.
[89] See my articles 'Micheli, Romano', and 'Scacchi, Marco', in *Die Musik in Geschichte und Gegenwart*, ix (1961), cols. 273–4, and xi (1963), cols. 1466–9, respectively, and 'Scacchi, Marco', in *The New Grove*, xvi, 542–4.

JEROME ROCHE

Monteverdi and the *prima prattica*

By First Practice he understands the one that turns on the perfection of the harmony, that is, the one that considers the harmony not commanded, but commanding, not the servant, but the mistress of the words, and this was founded by those first men who composed in our notation music for more than one voice, was then followed and amplified by Ockeghem, Josquin Desprez, Pierre de La Rue, Jean Mouton, Crequillon, Clemens non Papa, Gombert, and others of those times, and was finally perfected by Messer Adriano with actual composition and by the most excellent Zarlino with most judicious rules.[1]

Thus Monteverdi's brother, Giulio Cesare, outlines what Claudio himself meant by the term 'prima prattica', in a manifesto printed with the *Scherzi musicali* published in 1607. But what is our conception of the term? Is it synonymous with 'stile antico' or 'da cappella'? These questions inevitably pose themselves at the outset of a consideration of Monteverdi's relationship with the *prima prattica*, for the three terms have been used rather loosely and have even become interchangeable in writings on early seventeenth-century church music. The problem can be stated in another way: if we agree that the *prima prattica* represents seventeenth-century music written deliberately in a style that belongs to the previous century, then surely we shall have to decide at what date the style becomes anachronistic, at what date a composer writing polyphonically ceases to be with the times and becomes a reactionary? This crude over-simplification can lead us dangerously near to the viewpoint of historians several generations ago who treated 1600 as a 'great divide', whereas in reality the transition from late sixteenth-century church music to the *seconda prattica* is not nearly so abrupt. Just as the former has its anticipations of concertato techniques, the latter in its early stages still preserves characteristics of the older music. For instance, the motets of Viadana's *Cento concerti* of 1602, while breaking new ground as small-scale church music for a handful of solo voices with an indispensable basso continuo accompaniment, were composed with an attitude to the text that savoured of the *prima prattica*: that is, they

[1] Oliver Strunk, *Source Readings in Music History* (New York, 1950), 408.

had none of the emotionalism in their approach to the text that was essential to music of the Second Practice. The very reason why *prima prattica* is confined to church music is that the greater part of the liturgical texts of the Mass and psalms were of a neutral nature, not calling for the dramatic word-painting of the newer music. This is not to say that the best church music was composed according to the *prima prattica*; on the contrary most of the finest early seventeenth-century church music is essentially of the Second Practice.

Can the musical environment of Monteverdi's youth in Cremona and Mantua cast some light on his future development as a composer of *prima prattica* church music? His teacher in the 1580s was Ingegneri, who was not among the most progressive north Italian church musicians of the time, preferring a more flowing polyphony to the chordal tendencies in the music of Ruffo or Andrea Gabrieli. Monteverdi's *Sacrae cantiunculae* of 1582, which can be looked upon as contrapuntal exercises or possibly as spiritual madrigals—a form popular at the time—show a predilection for strict polyphony and are independent of musical trends in Venice. Had Monteverdi been born ten years later in Venice his whole musical upbringing, especially his attitude to polyphony, could have been utterly different. His style in the *Sacrae cantiunculae* was orientated towards the purer Roman kind of counterpoint. But in fact his concern during the period of his youth was less with church music than with the madrigal, in which field he was more progressive. It was probably not necessary for him to compose much church music for use until towards 1610, by which time the *Sacrae cantiunculae* were of the past.

It was by about this time that the transition to the concertato style in north Italian church music was more or less complete. Viadana's new conception of the small-scale motet for one to four voices and organ, written for the ordinary unambitious church choir, was beginning to have a wide influence precisely because it was a practical proposition in the average church where money was not plentiful. In Rome, on the other hand, the stylistic issue was more open: the *stile antico* was not a lost cause, since the full choirs necessary to its performance were more easily maintained financially, at least in the largest basilicas. Thus the two manners in church music were beginning to crystallize. 1610 was the year of Monteverdi's first publication of church music, historically unique in that it was the first to include *prima* and *seconda prattica* music within one cover. The publication of music in the two idioms within the same collection was to be a somewhat rare event, as a glance through a

list of mass publications after 1610[2] will show. In the first decade we
find only two collections of masses, by Pietro Lappi and Stefano
Bernardi, and in the 1620s four, by Ghizzolo, Ignazio Donati, Aloisi and
Bellazzi. An interesting point is that three of these publications include
parody masses upon madrigals; the parody mass was still very much the
norm where the concertato style was not adopted. More important is the
designation of the older-style masses as 'da cappella', used in antithesis
to 'concertato'. The term is also applied to the six-part mass in
Monteverdi's 1610 collection: its exact meaning has been widely
misconstrued. This is understandable since around this date its
meaning was changing. Praetorius[3] tells us that in Italy 'cappella'
signifies a choir with voices and instruments mixed, and Viadana, in
prefacing his polychoral psalms of 1612, asserts that unless the
'cappella', or foundation choir, has at least twenty voices and
instruments, it will produce a poor sound. This is the notion of 'cappella'
that was prevalent in the sixteenth century, when instruments never did
more than double the voices; but now that instruments were acquiring
their own obbligato parts, written in idiomatic style, the term 'cappella'
ceased to have any particular relevance to their use and slowly came to
mean simply full choir music without soloists. It was but a short step to
its modern, conventional meaning of unaccompanied choral music.
Thus, in these mass settings with the two idioms side by side, 'da
cappella' implies that soloists were not used.

The most striking difference between the *da cappella* style of
Monteverdi—at least in both the 1610 and *Selva morale* masses—and
that of his contemporaries is that he tried to be far more conservative. A
glance at one or two of the mass collections noted above will show that
the older-style masses stand at a point much closer along a line of
continuous evolution to the concertato ones: one or two of Bernardi's
works will be mentioned later. Monteverdi, on the other hand, went
right back to a motet of Gombert for the model of his parody mass *In illo
tempore* of 1610. At the time of composing it he was intent on proving to
the Roman world in general and Pope Paul V in particular that he had
mastered the intricacies of classical Netherlands polyphony. And yet
why should he consider that *this* was the kind of music the Romans
would like to see him writing? What really was the kind of music being
written for the Mass in Rome in 1610? The answer to this question can

[2] Taken from Gaetano Gaspari, *Catalogo della Biblioteca Musicale G. B. Martini
di Bologna* (repr. Bologna, 1961), ii.
[3] *Syntagma musicum*, iii (Wolfenbüttel, 1619), 113.

fortunately be found in a work that affords a most illuminating comparison with Monteverdi's Gombert mass—the Hexachord Mass (*Super voces musicales*) by Francesco Soriano, whose music Monteverdi must have got to know through his Mantuan connections.[4] This is written in the same Ionian mode and for the same six voices, and the 'Christe eleison' motif even bears a resemblance to the first of Gombert's points that Monteverdi uses:

Ex. 1[5]

Hereafter the likeness rapidly diminishes: Soriano displays the progressive trends typical of Palestrina's late manner—the interest in pure sonority rather than polyphony, especially in the *Gloria*, where rhythmic motifs replace conventional imitation points, as at 'Domine Deus':

Ex. 2

[4] Carl Proske, ed., *Selectus novus missarum*, i/2 (Regensburg, 1857), 205. Monteverdi's first mass and the Gombert motet *In illo tempore* on which it is based are printed in an Eulenburg score, ed. Hans F. Redlich (London, 1962).
[5] All musical examples except those in triple metre have (where necessary) been adjusted to 4/4 or 4/2 time with crotchet tactus to facilitate comparison. Organ continuo parts have not been quoted except when independent of the voices.

The *Gloria* begins chordally rather than imitatively, and almost at once the diatonic C major is tarnished by an unexpected A major harmony:

Ex. 3

This use of a strange chord is comparable with the sudden flatwards lean in bars 25–8 of Monteverdi's *Gloria*, though it is more dramatic because it comes so near the beginning. At 'Domine Deus Agnus Dei' Soriano actually juxtaposes the C and A major chords as a coloristic effect; the chromatic alteration in the top part is typical of the compromise of the Palestrina style with modern expressiveness:

Ex. 4

The whole wayward chord progression is thrown into relief by a return within three bars to a diatonic C major. It will be seen from these two quotations from Soriano's *Gloria* how much more angular and harmonically conceived is his bass line than Monteverdi's. His use of a modal B flat chord at 'Pater omnipotens' is similar to Monteverdi's at 'Jesu Christe' (see Ex. 5). But the 'Amen of his *Gloria* is full of clashes caused by the held G in the top part, again prompted by the desire for a touch of colour.

Soriano's melismas, in Palestrina's vein, have the effect of emphasizing the text, whereas Monteverdi's are more syncopated and

Ex. 5

(a) Soriano   (b) Monteverdi

rhythmically tortuous and recall earlier music: the type of writing can be seen at 'extollens vocem' or 'quinimo', in bars 14 and 31 of the Gombert motet:

Ex. 6

(a)

(b)   (c)

There is certainly no hint in Soriano's music of Monteverdi's obsession with sequences—the only suggestion of it occurs for three bars at 'resurrectionem mortuorum' in the *Credo*, where the patterns are almost exactly repeated, allowing minor differences demanded by the word-setting:

Ex. 7

There is also a sequence in actual sound if not part by part at the 'Amen'; both these instances, however, arise from the use of the hexachord motif, which invites sequential treatment, whereas Monteverdi evolves his sequences from non-sequential material, detaching and extending the first four notes of Gombert's second 'subject':

Ex. 8

sequence motif

Soriano's style, apart from the occasional chromatic alterations, reflects that of late Palestrina. A mass like the latter's upon the motet *Assumpta est Maria*[6] is even simpler harmonically, with a good deal of homophony in the *Gloria* and *Credo*, which is rare in Soriano. Palestrina's harmonic outline, as also his counterpoint, is infinitely clearer to the ear than Monteverdi's. The fact is that to a contrapuntist six parts are really less ideal for strict polyphonic writing than four;[7] the six-part texture allows for a more sonorous writing with extra, non-contrapuntal voices filling out the chording. This explains why Monteverdi's valiant attempt at completely independent part-writing results in a constantly lush texture lacking to some degree in clarity. He considered six parts to imply more, rather than less, complication. A study of his 'Crucifixus' section will demonstrate how much more clarity there is with just four parts and similar strictness of style.

[6] *Giovanni Pierluigi da Palestrina, Le opere complete*, xxv, ed. Lino Bianchi (Rome, 1958), 209.
[7] See Redlich, *Claudio Monteverdi* (English trans., rev., London, 1952), 123.

Gombert, the great master of Netherlands polyphony, does not have
to concern himself with sonority; it is the sheer command of
counterpoint that fires his motet *In illo tempore* with life. There are
several reasons why this music, too, has the clarity that Monteverdi
seemed to be unable to achieve. Firstly, Gombert is economical with the
six parts: the moments when all sing together are very brief, and for the
most part one or more voices are silent at any one time. Secondly, his
two lowest voices both function as bass lines in alternation since they
often cross: this means that a harmonic bottom line can be contrived
when, for instance, one part becomes conjunct and the other has a leap:

Ex. 9

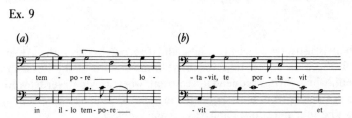

Here the lower bass has risen a fifth and relinquished harmonic control
to the quintus with its falling fourth (Ex. 9a); in bars 22–3 the
momentary modulation to F is supported by the quintus (Ex. 9b). Of
course, many of Gombert's 'subjects' contain rising fourths and fifths
that function harmonically in the lower parts. His overall harmonic
motion is more regular, cadences occurring on the strong beats of 4/4 in
Redlich's transcription. His economy with the voices leads to a clearer
chording: one has only to look at part of Monteverdi's *Kyrie II* to notice
some of the extraordinary clashes—some strangely beautiful—into
which an over-lush texture can lead him:

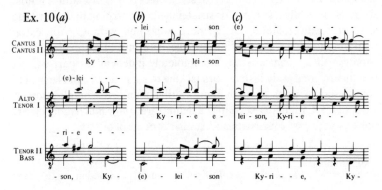

Monteverdi, used to the high level of unprepared dissonance in his *seconda prattica* madrigals, evidently finds it hard to manage the technique of conventional dissonance treatment and resorts to sequences as a solution (Ex. 10*c*).

This use of sequences gives rise to some of the clearest articulation in the Monteverdi mass. Though such a device might seem quite modern, and has no precedent in the music of Gombert (the continuous flow of which, as Tillman Merritt explains,[8] results from constant imitations), it was a composer even earlier than Gombert—Josquin Desprez—who made use of the sequence to preserve symmetry: an example of the device as he used it can be seen in Ex. 11:

Ex. 11. Josquin, *Missa Hercules Dux Ferrariae, Agnus*

Even so, sequences are on the whole a feature that further removes Monteverdi's music from the purity of Gombert's manner. His sequences are sometimes inspired by a strong feeling for modern tonality, especially at 'Domine Deus Agnus Dei' in the *Gloria* (Ex. 12*a*).

[8] A. Tillman Merritt, 'The Motet at the Time of Gombert', *Bulletin of the American Musicological Society*, vii (October 1943), 19. Ex. 11 is from *Missen*, ii, ed. Albert Smijers, Josquin des Prés: Werken (Leipzig, 1937), 38.

or they may be laid out with a vocal ornamentation typical of his madrigal style, as in *Agnus I(b)*:

Ex. 12

But unlike other important madrigal composers of the time, such as Wert, Vecchi and Marenzio, in their sacred music, Monteverdi did not allow the madrigalian idiom to influence his 1610 mass. Instead he put in a great amount of tiring work undergoing extensive studies to familiarize himself with an early style to which he was unsympathetic: in choosing that of Gombert, of all the Flemings, he displayed great discrimination.[9] Why should he choose Gombert as a model for a music that he hoped would be acceptable in Rome rather than the actual

[9] See Leo Schrade, *Monteverdi, Creator of Modern Music* (New York, 1950/ R1964), 249–50.

Roman music of the time? Firstly, because the collection of music at S. Barbara in Mantua contained motets by Gombert, but more significantly because this model would force him to adopt an old-fashioned style of greater contrapuntal purity. The 'subjects' of the motet *In illo tempore* were the very stuff of classical polyphony, and the six-part scoring was quite normal for *da cappella* music as Monteverdi would have known it in his youth. But the difficulties of composing the mass were immense, and the result is somewhat of a hotch-potch, not linked with anything else Monteverdi did, and falling short in several ways of being the perfect reincarnation of the music of the Netherlands master.[10]

A point that has been overlooked in the efforts of some writers to stress the modernity of the vespers psalms of Monteverdi's 1610 collection is that these psalms have at times a faint connection with the learned style of the mass: this can be seen from a comparison between 'et in Spiritum Sanctum' in the *Credo* and the 'Amen' of the psalm *Laudate pueri*:

Ex. 13

[10] For further discussion of the stylistic aspects of the 1610 mass, see Jeffrey G. Kurtzman, *Essays on the Monteverdi Mass and Vespers of 1610*, Rice University Studies, lxiv/4 (Houston, 1978), 47–68.

Likewise the vast polyphonic tuttis of the psalm *Nisi Dominus* are not at
all a 'modern' sound; they resemble parts of the Gombert mass in
texture, especially with their supernumerary syncopated inner parts.
The vespers psalms are not essentially ultra-progressive large-scale
church music like the later motets of Giovanni Gabrieli; they are rather
a synthesis between the boldness of Monteverdi's madrigal and operatic
writing (in *Orfeo*) and a late sixteenth-century type of *stile antico*. The
basic pull of styles can be witnessed in the way that the 'Amen' of
Laudate pueri is twisted back into a modern style by the intrusion of
sequences and then the florid duet manner.[11]

When he arrived in Venice to take up the post of *maestro di cappella* at
St. Mark's, Monteverdi was entrusted with the restoration of a 'canto
polifonico' which served to intensify his interest in what had by now
definitely become an old-fashioned church style.[12] As has already been
explained, the meaning of 'da cappella' was altering and becoming
more synonymous with 'stile antico'. It no longer signified merely the
type of ensemble required but implied a certain archaism of style as well.
The *stile antico* was now a deliberate phenomenon, in opposition to the
modern concertato style. The two four-part masses in the old style that
Monteverdi wrote during his Venetian period (1613–43) are more
natural and unforced than the Gombert mass: the four-part scoring is
now normal for the old style. Indeed, the publication by Giovanni
Francesco Anerio of Palestrina's *Missa Papae Marcelli* reduced to
four-part scoring[13] confirms that the six-part texture was becoming less
common. If colour and sonority were desired, the modern mixed vocal
and instrumental ensembles would provide it in the form of large-scale
music for big feasts. But for lesser Sundays or ferial days *stile antico*
masses filled the bill where the choir was still big enough to tackle them,
as in the larger churches of cathedral status. In these places the *stile
antico* was synonymous with an old-fashioned dignity, though lacking
the musical colour of Palestrina's style.

The Palestrinian polyphonic ideal inspires Monteverdi's *da cappella*
mass in the *Selva morale*[14] at the roots. If we compare it with a typical
Palestrina mass in four parts—the *Veni sponsa Christi* mass[15] is a good

[11] *Tutte le opere*, xiv/1, 168.
[12] Domenico De' Paoli, *Claudio Monteverdi* (Milan, 1945), 192.
[13] Recent Researches in the Music of the Baroque Era, xvi, ed. Hermann J.
Busch (Madison, 1973).
[14] Reprinted as an Eulenburg score, ed. Denis Arnold (London, 1962).
[15] *Palestrina, Le opere complete*, xxv, 30.

example of a fairly late work—we find that Monteverdi has the same
introduction of a point of imitation in pairs of voices: two parts state the
point in close canon, the other two following several bars later. Close
entry of all four parts is reserved for climaxes. Canzona-like points on
repeated notes (Ex. 14*a*), independent, harmonically angled bass lines
(Ex. 14*b*), the use of homophony at 'Et incarnatus' in the *Credo* and lively
triple time at 'Et resurrexit', and the greater smoothness of writing in the
Sanctus: all conform to the late Palestrina practice.

Ex. 14

(*a*)

(*b*)

But there are significant differences, of which the most important is
that Monteverdi is not in the least bit modal: in fact his mass is written in
an F major that is much more diatonic than the C major of the Gombert
mass. There is not one E flat in the whole work to suggest the
subdominant colouring, and only a few A major chords to hint at the
relative minor. Indeed the only point where a D minor feeling persists
for any length of time comes at 'Quoniam' in the *Gloria*, where it is
clearly ushered in by block chords:

Ex. 15

Monteverdi's rhythms are obsessively four-square, possessing none of
the suppleness of Palestrina's, where there are perpetual cross-accents
in individual lines. The start of the 'Crucifixus' is an instance of a
rhythmic interplay that is all too rare in Monteverdi's mass:

Ex. 16

This central part of the *Credo* lacks any of the pathos that its text
suggests, whereas Palestrina has melismas for 'Pilato' and a fine
descending 'passus' idea, with the soprano moving through an octave.
Again, Palestrina varies his *Sanctus* in the conventional manner, with a
tricinium at 'Pleni sunt' and a triple-time 'Osanna', but Monteverdi stays
in 4/4 and in four parts throughout, setting the 'Osanna' to yet another
statement of the cyclic theme which dominates the mass. Much of the
seconda prattica music that Monteverdi wrote during his Venetian period
shows his concern for thematic unity, but such a concern is somewhat
unnecessary in old-style polyphonic music: Palestrina, in the *Veni sponsa
Christi* mass, uses his cyclic theme only at the openings of movements,
and in the opening *Kyrie* has three different ideas treated in imitation.
Monteverdi's three sections of the *Kyrie* are, however, monothematic,
treating the ideas in various combinations in what is really a manner
more suited to the concertato idiom.

How does Monteverdi's four-part *Selva morale* mass compare with
other Italian masses in the *stile antico* for the same number of voices?
The only similarities between it and Felice Anerio's four-part mass[16]
(another typical contemporary Roman composition) consist in the short,
thwarted triple-time interjections in each *Gloria*:

Ex. 17

(*a*) Monteverdi

[16] Proske, ed., op. cit., i/1 (Regensburg, 1856), 35.

Ex. 17 cont.

(*b*) Anerio

Again, in the 'Amen' of the same movement, both have an interrupted-plus-perfect cadence:

Ex. 18

(*a*) Monteverdi

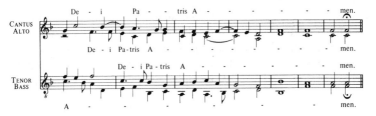

(*b*) Anerio

Monteverdi's endings are, however, curiously long-drawn-out, occasionally involving infelicitous harmony or awkward leaps. Anerio's mass is generally thicker in texture, reflecting the Roman interest in sonority. It has both the supple rhythms and the triple 'Osanna' movement of Palestrina, the former well exemplified in the opening of the work (Ex. 19*a*), where Anerio exercises a free approach to the duration of each note of the point, and in *Kyrie II*, where the canon is at a beat's distance (Ex. 19*b*):

Ex. 19

(a)

(b)

The important *prima prattica* composer in the north of Italy to whom
Monteverdi can be compared is Bernardi, whose mixed publication of
1615 has already been mentioned. His mass on *Praeparate corda vestra*[17]
(a contrafactum of his own madrigal *Quel rossignol, che si soave piange*) is
clearly in a modal D minor typical of the previous century, although the
harmonies at the end of the *Kyrie* and in the anguished 'Crucifixus' are
'affective':

Ex. 20

(a)

(b)

[17] Denkmäler der Tonkunst in Österreich, lxix, Jahrgang xxxvi/1, ed. K. A.
Rosenthal (Vienna, 1929), 1.

Ex. 20*b* cont.

Bernardi is again more interested in sonority than Monteverdi, using the four parts more continuously. His mass on Arcadelt's *Il bianco e dolce cigno* is a *missa brevis* in type, often chordal in the long movements; its tonality is not so obsessively F major as Monteverdi's, though it is perhaps more committed than that of Roman-school masses, so that a sudden A major chord at 'Et incarnatus' is very striking (this same point in Monteverdi's Gombert mass is marked by a mediant major chord). Here the 'Crucifixus' is a consciously Palestrina-like *tricinium*, more modal and polyphonic than the rest and showing how the old style in the rest of the mass had altered since about 1575. Despite its more old-fashioned sound, at least the conventional reduction in scoring is applied to this section of the *Credo*, whereas in the Monteverdi mass the music proceeds continuously in four parts. Although Bernardi did not completely succeed in capturing Palestrina's felicity of style, he showed a greater regard than Monteverdi for the true *stile antico* by avoiding four-square rhythms and by introducing modal colours into the tonality.

The third of Monteverdi's complete masses that survive, which was published posthumously by Vincenti in 1650 along with more modern-style psalm settings, is probably the finest *prima prattica* work of the whole early seventeenth century, and certainly Monteverdi's best.[18] For here he is, as it were, being himself and not trying desperately to be somebody else. If this results in the old style being compromised on all sides by the use of sequence, chromaticism, madrigalian part-writing and even occasional independence of the organ bass line, there is no cause for worry, since the music succeeds so much more than that of the other two masses. To couple this mass with the F major one and to assign both to 'the austere manner of Palestrina' is surely to do no justice to the vast difference between the two compositions. The F major mass is so austere that it bears less relation to Palestrina's music than some historians have perhaps imagined. On the other hand, the G minor

[18] Reprinted as an Eulenburg score, ed. Redlich (London, 1952).

mass, far from being a lifeless copy, constitutes a real reincarnation in seventeenth-century language of Palestrina's own intensity. Palestrina's restrained, mystical harmonic and rhythmic excitement is transformed, by a technical compromise of style, into the full-bloodedness to which seventeenth-century church-goers had become accustomed; still definitely *antico* in flavour yet having an immediacy relevant to the age; distinct in manner from the *seconda prattica*, yet with its own kind of up-to-date intensity. A strong characteristic of this mass is its consciously *thematic* musical development of a number of related ideas, of which the chromatic sequence figure that first occurs in the 'Christe' is the most striking.[19] The perfect use of the Dorian mode preserves the old spirit of Palestrina's modal colour; its E natural and associated harmonies are thrown into relief by the contradictory E flats in the chromatic sequence figure.

The madrigalian nature of some of the music can well be seen in the 'Christe', a perfectly balanced section opening and closing with the same succession of harmonies; it also uses the ornamental melismas of the madrigal style for the contrapuntal middle passage, at the start of which the imitation is treated by pairs of voices *à la* Palestrina. *Kyrie II* is concerned with sequences in many guises, including the lively cross-rhythms (bar 56) that were sadly lacking in the F major mass. In the *Gloria*, 'Qui tollis' (bar 32) has a madrigalian contrast of registers that can also be found in late Palestrina, followed by an imitative build-up to a homophonic climax at 'deprecationem nostram'. The 'Crucifixus' of the *Credo* has real pathos and respects the conventional reduction to three voices; the dovetailing of 'sepultus est' with the triple-time 'et resurrexit', though musically deft, makes rather strange sense of the text without the ritual pause to represent Christ's sojourn in the depths. Two passages show the middle Baroque feeling that sometimes comes out in the *Credo*: the varied triple time is much more advanced than in the old style (see Ex. 21). On the other hand Monteverdi's dissonance treatment is orderly and conventional. Most of the harmonic stringency is caused by typically sixteenth-century false relations, as at the heartfelt 'miserere' of the *Agnus Dei* (bar 16), which is characteristic of Monteverdi at his best. The use of sequence is in complete harmony with the overall style, not conflicting with its purity as in the Gombert mass. The G minor mass represents the real *prima*

[19] For a discussion of this aspect of the work, see Reginald Smith Brindle, 'Monteverdi's G minor Mass: an Experiment in Construction', *Musical Quarterly*, liv (1968), 352.

Ex. 21

(a)

(b)

prattica Monteverdi, borrowing from a *da cappella* manner of which he had had genuine experience in his early madrigals.

We are now left with the five *de cappella* psalm settings, three in the *Selve morale* of 1641 and two in the posthumous 1650 publication.[20] The three double-choir psalms pose special problems, while the other two are more comparable with the masses in their scoring. The four-part *Magnificat* from the *Selva morale* is a conventional *alternatim* psalm (polyphonic verses alternating with plainsong ones) in what would have been bold polyphony for the late sixteenth century. The *nota cambiata* figures at 'deposuit' (Ex. 22a) are very similar to the setting of 'reges' in the *Dixit Dominus* of the 1610 Vespers (Ex. 22b), again showing how Monteverdi unwittingly absorbed the traits of the *prima prattica* into his earlier concertato church music:

Ex. 22

(a)

[20] These five works can be found in *Tutte le opere* as follows: *Credidi*, xv/2, 544; *Memento*, xv/2, 567; *Magnificat*, xv/2, 703; *Dixit*, xvi, 94; *Laudate pueri*, xvi, 211.

Ex. 22 cont.

Besides a more lively rhythmic life than the F major mass, the *Magnificat* has added musical variety through its alternation with plainsong. The intermittent working of a plainsong *cantus firmus* into the top part is more convincing. It is also more consistent with the practice of the previous century than his attempt to graft it on to *seconda prattica* music, as in the 1610 Vespers, where its use militates against modernity of style. This *Magnificat* could well have been written early in Monteverdi's Venetian period, for there is little of the compromise with seventeenth-century idiom that we find in the G minor mass, nor indeed in the five-part *Laudate pueri* from the posthumous publication. The latter is a through-composed, not an alternating, psalm setting: sequences, bolder word-painting, homophony, sectionalization by well-defined pauses, and fine textural crescendos are well in evidence (Ex. 23*a*), though a slight archaism is maintained by the fact that the motifs are not in a thoroughly concertato vein. The 'Amen' sequences (Ex. 23*b*) are notably like those at the end of the *Gloria* of the G minor mass, with the written-out ritenuto implied in the decrease of movement.

Both the mass and the *Laudate pueri* seem to belong to the same creative period of Monteverdi's life, probably a late one: they show a maturity of invention, and a coming-to-terms with a *da cappella* idiom that he made his own—a genuine re-interpretation of the *prima prattica*.

Of the three *cori spezzati* psalm settings, the *Credidi* in the *Selva morale* is in a staid sixteenth-century Venetian manner, with much block chordal writing, syncopated entries and a lively triple-time 'Gloria Patri'. No plainsong *cantus firmus* is used except at the beginning in the top part, where it answers the plainsong intonation. Printed immediately following this is a setting of *Memento*, which has a crotchet rather than a minim tactus but is otherwise similar to the *Credidi*. Both use a *coro grave*

Ex. 23

(*a*)

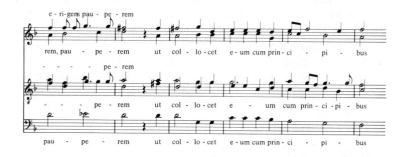

(*b*)

(ATTB) for the second choir; neither is really *prima prattica* music in the polyphonic sense. They are conceived in the lively double-choir style of the late sixteenth century, which is very close in spirit to the modern manner in all features except the use of soloists and was being used for non-concertato psalms by several lesser composers (such as Bellazzi, Leoni and Girelli) as late as the 1620s. The transition from this style to concertato was very smooth, although different cities had reached different stages along it. Girelli's psalms of 1620 include both *da cappella* and concertato settings, but apart from the use of soloists in the latter pieces the musical ethos of the two types is much the same in double-choir music. In music for single choir, both masses and psalms, two distinct idioms could coexist, especially in Venice; not only Monteverdi, but also Rovetta and Rigatti, included *da cappella* psalms in their publications of 1626 and 1640 respectively. Even so, not all these psalms are as entirely alien in conception to the seventeenth century as Monteverdi's first two masses seem to be.

Monteverdi shows himself to be a master of double-choir writing in the *da cappella Dixit* of the 1651 publication (marked 'alla breve'). The style is rendered more expressive by chromatic alterations ('confregit' and 'conquassabit'), contrasts between long and short notes, and harmonic chromaticism:

Ex. 24

Monteverdi is clearly much more imaginative with the forces at his disposal than the lesser church composers. Certainly these three double-choir psalms cannot be assigned to the *prima prattica*, although they are called *da cappella*, because the latter term is here used in the sense understood by Praetorius: it signifies the type of ensemble required, not the style in which the work is conceived, which, as we have seen, is not necessarily archaic in *cori spezzati* music. In single-choir music, however, the term became identified with *stile antico*, or indeed *prima prattica*. These signify any style that has its roots in the single-choir polyphony of the sixteenth century, used in deliberate antithesis to modern idioms by church composers from the time of Monteverdi's Gombert mass onwards. Monteverdi's own works show the various old styles that it was possible to select. He was surely the only composer to write in such divergent idioms with such unparalleled versatility: in this connection the interpolations for the *Credo* of the F major mass, also published in the *Selva morale*, are of great interest. Monteverdi, or rather his printer, indicates that these three short pieces may be inserted in place of the original settings of the relevant part of the text. All three are *seconda prattica* in conception: the 'Crucifixus' section is inspired by Monteverdi's madrigalian manner and is smoother than the more brilliant concertato of the 'Et resurrexit' and 'et iterum' sections, which are in the most up-to-date church style. Although to some ears all three might be stylistically incompatible with the mass itself,[21] a performance which included them could well make better music if only because of the much-needed element of variety introduced. The keys of the interpolations (D minor and C) are nicely related to the F major of the mass. It is quite possible that Monteverdi originally wrote the mass for a festive occasion (such as the thanksgiving for relief from the plague in 1631) and to be performed not only with the *Credo* interpolations but also with the magnificent *Gloria a 7*. The latter is printed *before* the interpolations in the *Selva morale*, suggesting that it too could be used instead of the original *Gloria* on special occasions. It was quite consistent with the practice of the day to mix styles of liturgical music within one service. The inventories of choir music in northern Italy, which contain modern motets but no modern masses, testify that concertato motets were often sung during masses in which the Ordinary was rendered in *stile antico*.[22] Today this idea is perpetuated in, for

---

[21] For example, Denis Stevens argues, in his *Monteverdi: Sacred, Secular and Occasional Music* (Cranbury, N.J., and London, 1978), 70, that they belong to a complete *Credo* whose tutti parts were mislaid.

[22] See also the fact that several composers wrote in different idioms for different forces or kinds of music; e.g., Frescobaldi wrote *antico* masses but up-to-date organ music, and Francesco Turini, who also wrote old-style masses (in his publication of 1643), wrote progressive church sonatas and canzonas.

example, the Anglican cathedral service, with responses, anthems, services and voluntaries drawn from different periods of music.

The mixing of styles in one movement—such as would happen if these *Credo* interpolations were sung—can be seen in the ceremonial mass of 1639 by Monteverdi's disciple Rovetta, where in a generally modern-sounding *Credo* there is a reversion to the *stile antico* at 'Et in Spiritum Sanctum'—the precise point where Monteverdi's modern insertions finish. This duality of style has already been discussed in relation to Monteverdi's vespers psalms of 1610, and it still persists in some of the other *Selva morale* music. The large setting of the *Magnificat*[23] has odd moments of old-style part writing:

Ex. 25

It seems to have been a chracteristic of Baroque church music generally to have included passages in a more learned, contrapuntal idiom than the rest of the music: this can be seen in Carissimi and Vivaldi, and it persists, indeed, in some of Haydn's earlier masses. Once the *stile antico* had become a deliberate phenomenon, its shadow could haunt composers whose work was otherwise 'modern' in manner.

[23] *Tutte le opere*, xv/2, 639. The missing parts in choir II are restored in the Novello edition by Denis Stevens and John Steele (Borough Green, Sevenoaks, 1969).

Monteverdi and the *seconda prattica*

i: MONODY

In his secular vocal music Monteverdi presents an apparent paradox. Here was an enthusiastic advocate of the *seconda prattica*, none more so, who constantly strove to illuminate and project words through music of the utmost expressiveness and who never bothered to write instrumental works at all. Yet he wrote very few solo songs at a time when song was so obvious a medium for the dissemination of the new style that after about 1600 it attracted all the Italian composers who shared his progressive humanist views, in some cases to the exclusion of all other music. Instead of writing songs Monteverdi first of all remained faithful to polyphonic madrigals. But even before he adopted the basso continuo in his fifth book he tended more and more to break up the traditional texture into smaller groups and to make the movement more discontinuous; this process was hastened in his continuo madrigals, in which he could also include contrasting solo sections; and in his later years it developed so radically that publications such as the seventh and ninth books of madrigals are packed with duets and trios that are really no longer madrigals at all.

The present chapter offers a survey of Monteverdi's songs in the context of the songs of the period and also shows how his operatic lament of Ariadne prompted other composers to write laments, the only type of song in which his influence as a song-writer can significantly be seen. The next chapter follows on from this. Its purpose is to show that by reacting as he did—by preferring ensemble music to monody—Monteverdi was probably indulging his love of sonorous textures not only for their own sake but also because they helped him to another of his chief concerns: the creation of satisfying large-scale forms that could also be enhanced by tonal contrasts. Some of his best monodies show the same tendencies, especially the convincing form that so many by lesser men fatally lack.

Hundreds of solo songs—or monodies, as they are often called—were published in Italy in the first four decades of the seventeenth century, the product of one of the most insistent crazes in the history of music.[1] Their two principal forms were still those of the ensemble music of the later sixteenth century: through-composed madrigals, which were particularly popular at first, and strophic forms such as aria and canzonetta. The epoch-making collection *Le nuove musiche* (1602) by Giulio Caccini, which decisively inaugurated the vogue, is prefaced by a long essay in which Caccini emphasizes the novelty of his songs, the madrigals in particular.[2] The words, he claims, are all-important. Solo performance with an accompanying instrument playing simple chords means that all the words can be clearly heard: this, he found, never happened in polyphonic madrigals. He was introducing 'a kind of music in which one could almost speak in tones';[3] the result is an arioso vocal line midway between the recitative of opera and the rhythmically defined tunes of arias. The sovereignty of the words demands that the music be sung in free time, and the more emotive ones are heightened by all manner of subtle embellishments. Caccini is acting here as polemical spokesman for the Camerata, the group of Florentine noblemen, thinkers, poets and musicians who from about 1570 forcefully argued the superior qualities of monodic music. He was also a singer, and singers such as Jacopo Peri (in Florence, like Caccini) and Francesco Rasi (at Mantua, like Monteverdi) were prominent among the composers who before long published monodies. They undoubtedly sang them themselves, an incentive to their composition denied to Monteverdi, who was not a singer.

Amateurs—both noblemen, like Claudio Saracini, and those who, like Domenico Maria Megli and Piero Benedetti, followed other professions—were another sort of men who quickly took to writing monodies. It is quite likely that professional composers of Monteverdi's generation who had had a hard grounding in the intricacies of polyphony considered monodies beneath them, because they were so 'easy' to write as to be within the powers of the dilettante and the part-time composer. Here, then, is another possible reason for Monteverdi's comparative indifference. It may be significant that the eminent theorist Giovanni Battista Doni, who championed monody, felt it necessary to ask, through rather a specious analogy, if it were really easier to paint a nude

---

[1] Nigel Fortune, 'A Handlist of Printed Italian Secular Monody Books, 1600–1635', *R.M.A. Research Chronicle*, iii (1963), 27.
[2] Translated in Giulio Caccini, *Le nuove musiche*, ed. H. Wiley Hitchcock, Recent Researches in the Music of the Baroque Era, ix (Madison, 1970), 43.
[3] Ibid., 44.

than a clothed body[4] and that even the best composers of vocal music born shortly after Monteverdi—Marco da Gagliano (born 1582) and Sigismondo d'India (born *c*. 1582)—though sympathetic to the 'new music' still composed more ensemble madrigals than songs in the heyday of monody. Gesualdo (born *c*. 1561) wrote no monodies at all, though he lived until 1613.

Solo arias were at first less self-consciously canvassed as 'new'. The meticulous expression of emotive words here yielded, in Caccini's phrase, to 'the sprightliness of song, as usually conveyed by the air itself',[5] and indeed many of their texts have been aptly summed up as amorous baby-talk. Some of Caccini's arias, however, are more serious and in mood are rather like strophic madrigals. In one or two he hinted at the technique of strophic variation, in which the vocal line varies from verse to verse over a more or less unchanged bass. This form proved to be a fruitful one for several later composers, especially in Rome, and with the bass moving briskly in crotchets it also characterized the earliest pieces to be called cantatas: these were published in the 1620s by Venetians such as Alessandro Grandi and Giovanni Pietro Berti, who worked under Monteverdi at St. Mark's.[6]

Only some fifteen monodies attributed to Monteverdi survive, and it is perhaps not surprising that five or six of them have overtones from the world of opera, where he was obviously so much at home. Nor is it surprising, in view of his preoccupation with formal unity, that in five songs he adopted the principle of strophic variation. Of the others, only one is a madrigal, and that for quite exceptional forces; one—possibly not authentic—is a lament (of Olympia), which, like Monteverdi's other laments, whether lost or in his last operas, doubtless stemmed from the immense success of his lament in *Arianna*; two are somewhat austere recitatives belonging to the genre of the *lettera amorosa* or musical love-letter (one of them originally called *partenza amorosa*); another, *Voglio di vita uscir*, is a suave and rounded aria, significantly (if it *is* by Monteverdi) founded on the strict form of the chaconne bass;[7] and six

[4] See Giovanni Battista Doni, *Compendio del trattato de' generi e de' modi della musica* (Rome, 1635), 124.

[5] *Le nuove musiche*, ed. Hitchcock, 50.

[6] See Fortune, 'Solo Song and Cantata', *New Oxford History of Music*, iv (London, 1968), 172–4.

[7] This aria and the lament of Olympia do not appear in Gian Francesco Malipiero's complete edition but may be found in *Monteverdi: 12 composizioni vocali profane e sacre (inedite)*, ed. Wolfgang Osthoff (Milan, 1958), 18 and 10 respectively. While the lament is quite possibly genuine Monteverdi, I have

are simple canzonettas. Hundreds of canzonettas, most of them in triple time, poured from the Venetian printing-presses in cheap books from 1618 onwards, and so popular were they that Monteverdi, the greatest musician in Venice, could hardly avoid writing a few, even if he rather despised them. But he left it to other men to publish them for him; indeed the only solo songs he bothered to see through the press himself are the four in the seventh book of madrigals.

It is worth looking at a few of these songs to see how far they reflect Monteverdi's principal preoccupations. His refusal to write convention-al solo madrigals is extremely pointed, for they were the monodists' favourite fare before being quickly superseded after about 1618 by the passion for canzonettas and arias. Since their non-strophic poems seemed to afford few opportunities for refrain-like repetitions, composers found it difficult to impose formal order on their madrigals; since, moreover, polyphony could no longer be used to conceal perfect cadences, continuity as often eluded them; and the amorphous and halting music that frequently resulted could no longer be enlivened by textural contrasts, which were beyond the power of a single voice and a neutral instrumental background to provide. Monteverdi was therefore perhaps unimpressed by whatever solo madrigals he knew. It is noteworthy that the masterly *Lamento d'Arianna* in its original solo version in the opera was interrupted from time to time by a chorus of fishermen (whose music is lost)[8] and is unified by reprises of two intensely despairing phrases which have a strong 'personal' quality on the lips of one who by that stage in the work (Scene 6) must have been established as a compelling tragic character.

There are over 50 pieces in the three madrigal-books Monteverdi brought out—in 1605, 1614 and 1619—during the first wave of enthusiasm for monody, and the only solo madrigal among them is *Con che soavità* (1619).[9] The poem is a typical amorous conceit by Giovanni Battista Guarini in praise of the beloved's lips as the source of both sweet words and kisses. Any other composer would have set it straightforwardly for the usual forces without worrying about problems of form and texture. But Monteverdi, possibly prompted in the first

---

[8] See J. A. Westrup, 'Monteverdi's "Lamento d'Arianna" ', *Music Review*, i (1940), 147.
[9] *Tutte le opere*, vii, 137.

---

reservations about the aria, which I am not otherwise considering in this chapter.

place by the seductive words, accompanied his soprano with three instrumental 'choirs', whose clefs are those favoured by Giovanni Gabrieli and other composers in polychoral works. The first is a continuo ensemble of two chitarroni, harpsichord and spinet; the second consists of three stringed instruments and harpsichord; and the third is a darker-hued string trio with an unspecified continuo instrument. From its scoring, the piece could be an offshoot from *Orfeo*; possibly it was written for the Accademia degli Invaghiti shortly after they had staged the opera. The movement of the vocal line is nicely varied between gently moving arioso and more rhythmic writing and is unusual in being almost entirely unornamented; the harmonic rhythm, too, is unusually slow, no doubt so that the instrumental sonorities could be heard to advantage. Monteverdi opens his setting with his first group of instruments. When the movement becomes livelier he adds his second group after half-a-bar's rest, and these upper strings tend to be used throughout to underscore the more incisive rhythms in the vocal part with a 'biting' homophonic texture. In his setting of the last seven lines of the poem he makes even more telling structural use of his instrumental forces. This is the text:

> Che soave armonia
> Fareste, O cari baci,
> Che soave armonia
> Fareste, O dolci detti,
> Se foste unitamente
> D'ambedue le dolcezze ambo capaci,
> Baciando i detti e ragionando i baci!

(What sweet harmony you would make, O beloved kisses, and you, O sweet words, if you were both together capable of both sweetnesses, words kissing and kisses speaking!)

At the important first pair of lines Monteverdi first of all brings in his third instrumental group for the first time, again after a half-bar's rest, and immediately adds the other two to reinforce a long-held note on 'O' with the first sound of his complete ensemble; he repeats all this a tone higher for the next matching pair of lines. He also uses his instrumental groups to organize his extended setting of the last three lines: he reserves his full ensemble for the idea of 'both together' and accompanies four statements of the final line with the first two groups in turn before again bringing everyone in for the last two repetitions of it. The exceptional length of the piece is entirely consistent with the size of the 'orchestra', which wonderfully illuminates the sentiments of the poem.

In the first of his strophic variations, *Tempro la cetra* (also from Book VII),[10] Monteverdi once again added rich instrumental sonorities to a conventional vocal form, which he had previously used in the better-known prologue to *Orfeo*. The instruments are an unspecified quintet with continuo. The poem opposes images of love and war, a theme that Monteverdi was of course to develop in his later madrigals; it is by Giambattista Marino, who, with Guarini, was the poet most often set by the early seventeenth-century monodists. The setting has something in common with the great song 'Possente spirto' in Act III of *Orfeo*,[11] especially in its still, portentous atmosphere and in the way the vocal embellishments become more elaborate from verse to verse as the variations unfold over the unchanging bass. The four verses are separated by a ritornello, which is the last of the three six-bar phrases of an introductory sinfonia; this sinfonia is also heard twice at the end, where, with a contrasting central dance, it forms a satisfying ternary structure that provides a fine culmination to the song. Certain structural and stylistic features of this work, and the inclusion in it of a dance, suggest affinities with stage music by Monteverdi, not only parts of *Orfeo* but one or two of the shorter works—notably the *ballo Movete al mio bel suon*[12]— and strongly suggest that *Tempro la cetra* too was conceived for stage performance.[13]

It was to be expected that Monteverdi would continue to employ a form in which the bass was so powerful a force for formal unity. Three more examples appear in the *Scherzi musicali* of 1632, a small collection mainly of solo songs assembled by the publisher Bartolomeo Magni almost as if he thought it about time so important a composer as Monteverdi had a few more songs in print. The best of them is *Et è pur dunque vero*,[14] in which variations appear over two basses, each heard seven times: one underpins the vocal sections, the other a ritornello whose varying melody is entrusted to a single unnamed instrument. The music of the seven verses has the characteristic madrigalian movement of strophic variations, and there is room for 'madrigalisms' such as the chromatic cadence expressing the jilted lover's tears, a clash of C natural

---

[10] Ibid., 1. 　　　　　　　　　　[11] *Tutte le opere*, xi, 84.

[12] *Tutte le opere*, viii, 157.

[13] For a penetrating comparative analysis, see Reinhard Strohm, 'Osservazioni su "Tempro la cetra" ', *Rivista italiana di musicologia*, ii (1967), 357.

[14] *Tutte le opere*, x, 82.

and C sharp for his torments, and slurred quavers for the murmuring of breezes. The brisk crotchet-and-quaver movement of the bass of the ritornello approaches the 'walking' bass usually found in the earliest strophic-bass cantatas. Monteverdi wrote one of these too, possibly the most distinguished of all, *Ohimè, ch'io cado*;[15] it appeared in either 1623 or 1624 in the *Quarto scherzo delle ariose vaghezze* of the minor composer Carlo Milanuzzi, who was then working in Venice. There are six verses, each preceded by the same short ritornello, of which we have only the bass. As in most strophic-bass cantatas,[16] the strict and steady progress of the bass, which moves almost entirely in crotchets, precludes the use of expansive 'madrigalisms'. But such a bass obviously acted as a challenge to Monteverdi, who triumphantly succeeded in devising over it six different melodies with the same general character, though there are here and there similarities in the lines from verse to verse. Ex. 1 shows the opening bars of each verse:

Ex. 1

Unless manuscript copies have not survived, Monteverdi must have been unwilling to develop his gifts as a writer of independent songs even in the 1620s when strophic songs were all the rage in Venice; but

[15] *Tutte le opere*, ix, 111.
[16] See the example by Berti given by Fortune, 'Solo Song and Cantata', 173-4.

he was kept very busy in St. Mark's and wrote a great deal of stage music, most of which is lost. He wrote no more strophic-bass cantatas and played no part in transforming the simple canzonetta into the rounded and sensuous triple-time aria, as junior associates such as Berti did with such success. However, we have of course the arias in his last operas, and the duet *Zefiro torna*, discussed in the next chapter, is to some extent a piece of this new kind. Monteverdi's six strophic songs are all quite simple, though one or two unusual, less simple features disrupt the innocuous tunes and tripping rhythms. For instance, he sets the last verse of *Più lieto il guardo*[17] as a recitative presumably because the words seemed to demand it, a step analogous to the contemporary development of the recitative and aria; and it was a madrigalian touch, for rather madrigalian words, to prolong and retard with chromatic minims the refrain 'languendo moro' of *La mia turca*.[18] Once at least, with the charming throw-away tune of *Maledetto*,[19] Monteverdi rivals the more self-conscious purveyors of tunes on their own ground, and the asymmetrical phrases and ternary form show that he could not help bringing craftsmanship and imagination to even the humblest task. But we may well wonder whether Monteverdi's lack of interest in arias and canzonettas, so conspicuously at odds with the musical climate in which he lived, was not connected with a dominant impression one gets from his work as a whole: that he was less interested in self-consciously melodic writing than in dramatic impact, form and texture; and it could have been this that kept him writing duets rather than monodies in his middle and later years. One instance should not be made to bear too much weight, but his setting of Gabriello Chiabrera's poem *Damigella* in the *Scherzi musicali* of 1607 and that by the minor Florentine Vincenzo Calestani illustrate succinctly the difference between an apt, quite attractive tune and a really catchy one and at the same time seem to sum up the difference between Monteverdi's attitude to tunes and those of a host of lesser contemporaries (see Ex. 20). It might of course be added that no great composer before this period had ever seen it as a main part of his function to write self-conscious tunes. As the first great composer influenced by the new 'harmonic' approach to

[17] *Tutte le opere*, xvii, 22; it was first published in *Arie de' diversi*, ed. Alessandro Vincenti (1634).
[18] *Tutte le opere*, ix, 117; it was first published in Milanuzzi's *Quarto scherzo* referred to above.
[19] *Tutte le opere*, x, 76.

Ex. 2[20]

(a)

Da-mi - gel - la Tut-ta bel - la, Ver -sa, ver - sa quel bel vi - no; Fa che ca - da La ru -

gia - da Dis-til - la - ta di ru - bi - no!

(b)

Da-mi - gel - la Tut-ta bel - la, Ver-sa, ver - sa quel bel vi - no; Fa che ca - da La ru -

gia - da Dis-til - la - ta di ru - bi - no!

composition. Monteverdi did so more readily than his forerunners. But Purcell is the first great master in the history of music whom we value as highly for his melodic gifts as for any other quality.

The two *lettere amorose*—*Se i languidi miei sguardi* and *Se pur destina* (strictly *partenza amorosa*)—have never been among Monteverdi's most admired compositions and are hardly ever performed. They are unusually long stretches of the kind of recitative devised by the Florentines for the earliest operas and rarely found outside operas before the Venetians developed the pairing of recitative and aria in their songs of the 1620s; and in these songs the recitatives are generally short. Monteverdi describes the *lettere* as being 'in genere rappresentativo', a definition that he and his contemporaries normally reserved for stage music: they can perhaps be seen as studies

[20] See respectively ibid., 40, and Vincenzo Calestani, *Madrigali et arie* (Venice, 1617), 35.

demonstrating the potential of this style.[21] It is worth noting that they
are settings of prose and that their vocal range is unemotionally
narrow. Schrade probably exaggerates when he says that the style of
the pieces was 'rather generally disapproved of by composers'[22] by
1619, since they reappeared in print in 1623 and several other *lettere
amorose* were printed between 1618 and 1633. These may well have
been written in emulation of Monteverdi's: even Biagio Marini, who
published one in his *Madrigali e symfonie* of 1618, may have known
Monteverdi's pieces in manuscript or have heard them. Since they
appeared in the print of 1623 only with the *Lamento d'Arianna*, then, as
now, Monteverdi's most famous piece, it might be inferred that they
also were included as being among his most popular works and not
simply as makeweights; however, they were his only songs for voice
and continuo available in print to the publisher Magni, and they are
mentioned on the title-page in type far smaller than that announcing
the lament. But they certainly made an impression on at least one
composer, Filippo Vitali, who published one of his own in 1629, when
he was probably living in Florence: it is headed in terms almost
identical with Monteverdi's and appears in a publication with the same
title, *Concerto*, as the one (the seventh book of madrigals) in which
Monteverdi's *lettere* were first printed. Monteverdi clearly took some
trouble over these pieces: he continually varies his pace, judiciously
repeats short phrases and is not afraid to introduce expressive roulades
at one or two cadences.

Monteverdi's *lettere*, then, may have given impetus to a rather
specialized sort of monody. There can be no doubt at all that the
resounding fame of the great lament of Ariadne initiated a more
rewarding kind of song, which enjoyed undiminished popularity
throughout the seventeenth century and beyond, and in other countries
besides Italy: before very long no opera was thought to be complete
without its lament, and a number of composers wrote chamber laments
vividly portraying the predicaments of those same characters—Dido,
Olympia, Jason—whose tragic stories dominated so many Baroque
operas. Although it was never published, *Arianna* was repeatedly
admired by eye-witnesses, composers, poets and theorists, whereas
Orfeo, published twice, was hardly discussed in print at all. It was clearly

[21] See Claudio Gallico, 'La "Lettera amorosa" di Monteverdi e lo stile
rappresentativo', *Nuova rivista musicale italiana*, i (1967), 287.
[22] Leo Schrade, *Monteverdi, Creator of Modern Music* (New York, 1950/R1964),
291.

Ariadne's lament that prompted these people to enthusiasm: for most of them the rest of the score need hardly have existed. Alas, for us it does not; but at least the activities of opportunist publishers and eager scribes ensured that we have six copies of the solo sections of the lament.

It is worth indicating briefly the enormous impact of this piece. It was published twice in 1623, as well as in Monteverdi's *Selva morale* in 1640 (with sacred words) and in his five-part arrangement in 1614. At least four composers produced their own less striking settings, Severo Bonini and Francesco Costa monodic ones in publications of 1613 and 1626 respectively, and Giulio Cesare Antonelli and Antonio Il Verso five-part ones, the former in Mantua in a manuscript that can perhaps be dated about 1611,[23] the latter in his fourteenth book of five-part madrigals in far-off Palermo in 1619. Also in Palermo in 1619 Claudio Pari entitled his fourth book of five-part madrigals *Il lamento d'Arianna*[24] after the opening work, a cycle of twelve madrigals; only parts of it are settings of the words by Rinuccini that Monteverdi set, but the musical debt to Monteverdi's lament is apparent. Marino wrote his own *Lamento d'Arianna, Misera, e chi m'ha tolto*, of which Pellegrino Possenti published a monodic setting in 1623 together with a fulsome eulogy of Monteverdi. Marino also refers to the original in his long poem *Adone* (vii, 68). Bonini, writing some thirty years after he tried to emulate Monteverdi as a composer, says that no musical household lacked its copy of the lament and refers to the 'peregrini vezzi' ('rare charms') in *Arianna*,[25] a phrase similar to one already used of it in 1620 by Vitali in the preface to his opera *Aretusa*.[26] Gagliano's preface to his *Dafne* (1608) reveals a fellow-composer's first flush of enthusiasm.[27] For Doni, writing about stage music, the lament was 'forse la più bella Composizione che sia stata fatta a' tempi nostri in questo genere' ('perhaps the most beautiful composition of our time in this field').[28]

---

[23] See Guglielmo Barblan, 'Un ignoto "Lamento d'Arianna" mantovano', *Rivista italiana di musicologia*, ii (1967), 217.

[24] *Musiche rinascimentali siciliane*, i, ed. Paolo Emilio Carapezza (Rome, 1970), with a substantial introduction.

[25] See Severo Bonini, *Prima parte de Discorsi e regole sopra la musica*, Florence, Biblioteca Riccardiana, MS 2218; trans. and ed. MaryAnn Bonino (Provo, Utah, 1979), 151.

[26] Reprinted in Emil Vogel, *Bibliothek der gedruckten weltlichen Vocalmusik Italiens* (repr. Hildesheim, 1962), ii, 332; the reference is omitted from *Il nuovo Vogel*.

[27] Reprinted in ibid., i, 265; again the reference is omitted from *Il nuovo Vogel*.

[28] Doni, *Trattato della musica scenica*, chap. ix, printed in his *De' trattati di musica*, ed. Antonio Francesco Gori (Florence, 1763), ii, 25.

Esteban Arteaga was still talking about it in 1783, likening its fame in its
day to that of Pergolesi's *La serva padrona* in his own.[29] Nor do these
references exhaust the catalogue. Mention should be made too of
laments by other composers clearly inspired by Monteverdi's example.
The finest are undoubtedly five by d'India, two published in 1621 and
three in 1623. They represent probably the most fruitful influence of
Monteverdi on any composer of the time and are worthy companions to
Monteverdi's own laments.[30] Another of the best monodists, Saracini,
published in his *Le seconde musiche* in 1620 not only a *Lamento della
Madonna* of Monteverdian cast but also an intensely sombre madrigal,
Udite, lagrimosi spirti d'Averno, which he dedicated to Monteverdi.[31]
There is another fine arioso lament, *Le lagrime d'Erminia*, in the
Madrigali concertati of 1629 by Giovanni Rovetta, Monteverdi's deputy
at St. Mark's. In the 1630s the number of laments increases, if anything.
They now tend to become aria-like pieces and are often built on ground
basses, the start of a tradition that was later to embrace, in Purcell's
lament of Dido, the only lament seriously to challenge the supremacy of
Monteverdi's great original. Many years later, a cantata, *Lasciatemi
morire*, by the contralto Francesco Maria Rascarini (died 1706) begins
with a clear evocation of Monteverdi's lament.[32]

Monteverdi was no doubt pressed for sequels. We know that in 1610
he intended the five-part version of the *Lamento d'Arianna* to form a
trilogy of laments with *Incenerite spoglie* and a setting of Marino's lament
of Hero and Leander. The first of these other two pieces is the one he
wrote in memory of Caterina Martinelli, who had she lived would have
sung the part of Ariadne, and he published it with Ariadne's lament in
his sixth book of madrigals;[33] either he did not finish the Marino lament
or it has been lost.[34] Of solo laments we have some magnificent examples

[29] See Esteban Arteaga, *Le rivoluzioni del teatro musicale italiano*, i (Bologna,
   1783), 254–5.
[30] See Fortune, 'Sigismondo d'India, an Introduction to his Life and Works',
   Proceedings of the Royal Musical Association, lxxxi (1954–5), 41–4. Also see
   above, 116. D'India's laments of Jason and Dido are printed in John J.
   Joyce, *The Monodies of Sigismondo d'India* (Ann Arbor, 1981), Musical
   Supplement, Nos. 11 and 16 respectively.
[31] Facsimile reprint of the complete volume (Siena, 1933); the two pieces are at
   pp. 25 and 1 respectively. The whole of the second piece and extracts from the
   first ed. in Robert Haas, *Die Musik des Barocks* (Potsdam, 1928), 53–5. For
   further discussion of Saracini's laments, see above, 115–16.
[32] See *The New Grove*, xv, 591.
[33] *Tutte le opere*, vi, 46.
[34] See Don Bassano Casola's letter to Cardinal Ferdinando Gonzaga, printed in

in the last operas, those of Penelope in *Il ritorno d'Ulisse* and Octavia in
L'incoronazione di Poppea,[35] and we have lost those of Apollo and Armida
of which we read in Monteverdi's letters.[36] We also have the little-known
Lamento d'Olimpia in a manuscript in the hand of Luigi Rossi, composer
to the Borghese family. As mentioned above, it is not certain that this
lament is by Monteverdi, but Osthoff plausibly suggests that he could
have written it for the great contralto Adriana Basile, who lived at
Mantua between 1610 and 1624 and who had connections in Rome with
Cardinal Scipione Borghese. Like so many sequels, the *Lamento
d'Olimpia* falls short of its model. But it is still a compelling work which
owes a good deal to its predecessor in text and organization, and even
in musical invention, as Ex. 3 shows. Here we see the opening of each
lament, (*a*) Ariadne's, (*b*) Olympia's, and also (*c*) that of a madrigal from
d'India's third book of *Musiche* (1618) to give an idea of the powerful
impression that Monteverdi's 'peregrini vezzi' must have made on a
responsive spirit:[37]

Ex. 3

(*a*)

(*b*)

[35] See *Tutte le opere*, xii, 14, and xiii, 49 and 229, respectively. Also see below,
Jane Glover, 'The Venetian Operas', *passim.*
[36] See above, 37, 39–40, 43, 76 and 80.
[37] Respectively *Tutte le opere*, xi, 161; *Monteverdi, 12 composizioni*, ed. Osthoff, 10;
and Sigismondo d'India, *Le musiche . . . libro terzo* (Milan, 1618), 6.

Vogel, 'Claudio Monteverdi', *Vierteljahrsschrift für Musikwissenschaft*, iii
(1887), 430.

Ex. 3 cont.

The common feature here is a drooping cadential figure, and so Monteverdi, in Olympia's lament as in Ariadne's, is able quite naturally to return to it at cadences as a unifying motif. In Olympia's lament we again see him building up tension through a mounting series of repeated notes:

Ex. 4[38]

The emotional and structural power of a tiny fragment repeated in a different melodic context can also be well illustrated at the more relaxed start of the third and last section:

Ex. 5[39]

---

[38] Osthoff, ed., op. cit., 11.   [39] Ibid., 16.

In most of his songs we have seen that Monteverdi exploits as far as he can at least one of the features that dominate so much of his music: dramatic possibilities, contrasts of texture, highly organized form. We can now go on to see in the next chapter how much truer this is of the music he wrote as he gradually transformed the traditional madrigal into the concertato textures so typical of the new century.

Monteverdi and the *seconda prattica*

ii: FROM MADRIGAL TO DUET

The tremendous popularity of monodies in Monteverdi's day is evident
from the great quantities printed and from the remarks of theorists and
of composers in their prefaces. However, at least 450 volumes of
ensemble madrigals appeared in the seventeenth century, and it would
be easy to assemble a rival anthology of observations pointing to their
continued popularity in the face of competition from monodies.[1] As one
would expect, they seem at first to have been favoured by older
composers and no doubt by people who preferred to sing themselves
rather than listen to professional soloists; in any case, if such people
wanted to sing monodies they probably found that many of them were
beyond their vocal powers. However, not all madrigals were old-
fashioned (nor were they easy to sing). In the later sixteenth century in
the hands of the most imaginative, forward-looking composers they
responded to influences similar to those that stimulated the art of
monody and shaped its development. Madrigalists grew more and more
anxious to project words, and so textures became increasingly
homophonic, with prominent top parts, more neutral inner parts and a
more harmonically conceived bass. As textures gradually became more
fragmented too there were more opportunities for varied sonorities and
more meaningful structural order; and the more changing sonorities
demanded repetition of words, the longer madrigals grew. Composers
such as Giaches de Wert who were Monteverdi's seniors at Mantua
were especially interested in developments of this kind and were very
likely prompted by the celebrated virtuoso singers at the court of
Ferrara.[2] The rise of virtuoso singing and a humanist concern with
words were parallel developments that fertilized each other.

[1] See Gloria Rose, 'Polyphonic Italian Madrigals of the Seventeenth Century',
Music & Letters, xlvii (1966), 153.
[2] See Anthony Newcomb, *The Madrigal at Ferrara 1579–1597*, Princeton
Studies in Music, vii (Princeton, 1980), *passim*; also Elio Durante and Anna

Even without his writings on the subject we could see from his middle-period madrigals that Monteverdi shared the ideals of the early monodists; and he convinces us that to transform the art of the madrigal from within instead of abandoning it and going over suddenly to monody was an equally valid way of fulfilling them. There are signs in his second set of madrigals, published in 1590 at about the time he settled in Mantua, that he had absorbed the new expressiveness of the Mantuans, especially as seen in Wert's eighth book. But for the purposes of this study there is no need to go back beyond his fourth book, published in 1603, to see his lively and sensitive handling of techniques that were soon to permeate so many of his continuo madrigals.

The opening of *Luci serene e chiare*[3] shows Monteverdi's new approach at its most expressive:

Ex. 1

The translucent chords in the first seven bars perfectly reflect the 'serene and clear' eyes. The two top parts sing in thirds, and Monteverdi may have been thinking of them as a duet against a neutral harmonic

---

[3] *Tutte le opere*, iv, 35.

Martellotti, *Cronistoria del concerto delle dame principalissime di Margherita Gonzaga d'Este* (Florence, 1979), *passim*.

background; as we shall see, homophony like this is one of the most
characteristic textures of his duets. Again, the slight increase in
movement from bar 7 in the three upper parts is a perfect match for the
lover's exclamation 'You inflame me'. Here the duet texture breaks
down, and the highest part becomes a 'solo'. The little lift on 'voi', one of
the simplest and most telling of emotional embellishments, is rather like
one that graces some early solo madrigals. Monteverdi also used it often.
Among other examples in the same book is one in the second bar of
Sfogava con le stelle, where the jump down of a third reminds one even
more forcibly of the form it usually assumes in monodies; in Ex. 2 this
passage can be compared with the opening of Caccini's song *Perfidissimo
volto*:

Ex. 2[4]

(a)   (b)

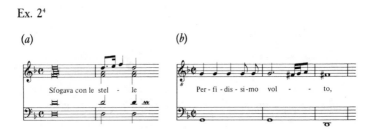

One more of Monteverdi's expressive 'solos' from these years is worth
mentioning: the opening of the lament *O Mirtillo* from his fifth book of
madrigals (1605), one of the innumerable settings at this time of the set
pieces in Guarini's *Il pastor fido*[5] (see Ex. 3). The very opening is not
unlike his setting of 'Voi m'incendete' in *Luci serene* with the important
exception that the opening note of the melody, now harmonized as a
concord, launches the new melodic interval of the major sixth, which
had hitherto been virtually excluded from polyphony and which
Monteverdi was beginning to use as one more way of heightening
emotional tension.

Declamatory series of repeated melody notes on the surface of a
homophonic texture are prominent in the last two examples. The words
are clearly audible, and the technique has the further advantage that it
builds up tension that needs to be released in some arresting dissonance

[4] Respectively ibid., 15, and Giulio Caccini, *Le nuove musiche* (Florence, 1602),
ed. H. Wiley Hitchcock, Recent Researches in the Music of the Baroque Era,
ix (Madison, 1970), 77.
[5] *Tutte le opere*, v, 5.

Ex. 3

or plangent melodic gesture. In this typical example from *A un giro sol*
(Book IV)[6] the alto moves up a semitone to start a chain of dissonant
suspensions sparked off by the emotive word 'crudele':

Ex. 4

This example also illustrates the duet texture we have already
noticed—here on two middle voices, but immediately transferred to the
top two with a nice sense of contrasting sonorities. The duet for two
sopranos that starts *Ah, dolente partita* in the same book[7] behaves in
precisely the same way: a monotone inflamed into acrid dissonance
under the stress of the composer's response to doleful words. When
Monteverdi was writing true duets with continuo he returned to this
highly effective technique, as we can see at the equally poignant opening
of *Interrotte speranze* in Book VII:[8]

Ex. 5

[6] *Tutte le opere*, iv, 52.   [7] Ibid., 1.   [8] *Tutte le opere*, vii, 94.

A good deal of the music in the examples we have been considering could after a fashion be reduced to monody. But this would remove the cunningly placed, affecting dissonances between two equal voices, which are precisely the sort of sound that fascinated Monteverdi and kept him for so long faithful to the duet and away from monody.

The repeated notes in Ex. 2a are of course of a peculiar kind: here and in five other places in *Sfogava* Monteverdi indicates only chords and leaves the singers to chant the rhythms freely as though they were singing psalms set in *falsobordone*. The cumulative tension here is even more powerful than that generated through 'normal' note-values, and the release from it when such values return can be all the more overwhelming. Indeed the last two pages of this madrigal are among the most arresting in the whole of Monteverdi. The poet, Ottavio Rinuccini, tells of a lover who is addressing the stars:

> La fareste col vostr'aureo sembiante
> Pietosa sì, come me fate amante.

(You would surely make her pitying with your golden mien, as you make me a lover.)

The first line and a half are declaimed three times in free chords, and the third is the most thrilling: in the first place the chord clashes with the one ending the previous phrase through the disruptive mediant relationship that Monteverdi so often exploited, and the three-note phrase that burgeons out of it, enhanced by the leaping dissonance, is charged with an emotional intensity that even he never surpassed:[9]

Ex. 6

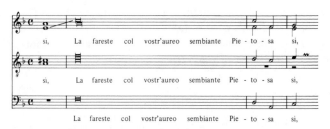

The music subsides to the final cadence through a quiet setting of the last few words in free imitation of a little scalic figure mingling with gently concordant treatment of the three-note outburst. Once again, we

[9] *Tutte le opere*, iv, 19.

can see Monteverdi in one of his later duets, *O come vaghi*,[10] generating emotional power at the same word 'pietosa' by not dissimilar, though simpler, means, after which he handles in a correspondingly bland way the technique of unison followed by dissonance—in this case a standard cadence—that we have just seen in other duets:

Ex. 7

It is not really true, as has been claimed, that in *Sfogava* Monteverdi reserves free chanting only for the less important parts of the poem. He does, however, distinguish clearly between homophony, which he uses for the setting of the scene at the start, and polyphony, which bursts in with the first direct speech as the poet starts to address the stars. The distinction is one that could within a few years be drawn by means of recitative and aria. Monteverdi possibly felt it a defect of monody that no such distinction could be made while preserving a reasonable degree of musical continuity, and indeed compared with his madrigal Caccini's flat setting[11] shows that simply to write for solo voice was no short cut to the attainment of imaginative *seconda prattica* ideals. Ex. 8 shows (*a*) the marked change Monteverdi makes while setting the words 'And, gazing at them, he said, "O fair images . . ."' and (*b*) Caccini's virtually undifferentiated setting of them.

As soon as he introduced an obligatory continuo part into his madrigals Monteverdi began to write monody, but significantly only in alliance with other textures in an attempt to create a new and convincing emotional and structural order. Let us next consider *T'amo, mia vita*, one of the last six madrigals in his fifth book for which the continuo was 'fatto particolarmente'.[12] The words of the title are sung five times by the first soprano, usually to a scale descending through a fifth, in alternation

[10] *Tutte le opere*, ix, 105. The piece was published in 1624 in the collection *Madrigali del Signor Cavaliere Anselmi posti in musica da diversi eccellentissimi spirti.*

[11] *Le nuove musiche*, ed. Hitchcock, 88. See also Imogene Horsley, 'Monteverdi's Use of Borrowed Material in "Sfogava con le stelle" ', *Music & Letters*, lix (1978), 316.

[12] *Tutte le opere*, v, 90.

Ex. 8

(a)

(b)

with homophonic declamation by the three lowest voices, often consisting of clearly articulated repeated notes of the type we have already seen. The two textures are utterly different, the trio rather matter-of-fact, the solo affectingly lyrical, especially when its last three statements come in quick succession in the middle of the piece: remembering *Sfogava*, the reader will not be surprised to learn that the solo represents a lover's direct speech, the trio a commentary. The madrigal is rounded off by nearly twenty bars of free polyphony for the full five-part ensemble. This climax, based on the refrain for 'T'amo, mia vita', now completed by the phrase 'La mia vita sia', indicates an imaginative new role for traditional polyphony when used in this concentrated way to crown and 'complete' a series of contrasting lighter textures. The work as a whole is like a study in the realistic textures of the celebrated *Lamento della ninfa* in Book VIII:[13] Monteverdi makes naturalistic use of monody but is still primarily intent on a rounded structure enhanced by interplay of textures. To turn the opening words into a refrain does no violence to the meaning of the poem: indeed it makes it more vivid, as do the comparable repetitions of two phrases in the *Lamento d'Arianna* that I mentioned in the last chapter. It is surprising that monodic madrigalists used repetition so rarely. Piero Benedetti brings back the opening phrase of his madrigal *Ho vist'al pianto mio* as a cadence to his first section, and Sigismondo d'India unifies his madrigal *E pur tu parti, ohimè* with nine more statements of the opening rhythm (Ex. 9), but these are isolated cases.[14]

Ex. 9

We can definitely say that in *T'amo, mia vita* Monteverdi was writing for solo voices, whatever may be true of his earlier madrigals. *Addio, Florida bella* in Book VI (1614)[15] is another piece obviously meant for one voice to a part. He described it by the fashionable new word 'concertato', and it is indeed more like a typical early seventeenth-century dialogue than a traditional madrigal. Two lovers, Florus and Florida, are saying good-bye on the banks of the Tiber. Dramatic realism now demands that each sing a solo, she as a soprano, he as a tenor; the solos are, moreover, heightened by the florid writing frequent in solo madrigals. Then they continue their farewells in an imitative duet. In between, the full five-part group of voices, again reduced to the role of commentator on the sidelines—or in the bushes, like the voyeurs of so much madrigal verse?—remark in plain words and amusingly 'confused' music on the confused noise of the lovers' sighing, kissing and talking, and they round off the piece by echoing the farewells in a coda as satisfying in terms of sense, form and texture as that of *T'amo, mia vita*.

[13] *Tutte le opere*, viii, 288.
[14] Piero Benedetti, *Musiche . . . libro quarto* (Florence, 1617), 17, and Sigismondo d'India, *Le musiche . . . libro terzo* (Milan, 1618), 16; the latter piece is also in John J. Joyce, *The Monodies of Sigismondo d'India* (Ann Arbor, 1981), Musical Supplement, No. 12, where the note-values are halved.
[15] *Tutte le opere*, vi, 38.

It is, however, not monody but the two-part textures of his middle madrigal books that Monteverdi later developed so intensively in independent pieces. One should really think of them primarily as three-part textures, certainly after he has adopted an instrumental bass. Even in his earlier books a passage for two adjacent voices is sometimes underpinned by a quasi-instrumental vocal bass. He has only to take the logical step of making the bass purely instrumental to produce the most characteristic forces of his duets—two equal voices and continuo. The vocal writing in his duets varies between homophony and a fairly free polyphony based on short melodic figures that also derives from passages (usually for more than two voices) in his ensemble madrigals; the bass nearly always moves independently. Monteverdi also wrote a number of trios: here the homophonic three-part textures of his ensemble madrigals are found much less often than loosely imitative polyphony for all three voices, and the instrumental bass either doubles the lowest one (nearly always a bass) or reproduces its essential harmony notes in the long values common in continuo lines. Monteverdi also of course wrote in his later years a number of madrigals for four or more voices, which are beyond the scope of this chapter; but, needless to say, in several of them he developed the important features I have pointed to in his earlier madrigals and his duets.

There are plenty of duet and trio sections in the madrigals of Monteverdi's fourth book and in those in the fifth book where the continuo is not yet obligatory. We have seen some of them already, and there is no point in multiplying examples. But there is one wonderful beginning, of *Era l'anima mia* in Book V,[16] that is well worth mentioning for its original, varied and outstandingly expressive use of the texture. Guarini's image of the soul at its last hour, in the context of a love poem, summoned from Monteverdi cavernous D minor chords for the three lowest voices in which the middle one acts as a pivot in third-textures with first the voice below and then the one above. The upper voices of this trio then sing drooping thirds, full of disturbing false relations. They also produce dissonances with a bass that from this point takes on an 'instrumental' character with long-held notes that act as successive dominants in a modern tonal way; when it drops out before the final resolution and leaves the other two voices on their own the effect is intensely chilling. Gloom is banished, however, by the sudden bright texture of the three highest voices and bass that follows at the words 'Quand'anima più bella, più gradita'—another striking textural contrast

[16] *Tutte le opere,* 'v, 9.

assuming structural importance as the major cadence of the new phrase blossoms into a series of polyphonic entries. Most of the 'trios' in Monteverdi's middle-period madrigals are homophonic and for three adjacent parts conceived as two-against-one. None of his works tells us so eloquently of his delight in this texture as the *Lamento d'Arianna*:[17] when he reworked his celebrated operatic monody as a five-part piece he added sixty-four bars and scored all but three of them for three voices. Contrasting trios more and more assumed structural functions: the appearance of four different three-part textures during less than twenty successive bars of *Ah, dolente partita*[18] is only one more example among many in which Monteverdi seems to have been concerned to expand his form in a satisfying way at least as much as to illuminate his text, which, however, certainly remained his starting-point. In the chamber duets in his seventh book of madrigals and elsewhere we constantly find him using homophonic textures of thirds over a free bass for varying emotional and structural ends: for example, as a still contrast to more elaborate imitative writing ('Gentil al par d'ogn'altre havete il core' in *Non è di gentil core*), or to emphasize points of repose or intensify cadences (two examples on the second page of *O come sei gentile*), sometimes creating a feeling of climax after alternating solos (second page of *Io son pur vezzosetta*).[19]

As soon as he adopted the continuo as an essential feature Monteverdi plunged into duet writing more eagerly than into solo writing, not only to exploit its sonorous potentialities but again to seek our new forms. *Ahi, come a un vago sol*, the first of his continuo madrigals,[20] is a marvellous illustration of what he could do with the new medium. The first twenty-three bars are a duet for the two tenors—as it were, the central characters in a miniature drama—now singing imitatively, now in thirds, over a slow-moving bass: the riot of embellishments at the protracted cadence affords a fine climax to those heard earlier in the duet. This proves to be the first of four duet sections, which get progressively shorter and plainer and are separated by a plaintive refrain to the final line of the poem, 'Ah! che piaga d'amor non sana mai' ('Ah! love's wound never heals'). This refrain is a remarkable example of the emotional power Monteverdi could wrest from quite ordinary chord progressions (see Ex. 10): it is as though a 'chorus'

[17] *Tutte le opere*, vi, 1.
[18] *Tutte le opere*, iv, 3 (bottom)–5.
[19] *Tutte le opere*, vii, 10–11, 36 and 42 respectively.
[20] *Tutte le opere*, v, 62.

were commenting on the plight of the two characters and pointing a moral.[21]

The first two statements of the refrain are for a trio consisting of the two highest voices and the lowest. The music of the refrain then invades the third duet, which flowers into five-part writing for the third statement proper of the refrain. This is a notably imaginative passage, which fuses the two main formal ideas of the piece: the new warmth generated as a result can burn itself out only through a development of the refrain in five parts interrupted only by the fourth duet section, now a mere four bars long. *Qui rise Tirsi*, in the next book,[22] is another fine concertato similarly opposing in a 'dramatic' manner a full but plain refrain and sections more lightly but also more exuberantly scored. The symmetrical schemes of these pieces, with their suggestions of rondo form, are of course similar to that of *T'amo, mia vita*, already discussed.

Ex. 10

As I mentioned above, we also find in his earlier madrigals the other important texture which shares the limelight with homophony in Monteverdi's fully fledged duets, as it also does in the first part of *Ahi, come a un vago sol*. This is the imitation of short, rhythmically incisive melodic phrases which are often developed sequentially and sometimes merge into characteristic textures in thirds. Spirited counterpoint of this nature, never developed at great length, was one of the newer techniques Monteverdi introduced into his earlier madrigals: it was one

[21] See the interesting view of this madrigal in John Whenham, *Duet and Dialogue in the Age of Monteverdi* (Ann Arbor, 1982), i, 96.

[22] *Tutte le opere*, vi, 77.

of the elements through which textures gradually became more
discontinuous as composers sought to express the meanings of their
texts more and more subjectively and in ever minuter detail.

The first page of *La piaga ch'ho nel core* in Book IV[23] (Ex. 11) vividly
illustrates the formal and emotional impact that such a texture can
create. Many other instances from Monteverdi's madrigals of this
period could be mentioned, all of them perhaps more 'normal': for this
is a particularly disruptive passage in which he approaches the neurotic
violence of the later Gesualdo:

Ex. 11

'The wound in my heart, lady, makes you happy', says the text, offering
the sort of sharp antithesis that must have delighted a composer of
Monteverdi's keen dramatic perceptions. So to start with he creates
'wounding' dissonance and harmonic dislocation (bars 2–3) in a context
of low spirits emphasized by the long values. The figure denoting the
lady's unseemly pleasure bursts in with the utmost force of surprise far
removed from the halting discontinuity of the weaker solo madrigals of
the day. For in every respect it is the exact opposite of the opening bars:

[23] *Tutte le opere*, iv, 41.

brief, sprightly, incisive, written in short values, repeated several times, treated imitatively. Monteverdi has no time now for strict and expansive imitative polyphony in a piece of this kind; the entries are sequential, and all of them are duets in thirds or tenths. Thus he announces his violently contrasting material at the outset, and he works out the rest of the madrigal as a synthesis of it.

There are innumerable instances in Monteverdi's duets of the imitative technique I have just illustrated in its five-part guise. Here is just one passage, from *Dice la mia bellissima Licori* in Book VII:[24]

Ex. 12

The vocal parts are a web of short interrelated phrases continuously heard in canon or close imitation, and the 'walking' bass, paralleled in a number of other duets, anticipates the basses of strophic-bass cantatas.

In the secular field Monteverdi wrote twenty-four duets and twenty-three trios.[25] The duets in particular belong to a genre that in prestige was second only to monody among many of the composers who were spreading the new music through Italy. There were several kinds of two-part music, two of which need not concern us here: imitative canzonettas without independent instrumental bass and thus little to the taste of modern-minded composers; and dialogues often consisting of alternating solos with a final duet. These types were popular, but less so

[24] *Tutte le opere*, vii, 59.
[25] The total of trios leaves out of account, of course, the *Canzonette* of 1584 and the *Scherzi musicali* of 1607, which are quite different types of piece.

than what are usually referred to as chamber duets—the balanced structure of homophony and imitation I have already referred to, nearly always in common time and sometimes on quite a large scale. Closely related to these works are an important group of duets in which strophic variations unfold from verse to verse over standard popular basses such as the *romanesca* and *Ruggiero*. There are more duets than monodies of this type: Antonio Cifra, rather a pedestrian composer, and d'India, a far more imaginative one, were especially attracted to it, but Monteverdi outclassed everyone else with his single example, *Ohimè, dov'è il mio ben* in his seventh book.[26] As in most works of this type, the text is an ottava (by Bernardo Tasso), a lament which stimulated Monteverdi to some of his most heartfelt writing, among which the agonized dissonance as the second voice enters is outstanding:

Ex. 13

Apart from this piece Monteverdi wrote fourteen chamber duets fairly strictly of the type I have mentioned; most of them are in his seventh book and account for half its contents. There are seven other duets, which probably date from the 1630s and reflect much more obviously than his solos the contemporary development of monodies into recitatives and triple-time arias and cantatas; the total is completed by two splendid isolated works which are discussed below. Several other composers at this period published collections largely devoted to chamber duets: d'India's *Musiche a due voci* (1615), especially rich in works founded on stock basses, and Giovanni Valentini's *Musiche a doi voci* (1622) are two of the most notable; and half the twenty pieces in Gagliano's fine *Musiche* (1615) are duets.

　　Duets, then, are the most representative contents of Monteverdi's seventh madrigal-book of 1619, as imaginatively discontinuous five-part madrigals are of the fourth book published sixteen years before. They are still, in essence, madrigals, but they are designated as such on the title-page only in small type as a subtitle to the significant word *Concerto*, which sums up Monteverdi's approach to the innovations

[26] *Tutte le opere*, vii, 152.

of the new century. Nearly all these duets, and the later ones, are exceptionally fine pieces which are still too little known. There is no space here to analyse them as they deserve. But the various technical features discussed above should be brought together in a study of a single complete piece; in choosing *Non vedrò mai le stelle*[27] I am aware of the equally pressing claims of such masterpieces as *O come sei gentile* and *O sia tranquillo il mare*[28] and two from which I have quoted above, *Interrotte speranze* and *O come vaghi*.

Non vedrò mai is the song of a betrayed lover. It begins with desolate recitative including many repeated notes over a static bass (e.g. eight bars of tonic pedal to start with). Monteverdi intensifies the feeling of grief by the texture in thirds, which stems from the fact that successive phrases enter a third higher; note also the satisfying way in which he completes the second phrase in bar 5 by twice repeating an earlier word:

Ex. 14

(I shall never look at the stars in the heavens, faithless woman, [without thinking of the eyes that attended the harsh cause of my torments or saying to them . . .])

The music progresses sequentially through shorter alternating phrases to a tonic cadence. The lover then addresses the stars, begging them to lend some of their light to the benighted mistress. At once Monteverdi introduces three telling changes—to monody, relative major and legato line (see Ex. 15). He proceeds to a little incisive duet of the type I have discussed above before expanding into a typically Venetian triple-time aria still imploring the 'luci belle'. This is a very significant change: it is

[27] Ibid., 66.
[28] Respectively ibid., 35, and *Tutte le opere*, ix, 36.

Ex. 15

one of the earliest suggestions of the later pairing of recitative and aria and, in so thoroughly upsetting the traditional movement of a duet, it makes this piece perhaps the most forward-looking in Book VII. Monteverdi returns to common time for the last page or so, during which imitation of short phrases again predominates. But before this there is a particularly cheerless moment when, as the poet still harps on the betrayal, he doubles solo tenor and continuo:

Ex. 16

It can be seen from this account that as in the great ensemble madrigals Monteverdi is still able to handle an expanded form with the utmost variety and consistency, to devise brilliant strokes memorable alike for imagination and truth and to reconcile these detailed responses to an emotional text with the claims of the total form.

It only remains to turn to Monteverdi's two most celebrated duets to show how in them he developed two other kinds of composition to new technical and imaginative heights. *Chiome d'oro*[29] is a canzonetta and as such appears at the back of Book VII away from the more serious duets; in both vocal and instrumental writing it is not unlike some of the *Scherzi musicali* of 1607. It is notable for the way in which he enriched a strophic form as he did in *Tempro la cetra*:[30] there are three ritornellos at the

[29] *Tutte le opere*, vii, 182.   [30] See above, 188.

beginning for two violins and continuo, and one of them in turn is heard between the five verses; and the entire piece—ritornellos as well as verses—is composed as strophic variations, an unusually serious form for a canzonetta. The vocal texture is mainly homophonic, which means that thirds predominate, and the bass throughout is of the 'walking' type found in the first cantatas. The text is very likely a parody of madrigal verse; if so it would make especially appropriate the weighty number of ritornellos and the 'learned' form and would certainly account for the comically exaggerated roulades on 'ferita' ('wound') just before the end. The invention all through shows Monteverdi at his happiest and most fertile.

This is of course equally true of *Zefiro torna*,[31] which technically is perhaps Monteverdi's greatest achievement. It is built almost entirely on a short chaconne bass, a type that had by 1630 supplanted in popularity the old type of longer bass such as the *romanesca* among composers interested in this sort of variation. It is the first great chaconne. To continue as long as he does with his bass, apparently so limiting of harmony and phrase structure, without once flagging is one more illustration of the way in which a stern technical challenge can release a composer's imagination. Monteverdi imposes larger paragraphs on his short-phrased structures and takes all sorts of word-painting in his stride without interrupting the onward flow. Or rather he interrupts it exactly when he wants to, at the only possible places—where the downcast lover can contain no longer the sorrows that contrast so sharply with the joys of spring he has been so lyrically describing. Monteverdi plunges into anguished recitative including at one appearance of the word 'piango' ('I weep') perhaps the most arresting and lugubrious of all harmonic progressions in that age of harmonic daring:

Ex. 17

[31] *Tutte le opere*, ix, 9.

Ex. 17 cont.

This work, first published in 1632, makes a fitting conclusion to the attempt to show the technical and emotional stresses that lay behind a great composer's personal transformation of a great musical genre, and to show too how strong were the claims of form, interpretation of text, texture and sonority in keeping him loyal to it even when surrounded by the fashionable sounds of monody. While serving and renewing, with such questing distinction, the form through which he grew to musical maturity Monteverdi showed himself to be the most imaginative humanist of his age.

JOHN WHENHAM

The Later Madrigals and Madrigal-books

The seventh book of madrigals marks a watershed in Monteverdi's published output of secular music. Although he had included concertato settings in his fifth and sixth books, these were published alongside madrigals cast in the traditional *a cappella* mould, and all were for five or more voices. All the settings in the seventh book, on the other hand, require continuo accompaniment, and the majority are scored for the newly fashionable small vocal ensembles of two, three and four voices, or for solo voice. The collection itself is a large and heterogeneous one, including not only madrigals but also 'altri generi de canti', among them several strophic arias and at least one ballet. In view of this, the eye-catching title that Monteverdi chose—*Concerto*—may have been intended as a rather elegant pun, suggesting not only that all the settings required instrumental accompaniment but also that the volume brought together 'in concert' various different kinds of music.

In deciding to publish a collection of this kind Monteverdi may simply have been responding to the changing musical climate of the second decade of the seventeenth century. For this was the decade that saw the first real efflux of monody books from the Italian presses, and it also witnessed the publication of the earliest madrigal-books devoted entirely to concertato music for small vocal ensemble. The first and most important of these was the *Madrigali concertati a due, tre, e quattro voci* (Venice, 1615) by Alessandro Grandi, then choirmaster of Ferrara Cathedral but later appointed by Monteverdi to the position of assistant choirmaster at St. Mark's, Venice. The success of Grandi's book can be judged by the fact that it was reprinted three times up to 1619 and twice more during the 1620s, and its success undoubtedly encouraged other composers to follow suit. Monteverdi can scarcely have been unaware of its existence or of the new type of lyrical madrigal that it contained.

Another factor that may have influenced Monteverdi's decision to compose and publish madrigals and arias for small concertato ensemble, however, was the potential of the new music in the Venetian context. As far as secular music was concerned, Monteverdi's position at

Venice was essentially that of a free-lance composer and performer. No longer the servant of a single aristocratic family, he was at liberty, within reason, to accept commissions from patrons both in and outside Venice and to supplement his income by directing performances of his own and other composers' music. His duties at St. Mark's were not onerous, as he himself admitted in a letter of 13 March 1620 to Alessandro Striggio,[1] and his outside activities brought him not only some 200 ducats a year—half as much again as his income from St. Mark's—but also additional prestige: in his own words, 'when I am about to perform either chamber or church music, I swear to Your Lordship that the entire city comes running'.[2]

In general, the professional concert life of Venice centred on the activities of the academies, whose performances sometimes included music used in conjunction with theatrical presentations,[3] and on musical evenings given at the houses of private citizens—at the homes of the Venetian nobility and at the residences of ambassadors and of the wealthy visitors who came to enjoy the many pleasures that the city afforded. Some of these visiting dignitaries brought their own musicians with them,[4] but none of the residents of Venice, as far as we know, maintained a musical staff. Rather, they would engage professional singers and instrumentalists as occasion demanded and finances allowed, and we can imagine that only rarely would the occasion have warranted the expense of hiring a large body of musicians. Under these circumstances, the new concertato music for solo voice and small ensemble may have seemed an ideal medium, allowing an evening of varied vocal and instrumental music to be given for the cost of engaging two or three of the choirmen of St. Mark's, two violinists from its orchestra, and the choirmaster or one of his deputies to direct the ensemble from the harpsichord. Singers and instrumentalists were readily available. A document of 1614 shows that the orchestra of St. Mark's then consisted of sixteen players, including at least three

[1] See above, 43–7.
[2] Ibid., 44.
[3] See Elena Povoledo, 'Una rappresentazione accademica a Venezia nel 1634', *Studi sul teatro veneto fra Rinascimento ed età barocca*, ed. Maria Teresa Muraro (Florence, 1971), 119–69. There is no evidence that Monteverdi was ever involved in any of these theatrical presentations.
[4] Among the retinue of more than 200 accompanying the Duke and Duchess of Mantua on their state visit to Venice in 1623, for example, was the renowned singer Adriana Basile: see *The Letters of Claudio Monteverdi*, trans. and ed. Denis Stevens (London, 1980), 272–3.

violinists, three trombonists and a performer on the *violone contrabasso*.[5]
As far as singers are concerned, by 1616 Monteverdi could call on the
services of some twenty-four men from his own choir alone; and these
included castratos, six of whom Monteverdi admitted to the choir
between 1613 and 1620.[6] There is no record, however, of female
virtuosos resident in the city before the 1630s and the advent of such
figures as Barbara Strozzi and Anna Renzi.[7]

Given the known vocal and instrumental resources at Monteverdi's
disposal, then, most of the music of the seventh book could certainly
have been performed at Venice. There is no reason, however, to
suppose that all the works that it contains were written in, or for, the city.
Indeed, in terms of the diversity of styles and resources represented, the
book gives every indication of being a retrospective collection,
containing music composed over a period of a decade or more. The duet
Ohimè, dov'è il mio ben, for example, a setting of one of Bernardo Tasso's
stanze di lontananza, which were written at a period when the poet was
separated from his wife, seems to me to belong to Monteverdi's later
years at Mantua, to the period following the death of his own wife, and to
the group of intensely personal utterances which includes the Petrarch
settings *Zefiro torna e 'l bel tempo rimena* and *Ohimè, il bel viso* (both
published in 1614 in Book VI).[8] Some of the other duets in Book VII may
also be Mantuan in origin, their publication having been delayed until a
market was established for small-scale concertato music.[9]

[5] See Eleanor Selfridge-Field, 'Bassano and the Orchestra of St. Mark's', *Early
Music*, iv (1976), 155–6.
[6] See James H. Moore, *Vespers at St. Mark's: Music of Alessandro Grandi,
Giovanni Rovetta and Francesco Cavalli* (Ann Arbor, 1981), i, 84.
[7] On Barbara Strozzi, see Ellen Rosand, 'Barbara Strozzi, *virtuosissima
cantatrice*: the Composer's Voice', *Journal of the American Musicological Society*,
xxxi (1978), 241–81. On Anna Renzi, see Claudio Sartori, 'La prima diva della
lirica italiana: Anna Renzi', *Nuova rivista musicale italiana*, ii (1968), 430–52.
[8] On the personal nature of Monteverdi's Petrarch settings, see Nino Pirrotta,
'Scelte poetiche di Monteverdi', *Nuova rivista musicale italiana*, ii (1968),
232–3.
[9] We know that Monteverdi wrote both sacred and secular duets at Mantua.
Some of them, of course, form parts of larger works such as *Orfeo*, the Vespers
of 1610 and five-part madrigals like *Ahi, come a un vago sol* (Book V, 1605), but
he may also have been writing independent duets. A duet and some arias of his
were, for example, praised by the Florentine poet Ottavio Rinuccini in a letter
of 24 June 1610 to Cardinal Ferdinando Gonzaga: see *The Letters of Claudio
Monteverdi*, 74–5. During the first decade of the seventeenth century, the new
type of solo song and duet seems to have been regarded by some composers as
music appropriate for court use but inappropriate for publication.

At the other end of the spectrum, larger-scale works like *Tempro la cetra*, *A quest'olmo* and *Con che soavità* also seem to call for the resources of court rather than city.[10] *A quest'olmo*, scored for six voices, two violins, two small flutes (recorders or fifes) and continuo, is the longest of the madrigals in the seventh book. It is a setting of a sonnet by Giambattista Marino, a poet well represented in the sixth book of madrigals, and it shares with some of the earlier-published Marino settings—*Qui rise, o Tirsi*, for example—a sense of nostalgic reminiscence. Marino's reminiscence is essentially sensual. He returns to a wooded grove because it reminds him 'of the time that Chloris, as a gift, gave herself and her heart to me' ('. . . all'hor che la mia Clori/Tutt'in dono se stessa e 'l cor mi diede'). These lines, the tenth and eleventh in the sonnet, form the core of the text, and Monteverdi makes them the main focus of his setting by allotting them to a solo voice accompanied by the two flutes and continuo. He, however, emphasizes not the gift of Chloris's body but the gift of her heart (Ex. 1), and he then caps the setting with a yearning chromatic phrase as he senses the flowers breathing around him the pleasures of past happiness. Though less intense than the Petrarch settings of Book VI, this work, too, contains an element of personal statement which is unusual in Monteverdi's output. The contrasts of scoring, the use of solo writing and the way in which instruments play an integral part in the counterpoint look forward to the large-scale madrigals of his later years; but the generally diatonic language of the piece harks back to the pastoral madrigal of the late sixteenth century.

Some of the smaller-scale polyphonic works of the seventh book reflect technical rather than emotional aspects of Monteverdi's Mantuan experience. *Parlo, misero, o taccio?* and, to a lesser extent, *Tu dormi*, for example, employ concerted ornamentation over slow-moving basses; and the wide leaps in the opening vocal lines of *Al lume delle stelle* are reminiscent of Wert. The similarities with Wert are, however, only superficial, for this setting of a madrigal by Torquato Tasso,[11] together

---

[10] The disposition of these larger works within the seventh book seems to have been determined by a wish to structure the book. It opens with *Tempro la cetra*, whose strophic-variation structure is akin to an operatic prologue (see above, 188. *A quest'olmo* initiates the section of the book devoted to madrigalian settings, and *Con che soavità* the section devoted to arias and monodies; and the grand conclusion is provided by the ballet *Tirsi e Clori*. Only the duet *Non è di gentil core*, which follows *Tempro la cetra*, seems to be misplaced in this scheme. See Pirrotta, op. cit., 238–9.

[11] The poet was identified by Pirrotta: ibid., 29.

Ex. 1

with the other four-part madrigal, *Tu dormi*, in fact demonstrate Monteverdian solutions to one of the most pressing problems for madrigalists working in the new styles of the early seventeenth century: how to combine in counterpoint lines which are melodically self-sufficient and either declamatory or tuneful in character. The opening paragraph of *Al lume delle stelle*, a narrative section in which Thyrsis is pictured lamenting by the light of the stars, is built from the constituent phrases of a single declamatory line, which is stated in full in the bass voice from bar 11. Bars 1–8 of Ex. 2 show the two main phrases combined in bass and soprano, with a third, short, motif in the alto voice which assumes importance towards the end of the paragraph. By never using more than three voices at a time, Monteverdi succeeds not only in producing workable counterpoint but also in allowing us to follow the

Ex. 2

individual lines quite clearly. The remainder of the setting is technically less complex, since Thyrsis' speech is set mainly for two pairs of voices. *Tu dormi*, on the other hand, employs a more consistently contrapuntal texture. Its opening paragraph is set for three voices, with short phrases treated in a dialogue-like manner before giving way to extended three-part treatment of the complete line. The second paragraph of the setting effectively (and affectively) combines a rising chromatic line for the words 'Io piango, e le mie voci lagrimose' ('I weep, and my tearful cries') with a plunging counter-theme for 'a te che sorda sei' ('to you who are deaf') (Ex. 3); and at the end of the work two pairs of voices combine to provide a climactic surge of emotion (Ex. 4). Though written on a smaller scale, this work is a worthy successor to those madrigals of Books III and IV that were designed to exploit the histrionic talents of the Mantuan ensemble.[12]

[12] For a description of the abilities of the Mantuan ensemble, see below, 256.

Ex. 3

Ex. 4

The problems of dating the polyphonic madrigals of Book VII on the basis of their style are complicated by two factors. The first is that, adaptable though Monteverdi undoubtedly was, we cannot assume that his style changed radically on his arrival at Venice, so that 'Mantuan' characteristics may not indicate Mantuan origins. The second is that Monteverdi's early years at Venice are, anyway, marked by a lingering involvement with the Mantuan court, so that we may, in some cases, be dealing with works which, though written at Venice, were intended for Mantua. Monteverdi continued to accept commissions from the court certainly until the late 1620s, and though the documented instances involve stage music only, madrigal settings may also have been requested. At all events, when Monteverdi published his seventh book he dedicated it to Caterina de' Medici, Duchess of Mantua, and sent her a presentation copy, for which he received in return the gift of a valuable necklace.[13]

One work in the seventh book was certainly written for performance at Mantua. This is the choral ballet *Tirsi e Clori*, a work in six movements (separated in the score by double bars and repeat marks) and a final *riverenza*, and with an introduction in dialogue for the shepherd Thyrsis and the shepherdess Chloris. From a purely musical point of view, it is not one of Monteverdi's finer inspirations, but it is one of the best-documented of his surviving works.

The commission for the ballet arrived in November 1615. Neither the forces to be used nor the length of the work were specified, nor was any text sent for Monteverdi to set. He had, however, already begun work on *Tirsi e Clori* without commission, with the intention of presenting it to the Duke of Mantua. Only two movements remained to be completed, and the manuscript was duly dispatched, with a covering letter in which Monteverdi discussed a number of technical details and offered to make any changes that might be required, including, if necessary, altering the text.[14] Since the published score of the work includes very few instructions for its realization, Monteverdi's letter is particularly valuable; and it shows, too, that he conceived the work not only in musical, but also in visual terms:

But if by good fortune the enclosed should be to his [the Duke's] liking, I would think it proper to perform it in a half-moon, at whose corners should be placed an archlute and a harpsichord, one each side, one playing the bass for Chloris and the other for Thyrsis, each of them holding a lute, and playing and singing themselves to their own instruments and to the aforementioned. If there could be a harp instead of a lute for Chloris that would be even better.

Then having reached the ballet movement after they have sung a dialogue, there could be added to the ballet six more voices in order to make eight voices in all, eight *viole da braccio*, a contrabass, a *spineta arpata*, and if there were also two lutes, that would be fine. And directed with a beat suitable to the character of the melodies, avoiding overexcitement among the singers and players, and with the understanding of the ballet-master, I hope that—sung in this way—it will not displease His Highness.[15]

[13] See Stevens, 'Monteverdi's Necklace', *Musical Quarterly*, lix (1973), 370–81.
[14] The text of *Tirsi e Clori* is not, as has sometimes been stated, by Alessandro Striggio.
[15] For the complete letter, of 21 November 1615, see above, 32–3.

This still leaves some questions unanswered—for example, the exact disposition of the eight voices in music which is scored for only five—but it indicates a much richer scoring than could be deduced from the published instructions. These state simply that Thyrsis and Chloris should each be accompanied by their own chitarrone or spinet, and that the ballet proper is 'a 5 con istrumenti e voci, concertato e adagio', that is, that the ballet should be performed slowly and with melody instruments doubling the vocal lines. Monteverdi's letter, then, serves to remind us that music that may appear quite thin on paper may in fact have been rich and colourful in performance.

On balance, the polyphonic madrigals in the seventh book that appear most obviously 'Venetian' in style and scoring are the three trios for male voices, *Augellin che la voce al canto spieghi*, *Vaga su spina ascosa* and *Eccomi pronta ai baci*, which are also among the most immediately attractive works in the collection. The first two employ a technique not developed in Monteverdi's earlier madrigals—the use of a bass line moving mainly in crotchets, coupled with an essentially tuneful style of melodic writing. The introduction of the so-called 'walking' bass and its associated melodic style is usually credited to Grandi, who employed it not only for his strophic-bass cantatas but also as one stylistic element in earlier works like his three-part aria *Mira fuggir le stelle* (1615):

Ex. 5

The association of the 'walking'-bass technique with aria writing which is evident in Grandi's work is also reflected in Monteverdi's *Vaga su spina ascosa*, a setting of great charm and delicacy in which a 'walking' bass is used for all but the last eight bars. Although Monteverdi's setting is through-composed and therefore, by definition, a madrigal, the text by Gabriello Chiabrera effectively consists of three four-line stanzas followed by a final stanza of six lines. This formal outline is marked in Monteverdi's music by the use of cadences followed by a rest at the end of each stanza. In a sense, then, the work could also be seen as a strophic aria in which each stanza is set to different music, and the slight subject matter of the poem is greatly enhanced by the way in which the composer contrasts long musical phrases for the first two stanzas with shorter ones in the third as the lover rejects the beauty of the flowers in favour of the blush on his beloved's cheek.

Grandi may well have done much to popularize the use of the 'walking' bass, but we should not be too hasty in attributing Monteverdi's use of the technique to his influence. In Monteverdi's own work the use of 'walking' basses can be traced back to some of the *Scherzi musicali* of 1607 (Ex. 6) and their employment in strophic

Ex. 6

variations to the aria 'Qual honor di te fia degno' in Act IV of *Orfeo*, which is a strophic-bass cantata in all but name. A comparison of the beginning of this aria (Ex. 7*a*) with the opening solo of the madrigal *Augellin* (Ex. 7*b*) shows not only a striking similarity of initial melodic gesture but also the source of the energetic style of melodic writing found in the later work, a style which is markedly different from Grandi's limpid, often short-breathed melodies. The text of *Augellin* is a genuine madrigal, and here Monteverdi uses a contrast of styles to highlight the ending of the poem. The first six lines of the text, in which the lover instructs the bird to carry a message to his beloved, are set in a generally lively style over a 'walking' bass. The last three lines—the words of complaint that the bird is to carry—however, are set as a delightfully exaggerated, passionate declamation.

Contrasts of style also form the basis of *Eccomi pronta ai baci*, though here the livelier styles derive not from the use of a 'walking' bass but

Ex. 7

(a)

Qual ho - nor____ di te sia de - gno, mia cet-ra on - ni - po -

ten - te.   s'hai nel tar - ta - reo re - gno

(b)

Au-gel-lin,   Au-gel - lin   che la   vo-ce al can - - - - - [-to]

from the 'scherzando' interplay of short motifs characteristic of
canzonetta writing. The text of the work, by Marino, depicts an
encounter between nymph and shepherd:

> Eccomi pronta ai baci.
> Baciami, Ergasto mio, ma bacia in guisa
> Che de' denti mordaci
> Nota non resti nel mio volto incisa,
> Perchè altri non m'additi e in esse poi
> Legga le mie vergogne e i baci tuoi.
> Ahi, tu mordi e non baci,
> Tu mi segnasti, ahi, ahi.
> Poss'io morir, se più ti bacio mai.

(Here I am, ready to be kissed. Kiss me, my Ergasto, but kiss me in such a
way that no mark from your biting teeth will be left on my face, so that no one
will point at me and read your kisses and my shame. Ah, you are biting, not
kissing; you have marked me, ah, ah. May I die before I ever kiss you again.)

Whatever we may feel about the quality and content of Marino's text,
Monteverdi succeeds admirably in conveying the ebb and flow of the
couple's love-play, from the nymph's importunate excitement (Ex. 8) to

her cry as Ergasto bites her (Ex. 9) and her final, not altogether convincing, resolution to have no more to do with him.

Ex. 8

Ex. 9

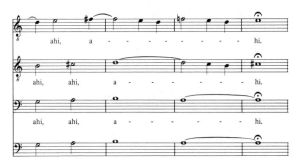

Eccomi pronta ai baci is the last setting of erotic verse that Monteverdi published, though several similar works survive from his career as a court composer. *Si ch'io vorrei morire* (Book IV, 1603), for example, also depicts a sexual encounter, and though its text is less explicit than Marino's, Monteverdi's setting makes the meaning quite clear. Texts of this kind, slight though they are, offered the composer an opportunity to create a vivid dramatization of the situations and emotions involved. A similar instance, though with different subject matter, is found in his three-part setting *Taci, Armelin*, which was published in the *Madrigali* (1624) of Giovanni Battista Anselmi, a Trevisan nobleman who commissioned for this volume settings of his own poetry by a number of north Italian composers. In Anselmi's text, Armelin is a dog which constantly interrupts a lover's suit with its barking. The lover begins by trying to soothe the dog but ends by rounding on it, calling it a 'malicious, treacherous little Cerberus':

Ex. 10

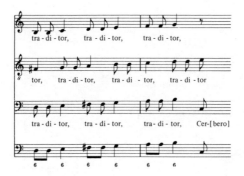

We have already seen that certain of the canzonettas in Monteverdi's *Scherzi musicali* of 1607 seem to anticipate his later use of 'walking' basses. This publication is, however, significant for his later work in two further respects: first as a background to the two strophic arias *Chiome d'oro* and *Amor che deggio far* included in Book VII, and secondly as the source of the term 'canto alla francese' which appears above the madrigal settings *Dolcissimo uscignolo* and *Chi vuol haver felice e lieto il core* in Book VIII.

The first of these relationships can be summarized simply by saying that the arias of Book VII represent a later, more sophisticated development of the performance manner indicated for the *Scherzi musicali*. Each of the *scherzi* is laid out as a three-part strophic canzonetta for two sopranos and bass, preceded by a ritornello for three instruments. The manner in which the pieces are to be performed is explained in a short preface to the book:

> Before one begins to sing, the ritornello must be played twice.
>
> The ritornellos must be played at the end of each stanza, the lines written in the soprano clef being taken by two violins, and the bass line by the chitarrone, or harpsichord, or some other similar instrument.
>
> The first soprano line (the first stanza having been sung by three voices with the violins) may be sung solo, [at pitch] or an octave lower, in the following stanzas, reverting in the last stanza, however, to three voices with violins.
>
> Where lines are seen drawn in place of words, the notes above the lines must be played, but not sung.[16]

Only the first and last stanzas of the *scherzi*, then, are intended to be sung by three voices, and in these the upper voice-parts are doubled by violins. The intervening stanzas may be sung as solos, with the chitarrone or harpsichord either doubling the vocal lines or providing a continuo realization.

The concertato arias of Book VII develop this basic ground-plan a stage further. *Amor che deggio far*, which is scored for four voices and two violins, with continuo realized on chitarrone or spinet, will serve as an

---

[16] 'Prima che si cominci à cantare, si dovrà sonare due volte il Ritornello. I Ritornelli dovranno esser sonati in fine d'ogni stanza ne i Soprani da due Violini da braccio, & nel Basso dal Chitarrone, ò Clavicembalo, ò altro simile instrumento. Il primo Soprano, cantata, che sia la prima stanza à tre voci con i Violini potrà esser cantato solo, ò vero all'ottava bassa nelle stanze che seguono, ripigliando però l'ultima stanza con l'istesse tre voci; & i violini stessi. Dove si vedranno tirate alcune linee nella sede delle parole, quelle note che sono ad esse linee sopraposte dovranno esser sonate, ma non cantate.'

example. Each stanza of the song is set as a variation over the same bass. The first two stanzas are set for solo voices, the third and fourth for two voices, and the fifth for three voices. The sixth stanza begins as a solo but is concluded by all four voices, singing together with violins and continuo to form a grand climax. The piece is preceded by three (repeated) ritornellos, each of which appears singly after stanzas 2, 4 and 5. The ritornellos are themselves variations over a bass, though a different one from that used for the vocal sections. The formal design of this work, and of its companion piece, the frothy strophic-bass cantata *Chiome d'oro*,[17] is undoubtedly more complex than that of the *scherzi*, and its use of strophic-variation technique more sophisticated. Nevertheless, the feature of its composition which seems most up to date in the context of Book VII—the way in which the melody instruments not only play ritornellos between the stanzas of the song but also join the voices at the end to provide a climax—can be seen as a natural extension of the same practice in the *scherzi*.

The term 'canto alla francese' presents an altogether thornier problem, and it has to be admitted at the outset that we may never know its precise meaning, especially since it seems to have been a term used only in Mantuan circles. It was first employed in print by Monteverdi's brother Giulio Cesare in the famous 'Dichiaratione' appended to the *Scherzi musicali* of 1607, and his remarks on the subject are worth reproducing in their full context, as a gloss on Monteverdi's claim to have invented the term 'seconda prattica':

I have wished to say this to you in order that the expression 'Second Practice' may not be appropriated by anyone else, and further, that . . .

My brother has made known to the world that this expression is assuredly his in order that it may be known and concluded that when his adversary said, in the second book of the Artusi: 'This Second Practice, which may in all truth be said to be the dregs of the First', he spoke as he did to speak evil of my brother's works. This was in the year 1603, when my brother had first decided to begin writing his defence of himself against his opponent and when the expression 'Second Practice' had barely passed his lips, a sure indication that his adversary was desirous of defaming in the same vein my brother's words and his music as well, although they were still in manuscript. And for what reason? Let him say it who knows; let him see it who can find it on the map! But why does the adversary show so much astonishment in that discourse of his, saying further: 'You show yourself as jealous of that expression as though you feared that someone would rob you

[17] On this piece, see above, 213–14.

of it', as though he meant to say, in his language: 'You should not fear such a theft, for you are not worth imitating, let alone robbing'? I inform him that, if the matter has to be considered in this light, my brother will have not a few arguments in his favour, in particular the *canto alla francese* in the modern manner that has been a matter of marvel for the three or four years since it first appeared in print, now applied to the words of motets, now madrigals, now canzonettas and arias. Who before him brought this to Italy until he returned from the baths of Spa in the year 1599? Who before him began to apply it to Latin words and to words in our vulgar tongue? Has he not now composed his *Scherzi*? There would be much to say of this to his advantage, and still more (if I wished) of other things, but I pass over them in silence since, as I have said, the matter does not need to be considered in this light.[18]

This passage has engendered a good deal of controversy. In his commentary, Giulio Cesare seems to imply that the new French manner or style which Monteverdi encountered on his journey to the Low Countries was represented in the *Scherzi musicali*. Taking this as his starting-point, Henry Prunières argued that in this volume Monteverdi was influenced by the *musique mesurée à l'antique* of Claude Le Jeune and others.[19] Doubt was cast on Prunières's theory by D. P. Walker,[20] and it was decisively rejected by Leo Schrade,[21] who even went so far as to doubt whether the *scherzi* were actually linked with the *canto alla francese*.[22] The two madrigals in Book VIII that are clearly marked as being 'sung with a full voice, in the French manner', and their sister piece, the third *Confitebor* of the *Selva morale*, are, in Schrade's view, a different matter. All use melodies that are stated by a solo voice and then repeated by the full choir, a practice for which there was a French precedent in, for example, the work of Pierre Guédron.[23]

A more moderate view of the subject was taken by Nino Pirrotta in his later discussion of it.[24] He noted that the texts by Chiabrera set in the *Scherzi musicali* were themselves based on French models and that Monteverdi's style in these pieces combines certain features from the *air de cour*—a 'measured self-possession, a prevalently quadruple

[18] Adapted from the translation in Oliver Strunk, *Source Readings in Music History* (New York, 1950), 410–11.
[19] Henry Prunières, *La Vie et l'œuvre de C. Monteverdi* (Paris, 1924, 2/1931); Eng. trans. (London, 1926/R1972), 46–51.
[20] 'The Influence of *musique mesurée à l'antique* particularly on the *airs de cour* of the Early Seventeenth Century', *Musica disciplina*, ii (1948), 148–9.
[21] *Monteverdi, Creator of Modern Music* (New York, 1950/R1964), 170–78.
[22] Ibid., 177–8.
[23] Ibid., 175–7.
[24] 'Scelte poetiche', 36–8.

rhythm, the frequent inflection of two quavers on a single syllable'—
with rhythms derived from Italian tradition.[25]

Schrade's doubt about the link between the *scherzi* and the *canto alla francese* can be dismissed immediately. Monteverdi was not the only composer to use the term 'alla francese': a colleague at Mantua, the singer, composer and poet Francesco Rasi, employed it to describe the final aria of the dialogue setting *Tu c'hai l'alba ne lumi* which he published in his *Dialoghi rappresentativi* of 1620. Ex. 11 shows the first stanza of Rasi's aria as transcribed by Alfred Einstein, with the text underlaid for the first soprano only.[26] The rubric to the aria reads 'Aria alla Francese. Si può Cantare all'unisono da due il primo soprano alla francese. E si può cantare a due voci' ('Aria in the French manner. The first soprano [line] may be sung in unison by two voices in the French manner; or it may be sung as a duet').

Ex. 11

O del ar - c'o de - gli stra - li Che mor - ta - li Fai le pia - gh'in me - z'al co - re Con-tra che non val ar - mar - si Ne sot - trar - si Per fug - gir l'em - pio fu - ro - re, [Per fug - gir l'em - pio fu - ro - re.]

[25] Ibid., 38.
[26] The only known copy of Rasi's publication was destroyed during World War II. Its contents survive in vol. 53 of Einstein's transcriptions, housed in the library of Smith College, Northampton, Massachusetts.

Rasi's double use of the designation 'alla francese' is interesting, since it separates performance manner from compositional style. The aria is 'in the French manner'. Its text (by Rasi himself) has the 8:4:8:8:4:8 pattern of syllables that Chiabrera derived from Ronsard; and its scoring and melodic style (including pairs of quavers for single syllables) are very similar to those employed by Monteverdi in Ex. 6 above, putting it beyond doubt that some at least of Monteverdi's *scherzi* are indeed 'in the French manner'. The first soprano line of Rasi's aria can also be sung by two voices in unison 'alla francese'. In this context the term may mean, as it does in Monteverdi's later work, 'to be sung with a full voice' rather than with the lighter, more restrained tone usually reserved for chamber music. What is interesting is that the melody line can be sung in unison by two voices, a notion that conflicts with the usual performing practice for continuo song. Here, however, we are dealing with a self-sufficient melody in regular rhythm, not the flexible arioso of the Florentine solo madrigal.

With this in mind, it is worth looking again at the passage from Giulio Cesare Monteverdi's 'Dichiaratione'. The main thrust of his argument was to establish that it was his brother, and not Artusi, who had first coined the term 'seconda prattica'. This was necessary because Artusi had used the term in print in 1603, two years before Monteverdi himself.[27] Monteverdi responded in the foreword to his fifth book of madrigals (1605) by claiming the term as his own, in the words that Giulio Cesare glosses. Artusi evidently replied in the now lost *Discorso musicale*, saying that the term was not worth stealing. The implication that Monteverdi's ideas were not worthy of imitation stung Giulio Cesare into drawing Artusi's attention to Monteverdi's precedence in the matter of introducing the new *canto alla francese* into Italy. His statement that the style first appeared in print some three or four years earlier clearly refers not to publications of French music but to the work of those Italian composers who had stolen Monteverdi's thunder by publishing sacred and secular works in the new French manner before he could do so himself.

The most obvious candidate for the role of 'thief', at least in the field of secular music, is the Florentine composer Giulio Caccini. In the preface to his *Le nuove musiche* (Florence, 1602), Caccini claimed not only that he had been the first to cultivate the new manner of

[27] Giovanni Maria Artusi, *Seconda parte dell'Artusi, overo Delle imperfettioni della moderna musica* (Venice, 1603), 16, 33. It is on the latter page that Artusi describes the Second Practice as 'the dregs of the first'.

declamatory solo song but also that he had introduced a new style of canzonetta writing:

Upon my return to Florence I reflected on the fact that also at that time certain canzonettas were common among musicians, for the most part with despicable words that appeared unseemly to me and were deprecated by men of sensibility. And it occurred to me, as a way of occasionally relieving depression, to compose some canzonettas in aria style that could be used in concert with several stringed instruments [*in conserto di più strumenti di corde*]. Having communicated this thought of mine to many gentlemen of the city, I was courteously gratified by them with many canzonettas in verses of various metres, as also later by Signor Gabriello Chiabrera, who favoured me with a great many, quite different from all the rest, offering me a fine opportunity for variety. All of these, set by me to divers arias from time to time, were not found displeasing anywhere in Italy: nowadays anyone who wants to compose for a solo voice uses this style.

He goes on:

In both madrigals and airs . . . I have hidden the art of counterpoint. I have formed chords on the long syllables, avoiding them on the short, and I have observed the same rule in making *passaggi*, although for a bit of decoration I have sometimes used, mainly on short syllables, a few quavers for as long as a quarter of one tactus or a half at the most. These are permissible since they pass by quickly and are not *passaggi* but merely an additional bit of grace.[28]

None of the strophic canzonettas in *Le nuove musiche* actually has an accompaniment for stringed instruments, and in most Caccini employs a madrigalian style replete with *passaggi*. In his setting of Chiabrera's *Belle rose porporine*, however, he does follow quite closely the rhythmic pattern produced by the 8:4:8:8:4:8 verse form; and he graces the aria not with *passaggi* but by dividing long notes into shorter note-values without disturbing the musical metre (Ex. 12). The result is a setting closely akin to those found in Monteverdi's *Scherzi*.

 Canto alla francese may, then, refer both to a manner of performance—singing with a full voice—and to a melodic style in which clear-cut phrases are graced with patterns that do not disturb the underlying musical metre. This melodic style is characteristic both of settings in the *Scherzi musicali* and of the two five-part madrigals *Dolcissimo uscignolo* and *Chi vuol haver felice e lieto il core* in Book VIII. Neither of the later settings is madrigalian in the usual sense of attempting a close match

[28] Adapted from the translation in Giulio Caccini, *Le nuove musiche*, ed. H. Wiley
 Hitchcock, Recent Researches in the Music of the Baroque Era, ix (Madison,
 1970), 46–7.

Ex. 12

between the meaning of the words and the musical setting. In *Dolcissimo uscignolo*, for example, Monteverdi ignores the poetic contrast between the nightingale's happy state and the lover's desolation, preferring instead to imbue the whole setting with a sense of wistful longing. Melody is the mainspring of the concept; and the melodies employ the quaver patterns which are also found in the *scherzi* (Ex. 13). A similar melodic style is used for the recurring theme in the large-scale setting of Petrarch's *Vago augelletto che cantando vai*, though this work is not described as being in the French manner, possibly because the passages using a 'French' style of melody are juxtaposed with passages employing the more usual madrigalian devices of declamation and word-painting.

The date of publication of the seventh book of madrigals—1619—may be taken as a convenient dividing line between two stages in Monteverdi's career as a madrigalist at Venice. The first was essentially a period of transition, as he established himself in his new environment, acquiring new patrons while retaining a close association with music at the court of Mantua. The transitional nature of these early years at Venice is reflected in the music of Book VII, in which works that are identifiably Venetian in character coexist with works that extend and develop the techniques and styles of Monteverdi's Mantuan music.

The 1620s and 1630s, however, saw a number of changes in Monteverdi's style and in his approach to madrigal writing. These changes were to some extent influenced by new patterns of patronage and by the work of the younger monodists and continuo madrigalists working in Venice and northern Italy during the third and fourth decades of the century. For even in his old age Monteverdi remained responsive to new developments in musical style. The nature of his response was, though, conditioned by his own long experience as a composer. In this respect it is worth noting, for example, that during his years at Venice the composition of light madrigals in general and strophic canzonettas in particular seems to have remained almost inextricably linked in Monteverdi's mind with the three-part texture of the late sixteenth-century canzonetta. The association of light madrigal and three-part texture is already evident in the three-part settings of Book VII, and it is continued in Book VIII (1638), where, with one exception (*Ogni amante è guerrier*), all the three-part works are either canzonettas (*Non partir ritrosetta, Su, su, pastorelli vezzosi*), or sectional arias (*Gira il nemico insidioso, Ninfa, che scalza il piede*), or madrigalian settings of strophic texts (*Perchè t'en fuggi, o Fillide*).

Ex. 13

One new style particularly associated with Venice during the 1620s and 1630s is the broad, *bel canto* type of triple-metre writing represented, for example, in Grandi's solo aria *Vientene, o mia crudel* from his fourth book of *Cantade et arie* (1629; Ex. 14). In Monteverdi's

Ex. 14

work, the new interest in triple-metre writing is reflected not so much in his music for solo voice as in his late three-part canzonettas, almost all of which are written in triple metre or contain extended passages of such writing.

Monteverdi wrote canzonettas throughout his career, though most were issued in anthologies or in collections of his work published by other men. Indeed, our picture of his output would be seriously distorted if we relied solely on the music that he himself chose to publish. The only publication of canzonettas in which he seems to have been directly involved was that of the *Canzonette a tre voci* of 1584. His *Scherzi musicali* of 1607 were collected for publication by his brother Giulio Cesare, the *Scherzi musicali* of 1632 by the publisher Bartolomeo Magni, and the *Madrigali e canzonette* of 1651 posthumously by the publisher Alessandro Vincenti.

This last volume contains nine of the sixteen three-part canzonettas that survive from Monteverdi's later years at Venice. There must, of course, always be some doubt about the authenticity of works published eight years after the composer's death. In the case of the *Madrigali e canzonette*, however, some of the contents can be authenticated from other sources, and the probability that the remainder are indeed by Monteverdi is increased by the close association that he enjoyed with Vincenti during his later years at Venice. Our knowledge of this association derives in part from the fact that Vincenti published Monteverdi's eighth book of madrigals, as well as the *Madrigali e canzonette* and the *Messa . . . et salmi* of 1650, but it is confirmed in a poem dedicated to the publisher by the Modenese poet–composer Bellerofonte Castaldi, a friend and admirer of Monteverdi. The poem is not dated but may have been written after 1638.[29] In addition to

[29] See Paolo Fabbri, 'Inediti monteverdiani', *Rivista italiana di musicologia*, xv (1980), esp. 81–3.

congratulating Monteverdi on his good sense in not accepting a post in Germany,[30] Castaldi reveals that Vincenti's shop was a regular meeting-place for musicians and lovers of music, among them Monteverdi,

> Il cui 'ngegno vie piu florido, e verde
> Quanto piu con l'età si và avvanzando,
> Piu nel compor leggiadro si rinverde.[31]

(whose genius becomes the more flourishing and green the more he advances in age, the more he renews himself in graceful composition.)

It is known that Monteverdi enjoyed talking about music,[32] and Vincenti's bookshop evidently provided him with a forum for this; and since the relationship between composer and publisher was more than a purely business one, it is quite likely that Vincenti would have had access to manuscripts of the composer's work over and above those delivered to him specifically for publication.

Taken as a group, the late canzonettas form a substantial and quite varied body of music. Most are scored for male voices and are simple strophic settings in which the same music is used for each stanza of the text. Some, however, attempt a more ambitious design. *Alcun non mi consigli* (1651), for example, is a set of strophic variations in which declamatory writing in duple metre is contrasted with a rich triple-metre refrain. And *Ninfa, che scalza il piede* (1638) is a sectional aria, with a different musical setting for each of its three sections (the *terza parte* is a setting of two stanzas of the text). Here Monteverdi builds progressively from one to three voices and varies the setting in response to the images of the text. In the first section of the aria the nymph's happy singing and

---

[30] Fabbri, op. cit., 82, suggests that Monteverdi had been invited to work in Poland rather than Germany.

[31] Loc. cit.

[32] See the letter of 27 November 1627 from Antonio Goretti to Marquis Enzo Bentivoglio, translated in Stuart Reiner, 'Preparations in Parma—1618, 1627–8', *The Music Review*, xxv (1964), 301, and also given by Stevens in *The Letters of Claudio Monteverdi*, 378–9. In this letter, written while Monteverdi was preparing stage works for performance at Parma, Goretti commented on Monteverdi's working methods: 'Signor Claudio composes only in the morning and evening: during the afternoon he does not wish to do anything at all . . . he is a man who likes to talk things over in company at great length (and about this, I make it a rule to take the opportunity away from him during working hours).'

dancing is conveyed by cross-rhythms between voice and bass; and in the last section, as she flees from her would-be lover, the tempo of the music quickens to *presto*, only slowing at the end as he hurls a curse after her. This essentially madrigalian response to the images of the text is typical of Monteverdi, and even in his simpler strophic settings he was rarely content, as were some of his younger contemporaries, simply to write appealing melodies.

It is impossible to date most of the late canzonettas precisely, though 1638 is obviously the terminus for the works in the eighth book and 1640 for the spiritual canzonettas in the *Selva morale*. More precise dates can, however, be suggested for two works. The first is *Ahi, che si partì il mio bel sol adorno*, for two sopranos and tenor, which survives in manuscript at Modena. This may just conceivably be one of the three-part canzonettas that Monteverdi sent, together with some madrigals, to Cesare I d'Este, Duke of Modena, in 1624.[33] The second datable work is *Come dolce hoggi l'auretta* (published in 1651). This graceful canzonetta, with its interweaving of three soprano voices reminiscent of music written for the consorts of ladies' voices at Ferrara and Mantua, is not, however, an independent work but a strophic chorus from the opera *Proserpina rapita*, which Monteverdi composed to a libretto by Giulio Strozzi for performance in 1630.[34]

The finest of Monteverdi's late settings of strophic texts, and one in

---

[33] See *The Letters of Claudio Monteverdi*, 283. For the correspondence concerning the madrigals and canzonettas that Monteverdi sent to Modena, see Fabbri, op. cit., 75–8. *Ahi, che si partì* is edited in *Tutte le opere*, xvii, 38. If this is one of Monteverdi's later works, then it is unusual among them in being called 'Villanella' and in being scored for three unaccompanied voices. Its style, too, seems more akin to that of the canzonettas in Monteverdi's 1584 book.

It is possible, though unlikely, that Monteverdi underestimated the degree of sophistication of music required by the Modenese court. In 1622, the Duke of Modena had purchased copies of nearly all Monteverdi's published madrigals, the *Scherzi musicali* of 1607 and *Orfeo* (Fabbri, op. cit., 74); and Sigismondo d'India, who worked at Modena between October 1623 and April 1624, wrote the complex virtuoso madrigals of his eighth book (Rome, 1624) for performance there. He stated in the dedication to the book that the Duke of Modena's singers were 'the best who today may be heard in Europe'. Even allowing for a measure of flattery in d'India's statement, it seems unlikely that the Duke of Modena would have required unsophisticated villanellas for his *concerto*.

[34] See Thomas Walker, 'Gli errori di "Minerva al tavolino": osservazioni sulla cronologia delle prime opere veneziane', *Venezia e il melodramma nel Seicento*, ed. Maria Teresa Muraro (Florence, 1976), 13.

which his ability as a melodist is to the fore, is the *Lamento della ninfa*
(1638). This is one of the 'opuscoli in genere rappresentativo', the 'little
theatrical works', which, according to the title-page of Book VIII, were
intended to be performed as brief episodes between songs that were
sung without gesture or theatrical action. At first sight, this work may not
appear to be based on a strophic text. Nevertheless, the poem, by
Rinuccini, was originally cast in regular stanzas with refrain and was set
as such by, for example, the Roman composer Giovanni Girolamo
(Johann Hieronymus) Kapsberger in his *Libro secondo di villanelle*
(Rome, 1619).[35] To give an idea of the original form of the text, here are
the first two stanzas:

> Non havea Febo ancora
> Recato al mondo il dì,
> Che del suo albergo fuora
> Una donzella uscì.
> Miserella, ah più, no, no,
> Tanto gel soffrir non può.
>
> Su 'l palidetto volto
> Scorgeasi il suo dolor.
> Spesso le venia sciolto
> Un gran sospir dal cor.
> Miserella, ah più, no, no,
> Tanto gel soffrir non può.

Unlike Kapsberger, Monteverdi saw the dramatic possibilities of the
text, which consists of two passages of narrative surrounding a central
lament. He set the narration (omitting the refrain) for three male voices
and the lament as a marvellously expressive solo above the descending
tetrachord ostinato which was to become the 'emblem' of the lament in
later operas and song-books.[36] The three male singers who introduce
and conclude the action are retained as onlookers during the lament and
interject the words of Rinuccini's refrain: 'Unhappy one, ah, no more
can she suffer such indifference.' (Ex. 15)

　Although Monteverdi continued to work for the Mantuan court after

[35] Transcribed in John Whenham, *Duet and Dialogue in the Age of Monteverdi*
(Ann Arbor, 1982), ii, 332–3.
[36] See Ellen Rosand, 'The Descending Tetrachord: an Emblem of Lament',
Musical Quarterly, lxv (1979), 346–59.

Ex. 15

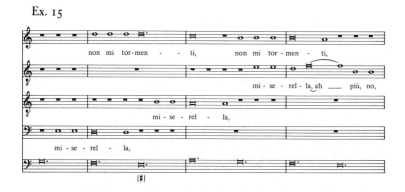

1619, the 1620s and 1630s saw a distinct broadening of the base of patronage that he enjoyed, with commissions for music coming from Modena, Parma and Ferrara,[37] performances of his music in Vienna, and important musical engagements within Venice itself. As the leading musician of the Venetian state, Monteverdi must have been the first choice as musical director for any aristocratic visitor to the city. Two examples of the private engagements that he undertook during the 1620s are recorded in his correspondence. The first is mentioned in a letter of 15 March 1625, when he excused his delay in replying to Alessandro Striggio by saying that he had been much occupied by serving King Sigismund of Poland 'both in his chapel and at his court'.[38]

[37] See *The Letters of Claudio Monteverdi*, 397–401, and Carlo Vitali, 'Una lettera vivaldiana perduta e ritrovata; un inedito monteverdiano del 1630 e altri carteggi di musicisti celebri, ovvero Splendori e nefandezze del collezionismo di autografi', *Nuova rivista musicale italiana*, xiv (1980), 410–12.

[38] *The Letters of Claudio Monteverdi*, 286.

The second, and more detailed reference occurs in a letter of 24 July 1627, again to Striggio:

I beg you to forgive me for missing the previous post, not having replied to Your Lordship's most kind and courteous letter; because the many tasks I had last Saturday (the post day) were the reason for my failure. There were two tasks: one was having to provide chamber music from 1 p.m. until 4 p.m. for the Most Serene Prince of Neuburg, who is staying incognito in the house of the English Ambassador; and this music being over, I then had to go—pressed by the entreaties of many friends—to the Carmelite Church, as it was the day of First Vespers of the Most Holy Madonna of that Order, and stay there fully occupied until almost 9 p.m.[39]

Occasionally, such music-making for distinguished visitors assumed a semi-official function, as in 1628, when Monteverdi supplied a setting of five sonnets by Giulio Strozzi—*I cinque fratelli*—for a banquet at the Arsenal given by the Venetian state to honour a visit by the Grand Duke Ferdinando II of Tuscany and his brother, Gian Carlo de' Medici.[40] There may have been other state occasions for which Monteverdi provided music. In 1623, for example, the Duke and Duchess of Mantua paid a state visit to Venice en route for Loreto. Their visit was described briefly in a letter of 9 June 1623 written by the English Ambassador to Venice, Sir Henry Wotton:

We had here ten days the Duke and Duchess of Mantova, Prince and Princess of Guastalla, with a train of as many as three great houses and the *foresterie* of two convents could harbour, at the public charge of some 1,500 crowns a day for their table. . . . At their approaching, they were attended in one of the nearer islands (having been first well feasted at Chioggia) with a great troop of the gravest senators to second the former reception, and to conduct them through the whole length of the Canal Grande. I may pass over *in cumulo* their journal entertainments, as a sight of the public rarities, a solemn dinner in the Arsenal, a banquet on a gilded galley of command, a *regata* or race of all kinds of boats, with forty gentlemen of the freest spirits and ablest purses, appointed to adorn that show with sundry liveries and inventions, and lastly a *festa* of 100 ladies, all in new gowns as rich as the season would suffer.[41]

[39] For the complete letter, see above, 68–9.
[40] Although the music of Monteverdi's settings is now lost, the texts of Strozzi's sonnets were published in 1628. A copy of this publication survives in Florence, Archivio di Stato, Carte Strozziane III, 171; I am grateful to James Chater for this information.
[41] Logan Pearsall Smith, *The Life and Letters of Sir Henry Wotton* (Oxford, 1907), ii, 270. In a footnote to his transcription of this letter, Pearsall Smith cites the (unpublished) dispatches of Francesco Sachetti, the Tuscan Resident at

Since their visit coincided with the Feast of the Ascension, the Duke and Duchess would, at the very least, have heard the music directed by Monteverdi for the ceremony of the marriage of Venice to the sea, but it seems unlikely that this represents the total extent of their contact with the former court choirmaster, especially since they had brought with them one of Monteverdi's favourite singers, Adriana Basile.

The most indulgent of Monteverdi's patrons within Venice itself was undoubtedly the Venetian senator Girolamo Mocenigo. It was Mocenigo who gave the composer his first opportunity to write an opera for Venice, by commissioning *Proserpina rapita* for the wedding of his daughter Giustiniana; the text which was to form the basis of the libretto of *La finta pazza Licori* (proposed for Mantua in 1627) was given its first reading at Mocenigo's palazzo (now the Danieli Royal Hotel);[42] and it was here, too, that the first performance of the *Combattimento di Tancredi e Clorinda* was first given in 1624. Mocenigo may also have given Monteverdi the opportunity to write some of the very large-scale madrigal settings published in Book VIII.

The *Combattimento* is the second of the 'opuscoli in genere rappresentativo' found in Book VIII. It was first performed during the Carnival of 1624 before 'all the nobility', and Monteverdi describes in some detail the manner in which it is to be performed. The two combatants are to be armed, and Tancredi rides in on a 'Cavallo Mariano' (a hobby horse?). The combat itself is to be depicted in movement and gestures that accord with the emotions of the text. Even

---

[42.] See *The Letters of Claudio Monteverdi*, 277, n.10. For the letter in which Monteverdi mentions Strozzi's having prepared *Licori finta pazza* for one of Mocenigo's musical evenings, see ibid., 322–4, and for Monteverdi's correspondence in general with Alessandro Striggio over *La finta pazza Licori*, see above, 63–9, 71. On the question of how much—or rather, how little—of the text Monteverdi may actually have set, see Gary Tomlinson, 'Twice Bitten, Thrice Shy: Monteverdi's "finta" *Finta pazza*', *Journal of the American Musicological Society*, xxxvi (1983), 303–11.

Venice, which have not been available to the present writer but which clearly offer a more detailed description of the Duke and Duchess's visit: 'Sachetti describes at length the reception of the Duke and Duchess at the island of S. Spirito, and all the festivities of this visit, and his dispatches are full of the splendour of Venetian fêtes as we see it in Venetian pictures, gilded barges, liveries of crimson and silver, gondolas covered with velvet and flowered brocade, and music on the waters. (*Arch. Med.* 3009, May 3, 6, 10, 13, 20, &c.).' See also the details supplied by Stevens in *The Letters of Claudio Monteverdi*, 271–3.

the way in which the piece is to be introduced into the evening's entertainment is theatrical in conception, since it is to begin without warning after the performance of conventional madrigals.[43]

The *Combattimento* is a crucial work in Monteverdi's output, not least because the style that it introduced—the *stile concitato*—was closely bound up with his more general thinking on the subject of musical rhythm. A section on rhythm was to have formed part of his treatise on the *seconda prattica*, and though this theoretical work seems to have remained incomplete at his death, part of it may survive in the preface to Book VIII, in which the genesis of the *stile concitato* is discussed. According to Monteverdi, the basis of the *stile concitato* itself consisted of the division of the semibreve into sixteen semiquavers:

After reflecting that according to all the best philosophers the fast pyrrhic measure was used for lively and warlike dances, and the slow spondaic measure for their opposites, I considered the semibreve, and proposed that a single semibreve should correspond to one spondaic beat; when this was reduced to sixteen semiquavers, struck one after the other, and combined with words expressing anger and disdain, I recognized in this brief sample a resemblance to the passion which I sought, although the words did not follow metrically the rapidity of the instrument.[44]

The *stile concitato* proper (Ex. 16, bars 1–3) is clearly important in the *Combattimento*, but in setting Tasso's story of the mortal combat between Tancredi and the Saracen maiden Clorinda, Monteverdi also introduced other musical motifs evoking the actions and sounds of war. These include rhythms imitating the galloping of a horse, the use of pizzicato for the blows delivered by the combatants (Ex. 16, bars 4–5), and triadic figures suggestive of trumpet calls; and it is these triadic figures, rather than the *stile concitato* itself, that are carried over into some of the *Madrigali guerrieri*, works like the lugubrious setting of Giulio Strozzi's *Gira il nemico insidioso*.[45]

In the context of the *Combattimento* the *stile concitato* is wholly successful. It is an essentially theatrical style, and the excitement of its rhythms provides an effective contrast to the slower pacing of the narrator's depiction of nightfall and the death of Clorinda. Its aptness in madrigalian contexts is more debatable. *Altri canti d'Amor*, for example, for all its bravura, is not wholly convincing, and one suspects that it was

[43] *Tutte le opere*, viii.i, 132–3.
[44] Preface to Book VIII, translated in Strunk, op. cit., 413–14.
[45] The text was also set by Nicolò Fontei in his first set of *Bizzarrie poetiche poste in musica* (Venice, 1635); he names its author as Strozzi.

Ex. 16

D'hor in hor più si me - - sce è più ri - stret - ta Si fa la pu - - gna, e

*Qui si lascia l'arco, e si strappano
le corde con duoi diti*

spa - - da o-prar non gio-va; Dan-si con po-mi e in fe-lo-ni - ti e cru-di

written simply to form a counterpart to *Altri canti di Marte* in the quasi-symmetrical double structure of Book VIII[46] and to provide an initial tribute in the collection to its dedicatee, the Emperor Ferdinand III.

In some of the other large-scale settings, however, *concitato* motifs are more successfully integrated into the overall concept. In both *Ardo avvampo* and *Altri canti di Marte*, for example, sections of *concitato* writing are used very effectively to paint a broad contrast between, in the first case, agitation and pleasure and, in the second, war and love. In both cases, though, the *concitato* sections appear at the beginning of the setting and do not sound as though they have been artificially grafted on

[46] On the symmetrical structuring of Book VIII, see Stevens, '*Madrigali guerrieri, et amorosi*: a Reappraisal for the Quatercentenary', *Musical Quarterly*, liii (1967), 161–87.

to an otherwise more conventional madrigalian style, as happens in *Hor che 'l ciel e la terra*.

Altri canti di Marte and *Hor che 'l ciel e la terra*, both of them settings of sonnets, are works of almost symphonic proportions and among the finest in Monteverdi's output. They are genuine madrigals, yet quite different in conception from the madrigals that he wrote at Mantua. Their scale and use of massive choral sonorities may owe more than a little to his experience as a composer of sacred music for St. Mark's. The striking sonority of the opening of *Hor che 'l ciel e la terra*, for example, is comparable with the setting of 'Et in terra pax' from the seven-part concertato setting of the *Gloria* (possibly composed in 1631) included in the *Selva morale* (1641). And Monteverdi's assured handling of madrigalian composition on an extended scale seems to me to derive from his experience in making coherent settings of long, and often unwieldy, psalm texts. In a very real sense, then, the late large-scale madrigals can be said to be Venetian in style and conception.

Monteverdi's eighth book of madrigals, as heterogeneous as the seventh book though more Venetian in content, is the largest of all his madrigal collections. Each half of its double structure of 'warlike' and 'amorous' madrigals follows a similar plan to that of the seventh book, opening with large-scale madrigals and closing with a ballet, in this case *Movete al mio bel suon*, possibly written to celebrate the election of Ferdinand III as Holy Roman Emperor, and the *Ballo delle ingrate*,[47] given not in its original version but in a version adapted for performance at Vienna.[48]

It has been said of the eighth book of madrigals that 'as a presentation of human passions and an example of the humanization of music, [it] sums up Monteverdi's art',[49] and there is, indeed, something of the quality of a final *magnum opus* about it. It was, too, published during a

[47] On this work, see below, 281–3.
[48] The date 1628 sometimes given for the Viennese performance of the *Ballo delle ingrate* seems to be based on Carl von Winterfeld's undocumented assertion that the work was performed at Vienna 'twenty years' after its first performance at Mantua (*Johannes Gabrieli und sein Zeitalter* (Berlin, 1834/R1965), ii, 39). Winterfeld may simply have meant that it was performed at Vienna at some time before the publication date of Monteverdi's eighth book of madrigals, though Theophil Antonicek ('Claudio Monteverdi und Österreich', *Österreichische Musikzeitschrift*, xxvi (1971), 268) adduces some circumstantial evidence which may point to a performance in Vienna around 1626–8.
[49] Schrade, *Monteverdi*, 335.

period which saw a gradual decline in the popularity of the madrigal. At Venice, however, the fate of the madrigal seems to have been linked with a more general decline in the popularity of vocal chamber music. Its place was taken by a new attraction—opera—and in this field Monteverdi still had a contribution to make.

IV

The Opera Composer

IAIN FENLON

The Mantuan Stage Works

Truely the view of this most sweet Paradise, this *domicilium Venerum &
Charitum*, did even so ravish my senses, and tickle my spirits with such inward
delight that I said unto my selfe, this is the Citie which of all other places in the
world, I would wish to make my habitation in, and spend the remainder of my
dayes in some divine Meditations amongst the sacred Muses

Thomas Coryate (1611)[1]

In the spring of 1607, Monteverdi's first opera, *Orfeo*, to a libretto by the
younger Alessandro Striggio, was given its première before members of
the Accademia degli Invaghiti, an aristocratic academy that had strong
connections with the Gonzaga court at Mantua, which the composer
had served for some eighteen years and was to continue to serve for a
further five. The work was successful, or at least sufficiently so to
encourage further performances in Mantua and elsewhere within a
short period, as well as the publication of two editions within eight years.
Yet all the evidence suggests that *Orfeo* was eclipsed, both in
Monteverdi's view and that of his audience, by his next opera, *Arianna*,
first given in 1608 as part of the lavish entertainments marking the
dynastically and politically important marriage of Prince Francesco
Gonzaga of Mantua to Margherita of Savoy. Monteverdi's own
satisfaction with *Arianna* is apparent from his later interest in it, his
reworking as a five-voice madrigal of the famous lament (the only part of
the opera to have survived), his readiness to revise the work in 1620 (and
perhaps again as late as 1640), and his lifelong admiration for Ottavio
Rinuccini, who wrote the libretto. Remarks that he made late in his
career suggest that he believed Ariadne's lament (the opera's 'most
essential part', as he described it on another occasion)[2] to be in a sense a
distillation of his attempts in the years 1607–8 to find 'the natural way of
imitation',[3] a musico-dramatic language in which words and music

---

[1] From the account of his visit to Mantua in *Coryat's Crudities* (London, 1611).
[2] Letter to Alessandro Striggio, 21 March 1620; see *The Letters of Claudio
Monteverdi*, trans. and ed. Denis Stevens (London, 1980), 197.
[3] Letter almost certainly to Giovanni Battista Doni, 22 October 1633; see above,
83–6.

would be intimately fused. Quite apart from his view that the lament was not only at the spiritual core of the work but (by implication) of a higher compositional order than anything in *Orfeo*, it was probably Monteverdi's most successful and popular work during his lifetime. Writing some thirty-five years after its composition, Severo Bonini claimed that no musical household lacked a copy,[4] and it is the only part of either of Monteverdi's two Mantuan operas to have been so popular as to circulate in manuscript. Thus from a number of points of view the varied, flexible and highly rhetorical recitative of Ariadne's lament stands at the centre of Monteverdi's operatic writing in the years 1607–8, in the composer's view no less than in the eyes of his colleagues who sought to emulate his success in laments of their own. It provides a key both to the traditional and innovatory aspects of Monteverdi's early operatic style and to the way in which the latter evolved from the former.

It is important not to overestimate the original at the expense of the traditional. Monteverdi's Mantuan operas are not of course the earliest examples of the new medium: that distinction belongs in a purely formal sense to the unimpressive surviving fragments of the Peri–Corsi *Dafne* (first performed in 1598) and to Caccini's *Euridice* (published in 1600) and *Il rapimento di Cefalo* (staged in that year),[5] and in a more meaningful sense to Peri's *Euridice*, produced three days before *Il rapimento di Cefalo* and over two years before Caccini's *Euridice*. Peri's *Euridice* ran to two editions, more than any other early opera score except Monteverdi's *Orfeo*; it was also the only one of these Florentine works to exert any influence on Monteverdi's own writing. Yet for all that some procedures of Monteverdi (and Striggio) in *Orfeo* are indebted to the example of Peri (and Rinuccini), the greater part of the music of *Orfeo* is forged out of the composer's experience with traditional musical and theatrical forms, above all the five-voice madrigal. We should not be misled by labels such

---

[4] *Prima parte de Discorsi e regole sopra la musica*, trans. and ed. MaryAnn Bonino (Provo, Utah, 1979), 151.

[5] For the few surviving fragments of *Dafne*, see William V. Porter, 'Peri and Corsi's *Dafne*: Some New Discoveries and Observations', *Journal of the American Musicological Society*, xvii (1965), 170–96. The libretto, which later served in revised form for Marco Da Gagliano's opera given in Mantua in 1608, was first published in 1600. Caccini published the final chorus (including three elaborate solos) from *Il rapimento di Cefalo* in his *Le nuove musiche* (Florence, 1602); details of the performance are given in Angelo Solerti, *Musica, ballo e drammatica alla corte medicea dal 1600 al 1637* (Florence, 1905/R1968, 1969), 26, and A. M. Nagler, *Theatre Festivals of the Medici, 1539–1637* (New Haven, 1964/R1976), 96–100.

as 'the first true opera' into believing that *Orfeo* represents a radical break with Monteverdi's previous music; much of the writing has its roots in new styles current at the Mantuan court in the years just before his arrival, in 1589 or 1590. The road to 'the natural way of imitation' properly begins in the 1580s, not so much in Mantua as in Florence and Ferrara, where the developing social and cultural interests of the Mantuan heir and Monteverdi's future patron, Vincenzo Gonzaga, were catered for rather more fully than in the oppressive Counter-Reformation gloom of his father's court.

After his sister Margherita married Duke Alfonso II d'Este in 1579, Vincenzo became a regular visitor to the Ferrarese court, partly on account of the legendary fascinations of Barbara Sanseverina, Countess of Sala, and partly because his growing interest in music, poetry and theatre was actively encouraged by both Alfonso and Margherita. It was at Ferrara during the 1580s that Vincenzo formed friendships with Tasso and Guarini, and it was mainly there that his musical tastes were formed. Ironically, the most notable composer associated with the Estensi during the same period was not a member of the Ferrarese court but another refugee from Mantua, Giaches de Wert, *maestro di cappella* to the Gonzagas for some twenty years. Partly for personal reasons, and partly because he too seems to have found cultural life there more stimulating, Wert spent a good deal of time at Ferrara, writing music for the court, while still retaining his appointment in Mantua. Musical life at Ferrara was dominated at that time by the *concerto di donne* (the so-called 'Three Ladies of Ferrara'), and it had been largely at Margherita Gonzaga's instigation that the four sopranos who performed in this ensemble had been attracted to the court at the beginning of the decade. Together with the renowned Neapolitan bass Giulio Cesare Brancaccio, this *concerto* rapidly acquired a reputation throughout Italy for brilliantly executed florid singing and particularly for simultaneously executed diminution.[6] What was novel about the ensemble was not so much that the vocal lines were heavily ornamented but that they were ornamented simultaneously, thus requiring an improvised practice to be written down and rehearsed. The essence of the Ferrarese virtuoso style

---

[6] For the most recent and complete history of the Ferrarese *concerto di donne*, see Anthony Newcomb, *The Madrigal at Ferrara 1579–1597*, Princeton Studies in Music, vii (Princeton, 1980), i, chaps. 2–4. Useful extra documentation is published in Elio Durante and Anna Martellotti, *Cronistoria del concerto delle dame principalissime di Margherita Gonzaga d'Este* (Florence, 1979).

is seen most clearly in Luzzasco Luzzaschi's *Madrigali . . . per tre soprani*, published in 1601 but almost certainly written for the *concerto di donne* some twenty years earlier (Ex. 1).[7]

Just as the performances of the *concerto di donne* were often held in private rooms before a carefully selected audience of *cognoscenti* (true *musica reservata*), so too some of the *concerto*'s repertory remained unpublished (true *musica secreta*), as had Luzzaschi's *Madrigali*.[8] The *concerto di donne* anticipates early opera not only through the presence of professional virtuoso performers but also in its aristocratic and élitist audience. But by far the greater part of the music that can be associated with the *concerto* was published. The fashion began with three contributions (by Lelio Bertani, Marenzio and Paolo Virchi) to the anthology *Il lauro secco* (Ferrara, 1582), compiled by Tasso and others in homage to a member of the *concerto*, the Mantuan soprano Laura Peperara. It was taken up by Wert in his seventh book of madrigals (Venice, 1581) and by the Ferrarese court composer Lodovico Agostini, whose third book of madrigals for six voices (Ferrara, 1582) is probably the first complete publication designed as a monument to the ensemble.[9] The widespread impact of the style after 1585 on the writing of composers working in various parts of north and central Italy is paralleled by the formation of virtuoso ensembles elsewhere, at least in the major centres of madrigal composition. This happened in Florence (under the direction of Caccini), in Ferrara itself and, towards the end of the decade, in Rome.[10] Not surprisingly, given the close interest and involvement of both Vincenzo Gonzaga and Wert in Ferrarese musical life, it also happened in Mantua shortly after Vincenzo came into his inheritance in September 1587.[11]

The expansion of the Gonzaga musical establishment that followed

---

[7] *Troppo ben può*, from *Luzzasco Luzzaschi ferrarese (1545–1607): Madrigali per cantare e sonare a uno, due e tre soprani (1601)*, ed. Adriano Cavicchi, Monumenti di musica italiana, ii/2 (Brescia and Kassel, 1965), 61.

[8] This is true of the entire contents of Modena, Biblioteca Estense, MS Mus. F. 1358, which probably dates from about 1581–2. Many of the madrigals in this collection show the interest of Ferrarese composers in the new virtuoso style; see my remarks in a review of Newcomb, op. cit., *Journal of the American Musicological Society*, xxxv (1982), 174–81.

[9] These madrigal publications are discussed in detail in Newcomb, op. cit., i, 67ff.

[10] Ibid., 90ff.

[11] See Iain Fenlon, *Music and Patronage in Sixteenth-century Mantua*, i (Cambridge, 1980), 126–46.

Vincenzo's assumption of power, and in particular the formation of a
Mantuan virtuoso *concerto* on the Ferrarese model, is of considerable
importance for the development of Monteverdi's musical style. By early
1589, the year in which Monteverdi may well have arrived at the

Ex. 1

Gonzaga court from Cremona, the ensemble had already been formed. In April of that year the Medici Resident in Ferrara wrote a description of a visit to the court by Vincenzo Gonzaga and his retinue. 'For entertainments', he reported to his masters in Florence, 'there were rich banquets and hours of exquisite music-making ... with the Duke of Mantua came four ladies from Vicenza who sing very well and play the cornett and other instruments.' These musicians may have appeared later in the year in the elaborate *intermedi* to Girolamo Bargagli's *La pellegrina*, given in Florence to celebrate the marriage of Christine of Lorraine and Grand Duke Ferdinando de' Medici,[12] and they were certainly established in Gonzaga service by 1592 at the latest. Some impression of the virtuosity of the Mantuan ensemble is vividly conveyed by Vincenzo Giustiniani (1564–1637), who, in a remarkable description of late sixteenth-century singing styles, singled out the Mantuan and Ferrarese *concerti* for special mention:

The Ladies of Mantua and Ferrara were highly competent, and vied with each other not only in regard to the timbre and training of their voices but also in the design of exquisite passages [*passaggi*] delivered at opportune points, but not in excess. (Giovanni Luca of Rome, who also served at Ferrara, usually erred in this respect.) Furthermore, they moderated or increased their voices, loud or soft, heavy or light, according to the demands of the piece they were singing; now slow, breaking off sometimes with a gentle sigh, now singing long passages legato or detached, now groups, now leaps, now with long trills, now with short, or again with sweet running passages sung softly, to which one sometimes heard an echo answer unexpectedly. They accompanied the music and the sentiment with appropriate facial expressions, glances and gestures, with no awkward movements of the mouth or hands or body which might not express the feeling of the song. They made the words clear in such a way that one could hear even the last syllable of every word, which was never interrupted or suppressed by passages and other embellishments.[13]

Composers' reactions to the possibilities of the Mantuan *concerto di donne* are easily traceable. Wert, a major influence on Monteverdi's

[12] For the complete music, see *Les Fêtes du mariage de Ferdinand de Médicis et de Christine de Lorraine (Florence, 1589)*, i: *Musique des intermèdes de 'La pellegrina'*, ed. D. P. Walker (Paris, 1963).
[13] Translated from Lucca, Archivio di Stato, Orsucci MS 48, as given in Fenlon, op. cit., i, 192. A complete English translation is published in *Hercole Bottrigari, Il Desiderio ... Vicenzo Giustiniani, Discorso sopra la musica*, trans. Carol MacClintock, Musicological Studies and Documents, ix (American Institute of Musicology, 1962), 67–80.

music during his first years in Mantua, had been writing for the Ferrarese *concerto* since its earliest days: his eighth book of five-part madrigals (1586), dedicated to Duke Alfonso d'Este, contains many pieces suggested by the style, some of which are known to have been written as early as 1583. Widespread use of florid passage-work and simultaneous diminution is carried over into the ninth book (1588), but whereas the eighth book is a product of Ferrarese experience and contains madrigals tailored to the vocal abilities of the Ferrarese *concerto*, as Wert admitted in the dedication,[14] the ninth book has a distinctly Mantuan flavour: it was dedicated to Vincenzo Gonzaga and opens with a piece performed at his coronation.[15] Once established, the virtuoso style remained a prominent feature of Wert's madrigal writing during his last years. A similar response can be seen in Benedetto Pallavicino's fourth book of five-part madrigals (1588), also dedicated to the new Mantuan Duke. The change is not total, and some pieces hark back, in their consistent use of rather stiff contrapuntal procedures, to Pallavicino's earlier manner. But in the use of slow-moving and at times quite violent dissonance (contrasting with the surrounding brisk polyphony), and in their emphasis on diminution, many pieces in the fourth book seem clearly intended for professional performers of considerable ability. As with Wert, so with Pallavicino: once integrated into his style, the virtuoso manner remained a vital and persistent aspect of his later writing.[16]

The startling differences in musical language and poetic taste that mark off the contents of Monteverdi's second and third madrigal-books, of 1590 and 1592 respectively, from his earlier pieces are largely explained by the influence of Wert, the new performance possibilities of the Gonzaga music establishment under Duke Vincenzo's patronage, and the example of Ferrara. But other forces too were at work on Mantuan musical developments, particularly the influence of Florentine music, which although at times less direct and on occasion less clear, was undoubtedly strong. Initially at least, it was again Vincenzo Gonzaga who provided the essential link. In 1584 he took as

[14] See above, 102. Further on Wert, Pallavicino and other composers in Mantua, see §II, above, generally.
[15] See *Giaches de Wert, Collected Works*, ix, ed. MacClintock (American Institute of Musicology, 1970), 1.
[16] See, for example, some of the passage-work in Pallavicino's *O come vaneggiate, donna* and *Una farfalla cupida e vagante*, published in Fenlon, op. cit., ii (Cambridge, 1982), 112ff, 133ff.

his second wife Leonora de' Medici, who, in contrast to his first, was interested in dancing and music, particularly in the lighter song styles that became so fashionable in the second half of the 1580s. Wert, in a unique departure from the publication of madrigals and sacred music, brought out a collection of *canzonette villanelle* dedicated to Leonora in 1589. It is only one of a large number of books of canzonettas and lighter madrigals published by Mantuan composers in the years immediately following Vincenzo's assumption of power, and while this new fashion undoubtedly reflects both the quality of the social life that ensued, as well as more general north Italian musical trends, it can partly be attributed to Leonora's own musical tastes.

It was also in Florence, where Duke Vincenzo was a frequent visitor after his second marriage, that he would have encountered the most technologically sophisticated and visually spectacular examples of court theatre anywhere in Europe, particularly in the elaborate *intermedi* that were used to frame the acts of spoken plays given on important public and dynastic occasions. Since the celebrations marking Cosimo de' Medici's marriage to Eleonora of Toledo in 1539,[17] the Medici had skilfully developed the *intermedio* as an aspect of statecraft, exploiting the possibilities of the medium for emphasizing princely virtues of liberality, erudition and magnificence, and using it to underscore the legitimacy of Medici rule by association with stock figures and scenes drawn from classical mythology. In Florentine terms the evolution of the *intermedio* is, in this sense, merely one aspect of Cosimo's keen appreciation of the value of the arts, particularly the visual arts (and above all statuary and large-scale paintings for public places) as a political device. The 1589 *intermedi* are a landmark in this Florentine tradition and were partly used as a showcase for Florentine artists; it is perhaps symbolic of the close links between the Medici and the Gonzagas that so many Mantuan performers also took part. Quite apart from *intermedi*, which while not exclusively cultivated in Florence were something of a local speciality, Vincenzo Gonzaga's taste for virtuoso singing, acquired largely in Ferrara, may well have been

---

[17] The music of these celebrations is published, together with other relevant material, in Andrew C. Minor and Bonner Mitchell, *A Renaissance Entertainment: Festivities for the Marriage of Cosimo I, Duke of Florence, in 1539* (Columbia, Missouri, 1968). For the most important discussions of the 1539 *intermedi*, see Nino Pirrotta and Elena Povoledo, *Li due Orfei* (2nd, rev. edn., Turin, 1975), trans. as *Music and Theatre from Poliziano to Monteverdi* (Cambridge, 1982), 154ff, and the bibliography cited there.

strengthened by performances of the Florentine *concerto* under Caccini.

Another important link between Mantuan, Florentine and indeed Ferrarese musical traditions was the elder Alessandro Striggio; he was the father of the librettist of *Orfeo* and was born into a Mantuan aristocratic family in 1536 or 1537. His principal connections seem to have been with the Medici court; he was employed there as a musician from 1559 and provided a good deal of state and ceremonial music. Nevertheless, he maintained close relations with the Gonzaga court throughout his Florentine years and spent most of his time after 1586 in Mantua, where he died in 1592.[18] It is clear that, like his contemporary Wert, he was impressed by the new styles of virtuoso singing and particularly by the *concerto di donne*. Following a visit to Ferrara in the summer of 1584, when he heard the *concerto* ('anzi angeli del paradiso'), Striggio composed a number of madrigals in the virtuoso style for Florentine performers. These pieces have not survived, but there can be little doubt that, since he was a respected composer who had experienced the most recent developments in both Florence and Ferrara, his presence in Mantua in the later 1580s must have been conducive to the changes in musical life that occurred under Duke Vincenzo's patronage.[19]

It was the traditional set pieces of the Florentine *intermedi* and the Ferrarese–Mantuan virtuoso madrigal as much as the new Florentine recitative that Monteverdi drew upon in *Orfeo*. The declamatory style, the passionate rhetoric and the taste for Tasso's verse, all three of them legacies of Wert's madrigals, make their first appearance in the third madrigal-book, which is also filled with evidence of the technical abilities of the Mantuan *concerto*, the 'Ladies of Vicenza' (Ex. 2).[20] If, in some of the pieces in Book IV in particular, there are glimpses of the duet textures not only of the seventh book but also of some of the duets in *Orfeo* and the *Ballo delle ingrate*, that serves as a reminder that duet and polyphonic textures and monody too should not be thought of as entirely

---

[18] Details based on new documentation and thus to some extent superseding the article on him in *The New Grove*, xviii, 271ff.

[19] Striggio's letters describing his impressions of the Ferrarese *concerto* were first published in Riccardo Gandolfi, 'Lettere inedite scritte da musicisti e letterati, appartenenti alla seconda metà del secolo XVI, estratte dal R. Archivio di Stato in Firenze', *Rivista musicale italiana*, xx (1913), 528ff. A further letter in the series is given in Fenlon, op. cit., i, Appendix II, document 68.

[20] Opening of *Lumi miei, cari lumi*, taken from Fenlon, op. cit., ii, 93–4.

separate techniques. Although the madrigal aesthetic might appear
absurd and unnatural to Vincenzo Galilei the theorist—however much
Galilei the composer found himself unable to renounce it in
practice—for Monteverdi monody and polyphony were not opposites
but part of the same language. Replying to the younger Striggio, who
had sent him verses to set, Monteverdi wrote in a letter of 1609: 'I

Ex. 2

Ex. 2 cont.

thought first of setting these words for a solo voice, but if later on His Highness [the Duke] orders me to re-arrange the air for five voices, this I shall do'.[21] He seems to have experienced no great qualms about recasting Ariadne's lament as a cycle of five-voice madrigals, and indeed it was published in that form in 1614 before it was twice issued as a solo in 1623. For Monteverdi, the two media were not distinct or even merely related but were rather differently constrained manifestations of a common language designed to serve the interests of 'poesia per musica'. It is with these influences on the development of Monteverdi's early madrigal style, the importance of that style for his cultivation of solo and duet writing, and the characteristics of late sixteenth-century (particularly Florentine) theatrical music in mind that we now turn to *Orfeo* and the circumstances in which it was written.

*   *   *

Tomorrow evening His Highness the Prince is to have performed . . . a piece that will be unique because all the performers speak musically (*posciachè tutti li interlocutori parleranno musicalmente*).

Carlo Magno, Mantua, 23 February 1607,
writing to his brother in Rome.[22]

Orfeo and *Arianna* were both commissioned (or rather required), the first by Prince Francesco Gonzaga, heir to the duchy and patron of the

[21] Letter to Alessandro Striggio, 24 August 1609; see *The Letters of Claudio Monteverdi*, 64.
[22] From Pietro Canal, *Della musica in Mantova* (Venice, 1881/R1977), 101.

academy in which it was first performed during Carnival, the second as part of the official court entertainments marking Francesco's marriage to Margherita of Savoy. Comparatively little is known about the composition of *Arianna* (though that little does reveal that Monteverdi was required to change the score in response to official criticism), but the growth of *Orfeo* can be traced in a series of letters, most of them only recently identified, between Prince Francesco and his brother Ferdinando. As well as being instructive about the pitfalls that befell the preparations for the first performance, these letters give an insight into some of the constraints that were at work and underline the essentially intimate character of the opera.[23]

In early January 1607 Francesco wrote to Ferdinando, then in Pisa, about 'una favola in musica' which he was attempting to organize for performance during the next Mantuan carnival season. Not all the performers could be provided from the court's own resources, and Francesco was now seeking his brother's help in finding a suitable castrato. Within a few days Ferdinando replied that he had been able to secure the services of a singer with some theatrical experience, a pupil of Giulio Caccini and an employee of the Grand Duke of Tuscany. From later letters in the series it emerges that the 'favola in musica' was Monteverdi's *Orfeo* and that the singer in question was Giovanni Gualberto Magli, whose participation in the first performance has been known about since the nineteenth century. Moreover, it was apparently intended from the start that *Orfeo* should be given before members of the Accademia degli Invaghiti, a body typical of courtly and aristocratic academies in its emphasis on quasi-chivalric ceremonial and the genteel arts of oratory and versification. Both Francesco and Ferdinando were members, and so was Striggio; Monteverdi, no doubt on account of his low rank, was not. Like some of the early Florentine operas (Peri's *Euridice*, for example, was given by a private citizen, Jacopo Corsi, in honour of Maria de' Medici's marriage to Henri IV of France and Navarre), *Orfeo* was originally conceived as an intimate aristocratic entertainment.

Perhaps the most useful specific information to be derived from the letters concerns the allocation of roles. In contrast to so many of the Medici *intermedi*, for *Orfeo* there are no surviving costume drawings or

---

[23] The complete correspondence is discussed in my chapter, 'The Mantuan *Orfeo*', in *Claudio Monteverdi 'Orfeo'*, ed. John Whenham, Cambridge Opera Handbooks (Cambridge, in preparation). Full texts and translations of the letters are given there as Appendix 1.

engravings of the sets.[24] The libretto presents the text but gives little help with the way the action proceeds. An anthology of poems by members of the Invaghiti reveals that the distinguished tenor Francesco Rasi took part (presumably he sang the title role),[25] and, as we have seen, Magli's participation has long been established, but otherwise the names of the performers are unknown. The two editions of the score produced during Monteverdi's lifetime list the instruments in a preface, but from the extra instruments called for in the course of the work it is clear that the list is incomplete. It is unclear which of the upper-voice roles were intended for castratos and which for sopranos. The newly identified letters add to this rather sketchy picture. It seems that from the start Magli had been allocated two roles, one unspecified (but conceivably that of the Messenger), the other that of the personification of Music, who occupies the stage alone for the Prologue. Moreover, at a late stage in the arrangements the singer who was to have taken the part of Proserpina was forced to withdraw and Magli was required to take on that as well. His participation was clearly crucial; as Francesco wrote to his brother only two weeks before the first performance: 'I am here waiting eagerly from day to day—without him [Magli] the *favola* will collapse in ruins.' Quite apart from the reassuring glimpse this affords of a seventeenth-century example of the traditional last-minute first night catastrophe (*Arianna* was to suffer an even more serious fate the following year), these remarks throw fresh light on Francesco Gonzaga's well-known description of *Orfeo* written the day before the first performance:

Giovanni Gualberto has acquitted himself so well that in the brief time he has been here he has not only memorized his entire part but has declaimed with so much grace and effect that we are very satisfied with him.

Francesco's praise had as much to do with feelings of relief as with genuine admiration for Magli's singing abilities.

[24] The 1589 *intermedi* are particularly well documented. See, both for these and for others in the Medici tradition, *Feste e apparati medicei da Cosimo I a Cosimo II*, ed. Giovanni Gaeta Bertelà and Annamaria Petrioli Tofani (Florence, 1969), and *Il luogo teatrale a Firenze. Spettacolo e musica nella Firenze medicea: documenti e restituzione*, ed. Mario Fabbri, Elvira Garbero Zorzi and Annamaria Petrioli Tofani (Milan, 1975), together with the literature cited there, particularly Aby Warburg, 'I costumi teatrali per gli intermezzi del 1589', with addenda by Gertrud Bing, in Warburg, *Gesammelte Schriften*, i (Leipzig, 1932), 259ff, 394ff.

[25] *Raccolta d'alcune rime di scrittori mantovani*, ed. Eugenio Cagnani (Mantua, 1612), introductory 'Lettera cronologica'.

At a more general level the most important point to come out of these letters concerns the intimate nature of *Orfeo*. Prevailing nineteenth-century notions of opera, together with the list of instruments printed at the front of the score, have often combined to produce rather grand performances, in opera houses on large stages and with large choruses and instrumental ensembles. But other evidence suggests that the work was first given in a small room, and this may explain the different endings provided by Striggio's libretto and Monteverdi's score. The libretto, which is known to have been available to the audience at the first performance, adheres quite closely to the ending in Poliziano's late-fifteenth-century version of the legend, but the published score of 1609 substitutes a happy ending in which, as a *deus ex machina*, Apollo descends to rescue Orpheus. It would have been impossible to install the machinery required to effect the appearance of Apollo in a room the size of that in which *Orfeo* was almost certainly performed; moreover the verse that Monteverdi set in the 1609 version is not sufficiently accomplished to be Striggio's work—it suggests rather the hand of some amateur such as Ferdinando Gonzaga himself.[26] The most likely explanation of these discrepancies is that Striggio's libretto relays the text of the original version and that Monteverdi subsequently revised the work before publication: as we shall see, there was at least one Mantuan performance planned for later in 1607 for which a happy ending might have seemed more appropriate.[27] If this suggests in turn that *Orfeo* was first devised as a small-scale work, the suggestion is supported by some of Francesco Gonzaga's letters. Giovanni Gualberto Magli finally sang three roles, including the Prologue and the equally taxing part of Proserpina. Other doublings of roles no doubt took place (particularly among the minor characters), and since the size of the court music establishment at this period can be calculated, it would seem that the available resources were small.[28]

As a chamber work designed for performance before members of an

---

[26] I am grateful to Gary Tomlinson for this suggestion.

[27] See below, 275–7.

[28] Of the five payrolls surviving from the period 1587–1627, only one applies to the early seventeenth century (actually *c.* 1603–8); see Fenlon, *Music and Patronage*, i, Appendix II, document 64. From other documents it is clear that other musicians may have been permanently employed at Mantua during this period, but, even so, it is clear that the establishment both at court and at the ducal chapel of S. Barbara was small (for the latter, see Pierre M. Tagmann, 'La cappella dei maestri cantori della basilica palatina di Santa Barbara a Mantova (1565–1630)', *Civiltà mantovana*, iv (1970), 376ff).

academy, *Orfeo* is clearly in the same mould as the early Florentine operas, above all Peri's *Euridice*, but the influence goes deeper than superficial similarities in function and audience to embrace details of dramatic shape and musical language. With the collapse of the Duchy of Ferrara in 1598, the musical contacts between Mantua and Florence—strong enough since the 1580s, as we have seen—became of greater and briefly paramount importance.[29] From about the end of the century, Florentine composers and performers became an increasingly prominent feature of musical life at the Mantuan court. One such was Francesco Rasi (1574–after 1620), poet, composer, virtuoso tenor, and chitarrone player, who entered Gonzaga service in late 1598. Much in the way that Magli was to be lent to the Mantuans in 1607, Rasi was borrowed to perform in the first performances of Peri's *Euridice* and Caccini's *Il rapimento di Cefalo* given in Florence in 1600. In Mantua he sang in both *Orfeo* and, in the following year, Gagliano's *Dafne*. His two collections of monodies, *Vaghezze di musica* (1608) and *Madrigali* (1610), show a preponderance of madrigals somewhat similar in style to those of Caccini who (according to Bonini)[30] had been Rasi's teacher. As a member of the first generation of monodists, and one with practical experience of early opera, Rasi may well have been of some importance to Monteverdi's assimilation and adaptation of the monodic style in *Orfeo*.

But without doubt the most significant factors in the Mantuan cultivation of the Florentine style were the musical tastes and active patronage of Ferdinando Gonzaga. As a second son, he had been destined from the start for a career in the Church and in 1605 embarked upon two years' study of law, theology and philosophy at the University of Pisa. Evidently he had taken an interest in music from an early age. Pisa was within the Medici domains (the court retired there for part of the year), and during his time at the university he developed strong contacts with Florentine musicians, particularly with members of the Accademia degli Elevati, including Luca Bati, Gagliano, Peri and Caccini; Gagliano may have taught him composition. During his time in Pisa he took a great interest in musical life there, to the extent of composing music for performance during Carnival. His letters home to Mantua are full of details of his musical and poetic compositions, and it is hardly surprising that Francesco should have turned to him for help in securing the services of Magli. As we shall see, Ferdinando's

---

[29] See Fenlon, *Music and Patronage*, i, chap. 4.
[30] Bonini, *Prima parte de Discorsi e regole*, trans. and ed. Bonino, 149–50.

enthusiasm for Florentine music and musicians was to have a crucial effect on the Mantuan marriage celebrations of 1608.[31]

Although it is not known whether Monteverdi was present at the performances of any of the first Florentine operas, it is clear that *Orfeo* was written with considerable knowledge of the Florentine operatic tradition. In view of the powerful influence of Florentine music on the Mantuan court during the early years of the seventeenth century, it is not difficult to see how easily Monteverdi might have become acquainted with Florentine operatic and monodic styles, perhaps through the agency of Rasi or Ferdinando Gonzaga as much as by studying printed scores. For in a more precise sense there can be no doubt that in writing *Orfeo* both composer and librettist took as their model the *Euridice* of Jacopo Peri and Ottavio Rinuccini, first performed in Florence in 1600 and published the following year.[32] The striking correspondences between some of the important speeches in Rinuccini's and Striggio's texts cannot simply be explained by their dependence on some common source of the Orpheus myth such as Poliziano's *Orfeo* and its imitators. Equally persuasive is the fact that extraneous characters in *Euridice*, present neither in Rinuccini's sources nor in the myth, have analogies in *Orfeo*. A good example is Venus, introduced by Rinuccini to escort Orpheus to the underworld in an episode clearly indebted to Dante's *Inferno*. Striggio uses the same device, renaming Venus as Speranza and making the reference to Dante even more explicit by quoting and then repeating the inscription over the gates of Hades, 'Lasciate ogni speranza voi ch'entrate'. In details such as these, as well as in matters of general organization such as the dramatic material of the first two acts, there are many parallels between the two librettos. Similarly, Monteverdi's music shows if not dependence on

[31] Details of Ferdinando's career are taken from Ippolito Donesmondi, *Dell'istoria ecclesiastica di Mantova*, ii (Mantua, 1616), 370, 391, and Giovanni da Mulla's *relazione* printed in *Relazioni degli ambasciatori veneti al senato*, ed. Arnaldo Segarizzi, i (Bari, 1912), 40–41, as well as from unpublished documents in the Archivio di Stato, Mantua. Ferdinando's connections with the Elevati are discussed at length in Edmond Strainchamps, 'New Light on the Accademia degli Elevati of Florence', *Musical Quarterly*, lxii (1976), 507-35.

[32] The relationship between the two works has often been noted. See, in particular, the discussion in Gary Tomlinson, 'Madrigal, Monody, and Monteverdi's "via naturale alla immitatione"', *Journal of the American Musicological Society*, xxxiv (1981), 60–108, and the literature cited in n. 1 there. I have drawn a good deal on this article in some of the following discussion.

Peri at least indebtedness to his example. Again this is sometimes noticeable in general procedures, such as the low tessitura of the Underworld choruses in the two works, or in structural outlines, as with both composers' organization of the lamenting chorus at the end of the second act; but the connections are also quite unmistakably present in matters of detail, particularly in extensive recitative sections.

This is not meant to suggest that there is little or no difference in character between the recitative style of the two works. Monteverdi's recitative is often more rhythmically varied, more flexible in its pace, than anything to be found in *Euridice*; at the same time it is frequently less abstract, more inclined to heighten the sense of individual words by using stock devices drawn from madrigalian rhetoric. In terms both of bass-line movement and harmonic progression Monteverdi's writing is at once more varied and wide-ranging than Peri's; whereas the latter is usually restrained in these respects, Monteverdi is more forceful, representing the sense of the words through directed melodic bass lines and unexpected chordal progressions. But perhaps the most obvious of Monteverdi's innovations in his recitative style is his use of sequence. In *Euridice* Peri uses sequence only rarely, relying more on repetition to achieve rhetorical effects. Monteverdi uses repetition too, though usually on a smaller scale and for reasons of syntax; one example occurs at the Messenger's announcement of Eurydice's death, another in the course of Proserpina's opening recitative in Act IV (Ex. 3).[33] In *Orfeo*

Ex. 3

(a)

[33] From *Monteverdi, Orfeo*, ed. Edward H. Tarr (Paris, 1974): (*a*) Act II, bars 205–14; (*b*) Act IV, bars 25–34.

Ex. 3 cont.

(b)

sequence is developed as a structural device, not only, of course, within recitative passages but also elsewhere, as in the instrumental ritornellos in the Prologue:[34]

Ex. 4

[34] Ibid., Prologue, bars 17–24.

I have already stressed that Monteverdi's recitative style is intimately related to his polyphonic writing, so it is not particularly surprising to find that many of the features that distinguish Monteverdi's recitative from Peri's are taken over from his madrigals. With the new interest in Tasso's poetry that he shows in the second and third books (1590 and 1592), Monteverdi seems to have discovered for the first time the purely sonorous qualities of verse and the need to project these qualities in music. Both in terms of poetic taste and in the technical means explored to meet the challenge, his models were certain pieces by his Mantuan colleagues, above all Wert's eighth book (1586, written for the Ferrarese *concerto di donne*), which contains twelve works on texts from Tasso's epic *Gerusalemme liberata*. Although Monteverdi seems to have consciously avoided setting any of the ottavas selected by Wert, the eighth book clearly helped to stimulate the interest of a young, provincially trained composer in a new poetry and in the flexible declamatory style employed to depict shifting emphases (Ex. 5).[35] The steps

Ex. 5

are short from a moment such as this to passages in Monteverdi's own madrigals where the effects are achieved by flexible declamation and carefully timed changes of the harmonic palette (Ex. 6),[36] and ultimately to the recitative sections of *Orfeo* and the *Lamento d'Arianna* (Ex. 7).[37]

[35] From *Qual musico gentil*, in *Wert, Collected Works*, viii, ed. MacClintock (1968), 46–7.
[36] *M'è più dolce il penar*, bars 22–7, from *Tutte le opere*, v, 57–8.
[37] *Orfeo*, ed. Tarr, Act II, 335–42.

Ex. 6

Ex. 7

Similarly, characteristic gestures of line which distinguish the recitative in *Orfeo* from Peri's can often be traced to Monteverdi's experience as a madrigalist. Whereas Peri's recitative is often comparatively unruffled, Monteverdi's relies on a much wider range of note-values and is consequently better able to respond to nuances of textual emphasis and moments of drama. A typical piece of Monteverdian rhetoric in *Orfeo* is the long-note exclamation followed by a series of rapid smaller notes (Ex. 8),[38] a procedure that has many precedents in the madrigals (Ex. 9).[39]

Ex. 8

[38] Ibid., Act IV, bars 257–9.
[39] From *Stracciami pur il core* (Book III), in *Tutte le opere*, iii, 29.

Ex. 9

In at least one instance the similarities extend beyond rhythm to melodic shape as well (Ex. 10).[40] In this sense Monteverdi's recitative, while a particular and intensely personal form of expression with characteristics of its own, is forged out of both an awareness of Peri's precedent and

Ex. 10

(a)

(b)

[40] (a) *Orfeo*, ed. Tarr, Act II, bars 308–10; (b) the opening of *O com'è gran martire* (Book III), from Fenlon, *Music and Patronage*, ii, 87.

aspects of an essentially Mantuan polyphonic tradition. Freed from the constraints of a five-voice medium, Monteverdi evolved from these elements a pliable, varied and urgent declamatory manner which goes beyond the more formal and technically limited recitative of Peri and Caccini. But the roots of Monteverdi's recitative, at least in its rhythmic and harmonic aspects, lie in the Mantuan traditions of serious madrigal-writing which he encountered, particularly in the madrigals of Wert, when he arrived at the Gonzaga court.

Some parts of *Orfeo* seem to have been planned with large-scale symmetries in mind. The extent and importance of these symmetries can be over-emphasized, but the effect of balance achieved in the first act, for example, can hardly be the result of coincidence:

This has more to do with the progress of text and action than with any supposed striving for abstract musical form (to envisage which would be to view the work anti-historically). Symmetry is achieved here by

[41] Based, with modifications and extensions, on the scheme proposed for the first half of the act only in Donald Jay Grout, *A Short History of Opera* (2nd, enlarged edn., London, 1965), 52. See also the words of caution about overstating the case for symmetries elsewhere in the work in Pirrotta and Povoledo, *Music and Theatre*, 268, n. 97.

framing the recitative within certain set pieces, most of which are based on theatrical conventions that predate opera (above all those of the *intermedio*) and many of which are cast in established musical forms and styles. Here again Monteverdi drew upon Mantuan secular traditions and his own experience as a madrigalist.

Thus the opening toccata, unnecessary in terms of the action, is played three times by all the instruments before the scene is revealed; the reappearance of this music underpinning a five-part vocal texture at the beginning of the 1610 Vespers suggests that it is no more than a formalization of a set fanfare, perhaps announcing the arrival or presence of the ducal family. By tradition the performance of such ceremonial flourishes was the duty of a group of resident court players, the *alta cappella*. The first chorus, 'Vieni Imeneo', is a homophonic madrigal which achieves its effect through sensitive declamation of the text allied to a wide-ranging harmonic palette capable of underscoring affective words by carefully calculated shifts in tension. It is a type of writing that Monteverdi had used before, as had some of his Mantuan colleagues (notably Salamone Rossi in his second madrigal-book, of 1602),[42] but yet again Wert was the true father of the style. The second chorus, 'Lasciate i monti', described in the score as a 'balletto', is reminiscent of the general tone of any number of light canzonettas written in the late 1580s and 1590s but particularly of the immensely popular ballettos by another Mantuan composer, Giovanni Giacomo Gastoldi.[43] Although never as engaging a composer in the lighter styles as Gastoldi, Rossi or even Wert (who in general preferred a more serious mode), Monteverdi did occasionally write such unpretentious pieces and the *Scherzi musicali* (1607) are conceived in a similarly light-hearted vein. With its imitative opening, textural contrasts and use of opposing triple and duple dance measures, 'Lasciate i monti' is more complicated than any of Gastoldi's *Balletti a cinque* (1591), more of a light madrigal than a true canzonetta and uncannily close to a piece by Alfonso Preti, compiler of the Mantuan anthology of madrigals *L'amorosa caccia* (Venice, 1588).

And so one could go on. It would not be difficult to describe ways in which the structure of each act is articulated by similar traditional means, whether the duets and trios which are such a feature of the first

---

[42] See, for example, Rossi's *Lumi miei, cari lumi*, printed in Fenlon, *Music and Patronage*, ii, 128–32.

[43] See, for example, many of the five-voice pieces in *G. G. Gastoldi: Balletti a cinque voci 1591*, ed. Michel Sanvoisin (Paris, 1968). Also see above, 112.

two acts, or the instrumental sinfonias (also derived from the *intermedio* tradition)[44] which assist the change in atmosphere from one act to another, or the final moresca, again dramatically irrelevant and yet another refugee from the *intermedio* (many plays with music since Poliziano's *Orfeo* had ended with one[45]). By contrasting, combining and recombining these means Monteverdi imparts balance, structure, and variety of expression to what, in the hands of the Florentines, had been sung drama overwhelmed by recitative.

By bringing together styles that he had explored since his arrival in Mantua (and on the whole not before), Monteverdi rooted *Orfeo* firmly in Mantuan traditions. But this is not to undervalue the highly original way in which these elements are welded together. Nor is it to understate the originality of some of Monteverdi's musical procedures, particularly in the use of ritornello or variation structures, above all in Orpheus's prayer 'Possente spirto', the spiritual, dramatic and literal centre of the opera. It is sometimes said that the ornamented and unornamented versions are presented in the score to allow the performer to add embellishments at will to the latter, perhaps using the former as an ideal model, but Nino Pirrotta is surely right to view the more elaborate version not as a schematic one but rather as the definitive realization following the principles of the early *stile rappresentativo*. The validity of both versions is expressly stated in the direction at the head of the piece in the published score: 'Orpheus sings only one [or 'either one'] of the two parts to the accompaniment of the wooden organ and one chitarrone'.[46] As Pirrotta says:

It took a stroke of genius, after having quite effectively conceived the whole series of strophic recitative variations on a repeated bass line, to give the same basic material . . . a completely new and more sophisticated twist,

[44] See, for example, Marenzio's curtain-raiser to the second of the 1589 *intermedi* (in *Les Fêtes du mariage*, ed. Walker, 36), a sinfonia cast as two opposing dance measures. Monteverdi was to use a similar device elsewhere, notably in the *entrata* which begins the finale of the *Ballo delle ingrate*.

[45] Just one example among many is the dance-song 'Bacco, bacco e u o e', which concludes the 1539 *intermedi* (see Minor and Mitchell, *A Renaissance Entertainment*, 350–51). The persistence of the tradition is shown by Cavalieri's monumental adoption of the idea in the sixth *intermedio* of the 1589 set and again at the end of his *Rappresentatione di Anima et di Corpo* (Rome, 1600).

[46] Claudio Monteverdi, *L'Orfeo: favola in musica . . . rappresentato in Mantova* (Venice, 1609, 2/1615); facsimile reprint of the 2nd edn. (Farnborough, 1972), with introduction by Denis Stevens, 52.

reworking it into an 'orphic' rite, a highly stylized and hieratically formalized incantation, through which a superhuman singer soothes and subdues the forces of darkness crossing his path.[47]

Both as a prayer and as an incantation aria, 'Possente spirto' is the forerunner of many early seventeenth-century set pieces, including the three prayers in Stefano Landi's *Sant'Alessio* (given at Rome, probably in 1631) no less than Medea's magic scene in Cavalli's *Giasone* (produced at Venice in 1649). Indeed Orpheus's song left its mark on history in a way that no other part of the work did, and in a manner that is broadly analogous to the impact of Ariadne's lament: both established strongly characterized set pieces (prayer, incantation, lament) that reappear time and again in early opera. And in terms of Monteverdi's approach to solo song in 'Possente spirto' it is not too fanciful to see the piece as an important landmark on the road to the 'natural way of imitation'.

* * *

Among the numerous admirable feasts that were ordered by His Highness upon the superb occasion of the wedding of the Most Serene Prince his son and Her Most Serene Highness the Infanta of Savoy he wished to have a 'favola in musica'. This was *Arianna*, written by Sig. Ottavio Rinuccini whom the Duke had summoned to Mantua for this purpose. Signor Claudio Monteverdi, the most famous musician, head of the music at the court of His Highness, composed the arias in so exquisite a manner that we can affirm in all truth that the power of ancient music has been restored because they visibly moved the audience to tears.

Marco da Gagliano, *La Dafne*
(Florence, 1608), preface

There is an instructive sequel to the difficulties that preceded the first performance of *Orfeo* on 24 February 1607.[48] A further letter from Francesco to his brother, written one week later, reveals that the first performance had greatly impressed Duke Vincenzo Gonzaga, while Magli's singing had been admired particularly by the Duchess. The Duke himself had now ordered a second performance to be given on 2 March, and Magli had been kept on. Nor was this the end of the matter. From letters between Francesco and Grand Duke Ferdinando de'

---

[47] Pirrotta and Povoledo, *Music and Theatre*, 277.
[48] For a fuller discussion of them, see Fenlon, 'The Mantuan *Orfeo*', *Claudio Monteverdi 'Orfeo'*, ed. Whenham, chap. 1.

Medici, it appears that Duke Vincenzo intervened to order yet another performance, and permission was sought to keep Magli in Mantua even longer. And although the reasons for this further performance were not divulged to the Grand Duke, they were clearly political rather than artistic.

Throughout the period when *Orfeo* was being prepared and performed, negotiations were in hand to arrange the marriage of Francesco Gonzaga and Margherita, daughter of Duke Carlo Emanuele of Savoy. Discussions had begun as early as 1604, and at first the prospects seemed good. Carlo Emanuele's concern about foreign involvements in Italy was no secret. The Venetian ambassador reported a characteristic expression of it in 1609:

When all is said and done, I am an Italian; and it is essential that we [Italians] come to terms with one another. These foreigners offer their friendship not in our interest but simply to take from us all that we own and to force us to serve their purposes, so that they can rule us all the more easily.[49]

This mistrust was no doubt sharpened by Savoy's geographical position, with a border shared with France and others touched by Switzerland and (to the east) Milan, which was governed by Spain. When the possibility of a Mantua–Savoy marriage alliance became known, it posed a threat to other interests, not least to the German Emperor Rudolf II, who became alarmed by a prospective union between two fiefs of the Holy Roman Empire. Another Habsburg, Philip III of Spain, was acutely conscious that his north Italian territories lay between Mantua and Savoy. Habsburg interests united and presented the somewhat unpleasant proposal that Rudolf himself should become Margherita's suitor, principally, or solely, to forestall the Mantua–Savoy match. As his dependants, both duchies had no alternative but to allow him to press his claim: it was decided that a deadline of 31 July 1607 be set for the successful conclusion of negotiations with the Emperor.

In the spring of that year, just after the first performance of *Orfeo*, it became known that a visit to Mantua, by Carlo Emanuele, was being planned. Vincenzo Gonzaga now arranged that all steps be taken to demonstrate the suitability of Francesco as bridegroom, and the power and wealth of the Mantuan state. It was as part of these schemes that he

---

[49] Cited in *Relazioni degli stati europei lette al senato dagli ambasciatori veneziani nel secolo decimosettimo*, ed. Nicolò Barozzi and Guglielmo Berchet, iii/1 (Venice, 1862), 102.

ordered a third performance of *Orfeo*, and it may not be too fanciful to suggest that the new ending may have been written for this occasion, the original having been considered unsuitable for the entertainment of a prospective father-in-law. In the end, though, Carlo Emanuele altered his plans and cancelled his visit to Mantua, and the third Mantuan performance of *Orfeo* seems not to have taken place.

The composition of *Orfeo* must have taxed Monteverdi considerably, and by the beginning of the summer of 1607 he had returned with his wife and two young sons to his father's house in Cremona. There he remained at least until early August, but by the end of that month he was in Milan, where his friend the court theologian Cherubino Ferrari was shown *Orfeo*, which prompted an enthusiastic letter to Mantua:

> Monteverdi has let me see the verses and hear the music of the comedy which Your Highness commissioned, and in truth poet and musician have represented the emotions of the spirit so well that none can better them. The poetry is beautiful in its invention, very good in construction and perfect in expression, and all in all it fulfils everything that could be expected of so exalted a mind as that of Signor Striggio. The music is also very creditable and serves the poetry so well that one could hear nothing better.[50]

Any satisfaction that Monteverdi may have felt at enthusiastic reactions of this sort was soon clouded by the news of the serious illness of his wife Claudia; he returned quickly to Cremona, where she died in early September. No sooner had this personal tragedy occurred than Monteverdi received an urgent letter from Federico Follino, who was in overall control of the forthcoming Mantuan wedding festivities, requiring him to return to Mantua to participate in the musical arrangements. By the end of October he was back there and had discussed matters both with Francesco and with Rinuccini, who was eventually to provide the texts for two of Monteverdi's contributions to the celebrations, *Arianna* and the *Ballo delle ingrate*. As in 1607, it was clear that these works and the other projected musical item, the *intermedi* to Guarini's play *Idropica*, could not be rehearsed and performed by Mantuan resources alone. Both Duke Vincenzo and the Duchess Eleonora turned again to the Grand Duke of Tuscany for assistance, but this time (perhaps the extended loan of Magli was fresh in the Grand Duke's mind) the reply was negative. By the end of December enquiries were being made elsewhere, more urgently now,

[50] See Fenlon, 'The Mantuan *Orfeo*'.

since the wedding was scheduled to take place at the end of Carnival, about 19 February 1608.

But there were other forces at work. It had been agreed by the parties that a new deadline for the Emperor Rudolf's claim for Margherita's hand would be set for 20 January. That date now passed without the Mantuans proceeding with all speed to a successful conclusion of the Savoy–Gonzaga match. There were a number of reasons for this apparently strange reluctance. One was that Rudolf was still procrastinating, and the Duke of Mantua had been instructed quite firmly 'not to hurry the marriage'. More persuasive was a careful strategy worked out by Spain which made haste suddenly seem less desirable. Under the terms of the proposed marriage agreement, Mantua and Savoy were to exchange certain territories in such a way that the boundaries of both states would be better consolidated, but in January Philip III announced that the planned exchange could not take place: it was illegal, since both Spain and Milan (Spain's deputy) had a latent claim on some of the lands specified in the agreement. The Mantuans were caught in a cleft stick. Should Mantua and Savoy carry out their territorial contract, then military action by Spain and Milan would almost certainly result, but to renege on an agreement with the fiery and impulsive Carlo Emanuele was equally perilous. The Mantuans were justifiably fearful and in desperation were reduced to writing pleas for divine intervention on the walls of the city. Whatever the final outcome, further postponement was inevitable, and it was now announced that the marriage would not take place until after Easter, leaving cynical observers to speculate wryly on which year was being contemplated. Officially, and somewhat improbably given the tradition of hedonism that had characterized the season during Duke Vincenzo's years, this further alteration to the arrangements was explained away by the imminence of Lent.[51]

The delay probably made little difference to Monteverdi. It is doubtful whether he had seen a word of Rinuccini's text before October 1607, yet according to Ferdinando Gonzaga most of the music had been written by the beginning of February.[52] This is more or less confirmed by one of Monteverdi's letters which mentions that the work, finally performed at the end of May, had taken five months to rehearse—it is

---

[51] For further details, see Stuart Reiner, 'La vag'Angioletta (and Others), Part I', *Analecta musicologica*, xiv (1974), 66ff.

[52] Quoted in Stefano Davari, *Notizie biografiche del distinto maestro di musica Claudio Monteverdi desunte dai documenti dell'Archivio Storico Gonzaga* (Mantua, 1884), 14, n. 1.

small wonder that twenty years later he could still recall that the composition of *Arianna* had worked him nearly to death.[53] And although there is no direct evidence, it may be that, having finished *Arianna*, he was able to find time to write (or perhaps to some extent assemble from pre-existing material) the so-called 1610 Vespers, which, in all probability, were first performed—if only in part—during the marriage celebrations.[54] Yet while the delay did not make the composition of *Arianna* more leisurely, it was certainly both embarrassing and expensive for the court. It was no doubt as a sop to the disappointed nobility who had gathered from many parts of Italy for nuptial celebrations that seemed increasingly imaginary as the days passed that Marco da Gagliano's *Dafne* was presented in the middle of February. *Dafne*, a setting of Rinuccini's reworked pastoral drama originally set by Peri and Corsi, had probably been intended as part of the wedding entertainment, but in the difficulties of the hour Gagliano had to content himself with one of the *intermedi* for *Idropica* and the composition of a *ballo*, *Il sacrificio d'Ifigenia*.

In the event, while the Spanish manœuvre succeeded in inhibiting progress for a while, it did not prevent Mantua and Savoy from finding a way round the difficulty. Eliminating from their formal agreement, though not from their minds, the areas disputed by Spain, they hastily concluded the marriage before further obstructive ploys could be devised. In mid-February Carlo Emanuele announced his acceptance of Francesco as a bridegroom for Margherita, and a few days later the marriage took place in Turin by proxy. Additional difficulties between Vincenzo Gonzaga and Carlo Emanuele delayed Margherita's departure for Mantua still further, and it was not until 24 May that 'the ceremonial barge carrying the Most Serene bride . . . was sighted',[55] and the long overdue celebrations finally got under way. Within a mere fifteen days the entire programme of entertainments—tournaments, stage works and feasts—was given.

Arianna was first performed on 28 May 1608, having been, on the composer's evidence, in rehearsal for some months. Certainly, the preparations had not been without difficulty. For one thing composer

[53] Letter to Alessandro Striggio, 1 May 1627; see above, 62–3.
[54] This is suggested, and such evidence as there is is produced, in Fenlon, 'The Monteverdi *Vespers*: Suggested Answers to Some Fundamental Questions', *Early Music*, v (1977), 380–87.
[55] Federico Follino, *Compendio delle sontuose feste fatte l'anno M.DC.VIII nella città di Mantova* (Mantua, 1608), 6–7.

and librettist had been forced to make revisions to the work as late as the end of February, when, at a meeting with them both, together with Follino and the stage designer, Antonio Maria Viani, the Duchess of Mantua proclaimed it 'very dry'.[56] But the most serious setback concerned Caterina Martinelli, a young singer who had earlier lodged for three years with Monteverdi and his family. She had been coached for the title role, but while learning it she contracted smallpox, and she died in early March. This was both a professional and a personal blow for Monteverdi. Martinelli was evidently the most accomplished female singer at court and had performed the role of Venus in Gagliano's *Dafne* earlier in the year. In the end Virginia Andreini, a member of a visiting theatrical troupe, the Comici Fedeli, was able to learn the title role and carry it off with some success.[57]

The stylistic differences between the recitatives in *Orfeo* and Ariadne's lament are striking. Repetition of key words and phrases, an essential part of Monteverdi's musico-rhetorical art, is achieved in *Orfeo* only at the expense of the destruction of the prosody, but in the lament such repetitions are carefully integrated into Rinuccini's poetic structure.[58] In place of the rhythmic complexity and sudden changes in harmonic rhythm of the earlier work, the rhetoric of *Arianna* is balanced, and rhythmic variety is more subtly achieved. Madrigalisms are now abandoned; drama is created through a fluid melodic style, simpler than that of *Orfeo* but capable of projecting a much greater range of textual nuance. In a more obvious way too the structure of the text has parallels in the music: the repetition of both the music and the text of the opening at the conclusion of the first part is the clearest example, and the repeated calls to Theseus which punctuate the work provide another.

The impact of Ariadne's lament was both powerful and long-lived and may have prompted Monteverdi's decisions to reissue the piece in various guises throughout his career. Other composers seem to have been fascinated by the possibilities of the idea as revealed by Monteverdi's example, and the interest in writing laments increased through the 1620s to reach its height in the 1630s. An extreme example of adulation came from Filippo Vitali in *Aretusa* (1620), the first opera produced in Rome, whose preface praises Monteverdi's 'peregrini

---

[56] Quoted in Solerti, *Gli albori del melodramma* (Milan, 1904/R1969), i, 92.
[57] For Gagliano's report of the impact of the music, see above, 275.
[58] See the discussion in Tomlinson, 'Madrigal, Monody, and Monteverdi's "via naturale . . ." ', 86ff.

pensieri' in *Arianna*.[59] Vitali's work consists of little else except a string of
laments: it opens with Alpheius telling of his unrequited love for
Arethusa, followed by Arethusa troubled by a disturbing dream, by her
father troubled by a premonition, by her brother troubled in case
premonition should turn into reality, by a distressed shepherd who
announces her death and Alpheius's grief, and finally by the
inconsolable Alpheius *in persona*. A mournful chorus brings the
proceedings to a close. More important than such consequences is the
fact that Monteverdi himself recognized the special character of the
language of Ariadne's lament in the famous letter of 1633, almost
certainly written to the philologist and music theorist Giovanni Battista
Doni, in which he describes the piece as the fruit of his search for the
'natural way of imitation' and, by implication, a more complete bonding
of words and music than anything he had written before.[60] Interestingly,
Doni himself attributed the success of the piece in part to the special
qualities that Rinuccini brought to the enterprise, 'even though he was
not skilled in music (making up for this with his fine judgment and keen
ear, as one knows from the character and form of his poetry)'.[61] Yet
although Monteverdi went on to make other settings of Rinuccini's
verse and maintained a close relationship with the poet until his death in
1621, the two did not collaborate again after 1608.

Following the performance of *Arianna* the next musical item of any
significance in the calendar of festivities celebrating the Mantua–Savoy
marriage came on 2 June, when Guarini's *Idropica* was given, with
intermedi by Gabriello Chiabrera. The musical work had been divided
between a number of composers, with Monteverdi providing the
Prologue; none of the music has survived. Two days later, Monteverdi's
Ballo delle ingrate was performed, the fruits of a further collaboration
with Rinuccini. It was by no means his first experience of writing staged
ballets; he may well have been present in 1598 when Gastoldi's setting
of the 'Giuoco della cieca' was performed as part of an elaborate
performance of Guarini's *Il pastor fido*, and in 1604 he was busy
composing two *entrate* and two dances. Writing in the 'Dichiaratione'
published as a preface to Monteverdi's *Scherzi musicali* of 1607, Giulio
Cesare Monteverdi apologized for his brother's neglect of the famous
dispute with the theorist Giovanni Maria Artusi, claiming that he was

[59] For this and further reactions to Ariadne's lament, see above, 193–4.
[60] See n. 3 above.
[61] Doni, *Trattato della musica scenica*, chap. 9, quoted from Solerti, *Le origini del
melodramma* (Turin, 1903/R1969), 214.

overburdened at court not only with his regular duties but also 'now with tourneys, now with ballets, now with comedies and various concerts'.[62] The composition of such occasional pieces may have been a frequent, though now largely invisible, aspect of Monteverdi's work at court.

The plot and some details of style and structure of the *Ballo delle ingrate* show obvious affinities with *Orfeo*, most noticeably the opening, which is set, as are the fourth and fifth acts of the opera, in Hades. The ballet begins with a dialogue between Venus and Amor in which Amor asks Venus to intercede with Pluto on behalf of the *ingrate* (women who have shown hard-heartedness to their lovers) so that they may return to earth. This Pluto eventually allows, partly since the spectacle can serve as a warning to the ladies in the audience (and principally of course to Margherita of Savoy). Slowly the *ingrate* emerge while Amor and Venus express their shock and pity at their fate. The *ballo* proper follows; except in the middle, the same material is used for the entire dance, but the basic rhythms, the steps and figures of the dance, change from section to section. This is often said to be a French procedure, but Monteverdi is far more likely to have been influenced by Italian precedents such as Gastoldi's *Giuoco della cieca* and, above all, Cavalieri's monumental and epoch-making final *ballo* for the 1589 Florentine *intermedi*.[63] Finally Pluto points the moral of the story in a long arioso section punctuated by a short instrumental ritornello. As the *ingrate* are commanded to return to Hades, one of them sings a final lamenting farewell to light and air ('Aer sereno e puro,/Addio, per sempre addio'), and a group of four others admonish the audience: 'Apprendete pietà, donne e donzelle'. The final lament is shorter than the *Lamento d'Arianna* but is close to it stylistically, particularly in its simple and rhythmically balanced melodic lines, underpinned by varied harmony. The textual 'point', contrasting the earthly air which the *ingrate* must now leave for ever with the cruelty of their fate, is made simply and effectively; the 'serene and pure' air is expressed with a slight rising gesture set consonantly, while the plaintive farewell is given a characteristic drooping phrase supported by a less settled harmonic sequence, which has obvious madrigalian parentage (Ex. 11).[64]

Although only twelve letters written by Monteverdi during his

<hr>

[62] English translation from Oliver Strunk, *Source Readings in Music History* (New York, 1950), 416; repr. (New York, 1965), iii, 46.

[63] For this tradition and its origins, see Fenlon, *Music and Patronage*, i, 146–62.

[64] (a) From the *Ballo delle ingrate* in *Tutte le opere*, viii, 346–7; (b) end of *Si ch'io vorrei morire*, from *Tutte le opere*, iv, 83.

Ex. 11

(a)

A - er   se - re - no e pu - ro,   Ad - dio per sem - pre, ad - di - o,

(b)

Si ch'io vor-rei mo - ri - re, ch'io vor - rei mo - ri - re, ch'io vor - rei __ mo - ri - re.

Si ch'io vor-rei mo - ri - re, ch'io vor - rei mo - ri - re, ch'io vor-rei mo - - ri - re.

Si ch'io vor-rei mo - ri - re, ch'io vor - rei mo - ri - re, ch'io vor - rei mo - ri - re.

Si ch'io vor-rei mo - ri - re, ch'io vor - rei mo - ri - re, ch'io vor-rei mo - ri - - re.

Si ch'io vor-rei mo - ri - re, ch'io vor - rei mo - ri - re, ch'io vor-rei mo - ri - - re.

Mantuan years survive, all from the years 1601–11, they suggest a state of almost permanent discontent. Almost without exception they are shot through with complaints of overwork, illness, poverty, inadequate payments and the ever-present suspicion that his abilities were not valued by the Gonzagas. So persistent and at times so forcibly expressed are these complaints that one might be forgiven for believing them ill-founded, motivated perhaps by insecurity and jealousy of other composers, were it not for the impressive amount of evidence supporting Monteverdi's case. By late 1606 matters had grown so serious that Claudia Monteverdi felt moved to add her voice to the catalogue of grievances, and by 1607–8, when he was composing *Arianna*, Monteverdi's difficulties had reached a point of crisis: financial hardship and ill-health had been aggravated firstly by the loss of his wife and then by the death of Caterina Martinelli, to whose memory the moving *Lagrime d'amante al sepolcro dell'amata* was composed in 1610 and published in his sixth book of madrigals in 1614. The physical discomforts and emotional strains of 1607–8, allied to the compositional struggles of writing *Arianna* itself, made a deep impression to which

Monteverdi often referred in subsequent years, and as late as 1627 he recalled that writing the opera had almost killed him.[65] The hardships, personal tragedies and bitterness of these years must be weighed in the balance when contemplating the final realization of the 'natural way of imitation' in the *Lamento d'Arianna*, for there can be little doubt that the extraordinary and particular qualities of the work, and Monteverdi's sense of achievement in writing it, were in part caused by a remarkable conjunction of personal, artistic and emotional circumstances.

The memory of these difficult years remained strong, and so too did some of the practical consequences of his long period of Gonzaga service. During his early years in Venice, and particularly during Ferdinando Gonzaga's time as Duke, his former masters frequently called upon him to provide music, mostly operas, for Mantuan civic and state occasions. Some of these works were uncompleted and others have not survived. Of those that have, the most substantial is the ballet *Tirsi e Clori*, commissioned by Ferdinando through the Mantuan Resident in Venice in late November 1615 and published in the seventh book of madrigals (1619) as one of the 'altri generi de canti' specifically advertised on the title-page.[66] Interestingly, Monteverdi had already begun work on the piece before the commission arrived, intending to present it to Ferdinando, presumably with an eye to the possibilities attendant on his coronation as Duke of Mantua in January 1616. Monteverdi's next Mantuan venture, a setting of Scipione Agnelli's *favola marittima, Le nozze di Tetide*, was also commissioned by Ferdinando. Monteverdi had set Agnelli's verse before, in the *Lagrime d'amante al sepolcro dell'amata*, but on reading *Le nozze di Tetide* he found it unsuitable as the libretto for a *favola in musica*. In fact, as it emerges from a number of his letters, his view was based on the mistaken belief that the piece was to be an opera rather than, as Ferdinando intended, a set of *intermedi*. Despite his doubts Monteverdi began work in late 1616 and continued with it well into January 1617 until it became apparent that Ferdinando, who had intended to present the work as part of the celebrations of his forthcoming marriage to Caterina de' Medici, had now abandoned the idea. The wedding itself took place in Florence in early February, and when the couple returned to Mantua in the first week of March the major musical celebration was *Gli amori d'Aci e di Galatea*, a play by Chiabrera with music by the

[65] See n. 53 above.
[66] For a discussion of this work, see above, 223–4.

Mantuan *maestro di cappella* Sante Orlandi. *Le nozze di Tetide* seems to have been neither completed nor performed.[67]

The frustrations of January 1616 can hardly have improved Monteverdi's already jaundiced view of the benefits of Gonzaga employment. Two years now elapsed before his next major involvement with the Mantuan court;[68] this time the prime mover seems to have been the Mantuan heir Prince Vincenzo Gonzaga. The proposals concerned a plan to set to music a libretto based on the legend of Perseus and Andromeda by the Mantuan court secretary, Ercole Marigliani, a scheme that may well have been prompted by Jacopo Cicognini's *Andromeda* 'per mettere in musica' of 1611, a text that was evidently known at the Mantuan court.[69] Monteverdi had already composed some of the music by the spring of 1618, but there then seems to have been a hiatus once it became clear that he would not be able to finish the piece in time for Carnival 1619. Following further pressure from the Mantuans the work was finally completed and presented during Carnival 1620, though it is clear that Monteverdi tackled the job with little relish. Like that of *Le nozze di Tetide*, the music has not survived, but the recent discovery of the libretto shows that *Andromeda* was given as a continuous drama (not even divided into acts) prefaced by a short prologue. It was performed during the carnival season of 1620, at about the time that Monteverdi also finished his other main Mantuan commission of 1619–20, the eclogue-with-ballet, *Apollo*, to a text by his old librettist, Striggio. Finally in March 1620 he was required to recopy *Arianna*, which Ferdinando Gonzaga now wished to perform as the artistic high point of Caterina de' Medici's birthday on 2 May. From Monteverdi's letters it is clear that parts of the score were also revised. Reworking and recopying continued throughout March and into April, but in the end *Arianna* was jettisoned by Ferdinando along with Peri's *Adone*.[70]

[67] See *The Letters of Claudio Monteverdi*, 113–29.
[68] In the meantime Monteverdi contributed an instrumental ritornello and the prologue to the music for *La Maddalena*, a *sacra rappresentazione* by the Florentine Giovanni Battista Andreini. This too may have been written for Mantua; two of the other three contributing composers, Muzio Effrem and Salamone Rossi, were employed there. The music was published in 1617.
[69] I discuss this point in 'Mantua, Monteverdi and the History of *Andromeda*', in the Festschrift for Reinhold Hammerstein (forthcoming).
[70] For *Andromeda* see also the discussion of the libretto in Albi Rosenthal, 'Monteverdi's "Andromeda": a Lost Libretto Found', *Music & Letters*, lxvi (1985), 1–8. I am grateful to Mr Rosenthal for allowing me to consult his

Against this background the history of Monteverdi's last substantial Mantuan stage work, *Licori finta pazza innamorata d'Aminta*, comes as no surprise.[71] As with *Le nozze di Tetide*, it was Striggio who first approached the composer with the proposal. This was in May 1627. In reply Monteverdi offered two pieces already composed or, alternatively, a setting of Giulio Strozzi's 400-line 'operina' *Licori*. When he saw Strozzi's play Striggio demanded extensive revisions, and on at least two subsequent occasions he made requests for a sight of the altered libretto. For his part Monteverdi progressed slowly with the work, and by the end of July only the first act had been attempted and even that was not yet finished. Not until early September was Striggio able to see the completed libretto; on reading it he summarily cancelled the entire project. By then Monteverdi was busy with a set of *intermedi* for the wedding of Odoardo Farnese, Duke of Parma,[72] and seems not to have worked much on the music of *Licori* since the end of July.

Monteverdi had, of course, dragged his feet before in his dealings with the Gonzagas, most notably over *Andromeda*, but over *Licori* he had every reason to be cautious. During the years of Vincenzo I he had suffered the hardships of overwork and sporadic pay in addition to personal tragedies. In addition, the pension promised by Vincenzo had never materialized, as Monteverdi frequently reminded his successors. Under Ferdinando's patronage he fared little better. The cancellation of *Le nozze di Tetide*, of which substantial portions had already been composed, may well have influenced Monteverdi's more languid approach to *Andromeda*, and Ferdinando's abrupt decision to abandon the plans to perform a revised version of *Arianna* must have been a bitter blow. Small wonder that, having been so indifferently treated by successive Gonzaga dukes, Monteverdi procrastinated over *Licori*. Though learned well, the lesson was learned late. At Christmas 1627, after little more than one year as Duke, Vincenzo II died, and with him went the last vestiges of a style of courtly patronage of the arts

[71] On this work, see now Tomlinson, 'Twice Bitten, Thrice Shy: Monteverdi's "finta" *Finta pazza*', *Journal of the American Musicological Society*, xxxvi (1983), 303–11.

[72] See Reiner, 'Preparations in Parma—1618, 1627–28', *Music Review*, xxv (1964), 273–301.

article in advance of publication and for arranging for me to consult the libretto itself. Previous knowledge of the piece has been derived solely from the composer's letters: see *Letters*, 37–41, 146–7, 159–63, 174–5. The plans for the revival of *Arianna* can be followed in ibid., 194–202.

which had been at its most brilliant under Vincenzo I but had been in a state of sad decline ever since. Spain and the Empire refused to recognize the succession, which now passed to Carlo of Nevers. The War of the Mantuan Succession, which brought in its wake the sack of the city and the plunder of the Gonzaga court, was in sight.

The Venetian Operas

Of Monteverdi's numerous full-length dramatic works, only three survive complete, *Orfeo* (1607), *Il ritorno d'Ulisse in patria* (1640) and *L'incoronazione di Poppea* (1642). During the 33 years that separate the first two he was by no means idle as a dramatic composer. It is true that, following his removal from Mantua to Venice in 1613, his new position at St. Mark's focused his attentions initially on sacred music. Yet he continued to keep his hand in with dramatic works, both large (such as *Proserpina rapita*, 1630) and small (*Combattimento di Tancredi e Clorinda*, 1624). The fact that none of the large-scale works has survived can almost be regarded as a tragedy contrived jointly by two of his later allegorical characters, Fortuna and Umana Fragiltà. The great stylistic gap that separates *Orfeo* and the last two operas would be more readily comprehensible if we knew the lost works. It would also help if more were known about the surviving sources of the two late works. Soon after the establishment of public opera houses in Venice in 1637, opera companies began to tour. Precisely how far afield they went is not known, but they certainly visited Austrian cities, and from 1650 Naples was a centre of opera second only to Venice. Thus it is not really surprising that the one known source of *Il ritorno d'Ulisse* survives in Vienna; while of the two sources of *L'incoronazione di Poppea* one is in Naples. None of the three scores agrees exactly with the librettos printed for performances at various places, and it must be assumed that changes were made to suit local tastes. Some of these, such as the four-part string textures in the Naples score of *Poppea*, no doubt reflect the resources available, and the Vienna performances of *Ulisse* are likely to have been on the grand scale fashionable at the court there. Deletions, and transpositions of vocal parts must likewise have been made to suit the available singers. All of this means that exactly what Monteverdi intended is sometimes problematical.[1]

Ulisse and *Poppea* differ from *Orfeo* in almost every respect: in dramatic format, subject matter, musical language and the forces required. The principal reason for these differences can only be the context of the

[1] Further on the sources and their interpretation, see below, 331.

performance of the works. The opening of the Teatro S. Cassiano at Venice for the presentation of opera in the carnival season of 1637 effectively transformed the history of opera overnight. Hitherto opera performances had been occasional, one-off extravaganzas for the entertainment of the privileged few, but now they were given nightly, in seasons, to a paying public in theatres that vied with one another for business and for star attractions. Where earlier operas—*Orfeo*, for example—had been financed by court treasuries, works such as *Ulisse* and *Poppea* were ultimately paid for by the nightly takings at the box-office and by a complicated subscription system which operated for the benefit of the wealthier, if not always patrician, Venetians.

Because of the different context, the demands made on both librettist and composer were quite different from those of thirty years earlier. But the manner in which the septuagenarian Monteverdi responded to these demands is astonishing. Instead of acknowledging that public opera was a new craze and retiring quietly into the background, Monteverdi, no doubt armed with the dramatic skills he had perfected over the years of the lost operas, greeted it with all the intelligence, humour and vigour of a young man. His music had always been refreshingly modern, and *Ulisse* and *Poppea* are no exception. Not only were they abreast of contemporary trends, they actually set precedents that were absorbed into the development and standardization of Venetian opera for much of the rest of the seventeenth century.

The first clear difference between *Ulisse* and *Poppea* and their illustrious predecessor is in the choice and treatment of the libretto. From about 1600, when the earliest operatic productions were mounted in Florence, mythological themes, in particular those of Orpheus and Eurydice and of Apollo and Daphne, dominated opera. Gradually, librettists and composers of operas in Rome introduced comic elements and brisker plots into the mythological format. Consequently, when opera reached Venice, starting with Francesco Manelli's *Andromeda*, mythological stories with a superimposed layer of comedy rapidly became the norm. The internal structure of the libretto was simplified by the Venetians. Where court and Roman operas were divided into five acts, with a prologue and possibly even an epilogue saluting the occasion or the distinguished guests, in Venice they were in three acts. Epilogues vanished completely; and prologues were considerably shortened and made relevant to the plot rather than being addressed to the audience.

For the first few seasons, Venetian opera theatres mounted productions of works with librettos adhering to this format. But

gradually the mythological element also came to be considered too
rarefied for an audience who needed to respond emotionally to real
people and the way they react to one another. Monteverdi firmly
endorsed this attitude. Even within the stylized mythological conventions of *Orfeo*, he had been moved to write 'Possente spirto' as an
impassioned plea from one human being to another.[2] Now he created
from the mythological figures of *Ulisse* and the historical ones of *Poppea*
characters who inhabit an emotional reality that in itself is sufficient to
elevate these works above their predecessors and even their successors.
Penelope, Ulysses, Telemaco, Octavia, Seneca and Ottone are all
recognizable human beings both in their actions and in their emotional
responses. This was the feature for which Venetian audiences
clamoured and at which Monteverdi in particular excelled.

Just as the librettos of *Ulisse* and *Poppea* show abundant differences
from their predecessors, so do the scores. The first clear indication of
change is in instrumentation. Where *Orfeo* uses relatively large
instrumental forces of strings, brass, woodwind and continuo, the scores
of *Ulisse* and *Poppea* show the barest possible instrumental accompaniment. In addition to continuo instruments, *Ulisse* requires strings in five
parts, and *Poppea* strings in three parts.[3] Clearly this diminution of
instrumental forces indicates an aesthetic move away from the kind of
music in which instrumental colours relate to particular types of scene.
In *Orfeo*, for example, strings and recorders play in pastoral scenes,
cornetts and trombones in infernal ones. But by now the musical
emphasis is entirely on the voice, and a varied sound-palette in the
accompaniment such as had been used before would only distract
attention from it. It was for this reason that the simplest of
accompaniments was employed in these and other Venetian operas. The
main burden of accompaniment is carried by the continuo instruments,
and string groups, whether in five parts or three, provide the most basic
of punctuation marks, in sinfonias and ritornellos. It is likely that the
string body was in fact used more than the surviving manuscript scores
indicate;[4] but clearly the role of instruments other than those playing the
continuo was drastically reduced from what had been normal in operas
at the courts of Florence or Mantua or in Rome.

[2] See his celebrated letter to Alessandro Striggio of 9 December 1616, above,
   33–5.
[3] For a discussion of string forces in seventeenth-century Venetian opera, and
   in particular of whether they consisted of five parts or three, see Jane Glover,
   Cavalli (London, 1978), 106–8.   [4] Ibid., 108–9.

A second immediate difference, in the number of characters, stems from the changed nature of the librettos. Whereas in *Orfeo* there are only a handful of main characters, with a chorus contributing other soloists (often very important), *Ulisse* has nineteen principal characters and *Poppea* twenty-one. The role of the chorus is negligible: there are two short passages in *Ulisse* and none in *Poppea*. This marked difference also highlights a move away from big concerted numbers and focuses attention entirely on the individual.

Thirdly, there are differences in musical technique. The material in *Orfeo* consists of madrigalian choruses, arias, recitative, and in-strumental movements. Now, of course, there are virtually no choruses, though madrigalian techniques are still evident, and there are far fewer instrumental pieces. The music consists mainly of recitative, punctu-ated by several self-contained closed forms (arias, duets and trios) of increasing substance and importance. As the seventeenth century progressed, the aria was to become the principal ingredient of Venetian opera; and already in *Ulisse* and *Poppea* there are some superb examples, such as Penelope's 'Illustratevi, o cieli' (*Ulisse*, Act III scene 10) and Arnalta's 'Oblivion soave' (Poppea, II, 12). But at this stage the importance and quality of the recitative is still supreme. In both *Ulisse* and *Poppea* the particularly tense, emotionally charged scenes are portrayed entirely in recitative, of infinite range and variety. Penelope's monologue in *Ulisse* (I, 1), or Octavia's self-introductory lament in *Poppea* (I, 5) are both recitative soliloquies of a distinction unsurpassed by Monteverdi himself or by any of his successors. For perhaps two decades after his death, his friend and pupil Francesco Cavalli continued to write in the manner he had learned from him, and, while Venetian audiences would permit it, attempted to retain the meticulous balance between closed forms and unmeasured music that Monteverdi had perfected. But able, lively and compassionate though Cavalli was as an opera composer, not even he could reach the level of distinction that Monteverdi achieved in his last two operas.

Il ritorno d'Ulisse

LIBRETTO AND STRUCTURE

Monteverdi's librettist Giacomo Badoaro[5] took his story from the latter part of Homer's *Odyssey*—Books XIII–XXII (with some narrative

[5] On Badoaro, see Thomas Walker, 'Badoaro, Giacomo', *The New Grove*, ii, 13.

embellishments omitted). But, despite the title of his work, he made Penelope the focal character rather than Ulysses himself. The story briefly relates the events that immediately precede the return of Ulysses, for whom Penelope has been waiting for twenty years; it is then concerned with her ability, or inability, to cope with the developing situation. It is a story that requires immense human understanding and compassion, which it certainly received at the hands of Badoaro and Monteverdi.

The work's three acts are introduced by a Prologue, which presents in symbolic form various aspects of Penelope's long ordeal. Umana Fragiltà (Human Frailty) sings of the terrors that cannot be concealed by mere courage: of Tempo (Time), Fortuna (Fortune) and Amor (Love). But the personifications of these three terrors together show no pity for mortal man.

Act I falls into four dramatic sequences. The first (scenes 1–2) begins with a long, slow-moving soliloquy for Penelope of remarkable dramatic and emotional intensity. It serves several dramatic functions: it introduces us to the main character; it reminds us who she is and what she has endured; and it indicates very clearly her state of exhaustion, in which she is sustained only by fragile, lingering hope. This intense monologue is relieved briefly by a gentle love scene between two of Penelope's servants, Melanto and Eurimaco; Eurimaco urges Melanto to try and persuade Penelope to accept one of the many suitors who are daily besieging her and so put an end to the considerable tension at court.

In the libretto, the second dramatic sequence begins with a scene (3) for the nereids and sirens on the sea, followed by a scene (4) in which Ulysses is brought to the shore of Ithaca by the Phaeacians. Monteverdi chose to omit these completely (or so it seems from the one extant score), merely supplying a simple repeated-chord sinfonia to be played while Ulysses is carried on to the stage. He did set the rest of this sequence (scenes 5–9). There is a long conversation between Neptune and Jove, who decide to punish the Phaeacians for saving Ulysses; this they proceed to do by turning their ship into stone, as occurs in Homer. Ulysses then wakes up, and in another protracted and multi-faceted soliloquy clearly articulates his own emotional and physical state: his exhaustion and confusion after his ordeal; his self-castigation for his misfortunes; his anger at the Phaeacians for (as he believes) not saving him; and a certain panic in contemplating his immediate future. The goddess Minerva then appears to him, disguised as a shepherd. After he has told his story to her, she reveals her true identity and outlines her plan to help him. He is disguised as an old beggar and sent into the company of the shepherd Eumete. She herself will go to Sparta to fetch Ulysses' son Telemaco, and the naiads are instructed to bury Ulysses' treasure. The third, and briefest, sequence (scene 10) returns to Penelope. Melanto is trying to persuade her to accept the fact that Ulysses must be dead, but she fails lamentably in this attempt, only inciting Penelope to further affirmations of constancy and even to violent insults against Love.[6]

The final sequence of the first act (scenes 11–13) begins by introducing the entirely sympathetic character of Eumete, the faithful old shepherd who is to stand beside Ulysses during the rest of the opera. Arguably the most straightforward and engaging character in either *Ulisse* or *Poppea*, Eumete is given a charming, lyrical solo scene, in which he reflects on the pleasures of a rustic existence as opposed to the stresses of court life. He is interrupted by the arrival of Iro, a character at once comic and yet unsympathetic. He is an incompetent, obese, stuttering coward,[7] who later has an important role in the unfolding of the drama and is clearly introduced here to provide a contrast with what follows. As instructed by Minerva, Ulysses comes to Eumete in his disguise as an old beggar and is received with characteristic humanity and generosity. When Eumete is informed by the 'old man' that Ulysses still lives, he ends the act with a delighted aria of rejoicing.

The second act falls into five sections, of which the first (scenes 1–3) opens with a charming scene as Minerva brings Telemaco from Sparta. He is seen as youthful, attractive and sincere, and he is gently cautioned by Minerva to be prudent. They are greeted by Ulysses (still disguised) and by Eumete, who joyfully passes on to Telemaco the old man's news that Ulysses is still alive. Telemaco sends Eumete ahead to the court to inform his mother of his arrival. At this point there is a dramatic stage effect: lightning flashes, and the disguised Ulysses is swallowed up by the earth. Telemaco is terrified that this portends the death of Ulysses.

---

[6] In this tirade Penelope refers to Theseus and Jason, who had been or were to be the subjects of celebrated seventeenth-century Italian operas: Monteverdi had already written his *Arianna* (1608); Cavalli was to write his *Giasone* in 1649.

[7] The *buffo* comic servant, often with strong bibulous tendencies, was to become a regular feature of Venetian operas in the ensuing decades. Iro himself seems to have been a prototype for a series of unfortunates (cripples, stutterers and so on) who were mocked by others in the cast and therefore by audiences. This is one of the least attractive aspects of such operas.

But Ulysses reappears in his own form, and there is a tender and moving duet of anagnorisis between father and son. Ulysses sends Telemaco to his mother. After a sequence of such spectacular action and intense emotion, brief respite is supplied by Melanto and Eurimaco (scene 4). Melanto reports to Eurimaco that she has been unable to persuade Penelope to take another lover. But the love between Melanto and Eurimaco themselves is secure.

The third sequence (scenes 5–8) begins with a superb scene in which the three suitors, Antinoo, Pisandro and Anfinomo, are continuing to bombard Penelope with marital offers, and she continues to resist them despite the fact that the pressure is clearly beginning to affect her stability. (Monteverdi cut scene 6, a *ballo* performed for Penelope by her suitors.) Eumete arrives to tell Penelope of Telemaco's imminent return and also that he has heard that Ulysses is still alive. Penelope, at such a low ebb, cannot decide how to react to this news, for which she has waited for so long. When she and Eumete have left, there is great consternation among the suitors, who decide they must kill Telemaco. At this point there is another *coup de théâtre*, an intervention from the gods in the form of an eagle which flies menacingly over them. Alarmed by this, the suitors modify their murderous plan to one of increasing their material offers of gifts and gold to Penelope. The fourth sequence (scenes 9–10) returns us briefly to Ulysses and his two protectors: the immortal Minerva, whom he thanks effusively for her support, and the mortal Eumete, who recounts with mirthful satisfaction the horrified reaction of the suitors to the mention of Ulysses' name.

The final sequence of the act (scenes 11–12) builds to a superb conclusion. Penelope is reunited with her son Telemaco, who recounts his adventures in Sparta. Penelope listens sympathetically, though she becomes incensed at Telemaco's description of his encounter with the notorious Helen of Troy. Eumete and Ulysses then arrive, and, again in close adherence to Homer, Eumete is chided by Antinoo for bringing an old beggar to the court. Iro, the glutton, picks a quarrel with Ulysses as a potential competitor for the court food supplies, and Ulysses' true strength is briefly glimpsed as he swiftly dispatches the coward. Penelope has seen and heard this encounter but has not recognized Ulysses. She welcomes him, as a courageous old man, to her court and offers him asylum. The suitors renew their pleadings with Penelope, and eventually, driven to make some move in the face of their persistent pressure, she produces Ulysses' bow. She says that if any of the suitors can draw it, she will yield. Each suitor in turn confidently tries to do so, and each fails ignominiously. Ulysses then tries and succeeds, calling on Minerva as he does so.

The final act similarly falls into five sections, of which the first is the shortest. The pathetic figure of Iro is seen fleeing the court and contemplating suicide. (Monteverdi omitted the second scene in the libretto.) The second sequence (scenes 3–5) shows Penelope totally confused and distracted. She is quite unable to accept or comprehend the fact that Ulysses' bow has been drawn. Severally, Melanto, Eumete and Telemaco try to convince her that the old man is in fact Ulysses, but with each attempt Penelope becomes more adamant that it cannot be he. In her distress she is uncharacteristically insulting to Eumete but almost rational to Telemaco. The third section (scenes 6–7) is a brief interlude among the gods. Minerva, seeing that not all has gone according to plan, appeals to Juno for clemency. Together with Jove and Neptune they agree that peace must be brought to Ithaca. Next comes an interesting little scene (8) which, again following Homer, finds the old nurse Ericlea caught in a dilemma. She has seen the 'old man' naked and recognized on him scars that she knows are from wounds inflicted on Ulysses by a boar. She cannot decide whether to tell anyone.

The denouement (scenes 9–10) finds Penelope still refusing to believe Telemaco and Eumete. Ulysses re-enters 'as himself' (to quote the scene heading), but still she doubts him, and even accuses him of being some sort of magician. At this point Ericlea makes her revelation, but this too is of no avail. Penelope refers to her own bed, which must be shared with none but Ulysses. He seizes on this reference and describes the bed and in particular its embroidered coverlet, woven by Penelope herself. Very gradually Penelope begins to be persuaded by him, and she moves from timid acceptance to emotional triumph. The opera ends with a duet for Ulysses and Penelope.

Badoaro's libretto for *Il ritorno d'Ulisse* is brilliantly constructed. The unfolding of the drama is abundantly clear; the proportions allotted to principal and secondary characters are superbly balanced; the contrasts between fast-moving and more reflective scenes are very well judged. Badoaro's task of both simplifying and expanding Homer was not an easy one, but he unquestionably accomplished it with a remarkable blend of scholarship, compassion and theatrical flair. Without a doubt, *Ulisse* has one of the outstanding librettos of seventeenth-century Venetian opera.

MUSIC

Monteverdi's music carries this superb plot by the means described above: a basis of recitative, embellished with arias and occasional ensembles (duets and trios). As ever with Monteverdi, the recitative shows deep sensitivity to the inflections of the text: all utterances, whether profound or mundane, remain entirely credible in their musical setting, and particularly in the context of the drama. The two major recitatives (surely among the greatest of all time) are those that introduce first Penelope and then Ulysses—it is interesting that Monteverdi did not yet find it necessary to introduce either of his principal characters by means of an aria. One of the most electrifying moments in the work is the point at which Penelope produces Ulysses' bow and hands it in turn to the three suitors (II, 12). Monteverdi's setting of her emotional line 'Ecco l'arco d'Ulisse' greatly enhances the intensity of the moment; it is low in her register, and each word is separated from the next by a resolute rest. But even among the lower orders of people, the musical setting of the text shows a total commitment to situation and emotion. A brief, almost random, example will illustrate this. In the scene where Melanto is trying to persuade Penelope to take a lover (I, 10), she begins rather hesitantly, her vocal line heavily punctuated by rests and repetitions (Ex. 1*a*). But as she gains in confidence, her music too becomes more secure, and she moves into a measured arietta (Ex. 1*b*). This is just one of countless places

Ex. 1

(*a*)

Ex. 1 cont.

(b)

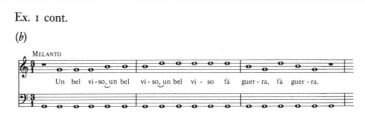

MELANTO

Un bel vi-so, un bel   vi-so, un bel   vi - so   fà   guer - ra,   fà   guer - ra.

where sophisticated dramatic awareness is translated into musical credibility.

The first of the two great recitative monologues is the opening of the opera itself, Penelope's 'Di misera regina'. The first two lines of text, and the way in which Monteverdi sets them, already tell the audience a great deal about Penelope. The slow pace of the opening five bars, mainly over a pedal; the sudden switch to rapid repeated semiquavers in the sixth bar; and the constant repetitions: all these combine to give the feeling that this is a daily ritual into which she has been ground by the passing of time. She goes on to describe her state of physical and emotional exhaustion in almost clinical terms, with words or phrases like 'zoppo' ('lame'), 'speranze . . . canute' ('white-haired hopes'), 'all'invecchiato male non promettete più pace o salute' ('you do not promise peace or health to the aged invalid'). Again these sentiments are portrayed in the slightly disturbing alternation between slow- and fast-moving notation. Penelope then embarks on her narrative, which almost seems matter-of-fact as she goes through her well-rehearsed review of her ordeal. When the story turns towards herself, she becomes more emotional, and a bitterness, even anger, begins to emerge; and she proceeds to her first imputation of failure to Ulysses: 'every departure implies a desired return; only you have failed to achieve the day of your return.'[8] Here again Monteverdi has supplied fast rhythms for the first of these lines, and slow rhythms with repetitions for the second (Ex. 2).

After Ericlea has introduced herself in a single line, Penelope attacks Fortune and her unfair wheel. Then she introduces her heart-rending refrain 'Torna, deh torna, Ulisse', which is to appear twice more. This too, by its very repetition, has the feeling of being part of a daily ritual utterance (Ex. 3). And so her private lament continues, flitting backwards and forwards between pleas to Ulysses, self-pity and

[8] It is touching that Badoaro supplies Penelope with the very words that, according to Homer, are on Ulysses' lips throughout his absence.

Ex. 2

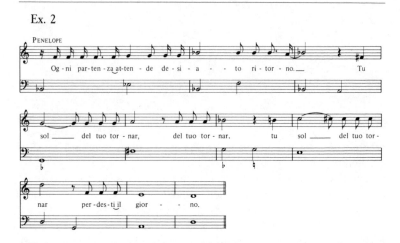

bitterness. Then, after Ericlea's second utterance, she suddenly
changes tack and launches into a most affecting arietta, 'Torna
tranquillo al mare', as she lists all the things that return to their rightful
place (sun, tides and so on). At this point the text becomes rich with
poetic imagery, and the gentle formality of the arietta is Monteverdi's
response to this textual shift. Penelope then breaks into this arietta, as
the list becomes uncomfortably long; but Ulysses still does not return.
Monteverdi gives Penelope an agonized chromatic rise through her
repeated accusation 'Tu sol del tuo tornar perdesti il giorno', and she
concludes with her 'Torna' refrain.

Ex. 3

It is important to remember that such a detailed exploration of
Penelope's psychological and emotional (even physical) state is only
possible in music with a recitative basis. Monteverdi faithfully absorbs
each manifestation of her distress and immediately translates it into
musical terms. But if an aria was inappropriate for this scene, it was
certainly right that an aria should contrast with it: that it is followed by
the Melanto–Eurimaco scene is a tribute to the sensitivity of both

librettist and composer, each aware of the need now for measured music and for memorable tunes. Constantly lyrical, and in well-contrasted sections, this scene is a perfect foil and release after Penelope's suffering.

Ulysses' introductory monologue (scene 7), though shorter, is built on the same principles as Penelope's and is thus equally successful. His initial confusion on waking is expressed in the first eleven bars by rests and repetitions; indeed, one can almost hear the question marks (Ex. 4a). Here again there is a quickening of pace for increase of agitation, for example where he shouts at the Phaeacians for not saving him as they promised (Ex. 4b). Like Penelope, Ulysses also has more serene

Ex. 4

(a)

passages, as when he apostrophizes Sleep. And, again as at the end of
Penelope's monologue, his prolonged soliloquy is immediately contrasted musically by the entry of a new character, in this case Minerva. A
cheerful ritornello introduces a two-stanza aria in *ABA* form, 'Cara e
lieta gioventù'. The whole sequence is thus a sophisticated musico-
dramatic structure.

Among the arias, 'Cara e lieta gioventù' is one of the most engaging
and successful. Quite apart from the felicity of its placing, it is well
shaped and instantly memorable. Another memorable aria is 'O
fortunato Ulisse' (I, 9), in which Ulysses rejoices in the fact that Minerva
has taken him under her aegis. Certainly the general optimism of this
bright G major aria contrasts brilliantly with his sombre state at the
beginning of his monologue. Yet even within this aria Monteverdi shows
his freedom with measured music. He breaks it at the reference to
'pianto dolce', a reversal of the way in which he often interrupts
unmeasured recitative with a few bars of measured music:

Ex. 5

But the most telling feature of the aria is that the audience is so well
prepared for it. On two occasions in the previous scene, Ulysses sang its
opening line before he went off to be disguised as an old man. When he
returns and sings the complete aria, the audience have a comfortable
sensation of familiarity. Monteverdi's versatility in arias is also shown on
two—very different—occasions where he lets his singers laugh in the
music, in each case writing appropriate directions above the stave. They
occur in Ulysses' aria 'Godo anch'io (II, 10) and, possibly to contrast
with this, in the dreadful Iro's soliloquy (III, 1), including ornaments on
the word 'rida' which fall naturally into laughter.

Ulisse is well supplied with ensembles, and among these the duets are
notably successful—not surprisingly, since Monteverdi was so accomplished a composer of chamber duets. One of the most affecting here is

the recognition between father and son, 'O padre sospirato' (II, 3). Their combined emotion initially inhibits articulate expression, but gradually their repeated embraces ('t'inchino', 'ti stringo') build up, the bass line becomes more active, and, very surreptitiously, the piece becomes a fully fledged duet. Elsewhere, 'Gli dei possenti', for Minerva and Telemaco (II, 1), or the final love duet between Penelope and Ulysses, 'Sospirato mio sole' (III, 10), are perfectly placed reminders of Monteverdi's skill as a composer of duets. They combine counterpoint and lyricism in the most fluent and enriching manner and yet never show any hint of artificiality, which would have impeded the flow of the drama.

Penelope's suitors are treated in a thoroughly madrigalian manner throughout. Here the sense of formality in their presentation is doubtless deliberate, for they all receive the same treatment. At their first appearance (II, 5) the refrain 'All'allegrezze' provides a sturdy structural backbone to the whole scene. The very relentlessness of its repetition serves to underline the ordeal Penelope is undergoing. Later in the same act, when the suitors are plotting their next move (II, 8), their music is even more madrigalian. 'Si, si, de' grandi amori', with its variations of tempo indicated by Monteverdi, is followed by the heavily contrapuntal 'Crediam', with its rapid semiquavers. Later, in the witty 'Amor è un'armonia', Monteverdi takes the text literally at its face value (Ex. 6). All these trios are reminders of the madrigal composer, and, again, perfected techniques are now turned to superb dramatic use.

Finally, there is the climax of the opera, so brilliantly handled by both Badoaro and Monteverdi. Ulysses returns 'as himself', and after many renewed protestations of disbelief, Penelope gradually accepts him. At first her refusal to accept him sounds no less automatic and blinkered than on every previous occasion throughout the opera, and once more she resorts to uncharacteristic insult. Ulysses' description of the marriage bed is the turning-point of the scene, and again Monteverdi's setting of the text is immaculate. From a low register Ulysses rises confidently as he describes the embroidery on the coverlet. Penelope's reaction is possibly one of the greatest moments in all opera. Very gradually the years of suffering fall away as she repeats, with growing certainty, 'Hor si, ti riconosco' (Ex. 7). He encourages her ('Sciogli la lingua'), and she bursts into the triumphant C major aria 'Illustratevi, o cieli', in two stanzas and with string interpolations. This is indeed a different Penelope: 'Illustratevi' is her first aria in the whole opera. But the joyful exuberance and sense of release that permeate this

Ex. 6

Ex. 7

remarkable piece provide the most glorious conclusion to her ordeal. After this, even the tender love duet seems a mere formality.

With *Il ritorno d'Ulisse* Monteverdi raised opera to a new level of musico-dramatic sophistication. One of the greatest stories in classical literature received a setting distinguished by nobility, compassion and rich dramatic sensitivity. Two years later he produced a final opera which surpassed even this achievement.

L'incoronazione di Poppea

Poppea is a remarkable opera by any reckoning, not least because it is so different from *Ulisse*. It shows signs that Venetian operatic tastes were drawing away from the classic, the formal, even the tragic, towards the more popular, earthy, even comic aspects of humanity. Where in *Ulisse* the happy ending results from the triumph of love and patience over all adversity, that in *Poppea* represents the defeat of reason by passion and unrelenting ambition. And yet for all its moral dislocation, *Poppea* survives as the most brilliant of all seventeenth-century operas, from every point of view: the structure of the plot, the variety of the music, the depth of musical characterization, and the portrayal of both tragedy and comedy.

LIBRETTO AND STRUCTURE

Monteverdi's librettist Giovanni Francesco Busenello[9] took the story of his opera from Book XIV of the *Annals* of Tacitus. It describes how the young and ambitious Poppea succeeds in turning the head of the Roman emperor Nero to such an extent that he abandons all reason, dignity and decorum, and crowns her as his empress. In so doing, he causes the death of his counsellor Seneca and the exile of his wife—the legitimate empress, Octavia—and of two others besides.

Like *Ulisse*, *Poppea* has three acts and a Prologue.[10] The allegorical characters in the Prologue are Fortuna, Virtù and Amor, the last of whom reappears at a crucial stage of the main action and dramatically alters the course of events. Fortune and Virtue are engaged in an acrimonious argument as to which of them is the stronger. Love subsequently reckons he controls both of them; and though Fortune and Virtue now unite against him, he prophesies that the events of the opera will prove him to be completely superior.

The first act falls into four sequences, the first of which (scenes 1–2) takes place outside Poppea's house. Ottone, betrothed to Poppea, is singing of his love for her, but the presence of two of Nero's soldiers (albeit asleep) can only mean that his worst fears are realized: she is in

---

[9] On Busenello, see Arthur Livingston, *La vita veneziana nelle opere di Francesco Busenello* (Venice, 1913); and Walker, 'Busenello, Giovanni Francesco', *The New Grove*, iii, 501.

[10] There is some conflict in the numbering of scenes in the two surviving sources of the work (see above, 288); the account below follows the numbering of *Tutte le opere*, xiv.

bed with Nero. As he leaves in distress, the soldiers wake and discuss the political consequences of their emperor's dissolute behaviour. By the end of these scenes, the audience has been made fully aware of both the emotional and the political stakes involved. The second sequence (scenes 3–4) occurs in Poppea's bedroom: she is now seen to be in bed with Nero. They enact a very flirtatious and sensuous love scene, and, after they refer tersely to Octavia, Nero takes a lengthy, lyrical leave of Poppea. We then witness her delight at the expected achievement of her ambition; although her nurse Arnalta cautions her, she cheerfully takes no notice.

The third sequence (scenes 5–9) begins with Octavia, of whom we have already heard twice—not only from Nero and Poppea but also from the soldiers. She sings a long monologue, very similar to Penelope's at the beginning of *Ulisse*: she reveals a great deal about her situation—that she is wronged and wretched, even distracted and confused, and that she is doomed to be the victim and knows it. These are the private, desolate thoughts of a woman whose husband has left her for someone younger and more attractive; as such, they cover an even wider gamut of emotion than did those of Penelope. Octavia's nurse tries to console her, in a scene that seems a curious reversal of the previous one, but to little avail. Octavia is in no doubt as to whether she or Nero is the one disgraced, but she ends on the same resigned note of the start of the scene: 'my heart is torn between innocence and tears'. Seneca and a page come to try and bring her comfort. Seneca shows that he is still on her side, and he addresses her as 'glorious empress of the world'. He points out that she has actually grown in her misfortune to a strength and fortitude of much greater worth than beauty. Such gentle flattery and encouragement seem to work, and she is momentarily comforted and grateful. But the page is outraged at Seneca's attitude, thinking that he is deluding her. In his youthful passion he shows himself effusive and headstrong. Seneca is left alone, reflecting briefly that pomp and splendour go hand in hand with torment and suffering. Then Pallas Athene appears to tell him that he must die; he accepts this calmly and with dignity. Nero then enters, and there follows one of the most remarkable encounters in the opera. He nonchalantly informs Seneca that he intends to banish Octavia and marry Poppea; Seneca calmly accuses Nero of disobedience, irrationality, even insanity. A fierce argument ensues, Seneca's quiet reasoning gradually arousing Nero to ever greater levels of hysterical petulance. The ultimate irony of this scene (which is described in greater detail below) is that, though Seneca unequivocally wins the argument, in doing so he effectively signs his own death-warrant.

The fourth section (scenes 10–13) begins with another, equally explicit, love scene between Nero and Poppea. But business takes over from pleasure, and they discuss the problem of Seneca. Poppea refers to him in sarcastic tones ('quel filosofo astuto') and declares that he is constantly undermining Nero's authority. Enraged, Nero rushes off to order Seneca's death. Ottone comes to Poppea, pleading with her to take him back. She is very offhand with him and coldly tells him that his misfortunes are of his own making. Left alone, he becomes desperate and decides that he must kill Poppea. He transfers his affections to Drusilla, a lady of the court who has long loved and wanted him. She is overjoyed and cannot believe her change of fortune. She is right to question it; as Ottone holds her in his arms, he utters the devastating last words of the act: 'Drusilla's name is on my lips, Poppea is in my heart.'

The second act falls into six sections. The first (scenes 1–3) begins with Seneca alone. The god Mercury comes to tell him, gently and tenderly, that he is to die. Seneca is overjoyed, partly because it means an end to tension and suffering, partly because, according to his own philosophical thinking, there is life after death for those whose death is announced by a god. Then Nero's captain too appears, sent by Nero and against his will, to tell Seneca of his impending death. He is amazed to find Seneca already calmly aware of it; indeed, he proposes to effect it himself. Despite the most moving of pleas from his family, Seneca is resolved. At this most touching moment, when he gives his family an untroubled explanation, the poetry becomes profound and affecting. After this highly charged emotional scene, the libretto provides another for Seneca, with Virtue. But Monteverdi omitted it, evidently wishing to have Seneca depart at this point and to break the tension with a strongly contrasted scene. His contrast is supplied perfectly in the scene (5) showing the page with his sweetheart, a maid of honour at court. It is a charming love scene between two lively young people, a direct parallel to those for Melanto and Eurimaco in *Ulisse*. It succeeds not simply as a lyrical contrast to the previous tension but as a means of pointing up the unsuccessful love affairs of those whom the two characters serve. The maid's role begins and ends here: she was clearly included for precisely this dramatic contrast. The third section (scene 6), equally brief, shows Nero and the poet Lucan celebrating the news of Seneca's death. At this point Busenello supplied another love scene for Nero and Poppea, but Monteverdi cut it.

The fourth sequence (scenes 8–9) is a telling encounter between Ottone and Octavia, two individuals suffering personal despair. At first Ottone is alone, vacillating between his longing to kill Poppea and his total inability to contemplate the reality of doing so. Octavia comes to plead with him to kill Poppea for her sake. One might expect this to decide the matter for him, but he completely renounces the idea. There is then a tense argument, and it is only when Octavia threatens him that he gives in. She advises him to wear female clothes so that he may not be recognized. He weakens again, but she threatens again; and once more he agrees to the act. This episode encapsulates the change that the Venetian libretto had undergone in just two years. On one level the audience must now come to terms with the prospect of considerable physical violence, as a murder plot is hatched. On another, psychological level, it is witnessing a confrontation between two characters who are both in a greatly distressed state. It is true that there was a murder plot in *Ulisse* (the suitors discussed the possibility of killing Telemaco), but this was swiftly undermined by the gods. Here Ottone's plot is actually encouraged by Octavia. It is also true that in *Ulisse* we witnessed, various manifestations of human distress, in the long monologues of Penelope or Ulysses for instance. But here two people are under stress, and it is their combined agonies that give the scene its emotional impetus. These differences are subtle but of deep significance.

The fifth sequence (scenes 10–11), again, opens with a sharp contrast to what has gone before. Drusilla is still expressing her new-found joy, and there is a series of comic exchanges between the page and an old nurse.[11] As they leave, Ottone comes to Drusilla. He is still distraught but eventually takes her into his confidence and borrows her clothes for his disguise. Drusilla, all too happy to be of some use to him, repeats the joyful words with which she opened this sequence. The last, brilliant scenes (12–15) of the act take place in Poppea's bedroom. She is preparing for bed with the help of Arnalta. Arnalta begs to be taken to the court if Poppea achieves her ambition of becoming empress. In an aphorism of glorious bathos, she declares that, unlike most people at court, she can be trusted: 'Jove is powerless in two things: he cannot guarantee that the dead go to Heaven, nor that trusty people are found at court.' Poppea expresses a desire to sleep in the fresh air and orders that

[11] This conversation was surely the prototype for many such scenes in later operas, where old maids are similarly teased about the departure of youth and therefore of opportunities for joys they have never experienced, merely imagined.

no one except Drusilla be allowed near. Poppea is very sleepy, and Arnalta sings her a lullaby. As Poppea sleeps, Love arrives; he expresses his contempt for humans and their unawareness of potential danger but declares that he will protect Poppea. Ottone duly arrives, disguised in Drusilla's clothes. Still in a distracted state, he panics at the sight of his victim but eventually steels himself to do the deed. Love prevents him, Poppea wakes up, and Arnalta screams for assistance. The act ends with a triumphant aria for Love.

The final act falls into four sections. In the first (scenes 1–5), poor Drusilla still believes that everything is well when Arnalta and the guards come to arrest her as a murderess. She works out what must have happened. She is brought to Nero, who tries to make her confess to the murder plan. She protests her innocence, to his increasing rage; but she admits to having desired Poppea's death. This is enough for Nero, who orders her to be taken away for torture. Ottone bursts in, trying to claim that it was all his work. To protect him, Drusilla declares that she is guilty, and the claims and counter-claims continue for some time. Ottone then appeals directly to Nero, who has begun to believe the truth and now partly relents, revealing some clemency and humanity. Rather than kill Ottone and Drusilla he merely exiles them. But when he learns that Ottone's plot was instigated by Octavia he realizes that he can now legitimately banish her for being a scheming murderess. He then recounts his actions to Poppea and declares that he is free to marry her. She can hardly believe that she has indeed fulfilled all her ambitions and makes him swear to it. A further love duet ensues. In a brief contrasting scene (6), Arnalta presents a philosophical disquisition about her status in life: she was born a servant, but after the events of the night she will die a matron of the court. The third sequence (scene 7) is the final harrowing appearance of Octavia, who must take leave of her home and her family. She has an anguished soliloquy, which reflects her opening monologue (I, 5). She is so drained that she can barely utter the words; nor has she the strength even to weep. The opera culminates in a magnificent coronation sequence (scene 8). In the true Venetian tradition of spectacle, there are crowds of people for this event: consuls and tribunes in addition to Poppea and Nero themselves, and also Love, Venus and a chorus watching from above. After the coronation, the spectacle recedes, and the opera ends on an intimate note with one of the most alluring love duets ever written.

MUSIC

As in *Ulisse*, the story of *Poppea* unfolds through recitative, together with arias and ensembles. It is a more lyrical score than *Ulisse*, with even more closed forms. But there is no loss of quality in the recitative: in handling it Monteverdi shows spontaneous, wide-ranging brilliance. Of many outstanding sections, two in particular merit detailed examination.

The first is Octavia's initial lament, 'Disprezzata regina', in Act I scene 5. It is a long speech, lasting about four and a half minutes; but it is clearly structured in five sections preceded by a short introductory passage in which, quite simply, she says who she is. She then asks herself three pertinent questions: 'What am I doing? Where am I? What am I thinking?' Then she launches into a tirade about the misery of the female sex: how matrimony enchains women, who themselves create their own captivity by giving birth to the men who will ultimately dominate them. It is an irrational, deeply confused statement, but uttered in music of such passion that one is compelled almost to believe her. Her initial cry, 'O delle donne miserabil sesso', is repeated, practically in mid-sentence, as she claws her way through her dubious philosophy. But having overcome that, she becomes more specific about her own suffering, and in the passage beginning 'Nerone, empio Nerone', she spells out the name of her tormentor. Again Monteverdi uses rests and repetitions to underline the violence of her attitude, and rapid note-values as she hurls insults at Nero:

Ex. 8

When Octavia herself answers her question 'where are you?' with 'in Poppea's arms', Monteverdi devises a brilliant stroke. He alters the metre and the tactus; and he makes Octavia repeat the statement again and again, the phrases separated by aggressive rests. Here surely she is turning the knife in her wound:

Ex. 9

But she breaks out of this appalling outburst as suddenly as she entered it, and turns the subject to herself. There is a glorious poetic image of her weeping a river of mirrors in which Nero can see her torments reflected. Again Monteverdi supplies a telling vocal line, gradually falling from the relatively high notes for 'specchi' ('mirrors') through sobbing repetitions of 'i miei' ('my') to 'martiri' ('torments'). She then cries out to the gods to do something, to send down thunderbolts on Nero, and Monteverdi interprets the thunderbolts in furious vocal scales. Octavia goes on to make two chilling accusations: the gods are powerless, and they are unjust. These two statements themselves break the ferocity of her utterances, and from their C major the harmony collapses on to a barely prepared seventh on E flat at the exclamation 'Ahi'. From that point the vocal line gradually descends as Octavia realizes the enormity of what she has said, apologizes for it and sinks back into herself and into the area of her voice and psychological state where she started her speech:

Ex. 10

At the end of this remarkable monologue, we know everything we need to know about Octavia. Together with Penelope's monologue from the opening of *Ulisse*, this scene marks the summit of achievement in Italian recitative. The text and music are quite inseparable: each enhances the other, so that the whole exceeds the sum of the parts.

The second outstanding section of recitative is the argument between Seneca and Nero (I, 9). Seneca calmly and rationally deflates all Nero's excuses for his proposed plan of action: his banishing Octavia and marrying Poppea will irritate the Senate and the Roman people and will be unjust and insane, even unsafe. After a while, Seneca changes tack a little and turns to more basic insult. To Nero's 'the most powerful will always be the most just' he replies: 'he who does not know how to reign always achieves less.' Eventually Nero explodes uncontrollably. In the speech beginning 'Tu mi sforzi allo sdegno' Monteverdi exploits all the elements of hysteria. There are abrupt rests, rapidly repeated notes and several verbal repetitions, all clearly indicating a man on the edge of insanity:

Ex. 11

Seneca's reply, over a slow-moving bass, is all the more devastating for
its quiet delivery. Nero storms off the stage, hurling more insults at
Seneca, whose calm conclusion—'the worse cause always prevails when
force and reason are opposed'—sums up the strength of his argument.
Monteverdi accentuates this strength and Seneca's authority by giving
him a vocal line with a wide, imposing range:

Ex. 12

Poppea abounds in rich arias and other closed forms, not least in the
very explicit love scenes between Poppea and Nero. There is one rather
surprisingly beautiful aria, the lullaby for Arnalta, 'Oblivion soave', in
Act II scene 12. Its dramatic purpose is quite understandable—to slow
the pace of the action before the murder attempt. What is surprising is
that it is a relatively minor character who receives what is perhaps the
most beautiful aria in the opera, with its long, sustained vocal line over a
caressing, undulating bass. All the main characters, with the notable
exceptions of Octavia and Seneca, have their lyrical moments, from
Ottone's opening aria to Drusilla's aria at the beginning of Act III, not
forgetting the delightful scene between the page and the maid.

The most concentrated lyricism is inevitably found in the scenes
between Poppea and Nero (I, 3, I, 10 and III, 5, and reaching its height
in III, 8). From the start, there are heavily sensuous vocal lines for her,
and much measured but contrasted music. She is constantly flirtatious;
in their first scene, for instance, Monteverdi makes her repeat her
question 'Tornerai?' throughout their slow and tender parting. The
lyricism of their second encounter is particularly effective after the
aggression of the preceding scene (I, 9). There is also a ground-bass
aria, 'Ma che dico', for Nero, based on two consecutive bass patterns.
Act III scene 5 follows the pattern of the other love scenes in
concentrating on sensuality but including a section of more prosaic

discussion. But where before Poppea and Nero discussed Octavia (in I, 3) and Seneca (in I, 10), here they are concerned with Poppea herself. Her mood to begin with is, as ever, endearing, even vulnerable. But when she learns of Octavia's hand in the plot to kill her, she realizes that she has achieved her ambition. This seems temporarily almost to take her breath away, but she recovers quickly and triumphantly, her vocal line borne aloft by a rising scale in the bass:

Ex. 13

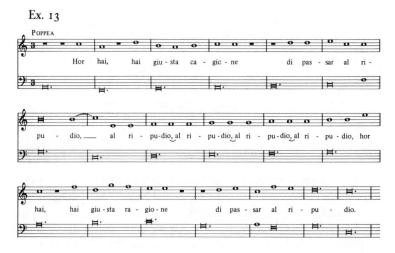

Then comes her repeated insistence that Nero must swear to her that she will soon be crowned; the scene culminates in the duet 'Non più s'interporra'. Finally, at the end of the opera, there is the duet 'Pur ti miro', over a descending-tetrachord ground bass. Doubts have recently been expressed as to whether this duet is by Monteverdi,[12] but in the context of the other scenes between Nero and Poppea it is by no means out of place; it is in an immaculately built *ABA* form and certainly provides a superb and fitting conclusion to the opera.

Turning to music for more than two singers, the entreaty of the three members of Seneca's family (II, 3) provides a tragic equivalent to the ensembles for Penelope's suitors in *Ulisse*. The madrigalian manner is common to both. The scene in *Poppea* is sectional and increasingly

[12] See, for example, Alessandra Chiarelli, '*L'incoronazione di Poppea* o *Il Nerone*: problemi di filologia testuale', *Rivista italiana di musicologia*, ix (1974), 150f. Continuing research may eventually throw more light on this tantalizing problem and even indicate whether other parts of the score too may not after all be by Monteverdi.

moving. It begins with a chromatically rising refrain, treated contrapun-
tally, and then passes through various ritornellos and identical stanzas
before returning to the initial refrain and ritornello. It is entirely
successful on every level. It goes without saying that it is dramatic and
emotional; but it also succeeds on the musical level, not least simply
because of the contrast between the music of the rest of the opera and
this restrained, formal trio, with its perfectly judged matching of musical
style to dramatic requirements.

Ulisse and *Poppea* display the consummate artistry of a great composer in
the last years of his life. They illuminate virtually every facet of
humanity, translated into musical terms with remarkable compassion
and insight. The very spontaneity and vivacity of both scores reveal
Monteverdi's sensitive responses to the smallest nuances of text and
drama. Every musical device available to him is turned to dramatic
effect, and there is no emotion or activity for which he fails to supply an
apt musical setting. For example, he portrays laughter (Ulysses in *Ulisse*,
II, 10, or Iro in *Ulisse*, III, 1) and weeping (Octavia in *Poppea*, III, 7);
flirting (Poppea in *Poppea*, I, 5, etc.) and raging (Nero in *Poppea*, I, 9);
even waking up (Ulysses in *Ulisse*, I, 7) and falling asleep (Poppea in
Poppea, II, 12).
   But Monteverdi's dramatic talents are by no means limited to the
passing moment. He possessed a supreme ability to shape a scene, not
only according to the dictates of the libretto but also through the
devising of cogent musical schemes. By means of refrains, ritornellos
and repetitions, he can impose a tighter and yet more fluent structure on
a scene than his librettist provided for him. The first suitors' scene in
Ulisse (II, 5) is a distinguished example. It is bound by the refrains 'Ama
dunque, si, si' from the suitors and 'Non voglio amar, no, no' from
Penelope. The two refrains intertwine, and are laced about with pleas
from individual suitors. Each return of the refrains serves to build the
pressure on Penelope, with the result that her last 'Non voglio amar' is
quite different from the others. The disintegration of her resistance is
thus made perfectly understandable. Likewise in *Poppea*, the structuring
of several individual scenes demonstrates similar distinction. An apt
example occurs in one of the less important scenes, Act I scene 4,
between Poppea and Arnalta. Here Poppea has two refrains: the rising
sequence 'No, no, non temo, no' and the more 'war-like' 'Per me
guerreggia Amor e la Fortuna'. Both emerge almost casually at the end
of her aria 'Speranze', which in itself is well constructed, the first

line being anticipated between two statements of a ritornello. Arnalta appeals to her mistress for caution; but no sooner has she begun to do so than she is put down by one of Poppea's refrains. By her third attempt Arnalta is more insistent, and she sings what are in effect two stanzas of strophic recitative separated by a ritornello. Again Poppea brushes her aside. At her fourth appeal Arnalta is even more pressing and achieves three stanzas of strophic recitative separated by ritornellos. But these too meet the inevitable refrain from Poppea. For her fifth and final plea Arnalta tries a new approach, moving into lyrical and measured music. But when this meets both of Poppea's refrains one after the other, Arnalta gives up. 'Ben sei pazza', she declares in impatient disgust; and one can fully sympathize with her.

Monteverdi further enhances characterization through the types of music he writes. The most serious and solemn characters, Penelope and Octavia, Ulysses and Seneca, are all granted the privilege of dramatic monody. Further down the hierarchy, the most effervescent, light-hearted music is given to those whose function is generally to provide contrast with the principals: Melanto and Eurimaco, the page and the maid, even Telemaco and Drusilla. Groups of suitors or mourners are treated collectively with madrigal techniques. Gods, on the other hand, have a special prominence: their music tends to be much more florid than that of the mortals whose escapades they are witnessing, if not controlling. And for characters who at times have to provide pure comedy, unrelated to the plot (Iro with his gluttony or Arnalta with her advancing years) there is yet another type of music: virtually slapstick, instantly amusing and of little more than passing significance.

In writing *Ulisse* and *Poppea* at the end his life, Monteverdi did much more than merely provide a brilliant conclusion to a brilliant career. He actually set several standards and precedents which his pupils and successors adopted and developed in the 1640s and 1650s, when the whole format of Venetian opera was being standardized. Firstly, the increasing concentration on aria and other closed forms was to develop strikingly in these decades, and by the 1660s it was actually to swamp the whole aesthetic of opera construction. Secondly, the device of concluding an opera with a love duet, as in both *Ulisse* and *Poppea*, became standard in the ensuing years; it can be seen to have been launched by the popularity of 'Pur ti miro'. Thirdly, the meticulous balance and proportion between serious and comic scenes, between reflective scenes and those with much action, between ensembles and

soliloquies, were imitated in the operas of Monteverdi's successors.
Even if he had not written *Ulisse* and *Poppea*, the immense popularity of
opera would certainly have ensured its survival in the feverish activity of
the Venetian theatres. What is less certain is that Monteverdi's
successors, such as Cavalli or Cesti, would themselves have continued
to produce distinguished works if they had not been able to profit, even
subconsciously, from the examples of *Ulisse* and *Poppea*.

V

Performing Practice

DENIS ARNOLD

Performing Practice

Monteverdi was the first of the forgotten great composers of the early Baroque era to be rediscovered; as such he has suffered most at the hands of the restorer. Other early composers have received better treatment because the traditions in which they worked did not completely vanish. The church music of Byrd and Palestrina never went entirely out of use and cathedral and other choirs always inherited some idea about its proper performance. Monteverdi's operas were never given for more than 250 years; his madrigals for longer than that; his church music for nearly 300 years. When the time for disinterment came, the appropriate traditions had disappeared and others had replaced them. When he was rediscovered in the 1920s and 1930s he was immediately recognized as a major figure, and professional performers took him up; there was little of that amateurism that marked the revival of viol music or the English madrigal. The operas were taken up by the men of the opera houses, familiar only with a much later repertory. The church music—in this context, the Vespers published in 1610—was too demanding for the ordinary cathedral choir, so it became the province of the choral societies under their professional trainers and conductors. This should have been all to the good; in the event, they transferred their modern ways to this older music, with sometimes disastrous results. Gradually, understanding has improved: today's performances are not only more musicologically 'correct' than those of thirty years ago, they also show a greater sense of Monteverdi's aims. But there is still much to explore, more experiments to be tried.

The main stumbling-block has been the failure to realize that there is no single 'Monteverdi style'. Monteverdi lived for seventy-six years at a time of musical revolution. Perhaps the only comparable figure in musical history is Stravinsky. The difference between the musical, social and intellectual conditions known to a young man of 1900 and an ageing master of the 1950s is enormous. Would a pupil of Rimsky-Korsakov really have imagined that half a century on he would be influenced by the as yet unborn musical methods of Webern? Similarly would a young man being taught counterpoint by the *maestro di*

cappella of Cremona Cathedral have thought of delighting the audiences
of the Teatro di SS. Giovanni e Paolo sixty years later? In fact, the old
world had gone by 1630—gone with the wealth of the Este and Gonzaga
courts, gone with the invention of opera and its virtuoso divas, gone with
the use of the continuo. No doubt their youthful identities survived in
both: late Stravinsky is as typical of the man as is late Monteverdi.
Nevertheless, media change in the course of a lifetime; and just as the
big symphony orchestra, the natural means for the early twentieth-
century composer, was succeeded by the smaller forces used by the
mature master, so the big Renaissance ensemble gave way to that of the
Venetian theatres of the 1640s. In deciding how to perform
Monteverdi's music, we must take such radical changes into account.
To perform *L'incoronazione di Poppea* with the means of *Orfeo* is to
commit a solecism.

Perhaps the best way of determining the essential differences within
Monteverdi's *œuvre* is to divide his career into two. The first phase is that
of the late Renaissance court musician, his role at Mantua. The other is
that of the Baroque *maestro di cappella*, his role in Venice. In both roles he
found himself in what were, for the time, ideal circumstances. There
was no shortage at Mantua of money or the resources it could buy. We
do not know the cost of producing *Orfeo* or details of the massive
expenditure on the celebrations in 1608 during which *Arianna* was
performed. Nevertheless, we may assume that anything Monteverdi
wanted for either was available. At St. Mark's he was in charge of the
largest ecclesiastical musical establishment in Italy. He was acknowledged as a master by his employers, made changes at will (as the letter
of 13 March 1620 shows[1]) and can thus be assumed to have had his
favourite media to hand. There may have been more financial
restrictions in the opera houses of the late 1630s and early 1640s. Even
so, he was by that time a Grand Old Man and probably got his own way
in most things. Thus we may assume that he could attain his ideal, as far
as man, and musician, could. If, therefore, we examine the means at his
disposal, as revealed both by documents and by the evidence in the
music itself, we shall find a good guide to 'authentic' performance. It
must also be said that Monteverdi was by no means a vague idealist who
wrote regardless of the capabilities of his performers. His letters reveal a
very practical composer who sought to fit his music to very precise
circumstances. To alter his music on the grounds that we can 'improve'
it is both arrogant and silly.

[1] See above, 43–7.

The Renaissance composer

Monteverdi arrived at Mantua as a string player. This probably meant that he was one of the quintet who played for *balli*. This type of ensemble was known elsewhere, for example at the Florentine court, where the French taste for dancing was well developed.[2] There is no sign that the parts were doubled, for the court lists of musicians, though spasmodic and incomplete, mention at one stage only four 'suonatori'[3] (to which Monteverdi must surely be added) and never suggest any more. When in *Orfeo* he demands ten strings, it is less to swell the sound than to allow theatrical effects such as echoes to involve them. Certainly, for *Tirsi e Clori* (1616) he asks for eight *viole da braccio* and also a double bass; but how these were to play five-part music is not explained in the relevant letter,[4] and one wonders whether they were more for visual effect than sonority. Be this as it may, at Mantua there was no 'orchestra', and a string section of a modern type was never used.

Before 1600 there is no evidence for continuo instruments. Nevertheless, their deployment in *Orfeo* and the mention of them in Monteverdi's earliest extant letters seem to imply that lutes, harpsichords and organs were often employed. Since instruments of this kind were used in *intermedi* (for example the famous ones to *La pellegrina* performed in Florence in 1589), we may assume that they were employed in theatre music at least from the latter years of the sixteenth century. It is, however, impossible to say what they played. The evidence of Agazzari's booklet *Del sonare sopra 'l basso con tutti li stromenti e dell'uso loro nel conserto* (Siena, 1607) suggests that they improvised freely, producing a rich web of sound. But all the evidence in vocal music—Caccini's *Le nuove musiche* and Viadana's introduction to his *Cento concerti ecclesiastici* (both published in 1602)—is that continuo realizations were chordal and simple. It could easily be that purely instrumental music, such as the dances in ballets, was embellished, while the accompaniments to madrigals, songs and the vocal sections of operas were kept plain. Certainly nothing should detract from the voice, and in the solo music of operas anything that ties the singer to rigid time-keeping must be avoided if Caccini's ideal of the 'nobile

---

[2] See Frederick Hammond, 'Musicians at the Medici Court in the Mid-seventeenth Century', *Analecta musicologica*, xiv (1974), 151.
[3] See Iain Fenlon, *Music and Patronage in Sixteenth-century Mantua*, i (Cambridge, 1980), 192f.
[4] See above, 32–3.

sprezzatura di canto', the *rubato* freedom of expression, is to be achieved. It is noticeable, both in the fully marked score of *Orfeo* and in his letters, that Monteverdi liked combinations of harmony instruments rather than a single harpsichord or lute. In the letter of 28 December 1610, he looks forward to receiving a cantata 'with accompaniment for two arch-lutes'.[5] For a concert in 1611, he says:

I shall have the theorbos played by the musicians from Casale, to the accompaniment of the wooden organ (which is extremely suave), and in this way Signora Adriana and Don Giovanni Battista will sing the extremely beautiful madrigal *Ahi, che morire mi sento*, and the other madrigal to the organ alone.[6]

The frequent references to the organ and to lutes show that the harpsichord was by no means the standardized continuo instrument it became in the later Baroque period. The organ was generally a portable instrument in the early seventeenth century (in Venice organs were continually being moved into St. Mark's or the Scuola di S. Rocco), and its use shows that Monteverdi liked sustained harmonies against which the dissonances of the vocal line could make a strong effect. The fact that he also liked a chitarrone with the organ indicates that the continuo role was often taken by a team. But there is no suggestion that a cello or violone played the bass line itself; Monteverdi was concerned to maintain flexibility, which the stress on a single melodic part often inhibits.

As for singers, Monteverdi had at Mantua a consort that was among the finest of its time. It was probably modelled on the *concerto di donne* of Ferrara, where small groups of noblewomen were taught to perform the upper parts of madrigals using elaborate embellishments. At Mantua the ladies may have been less noble and more professional, for a 'Rollo de' salariati del Prencipe'[7] includes the names of Signora Lucia Pellizari, Signora Isabetta Pellizari, Signora Lucretia Urbana and Signora Caterina Romana; and Signora Lucretia was paid very well indeed. The Friday night madrigal concerts in the Hall of Mirrors in the Palazzo Ducale were therefore sung by a virtuoso consort, and there is no suggestion that a choir was ever used. This indeed is evident from the style of Monteverdi's third, fourth and fifth madrigal-books, which demand more skilled performers than those of Marenzio or the

[5] *The Letters of Claudio Monteverdi*, trans. and ed. Denis Stevens (London, 1980), 78.
[6] For the complete letter, see above, 27–8.
[7] See Fenlon, op. cit., 194, including n. 3.

Gabrielis. The *falsobordone* parts of *Sfogava con le stelle*, for example, demand the utmost coordination; to have them written out in modern editions with firm rhythms imposed on them for choral performance is to miss the point, which is the verbal flexibility that caused Monteverdi to adopt a notation unusual in secular music.[8]

We gain from his letters some idea about Monteverdi's demands on his singers. He was not on the whole concerned with the size of a voice, though the references to the suitability of individual singers for various posts indicate that he was well aware of the difference between church and chamber music. But he did not like a forced tone.[9] He was very concerned about clarity of tone (he criticized one contralto who 'swallows his vowel'[10]) and—though his meaning is not entirely clear—also about the proper control of 'middle' and 'chest' voices.[11] His other great concern was for the articulation of ornaments. In nearly all his references to ornamentation he separates the *gorgia* from the *trillo*. No doubt Caccini's publicity for the latter had left its mark on Monteverdi, who used it frequently and justifies to some extent the modern performer's reliance on it to make an 'authentic' seventeenth-century sound.

Although the new ornaments current in monody interested him, Monteverdi's attitude to ornamentation is much nearer to that of the sixteenth-century writers of books on *gorgia* or what the English called 'divisions'. The examples of ornamentation in, for example, Giovanni Bassano's *Ricercate, passaggi et cadentie* (1585) show continuous embellishment, whereas Caccini wanted to restrict ornaments to important words and suitably open vowel sounds. It is significant that Monteverdi uses a continuous stream of ornament both in the *preghiera* 'Possente spirto' in *Orfeo* and in *Audi coelum* in the Vespers music. But it is in the ensemble music that we see Monteverdi's typically sixteenth-century education coming out most strongly. In the madrigals of the fifth book and the ensemble motets of the Vespers, the main difference between the sections in which ornaments are liberally used and Caccini's ornamental songs lies in the regularity of Monteverdi's ornamental patterns. Naturally, in ensembles that 'nobile sprezzatura di canto' of which Caccini was so proud is impossible. Thus Monteverdi makes even the *trillo*, as free an ornament as could be invented, part of a

[8] See above, 200, Ex. 2a, and 202, Ex. 6.
[9] See above, 26.
[10] Loc. cit.
[11] See above, 68–9.

strict rhythmic pattern in *Duo seraphim*:

Ex. 1

One notices his 'musicality' of approach in such passages. He rarely uses any ornament, or rhythm, merely once: he integrates it firmly into the whole melodic pattern and in doing so differs from many composers of the time.

We must also be aware of his attitude to harmony. When he ornaments a passage, the basic chords are rarely obscured. He does not favour appoggiaturas or the appoggiatura principle of making an ornament deliberately cause a dissonance (it was only much later that the appoggiatura became a favourite ornament). He occasionally uses the slide of an upward third to a high note (a practice castigated by Caccini), as is indicated in *Nigra sum* from the Vespers:

Ex. 2

His main use of dissonance by ornamentation arises from making the melody anticipate the next chord; this sometimes results briefly in a harsher sound, yet it always resolves satisfactorily, simply by being integrated into the following harmony. This is something worth considering in adding ornaments to any of his music, though it should be noted that he does it mainly for expression of the words; he never uses dissonance casually, and since he does sometimes write out ornamental passages in madrigals, opera and church music, the performer should perhaps observe discretion.

A less easily resolvable matter is that of pitch. We have, in fact, little idea of pitch or pitches at Mantua—the plural is necessary since we must not assume that church and chamber pitch were identical or even that each church organ was tuned to some standard pitch. Two factors may help us. The first is that the vocal parts of *Orfeo* seem to be a shade low. Certainly the title role, given to a light tenor voice (and not only the use of the tenor clef indicates that it was not meant for the modern baritone), would suffer if transposed downwards to what is now known as 'Baroque pitch'. Indeed, if anything, a modest transposition upwards (perhaps by a tone) might give better results for the principal parts and would not make those of the chorus impossible. The second factor worthy of consideration is that quite a large number of madrigals from the third book (that is, from about the date of Monteverdi's arrival in Mantua), as well as several works in the 1610 volume of church music—the Gombert mass, and the psalm *Lauda Jerusalem* and the seven-part *Magnificat* from the Vespers music—are written in the 'high *chiavette*' clef combination.[12] This usage indicates a transposition of a fourth or fifth, according to contemporary treatises; and indeed some transposition is usually thought desirable, for in practice the strain on the choir in all these works makes keeping in tune difficult. Nevertheless, so great a transposition poses problems for the lower voices, to the extent of altering their very nature. If we accepted normal Mantuan pitch as higher than present-day pitch, such transpositions would seem more natural: the uppermost voices in the church music might be taken by falsettists (which is probably what happened originally) and the alto line by tenors. This solution would help the rather low-lying tessitura in such pieces as the *Dixit Dominus* of the 1610 volume and even *Nigra sum*, which would go well at a higher pitch.

Finally, there are problems of overall proportion, especially in the dramatic works of this early period. The most obvious example is that of the *Ballo delle ingrate*, published in the eighth book of madrigals (1638) in a version revised from the original of 1608 (probably as the result of a later performance). Here Monteverdi provides an ample quasi-operatic work, including an extended dialogue between Venus and Cupid and a lengthy aria for Pluto, but relatively little dance music. Yet it is clear that

[12] See Siegfried Hermelink, 'Chiavette', *The New Grove*, iv, 221, and also Gustave Reese, *Music in the Renaissance* (New York, 2/1959), 530ff, for explanations of this puzzling term.

the ballet was the principal part of perhaps a whole evening's entertainment (performed literally as printed it takes only about forty minutes). There is obviously a need to extend the dances. This can be done merely by simple repetition (there are repeat marks at the end of each section), perhaps with embellishments in the manner of divisions. We know from the court chronicler Follino that 'all kinds of instruments' were used at the 1608 performance;[13] but we are not told how they were employed. Before we succumb to the temptation to orchestrate the dances in a vivid way, we should remember that dance music was the prerogative of the string quintet (which is what the dances are scored for in the 1638 version); no other family of instruments (except perhaps a mixture of cornetts and trombones) was similarly consistent. It seems more likely, therefore, that Follino was referring to the continuo team—the *organo di legno*, chitarrone, harpsichord and regal—which, as in *Orfeo*, might well be used during the dialogue sections to give character and atmosphere.

The Baroque *maestro di cappella*

When Monteverdi was dismissed from Mantua in 1612 he can hardly have known that the apparently rich ambience he was leaving was nearing the end of its life. In fact, the artistic lavishness of the Renaissance courts of northern Italy was in decline: Ferrara had already gone, taken over by the Papal States; Mantua, and much of the Po valley, were to be ruined by the War of the Spanish Succession and the ensuing plague. Monteverdi was fortunate to be employed in such a relatively unchanging institution as the *cappella* of St. Mark's, Venice.

The fundamental musical changes of the early seventeenth century stemmed almost entirely from the invention of the basso continuo. We have seen that in the first decade the employment of harmony instruments had been normal; nevertheless, the true nature of continuo music had not yet been appreciated. From about 1620, harmony instruments strongly implied a soloist (or perhaps two) to be accompanied. Thus in vocal music the aria and duet flourished; in instrumental music the solo or trio sonata soon dominated the scene. Thus upper voices and instruments survived while the middle instruments disappeared. Whereas in the late Renaissance whole families of instruments were played—flutes, recorders, bassoons and so

[13] Federico Follino, *Compendio delle sontuose feste fatte l'anno M.DC.VIII nella città di Mantova* (Mantua, 1608).

on—by the mid-seventeenth century it was the 'sopranos' of each family that had survived. The most important of these 'soprano' instruments was undoubtedly the violin, though it is difficult to say why it should have emerged so strongly. The usual story—that it was more suitable for large halls than the viol—will not do, since the churches in which instruments were used were the same throughout the sixteenth and seventeenth centuries, while such secular surroundings as the Hall of Mirrors in the Palazzo Ducale at Mantua were not markedly different from those in later, seventeenth-century palaces. Nor can it really have been easier to perform the intricate, sometimes chromatic music of the Baroque era on an unfretted instrument. Whatever the reason, the fact remains that, as the century progressed, the violin became the favoured melody instrument, enhanced by such excellent virtuosos as Salamone Rossi, Biagio Marini and G. B. Fontana. As the violin gained ground the cornett disappeared, which is surprising, because by all accounts it could match the expressiveness of the human voice required by the New Music. Yet apparently by 1640, Venice, where it had flourished during the high and late Renaissance, could not find a single player for St. Mark's; nor do we hear much about its employment in Italy generally, though it did persist in Germany and England.

In fact, the development of the orchestra at St. Mark's is in several ways typical of what occurred in Italy. Monteverdi inherited the Gabrielian orchestra of cornetts and trombones. The total band was about fifteen, and Monteverdi, finding that they were paid on a daily basis, persuaded the authorities to put them on the permanent payroll. As one player retired or died, he could then replace him as he preferred, which meant that gradually the group became mainly one of string players, with some trombones, a bassoon and perhaps one or two other wind instruments. Indeed as early as 1617, a violinist, rather than a cornettist, became its leader. Monteverdi also seems to have been able to increase the total number. His assistant Giovanni Rovetta, in the preface to his *Salmi concertati* Op. 1 (1626), refers to 'not just thirty or more singers [of the St. Mark's *cappella*] but twenty and more instrumentalists playing wind and strings'.

If one looks at the music that Monteverdi wrote for this ensemble—which played only on the major festivals—several new features of his treatment of the orchestra become apparent. Firstly, the only instrumental parts to be written out for every psalm setting (or for the great concerted seven-voice *Gloria*) are those for two violins and, of course, the bass. The rest are generally alluded to in the title, as, for example, with the *Magnificat* 'a 8 voci et due violini et quattro viole overo quattro Tromboni quali in acidente si ponno lasciare' ('for eight voices and two violins and four viols or four trombones, which can be omitted if need be'). Given the size of the ensemble at St. Mark's, the natural conclusion to be drawn is that the violin lines were doubled; indeed each part could have been played by up to eight instruments. Whether the middle parts—surely akin to the *parties de remplissage* that Lully left to be provided by his assistants—were also doubled by multiple trombones must surely be more doubtful. Here the conclusion is that they supported the voices in the Renaissance tradition. A matter of vital moment in reconstructing these *parties de remplissage* is whether they should expand the duet texture of the passages for violins into five-part writing. The answer must be a qualified 'no': qualified simply because we cannot be sure, 'no' because these middle parts are, by Monteverdi's own titling of the works, optional (and therefore of no essential harmonic import), and also because so much Italian music of the period relies on the trio texture of two melodic lines and a bass. Monteverdi was a master of the chamber duet, and it is inconceivable that he would not have been happy with the written notes in three parts. In fact, the additional parts for trombones or lower strings are easily made up from the vocal parts, which means that generally they are employed in tutti passages. There is no evidence for the reorchestration or thickening of middle parts in Monteverdi's Venetian church music.

Exactly what instruments played the bass line is unknown. That a stringed instrument was employed is fairly certain; that this was more likely to be a violone than a violoncello is indicated by such documents as Cavalli's (admittedly later) instructions for the performance of his own *Requiem* with instruments.[14] Whether it played at the lower octave, in the manner of the modern double bass, is problematical. If it did, no doubt a bassoon (which Cavalli also required) presented the line at written pitch. The harmony instruments were probably organs. By this time, the idea of a team including plucked strings seems to have faded away. Certainly there seems to have been no harpsichord in regular use at St. Mark's, since the procurators customarily hired one for Holy Week, when it seems to have played some special part. But two or three organs may have been used. At the festivals that the orchestra attended, both of the organists were present, and at times there was a third organist on the payroll.

[14] See Jane Glover, *Cavalli* (London, 1978), 31.

The nature of the spatial separation of these forces in the manner of *cori spezzati* is uncertain. Monteverdi's psalm settings for double choir lack instrumental parts and are in a retrospective style. Recent research suggests that they would have been sung 'in Bigonzo' (literally, 'in [the] tub' (*bigoncio*—an octagonal platform)),[15] that is, with the first 'choir', a solo quartet, in one of the pulpits, and the second 'choir', the ripieno, in the other pulpit or on the floor of the church. Usually, however, the employment of the orchestra seems to have been 'in organi'—that is, using the organ lofts—which, in turn, implies separation of the forces, if only because there is too little space in either loft to take all the performers. The duet and trio sections of the psalm settings may have been sung by soloists, with the ripieno joining in the tutti passages, in which case perhaps seven or eight singers were in one loft with the organist (the other would still have been very crowded); or perhaps the choir were in one and the orchestra in the other. But these works do not demand such separation, nor need they be divided between solo and tutti groups (though this can sometimes work very happily).

Compared with the conditions of St. Mark's, those of the Venetian opera houses during Monteverdi's last years are obscure. Although they rose as quickly as mushrooms, and although there are two invaluable files of papers concerning them in the Venetian State Archives,[16] we know little about the details of their operations. One thing can be said: their productions bore little resemblance to the spectacular stage productions of the Renaissance courts. The opera houses were commercial organizations with different priorities. True, the dukes of Mantua and the great Venetian public alike enjoyed star singers; but at Mantua they were members of the household, paid a salary for whatever they did. In Venice they soon learned their value and pressed hard for high fees. It is also true that there was a common link in the delight in opulent sets and ingenious stage machines. The difference is that the monarch hardly noticed the cost whereas the impresario worried about balancing the books.

The casualties in the opera houses were the chorus and the orchestra. No one went to the theatre specially to attend to either. The chorus therefore more or less disappeared in Venetian opera, whereas in *Orfeo* it had had a major role. The orchestra became more restricted and distinctly smaller. The papers of Marco Faustini, who ran the S.

---

[15] See James H. Moore, *Vespers at St. Mark's: Music of Alessandro Grandi, Giovanni Rovetta and Francesco Cavalli* (Ann Arbor, 1981), i, 103ff.

[16] Venice, Archivio di Stato, Scuola Grande di S. Marco, buste 188 and 194.

Cassiano theatre in the 1650s and 1660s, include two orchestra lists.[17]
One dates from the 1658–9 season:

Violin	17 lire
D. Gio: Battista	18 lire, 12 soldi
Second violin	12 lire
Tomini	12 lire
D. Lorenzo violin	10 lire
Violetta	4 lire, 13 soldi
Theorbo from Padua	14 lire
The priest who plays the theorbo	13 lire
The tuner	4 lire, 13 soldi
Total	105 lire, 15 soldi [= *c.* 15 ducats]

The other refers to the 1665 season:

To Sig. Antonio first keyboard instrument	24 lire, 16 soldi
To the second keyboard instrument	10 lire
To Sigra Prudenza third keyboard instrument	10 lire
Sig. Carlo Savion	15 lire
To the first violin, Sig. Rimondo	18 lire, 12 soldi
Sig. Domenico, second violin	14 lire
To Sig. Marco, viola da brazzo	12 lire
To Ruzzier, violetta	4 lire
To the first theorbo	18 lire, 12 soldi
To the second theorbo	11 lire
Total	138 lire

There are difficulties in interpreting these documents. The payments
are small, but we do not know precisely how many performances they
refer to, and we cannot compare them with other expenses at the opera
house. Nor can we be sure that the players named made up the complete
orchestra, for the Faustini papers are not orderly and many may have
been lost. They also date from several years after Monteverdi was
involved with the opera houses. Nevertheless certain conclusions may
be drawn. Firstly, the orchestras were probably small, perhaps even to
the extent of a single instrument for each part. Secondly, there was little
variety of tone colour. Strings were the basis (the word 'violetta' at this
period may refer to what we would call the violoncello). Brass may have
been brought in for fanfares (there are payments for the military that can

[17] See Denis Arnold, '"L'incoronazione di Poppea" and its Orchestral
Requirements', *Musical Times*, civ (1963), 176 (see also correction, p. 255).

be so interpreted), but of the vast panoply of the Renaissance orchestra little is left. This applies also to the continuo instruments, now harpsichords and theorbos without regals or *organi di legno* or diverse members of the lute family. That the continuo players bore the brunt of orchestral performance is surely denoted by the presence of several harpsichord and theorbo players. Whether they divided the task by each accompanying a singer or group of singers, or whether they took part in a whole scene each is not known. But in any case it can hardly have mattered much, for the tone quality changes little. The idea of 'characterization' by sonority and of the delineation of the atmosphere of a scene, as occurs in *Orfeo*, is impossible.

The broader issues raised by performance of the late operas bring to light still greater puzzles. It has been held that the scores that have survived—the Vienna score of *Il ritorno d'Ulisse* and those at Venice and Naples of *L'incoronazione di Poppea*—are no more than sketches of what actually happened and that the modern editor is therefore entitled to alter them almost at will. Each of these scores was probably made for a particular company and performance. That of *Il ritorno d'Ulisse* may well have been for the Viennese court, where grand spectacles like those mounted by Renaissance princes still survived, for it has choruses and some indications that suggest the lavish orchestration that Monteverdi was still using as late as the 1620s in works commissioned from Mantua. Of the two scores of *L'incoronazione di Poppea*, that preserved in the Biblioteca Marciana, Venice, seems to have been 'edited' (or 'doctored') by Cavalli. It shows many crossings-out, transpositions and alterations to suit particular singers. It is noticeable that the instrumental parts make up a trio texture[18] (though the instruments are not named) and that the vocal music is accompanied only by the continuo bass. The Naples score includes some entirely different music, and the instrumental ritornellos are generally in four parts; it was obviously meant for different circumstances from those obtaining in Venice. Both scores probably date from after Monteverdi's death; neither can be said to be completely 'authentic'. A comparison of the librettos for various performances indeed implies that not all the music is by Monteverdi; and if it is true that the final duet was written by another composer, as has been suggested,[19] nothing can be certain about unity of style.

[18] Nor does the score provide blank staves for middle parts, as do other scores in the same Contarini collection.

[19] See Alessandra Chiarelli, '*L'incoronazione di Poppea o Il Nerone*: problemi di filologia testuale', *Rivista italiana di musicologia*, ix (1974), 149ff.

This gives the modern performer considerable freedom, though not a blank cheque. The cutting out of particular scenes is possible, though editors and conductors would do well to read the original librettos to maintain the balance of elements. *L'incoronazione di Poppea* is not a simple human story, and to cut down the intervention of the gods deprives the work of its backbone, leaving the final victory of evil totally inexplicable. On the other hand, transposition of music to suit individual voices is sometimes to be recommended. Here it must be said that although Monteverdi did not have the highly developed sense of key of later composers, he was by no means insensitive to a smooth progression of tonality. He was very concerned for the music to flow, and he would have avoided the abrupt changes of gear that can sometimes be heard in performances of his late operas today. As for the addition of music (and presumably words) to fit in with an editor's wish to add comedy or heighten emotion, it must be said that although an expert pasticheur can get away with it in front of an inexperienced audience, it takes more than ordinary arrogance to try it. Nor is there any necessity for it. There is quite enough in the existing scores to convey Monteverdi's meaning; and quite enough to engage our intellects in deciding what he meant.

Modern editions and performances

To have too great a reverence for the written notes in the music of Monteverdi's era is to graft twentieth-century thinking on to the mentality of the seventeenth-century musician. There can be no 'authenticity' in the strictest sense. Nevertheless, the written notes are the main guide to knowing Monteverdi's music—the sound of 'original' instruments and the conventions of musical theory are others—and the overriding purpose must be to interpret the score as best we can in the light of existing information. When Monteverdi's music was first revived it was sometimes in an antiquarian spirit, and sometimes by musicians who thought it needed bringing up to date. Few people today would be able to withhold a shudder at seeing the score of Respighi's version of *Orfeo*, made for La Scala in 1935, with its free interpolations of other music by Monteverdi, its rescoring for full-scale modern orchestra of music already clearly marked in detail. And it is difficult to see what Carl Orff hoped to achieve in a quite dreadful version of the lament from *Arianna* dating from 1924 and revived as late as the 1950s. Raymond Leppard's version of *L'incoronazione di Poppea* is more forgivable in its adaptation of the length and general shape of the work to the conditions of the modern opera house. But reorchestration, especially of the recitative passages, has in recent years been proved totally unnecessary; indeed it impedes the sense of drama of the original, with its total emphasis on the singers.

The lesson to be learned is: trust the composer. Monteverdi wrote for particular resources, most of which are recreatable today. His use of ornaments is clear from existing scores, and if singers who wish to embellish their lines look through his music to find out what he prescribed they will discover sufficient variety without looking elsewhere. There is no need for the symphony orchestra, indeed for any more than single players on most of his instrumental parts: our buildings are not necessarily larger than the churches and halls of Mantua and Venice. It is as well to remember that Monteverdi was a connoisseur of singers and that those who sang for him were probably just as competent as those of today. He demanded of them a capacity to express human emotions and provide beautiful tone. To perform his music mechanically, in either rhythm or expression, is to miss the point. With sympathy and taste it is amazingly easy to fulfil his great aim: 'muovere gli affetti'.

VI

A Monteverdi Bibliography

A Monteverdi Bibliography

Compiled by Denis Arnold and Nigel Fortune

A complete bibliography of works dealing with Monteverdi would include virtually every history of music, most books on the various genres in which he composed and a great number of articles on many subsidiary themes. To reduce this vast literature to manageable proportions we have included only writings which add something new to a study of Monteverdi's music, life or ambience, or are in some way significant for the historiography of the subject; there is a bias towards more recent writings. Similarly, in compiling the list of printed editions we have generally excluded editions of single madrigals and motets and those to be found in anthologies; most of those cited are thus of the larger works or of collections of shorter ones.

Editions

COLLECTED EDITIONS

Tutte le opere di Claudio Monteverdi, ed. Gian Francesco Malipiero, i–xvi (Asolo, 1926–42); 2nd edn. with revisions only in viii, xv and xvi (Vienna, 1954–68); supplementary vol. xvii (Venice, 1966)

Monteverdi: 12 composizioni vocali profane e sacre (inedite), ed. Wolfgang Osthoff (Milan, 1958)

Claudio Monteverdi: Opera omnia, ed. Fondazione Claudio Monteverdi, Instituta et monumenta, *Monumenta*, v (Cremona, 1970–)

DRAMATIC MUSIC

L'Orfeo, ed. Robert Eitner, Publikationen älterer praktischer und theoretischer Musikwerke, x (Leipzig, 1881)

—— ed. Vincent d'Indy (Paris, 1905)

—— ed. Giacomo Orefice (Milan, 1909)

—— ed. Gian Francesco Malipiero (London, 1923)

—— ed. Carl Orff (Munich, 1923; rev. edns. Mainz, 1929, 1931, 1940): 'in freier deutscher Neugestaltung'

L'Orfeo (Augsburg, 1927): facsimile of the original edition of 1609, with introduction by Adolf Sandberger

——ed. Giacomo Benvenuti (Milan, 1934): 'trascrizione ritmica, realizzazione e strumentazione'

——ed. Ottorino Respighi (Milan, 1935): 'realizzazione orchestrale'

——ed. Giacomo Benvenuti (Milan, 1942)

——ed. August Wenzinger (Kassel, 1955)

——ed. Bruno Maderna (Milan, 1967)

——ed. Denis Stevens (London, 1967)

——(Farnborough, 1972): facsimile of the 1615 edition, with introduction by Denis Stevens

——ed. Edward H. Tarr (Paris, 1974)

——ed. John Eliot Gardiner (London, in preparation)

L'Arianna (the surviving lament in its solo version), ed. François-Auguste Gevaert (Paris, 1868)

——ed. Angelo Solerti, in *Gli albori del melodramma* (Milan, 1904/R1969), i

——ed. Ottorino Respighi (Leipzig, 1910): 'armonizzato e orchestrato'

——ed. Carl Orff (Mainz, 1931): 'in freier deutscher Neugestaltung'

——ed. Carl Orff (Mainz, 1952): 'trascrizione libera'

——ed. Hans Joachim Moser (Kassel, 1961): 'für Alt Solo, fünfstimmigen gemischten Chor, Cembalo und Basso continuo'

——ed. Helmut Bornefeld (Kassel, 1962)

——in Günter Hausswald, ed., *The Music of the Figured Bass Era*, Anthology of Music, xlv (Cologne, 1974)

Ballo delle ingrate, in Luigi Torchi, ed., *L'arte musicale in Italia*, vi (Milan, 1907)

——ed. Carl Orff (Mainz, 1931): as *Tanz der Spröden*

——ed. Alceo Toni (Milan, 1932)

——ed. Denis Stevens (London, 1960)

Tirsi e Clori, ed. Kenneth Cooper (University Park, Pennsylvania, 1968)

Combattimento di Tancredi e Clorinda, in Luigi Torchi, ed., *L'arte musicale in Italia*, vi (Milan, 1907)

——ed. Alceo Toni (Milan, 1921)

——ed. Gian Francesco Malipiero (London, 1931)

——ed. Gian Francesco Malipiero, trans. Peter Pears (London, 1954)

——ed. Denis Stevens (London, 1962)

——ed. Luciano Berio (London, 1968)

Ballo: Movete al mio bel suon, ed. Denis Stevens (London, 1967)

Il ritorno d'Ulisse in patria, ed. Robert Haas, Denkmäler der Tonkunst in Österreich, lvii, Jg. xxix (Vienna, 1922)
——ed. Vincent d'Indy (Paris, 1926): 'adaptation musicale'
——ed. Luigi Dallapiccola (Milan, 1942): 'trascrizione e riduzione per le scene moderne'
——extracts ed. J. A. Westrup (London, 1929)
L'incoronazione di Poppea, ed. Hugo Goldschmidt, in *Studien zur Geschichte der italienischen Oper im 17. Jahrhundert*, ii (Leipzig, 1904/R1967)
——ed. Vincent d'Indy (Paris, 1908)
——ed. Charles van den Borren (Brussels, 1914)
——ed. Giacomo Benvenuti (Milan, 1937)
——ed. Ernst Krenek (Vienna, 1937)
——(Milan, 1938): facsimile of the Venice manuscript, with introduction by Giacomo Benvenuti
——ed. Giorgio Federico Ghedini (Milan, 1953)
——ed. Hans F. Redlich (Kassel, 1958)
——ed. Walter Goehr (Vienna and London, 1960)
——ed. Raymond Leppard (London, 1966)
——(Bologna, 1969): facsimile of the Venice manuscript

SECULAR CHAMBER MUSIC

12 fünfstimmige Madrigale, ed. Hugo Leichtentritt (Leipzig, 1909)
12 fünfstimmige Madrigale, ed. Arnold Mendelssohn (Leipzig, 1911)
15 madrigals, ed. Hans F. Redlich (London, 1954ff)
Collected madrigals in practical editions, ed. Gian Francesco Malipiero (Vienna, 1967)
Madrigali a 5 voci, libro primo, ed. Bernard Bailly de Surcy (Paris, 1972)
——(Paris, 1972): facsimile of the five part-books with introduction by Bernard Bailly de Surcy
Ten Madrigals, ed. Denis Stevens (London, 1978)
6 duets, ed. Ludwig Landshoff (Leipzig, 1927)
Canzonette a tre voci, ed. Gaetano Cesari, Istituzioni e monumenti dell'arte musicale italiana, vi (Milan, 1939)
——ed. Hilmar Trede (Basle, 1951)
Scherzi musicali, ed. Hilmar Trede (Kassel, n.d.)
Arie, canzonette e recitativi, ed. Gian Francesco Malipiero (Milan, 1953)
Scherzi musicali [a una voce], ed. Marius Flothuis (Amsterdam, 1958)
5 songs, ed. G. Hunter and Claude V. Palisca (Bryn Mawr, 1963)

CHURCH MUSIC

Sacrae cantiunculae, ed. G. Terrabugio (Milan, 1910)
——ed. Gaetano Cesari, Istituzioni e monumenti dell'arte musicale italiana, vi (Milan, 1939)
——ed. János Gábor (Budapest, 1943)
Vespro della Beata Vergine, ed. Hans F. Redlich (Vienna, 1949; rev. edn., Kassel, 1958)
——ed. Giorgio Federico Ghedini (Milan, 1952)
——ed. Gottfried Wolters, excerpts (Wolfenbüttel, 1954ff); complete in 1 vol. (Wolfenbüttel and Zurich, 1966)
——ed. Walter Goehr (Vienna, 1957)
——ed. Denis Stevens (London, 1961)
——ed. Jürgen Jürgens (Vienna, 1977)
——*Magnificat a sei voci*, ed. Denis Arnold (London, 1967)
Missa 'In illo tempore' a 6 [1610], ed. H. F. Redlich (London, 1962); including Gombert's motet *In illo tempore*
Messa a 4 voci da cappella [1641], ed. Rudolf Walter (Stuttgart-Hohenheid, 1972)
Christmas Vespers, ed. Denis Stevens (Borough Green, Sevenoaks, 1979); a selection of pieces from *Selva morale et spirituale* (1641) and *Messa ... et salmi* (1650)
Selva morale: Magnificat I, ed. Denis Stevens and John Steele (Borough Green, Sevenoaks, 1969)

Books

Abert, Anna Amalie, *Claudio Monteverdi und das musikalische Drama* (Lippstadt, 1954)
Ademollo, Alessandro, *La bell'Adriana ed altre virtuose del suo tempo alla corte di Mantova* (Città di Castello, 1888)
Adrio, Adam, *Die Anfänge des geistlichen Konzerts* (Berlin, 1935)
Anfuso, Nella, and Gianuario, Annibale, *Preparazione alla interpretazione della ποίησις [poiēsis] monteverdiana* (Florence, 1971)
Arnold, Denis, *Monteverdi*, The Master Musicians Series (London, 1963; rev. 2/1975)
——*Monteverdi Madrigals*, BBC Music Guides (London, 1967)
——*Monteverdi Church Music*, BBC Music Guides (London, 1982)
Artusi, Giovanni Maria, *L'Artusi, overo Delle imperfettioni della moderna musica*, i (Venice, 1600); ii (Venice, 1603/R1969)

Artusi, Giovanni Maria, *Discorso secondo musicale di Antonio Braccino da Todi* (Venice, 1608); facsimile reprint (Milan, 1924)

Banchieri, Adriano, *Lettere armoniche* (Bologna, 1628; 2/1630 as *Lettere scritte a diversi patroni et amici*)

Barblan, Guglielmo; Gallico, Claudio; and Pannain, Guido, *Claudio Monteverdi sul quarto centenario della nascita* (Turin, 1967)

Bertolotti, Antonio, *Musici alla corte dei Gonzaga in Mantova dal secolo XV al XVIII* (Milan, n.d., [1890]/R1969)

Caffi, Francesco, *Storia della musica sacra nella già cappella ducale di San Marco in Venezia dal 1318 al 1797* (Venice, 1854–5; repr. 1931)

Canal, Pietro, *Della musica in Mantova* (Venice, 1881/R1977)

Davari, Stefano, *La musica a Mantova*, ed. Gherardo Ghirardini: see under 'Articles', below

——*Notizie biografiche del distinto maestro di musica Claudio Monteverdi desunte dai documenti dell'Archivio Storico Gonzaga* (Mantua, 1884)

De' Paoli, Domenico, *Claudio Monteverdi* (Milan, 1945)

——*Claudio Monteverdi* (Milan, 1979)

——ed., *Claudio Monteverdi: lettere, dediche, e prefazioni* (Rome, 1973)

Einstein, Alfred, *The Italian Madrigal* (Princeton, 1949/R1971)

Fenlon, Iain, *Music and Patronage in Sixteenth-century Mantua* (Cambridge, 1980–82)

Gallico, Claudio, *Monteverdi: poesia musicale, teatro e musica sacra* (Turin, 1979)

Gianturco, Carolyn, *Claudio Monteverdi: stile e struttura* (Pisa, 1978)

Goldschmidt, Hugo, *Studien zur Geschichte der italienischen Oper im 17. Jahrhundert* (Leipzig, 1901–4/R1967)

Jung, Hermann, *Die Pastorale: Studien zur Geschichte eines musikalischen Topos* (Berne and Munich, 1980)

Kreidler, Walter, *Heinrich Schütz und der stile concitato von Claudio Monteverdi* (Stuttgart, 1934)

Kurtzman, Jeffrey G., *Essays on the Monteverdi Mass and Vespers of 1610*, Rice University Studies, lxiv/4 (Houston, 1978)

Leopold, Silke, *Claudio Monteverdi und seine Zeit* (Laaber, 1982)

Le Roux, Maurice, *Claudio Monteverdi* (Paris, 1951)

Malipiero, G. Francesco, *Claudio Monteverdi* (Milan, 1929)

Maniates, Maria Rika, *Mannerism in Italian Music and Culture, 1530–1630* (Chapel Hill, 1979)

Martini, Giovanni Battista, *Esemplare, ossia Saggio fondamentale di contrappunto* (Bologna, 1774–5); facsimile reprint (Farnborough, 1965)

Monterosso, Raffaello, ed., *Claudio Monteverdi e il suo tempo* (Verona, 1969); certain of the papers it contains are listed separately under 'Articles', below

Moore, James H., *Vespers at St. Mark's: Music of Alessandro Grandi, Giovanni Rovetta and Francesco Cavalli* (Ann Arbor, 1981)

Müller, Karl Friedrich, *Die Technik der Ausdrucksdarstellung in Monteverdis monodischen Frühwerken* (Berlin, 1931)

Newcomb, Anthony, *The Madrigal at Ferrara 1579–1597*, Princeton Studies in Music, vii (Princeton, 1980)

Osthoff, Wolfgang, *Das dramatische Spätwerk Claudio Monteverdis* (Tutzing, 1960)

Passuth, László, *A mantuai herceg muzsikusa: Claudio Monteverdi korának regényes története* (Budapest, 1959, 5/1964); Ger. trans. as *Monteverdi: der Roman eines grossen Musikers* (Vienna, 1959; 2/ed., Leipzig, 1982, as *Divino Claudio: ein Monteverdi-Roman*)

Pirrotta, Nino, *Scelte poetiche di Monteverdi* (Rome, 1968); see also under 'Articles', below

Pirrotta, Nino, and Povoledo, Elena, *Li due Orfei* (Turin, 1969; rev. 2/1975); trans. as *Music and Theatre from Poliziano to Monteverdi* (Cambridge, 1982)

Pontiroli, Giuseppe, *Notizie sui Monteverdi* (Cremona, 1968)

Prunières, Henry, *La Vie et l'œuvre de C. Monteverdi* (Paris, 1924, 2/1931; Eng. trans., London, 1926/R1972)

Redlich, Hans Ferdinand, *Claudio Monteverdi. Das Madrigalwerk: ein formengeschichtlicher Versuch* (Berlin, 1932)

——*Claudio Monteverdi: Leben und Werk* (Olten, 1949; Eng. trans., rev., London, 1952)

Roche, Maurice, *Monteverdi* ([Paris], 1960)

Sadie, Stanley, ed., *The New Grove Dictionary of Music and Musicians* (London, 1980); besides 'Monteverdi, Claudio' (see 'Articles', below, 344), relevant articles include 'Gonzaga', 'Mantua', 'Venice'

Santoro, Elia, *La famiglia e la formazione di Claudio Monteverdi: note biografiche con documenti inediti* (Cremona, 1967)

——*Iconografia monteverdiana* (Cremona, 1968)

Sartori, Claudio, *Monteverdi* (Brescia, 1953)

Schneider, Louis, *Un Précurseur de la musique italienne aux XVIe et XVIIe siècles: Claudio Monteverdi: l'homme et son temps* (Paris, 1921)

Schrade, Leo, *Monteverdi, Creator of Modern Music* (New York, 1950/R1964)

Stevens, Denis, *Monteverdi: Sacred, Secular and Occasional Music* (Cranbury, N.J., and London, 1978)
——trans. and ed., *The Letters of Claudio Monteverdi* (London, 1980)
Tellart, Roger, *Claudio Monteverdi: l'homme et son œuvre* (Paris, 1964)
Tiby, Ottavio. *'L'incoronazione di Poppea' di Claudio Monteverdi* (Florence, 1937)
——*Claudio Monteverdi* (Turin, 1944)
Vecchi, Giuseppe, *Le accademie musicali del primo Seicento e Monteverdi a Bologna* (Bologna, 1969)
Westerland, Gunnar, and Hughes, Eric, *Music of Claudio Monteverdi: a Discography* (London, 1972)
Whenham, John, *Duet and Dialogue in the Age of Monteverdi* (Ann Arbor, 1982)
——*ed., Claudio Monteverdi 'Orfeo'*, Cambridge Opera Handbooks (Cambridge, in preparation)

Articles

Abbreviations

AcM	*Acta musicologica*
AMw	*Archiv für Musikwissenschaft*
AnMc	*Analecta musicologica*
CMST	*Claudio Monteverdi e il suo tempo* (see under Monterosso, Raffaello, ed., in 'Books', above)
JAMS	*Journal of the American Musicological Society*
ML	*Music & Letters*
MMR	*Monthly Musical Record*
MQ	*Musical Quarterly*
MT	*Musical Times*
NRMI	*Nuova rivista musicale italiana*
RIM	*Rivista italiana di musicologia*
SIMG	*Sammelbände der Internationalen Musik-Gesellschaft*

Allorto, Riccardo, 'Il prologo dell'*Orfeo*: note sulla formazione del recitativo monteverdiano', *CMST*, 157
Antonicek, Theophil, 'Claudio Monteverdi und Österreich', *Österreichische Musikzeitschrift*, xxvi (1971), 266
Apel, Willi, 'Anent a Ritornello in Monteverdi's Orfeo', *Musica disciplina*, v (1951), 213

Arnold, Denis, 'A Background Note on Monteverdi's Hymn Settings', *Scritti in onore di Luigi Ronga* (Milan and Naples, 1973), 33

—— 'Alessandro Grandi, a Disciple of Monteverdi', *MQ*, xliii (1957), 171

—— 'Formal Design in Monteverdi's Church Music', *CMST*, 187

—— '"Il ritorno d'Ulisse" and the Chamber Duet', *MT*, cvi (1965), 183

—— '"L'incoronazione di Poppea" and its Orchestral Requirements', *MT*, civ (1963), 176 (also 255)

—— 'Monteverdi's Church Music: Some Venetian Traits', *MMR*, lxxxviii (1958), 83

—— 'Monteverdi's Singers', *MT*, cxi (1970), 982

—— 'Music at a Venetian Confraternity in the Renaissance', *AcM*, xxxvii (1965), 62

—— 'Notes on Two Movements of the Monteverdi "Vespers" ', *MMR*, lxxxiv (1954), 59

—— ' "Seconda pratica": a Background to Monteverdi's Madrigals', *ML*, xxxviii (1957), 341

—— 'The Monteverdi Vespers—a Postscript', *MT*, civ (1963), 24

—— 'The Monteverdian Succession at St. Mark's', *ML*, xlii (1961), 205

—— 'The Significance of "cori spezzati" ', *ML*, xl (1959), 4

—— with Elsie M. Arnold, 'Monteverdi, Claudio', *The New Grove Dictionary of Music and Musicians*, ed. Stanley Sadie (London, 1980), xv, 514

Beat, Janet E., 'Monteverdi and the Opera Orchestra of his Time', *The Monteverdi Companion*, ed. Denis Arnold and Nigel Fortune (London, 1968), 277

Bianconi, Lorenzo, 'Struttura poetica e struttura musicale nei madrigali di Monteverdi', *CMST*, 335

Biella, Giuseppe, 'I "Vespri dei Santi" di Claudio Monteverdi', *Musica sacra*, 2nd ser., xi (1966), 144

—— 'La "Messa", il "Vespro" e i "Sacri concenti" di Claudio Monteverdi nella stampa Amadino dell'anno 1610', *Musica sacra*, 2nd ser., ix (1964), 104

Bonta, Stephen, 'Liturgical Problems in Monteverdi's Marian Vespers', *JAMS*, xx (1967), 87

Boyden, David D., 'Monteverdi's *violini piccoli alla francese* and *viole da brazzo*', *Annales musicologiques*, vi (1958–63), 387

Brizi, Bruno, 'Teoria e prassi melodrammatica di G. F. Busenello e

"L'incoronazione di Poppea"', *Venezia e il melodramma nel Seicento*, ed. Maria Teresa Muraro (Florence, 1976), 51

Cammarota, Lionello, 'L'orchestrazione dell'"Orfeo" di Monteverdi', *Venezia e il melodramma nel Seicento*, ed. Maria Teresa Muraro (Florence, 1976), 21

Cesari, Gaetano, 'L'"Orfeo" di Cl. Monteverdi all'"Associazione di Amici della Musica" di Milano', *Rivista musicale italiana*, xvii (1910), 132

Chiarelli, Alessandra, '*L'incoronazione di Poppea* o *Il Nerone*: problemi di filologia testuale', *RIM*, ix (1974), 117

Dangel-Hofmann, Frohmut, 'Eine bisher unbekannte Monteverdi-Quelle', *Die Musikforschung*, xxxv (1982), 251

Davari, Stefano, 'La musica a Mantova: notizie biografiche di maestri di musica, cantori e suonatori presso la corte di Mantova nei secoli XV, XVI, XVII, tratte dai documenti dell'Archivio Storico Gonzaga', *Rivista storica mantovana*, i (1884), 53; ed., with appendices, by Gherardo Ghirardini (Mantua, 1975)

Degrada, Francesco, 'Gian Francesco Busenello e il libretto della *Incoronazione di Poppea*', *CMST*, 81

Della Corte, Andrea, 'Aspetti del "comico" nella vocalità teatrale di Monteverdi', *RIM*, ii (1967), 255

De Logu, Giuseppe, 'An Unknown Portrait of Monteverdi by Domenico Feti', *Burlington Magazine*, cix (1967), 706

Donington, Robert, 'Monteverdi's First Opera', *The Monteverdi Companion*, ed. Denis Arnold and Nigel Fortune (London, 1968), 257

Einstein, Alfred, '*Orlando furioso* and *La Gerusalemme liberata* as Set to Music during the 16th and 17th Centuries', *Notes*, viii (1950–51), 623

Epstein, Peter, 'Zur Rhythmisierung eines Ritornells von Monteverdi', *AMw*, viii (1926), 416

Fabbri, Paolo, 'Inediti monteverdiani', *RIM*, xv (1980), 71

—— 'Tasso, Guarini e il "divino Claudio": componenti manieristiche nella poetica di Monteverdi', *Studi musicali*, iii (1974), 233

Fano, Fabio, '*Il combattimento di Tancredi e Clorinda* e *L'incoronazione di Poppea* di Claudio Monteverdi', *Studi sul teatro veneto fra Rinascimento ed età barocca*, ed. Maria Teresa Muraro (Florence, 1971), 345

—— 'Il Monteverdi sacro, la "prima prattica" e la scuola veneziana', *RIM*, ii (1967), 264

Federhofer, Hellmut, 'Die Dissonanzbehandlung in Monteverdis kirchenmusikalischen Werken und die Figurenlehre von Christoph Bernhard', *CMST*, 435

Fenlon, Iain, 'The Monteverdi *Vespers*: Suggested Answers to Some Fundamental Questions', *Early Music*, v (1977), 380

Ferrari Barassi, Elena, 'Il madrigale spirituale nel Cinquecento e la raccolta monteverdiana del 1583', *CMST*, 217

Fortune, Nigel, 'Duet and Trio in Monteverdi', *MT*, cviii (1967), 417

—— 'Italian Secular Monody from 1600 to 1635: an Introductory Survey', *MQ*, xxxix (1953), 171

Frobenius, Wolf, 'Zur Notation eines Ritornells in Monteverdis *L'Orfeo*', *AMw*, xxviii (1971), 201

Gallico, Claudio, ' "contra Claudium Montiuiridum" ', *RIM*, x (1975), 346

—— 'Emblemi strumentali negli "Scherzi" di Monteverdi', *RIM*, ii (1967), 54

—— 'I due pianti di Arianna di Claudio Monteverdi', *Chigiana*, xxiv (1967), 29

—— 'La "Lettera amorosa" di Monteverdi e lo stile rappresentativo', *NRMI*, i (1967), 287

—— 'Monteverdi e i dazi di Viadana', *RIM*, i (1966), 242

—— 'Newly Discovered Documents concerning Monteverdi', *MQ*, xlviii (1962), 68

—— 'Strutture strumentali nella musica da camera di Monteverdi', *RIM*, ii (1967), 282

Ghisi, Federico, 'L'orchestra in Monteverdi', *Festschrift Karl Gustav Fellerer zum sechzigsten Geburtstag*, ed. Heinrich Hüschen (Regensburg, 1962), 187

Godt, Irving, 'A Monteverdi Source Reappears: the "Grilanda" of F. M. Fucci', *ML*, lx (1979), 428

Goldschmidt, Hugo, 'Claudio Monteverdi's Oper: Il ritorno d'Ulisse in patria', *SIMG*, ix (1907–8), 570

—— 'Monteverdi's Ritorno d'Ulisse', *SIMG*, iv (1902–3), 671

Hell, Helmut, 'Zu Rhythmus und Notierung des "Vi ricorda" in Claudio Monteverdis *Orfeo*', *AnMc*, xv (1975), 87

Hermelink, Siegfried, 'Das rhythmische Gefüge in Monteverdis ciaccona "Zefiro torna" ', *CMST*, 323

Heuss, Alfred, 'Die Instrumental-Stücke des "Orfeo" ', *SIMG*, iv (1902–3), 175

—— 'Die venetianischen Opern-Sinfonien', *SIMG*, iv (1902–3), 404

Holschneider, Andreas, 'Zur Aufführungspraxis der Marien-Vesper von Monteverdi', *Hamburger Jahrbuch für Musikwissenschaft*, i (1974), 59

Horsley, Imogene, 'Full and Short Scores in the Accompaniment of Italian Church Music in the Early Baroque', *JAMS*, xxx (1977), 466

——'Monteverdi's Use of Borrowed Material in "Sfogava con le stelle"', *ML*, lix (1978), 316

Jürgens, Jürgen, 'Urtext und Aufführungspraxis bei Monteverdis *Orfeo* und *Marien-Vesper*', *CMST*, 269

Kurtzman, Jeffrey G., 'Some Historical Perspectives on the Monteverdi Vespers', *AnMc*, xv (1975), 29

Leichtentritt, Hugo, 'Claudio Monteverdi als Madrigalkomponist', *SIMG*, xi (1909–10), 255

Leopold, Silke, 'Die Hierarchie Arkadiens: soziale Strukturen in den frühen Pastoralopern und ihre Ausdrucksformen', *Schweizer Jahrbuch für Musikwissenschaft*, new ser., i (1981), 71

Lesure, François, 'Un nouveau portrait de Monteverdi', *Revue de musicologie*, liii (1967), 60

Lowell, John K., 'Aspects of Psalmody and Text Setting in Monteverdi's Marian Vespers', *Musical Analysis*, ii/2 (Summer 1974), 15

Mace, Dean T., 'Tasso, *La Gerusalemme liberata*, and Monteverdi', *Studies in the History of Music, i: Music and Language* (1983), 118

Mondolfi Bossarelli, Anna, 'Ancora intorno al codice napoletano della *Incoronazione di Poppea*', *RIM*, ii (1967), 294

Noske, Frits, 'An Unknown Work by Monteverdi: the Vespers of St. John the Baptist', *ML*, lxvi (1985), 118

Osthoff, Wolfgang, 'Die venezianische und neapolitanische Fassung von Monteverdis "Incoronazione di Poppea"', *AcM*, xxvi (1954), 88

——'Monteverdi-Funde', *AMw*, xiv (1957), 253

——'Monteverdis Combattimento in deutscher Sprache und Heinrich Schütz', *Festschrift Helmuth Osthoff zum 65. Geburtstage*, ed. Lothar Hoffmann-Erbrecht and Helmut Hucke (Tutzing, 1961), 195

——'Neue Beobachtungen zu Quellen und Geschichte von Monteverdis "Incoronazione di Poppea"', *Die Musikforschung*, xi (1958), 129

——'Per la notazione originale nelle pubblicazioni di musiche antiche e specialmente nella nuova edizione Monteverdi', *AcM*, xxxiv (1962), 101

——'Trombe sordine', *AMw*, xiii (1956), 77

——'Unità liturgica e artistica nei *Vespri* del 1610', *RIM*, ii (1967), 314

Osthoff, Wolfgang, 'Zu den Quellen von Monteverdis Ritorno d'Ulisse in patria', *Studien zur Musikwissenschaft*, xxiii (1956), 67

—— 'Zur Bologneser Aufführung von Monteverdis "Ritorno d'Ulisse" im Jahre 1640', *Österreichische Akademie der Wissenschaften: Anzeiger der phil.-hist. Klasse*, xcv (1958), 155

Palisca, Claude V., 'Vincenzo Galilei's Counterpoint Treatise: a Code for the "seconda pratica"', *JAMS*, ix (1956), 81

Pestelli, Giorgio, 'Le poesie per la musica monteverdiana: il gusto poetico di Monteverdi', *CMST*, 349

Petrobelli, Pierluigi, '"Ah, dolente partita": Marenzio, Wert, Monteverdi', *CMST*, 361

Pirrotta, Nino, 'Early Opera and Aria', *New Looks at Italian Opera: Essays in Honor of Donald J. Grout*, ed. William W. Austin (Ithaca, NY, 1968), 39; It. trans. in Nino Pirrotta and Elena Povoledo, *Li due Orfei* (see under 'Books', above), chap. 6 (original Eng. version, modified, used in trans. of this book)

—— 'Early Venetian Libretti at Los Angeles', *Essays in Honor of Dragan Plamenac on his 70th Birthday*, ed. Gustave Reese and Robert J. Snow (Pittsburgh, 1969), 233

—— 'Monteverdi e i problemi dell'opera', *Studi sul teatro veneto fra Rinascimento ed età barocca*, ed. Maria Teresa Muraro (Florence, 1971), 321

—— 'Scelte poetiche di Monteverdi', *NRMI*, ii (1968), 10, 226; also published separately (see under 'Books', above)

—— 'Teatro, scene e musica nelle opere di Monteverdi', *CMST*, 45

Redlich, Hans F., 'Claudio Monteverdi (1567–1643): Some Editorial Problems of 1967', *The Consort*, xxiv (1967), 224

—— 'Claudio Monteverdi: Some Problems of Textual Interpretation', *MQ*, xli (1955), 66

—— 'Notes to a New Edition of Monteverdi's Mass of 1651', *MMR*, lxxxiii (1953), 95

Reiner, Stuart, 'La vag'Angioletta (and Others), Part I', *AnMc*, xiv (1974), 26

—— 'Preparations in Parma—1618, 1627–28', *Music Review*, xxv (1964), 273

Riemann, Hugo, 'Eine siebensätzige Tanzsuite von Monteverdi v. J. 1907', *SIMG*, xiv (1912–13), 26

Roche, Jerome, 'The Duet in Early Seventeenth-century Italian Church Music', *Proceedings of the Royal Musical Association*, xciii (1966–7), 33

Rose, Gloria, 'Agazzari and the Improvising Orchestra', *JAMS*, xviii (1965), 382

Rosenthal, Albi, 'A Hitherto Unpublished Letter of Claudio Monteverdi', *Essays Presented to Egon Wellesz*, ed. Jack Westrup (Oxford, 1966), 103

——'Monteverdi's "Andromeda": a Lost Libretto Found', *ML*, lxvi (1985), 1

Salzer, Felix, 'Heinrich Schenker and Historical Research: Monteverdi's Madrigal *Oimè, se tanto amate*', *Aspects of Schenkerian Theory*, ed. David Beach (New Haven and London, 1983), 135

Sartori, Claudio, 'Monteverdiana', *MQ*, xxxviii (1952), 399

Schmitz, Eugen, 'Zur Geschichte des italienischen Continuo-Madrigals im 17. Jahrhundert', *SIMG*, xi (1909–10), 509

——'Zur Geschichte des italienischen Kammerduetts im 17. Jahrhundert', *Jahrbuch der Musikbibliothek Peters*, xxiii (1916), 43

Sirch, Licia, ' "Violini piccoli alla francese" e "canto alla francese" nell' "Orfeo" (1607) e negli "Scherzi musicali" (1607) di Monteverdi', *NRMI*, xv (1981), 50

Smith Brindle, Reginald, 'Monteverdi's G minor Mass: an Experiment in Construction', *MQ*, liv (1968), 352

Sopart, Andreas, 'Claudio Monteverdis "Scherzi musicali" (1607) und ihre Beziehungen zum "Scherzo"-Begriff in der italienischen Barocklyrik', *AMw*, xxxviii (1981), 227

Spinelli, Gianfranco, 'Confronto fra le registrazioni organistiche dei *Vespri* di Monteverdi e quelle de *L'arte organica* di Antegnati', *CMST*, 479

Stevens, Denis, 'Claudio Monteverdi: *Selva morale e spirituale*', *CMST*, 423

——'*Madrigali guerrieri, et amorosi*: a Reappraisal for the Quatercentenary', *MQ*, liii (1967), 161; slightly modified version, as '*Madrigali guerrieri, et amorosi*', *The Monteverdi Companion*, ed. Denis Arnold and Nigel Fortune (London, 1968), 227

——'Monteverdi, Petratti, and the Duke of Bracciano', *MQ*, lxiv (1978), 275; It. trans., *Studi musicali*, vi (1977), 69

——'Monteverdi's Double-choir Magnificat', *MT*, cx (1969), 587

——'Monteverdi's Necklace', *MQ*, lix (1973), 370

——'Monteverdi's Other Vespers', *MT*, cxx (1979), 732; It. trans., *NRMI*, xiv (1980), 167

——'Ornamentation in Monteverdi's Shorter Dramatic Works', *Bericht über den Siebenten internationalen musikwissenschaftlichen Kongress, Köln 1958* (Kassel and Basle, 1959), 284

Stevens, Denis, 'Where are the Vespers of Yesteryear?' *MQ*, xlvii (1961), 315

Strohm, Reinhard, 'Osservazioni su "Tempro la cetra"', *RIM*, ii (1967), 357

Szweykowski, Zygmunt M., '"Ah dolente partita": Monteverdi, Scacchi', *Quadrivium*, xii/2 (1971), 59

Tagliavini, Luigi Ferdinando, 'Registrazioni organistiche nei Magnificat dei "Vespri" monteverdiani', *RIM*, ii (1967), 365

Tiepolo, Maria Francesca, 'minima monteverdiana', *Rassegna degli archivi di stato*, xxix (1969), 135

Tomlinson, Gary, 'Madrigal, Monody, and Monteverdi's "via naturale alla immitatione"', *JAMS*, xxxiv (1981), 60

——'Twice Bitten, Thrice Shy: Monteverdi's "finta" *Finta pazza*', *JAMS*, xxxvi (1983), 303

Vitali, Carlo, 'Una lettera vivaldiana perduta e ritrovata; un inedito monteverdiano del 1630 e altri carteggi di musicisti celebri, ovvero Splendori e nefandezze del collezionismo di autografi', *NRMI*, xiv (1980), 404

Vogel, Emil, 'Claudio Monteverdi', *Vierteljahrsschrift für Musikwissenschaft*, iii (1887), 315

Walker, Thomas, 'Gli errori di "Minerva al tavolino", osservazioni sulla cronologia delle prime opere veneziane', *Venezia e il melodramma nel Seicento*, ed. Maria Teresa Muraro (Florence, 1976), 7

Westrup, J. A., 'Monteverde's "Il ritorno d'Ulisse in patria"', *MMR*, lviii (1928), 106

——'Monteverde's "Orfeo"', *MT*, lxvi (1925), 1096

——'Monteverde's "Poppea"', *MT*, lxviii (1927), 982

——'Monteverdi and the Madrigal', *The Score*, i (1949), 33

——'Monteverdi and the Orchestra', *ML*, xxi (1940), 230

——'Monteverdi's "Lamento d'Arianna"', *Music Review*, i (1940), 144

——'The Originality of Monteverde', *Proceedings of the Musical Association*, lx (1933–4), 1

Witzenmann, Wolfgang, 'Stile antico e stile nuovo nella musica sacra di Claudio Monteverdi', *RIM*, ii (1967), 372

Zimmerman, Franklin B., 'Purcell and Monteverdi', *MT*, xcix (1958), 368

The following book appeared too late for inclusion in the foregoing bibliography:

Pirrotta, Nino, *Music and Culture in Italy from the Middle Ages to the Baroque: a Collection of Essays*, Studies in the History of Music, i (Cambridge, Mass., and London, 1984)

Of the essays by Pirrotta listed on page 348, above, it includes a reprint of the second (at page 317) and translations of the last three: 'Monteverdi and the Problems of Opera' (p. 235), 'Monteverdi's Poetic Choices' (p. 271) and 'Theater, Sets, and Music in Monteverdi's Operas' (p. 254).

Index

Compiled by Elsie Arnold

indicates that there are one or more musical examples on the page